DATE DUE

			PRINTED IN U.S.A.

Authors
& Artists
for Young
Adults

ISSN 1040-5682

Authors & Artists for Young Adults

VOLUME 21

Thomas McMahon
Editor

GALE

DETROIT • NEW YORK • TORONTO • LONDON

Thomas McMahon, *Editor*

Joyce Nakamura, *Managing Editor*

Hal May, *Publisher*

Diane Andreassi, Ken Cuthbertson, Ronie-Richele Garcia-Johnson, Marian C.
Gonsior, Janet L. Hile, J. Sydney Jones, Marie J. MacNee, Laurie A. Jenkins McElroy,
Irene McKnight-Durham, Nancy Rampson, Megan Ratner, Peggy Saari, Pamela L.
Shelton, Kenneth R. Shepherd, Tracy J. Sukraw, and Kathleen Witman,
Sketchwriters/Contributing Editors

Victoria B. Cariappa, *Research Manager*
Cheryl L. Warnock, *Project Coordinator*
Gary J. Oudersluys and Maureen Richards, *Research Specialists*
Laura C. Bissey and Sean R. Smith, *Research Associates*

Susan M. Trosky, *Permissions Manager*
Maria L. Franklin, *Permissions Specialist*
Michele Lonoconus, *Permissions Associate*
Andrea Grady, *Permissions Assitant*

Mary Beth Trimper, *Production Director*
Deborah Milliken, *Production Assistant*

Randy Bassett, *Image Database Supervisor*
Mikal Ansari, *Macintosh Artist*
Robert Duncan, *Imaging Specialist*
Pamela A. Reed, *Photography Coordinator*

The paper used in this publication meets the minimum requirements of
American National Standard for Information Sciences—Permanence Paper
for Printed Library Materials, ANSI Z39.48-1984.

Library of Congress Catalog Card Number 89-641100
ISBN 0-7876-1137-9
ISSN 1040-5682

10 9 8 7 6 5 4 3 2 1

Printed in the United States of America

Authors and Artists for Young Adults

TEEN BOARD

The staff of *Authors and Artists for Young Adults* wishes to thank the following young adult readers for their teen board participation:

Contents

Introduction

Authors and Artists for Young Adults is a reference series designed to serve the needs of middle school, junior high, and high school students interested in creative artists. Originally inspired by the need to bridge the gap between Gale's *Something about the Author,* created for children, and *Contemporary Authors,* intended for older students and adults, *Authors and Artists for Young Adults* has been expanded to cover not only an international scope of authors, but also a wide variety of other artists.

Although the emphasis of the series remains on the writer for young adults, we recognize that these readers have diverse interests covering a wide range of reading levels. The series therefore contains not only those creative artists who are of high interest to young adults, including cartoonists, photographers, music composers, bestselling authors of adult novels, media directors, producers, and performers, but also literary and artistic figures studied in academic curricula, such as influential novelists, playwrights, poets, and painters. The goal of *Authors and Artists for Young Adults* is to present this great diversity of creative artists in a format that is entertaining, informative, and understandable to the young adult reader.

Entry Format

Each volume of *Authors and Artists for Young Adults* will furnish in-depth coverage of twenty to twenty-five authors and artists. The typical entry consists of:

—A detailed biographical section that includes date of birth, marriage, children, education, and addresses.

—A comprehensive bibliography or filmography including publishers, producers, and years.

—Adaptations into other media forms.

—Works in progress.

—A distinctive essay featuring comments on an artist's life, career, artistic intentions, world views, and controversies.

—References for further reading.

—Extensive illustrations, photographs, movie stills, cartoons, book covers, and other relevant visual material.

A cumulative index to featured authors and artists appears in each volume.

Compilation Methods

The editors of *Authors and Artists for Young Adults* make every effort to secure information directly from the authors and artists through personal correspondence and interviews. Sketches on living authors and artists are sent to the biographee for review prior to publication. Any sketches not personally reviewed by biographees or their representatives are marked with an asterisk (*).

Highlights of Forthcoming Volumes

Among the authors and artists planned for future volumes are:

Michael Bedard	E. L. Doctorow	Geraldine McCaughrean
Margaret Buffie	Alexandre Dumas	Toni Morrison
Michael Cadnum	Nikki Giovanni	Colby Rodowsky
Chris Carter	Amy Heckerling	Margaret Rostkowski
Mary Cassatt	Alfred Hitchcock	Gillian Rubenstein
John Christopher	Jan Hudson	Sir Walter Scott
James Fenimore Cooper	M. E. Kerr	Ivan Southall
Karen Cushman	Daniel Keyes	Bram Stoker
Salvador Dali	Elmore Leonard	T. H. White
Charles Dickens	George Lucas	Rita Williams-Garcia
Emily Dickinson	Gregory Maguire	Tim Wynne-Jones
Walt Disney	Carol Matas	Jane Yolen

Contact the Editor

We encourage our readers to examine the entire *AAYA* series. Please write and tell us if we can make AAYA even more helpful to you. Give your comments and suggestions to the editor:

BY MAIL: The Editor, *Authors and Artists for Young Adults*, Gale Research, 835 Penobscot Building, 645 Griswold St., Detroit, MI 48226-4094.

BY TELEPHONE: (800) 347-GALE

BY FAX: (313) 961-6599

BY E-MAIL: CYA@Gale.com@GALESMTP

Authors & Artists for Young Adults

Janet Bode

■ Personal

Surname is pronounced *Boe*-dy; born July 14, 1943, in Penn Yan, NY; daughter of Carl J. (a writer and professor) and Margaret (Lutze) Bode. *Education:* University of Maryland, B.A., 1965; graduate study at Michigan State University and Bowie State College.

■ Addresses

Home—New York, NY.

■ Career

Writer, since 1972. Has worked in Germany, Mexico, and the United States as personnel specialist, program director, community organizer, public relations director, and teacher. *Member:* PEN, National Writers Union, Authors Guild.

■ Awards, Honors

Outstanding Social Studies Book Award, National Council for Social Studies (NCSS), for *Rape: Pre-*

venting It; Coping with the Legal, Medical and Emotional Aftermath; Notable Children's Trade Book in the Field of Social Studies, NCSS, Best Books for Young Adults Citation, American Library Association (ALA), Book for the Teen Age selection, New York Public Library (NYPL), 1981 and 1982, all for *Kids Having Kids: The Unwed Teenage Parent;* Best Books for Young Adults selection, ALA, Outstanding Merit Book, NCSS, 1990 Books for the Teen Age selection, NYPL, all for *New Kinds on the Block: Oral Histories of Immigrant Teens;* Best Books for Young Adults selection, ALA, 1991 Books for the Teen Age, NYPL, Blue Ribbon Book, *Bulletin for the Center of Children's Books,* Best Book citation, *School Library Journal,* Editor's Choice, *Booklist,* all for *The Voices of Rape;* Best Books for Young Adults selection, ALA, 1992 Books for the Teen Age, NYPL, Recommended Books for Reluctant Young Readers, Young Adult Library Services Association (YALSA), all for *Beating the Odds: Stories of Unexpected Achievers;* Notable Children's Trade Book in the Field of Social Studies, NCSS, 1993 Books for the Teen Age, NYPL, both for *Kids Still Having Kids: People Talk about Teen Pregnancy;* Quick Picks—Best Books for Reluctant Readers selection, YALSA, 1993 Books for the Teen Age, NYPL, Young Adults' Choice for 1995, International Reading Association, all for *Death Is Hard to Live With: Teenagers Talk about How They Cope with Loss;* Best Books for Young Adults selection, ALA, 1995 Books for the Teen Age, NYPL, both for *Heartbreak and Roses: Real Life Stories of Troubled*

Love; Quick Picks—Best Books for Reluctant Readers, YALSA, 1995 Books for the Teen Age, NYPL, both for *Trust and Betrayal: Real Life Stories of Friends and Enemies*; Best Books for Young Adults selection, ALA, Top Ten Quick Picks—Best Books for Reluctant Readers, YALSA, 1997 Books for the Teen Age, NYPL, all for *Hard Time: A Real Life Look at Juvenile Crime and Violence*.

■ Writings

Kids School Lunch Bag (on the National School Lunch Program), Children's Foundation, 1972.

View from Another Closet: Exploring Bisexuality in Women, Hawthorn, 1976.

Fighting Back: How to Cope with the Medical, Emotional and Legal Consequences of Rape, Macmillan, 1978.

Rape: Preventing It; Coping with the Legal, Medical and Emotional Aftermath (young adult), F. Watts, 1979.

Kids Having Kids: The Unwed Teenage Parent (young adult), F. Watts, 1980.

Different Worlds: Interracial and Cross-Cultural Dating, F. Watts, 1989.

New Kids on the Block: Oral Histories of Immigrant Teens, F. Watts, 1989, reprinted by Scholastic as *New Kids in Town*.

The Voices of Rape, F. Watts, 1990.

Truce: Ending the Sibling War, F. Watts, 1991.

Beating the Odds: Stories of Unexpected Achievers, graphic stories by Stan Mack, F. Watts, 1991.

Kids Still Having Kids: People Talk about Teen Pregnancy, graphic stories by Stan Mack, F. Watts, 1992.

Death Is Hard to Live With: Teenagers Talk about How They Cope with Loss, graphic stories by Stan Mack, Delacorte, 1993.

Heartbreak and Roses: Real Life Stories of Troubled Love, graphic stories by Stan Mack, Delacorte, 1994.

Trust and Betrayal: Real Life Stories of Friends and Enemies, Delacorte, 1995.

(With Stan Mack) *Hard Time: A Real Life Look at Juvenile Crime and Violence*, Delacorte, 1996.

Food Fight: A Guide to Eating Disorders for Pre-Teens and Their Parents, Simon & Schuster, 1997.

Co-author of "Women against Rape" (television documentary film), 1975. Contributor of magazine articles to periodicals, including *New York Times*, *Cosmopolitan*, *Redbook*, *New York*, and *Mademoiselle*.

■ Adaptations

Different Worlds: Interracial and Cross-Cultural Dating was made into a CBS-TV *Schoolbreak Special* entitled *Different Worlds: A Story of Interracial Love*.

■ Sidelights

I just graduated from high school. I feel we had a curse on my class. Six people died. The worst was Shannon, my best friend. She was free-spirited, the last person you'd expect to die.

One day she's great.

The next day she's dead.

I wasn't prepared for it.

Leticia, age seventeen, the narrator in a chapter entitled "Death Hurts" in Janet Bode's book *Death Is Hard to Live With: Teenagers Talk about How They Cope with Loss*, discusses the death of her friend Shannon. She was killed in a hit-and-run accident involving a pair of teens who stole a car. "Actually, Tommy, the one driving, went to elementary school with us," Leticia explains. "He loses control of the car, hits a group of people on the sidewalk. Shannon gets pinned against the wall."

The story that Leticia tells is not really Shannon's story but Leticia's own. She goes on to tell about how she put her life back in shape after the death of her best friend. Leticia is a survivor, the sort of person that Bode's book celebrates. "Some of you don't want to think about death," Bode writes in her introduction, "Death Is Not Optional." "You want to forget that everything alive must die. Plants, ants, snakes, fish, dogs, cats—and people. You want to believe that you and those you love are somehow going to live forever."

"This book," the author continues, "is a place to start sorting out your emotions and making sense of your world. Think of it as a survival guide. This book will help answer the question: How do I cope with the death of someone special? Wherever that person is, whether there's a soul, eternity, reincarnation—you're still here. How do you deal with your conflicting emotions and get on with your life? To help you on your own journey, teenagers from across the country recount how they face these questions head on."

Issues like those described in *Death Is Hard to Live With* are the sort of problems that Janet Bode confronts in her award-winning books. Titles such as *Rape, Kids Having Kids: The Unwed Teenage Parent, Different Worlds: Interracial and Cross-Cultural Dating, Truce: Ending the Sibling War, Heartbreak and Roses: Real Life Stories of Troubled Love,* and *Hard Time: A Real Life Look at Juvenile Crime and Violence* look at problems faced by modern teens and suggest solutions, often through the wisdom of other teenagers. Bode's work is often presented with the illustrations of cartoonist Stan Mack, which also present the stories of teens in crisis. "Bode uses the young adults' own words as much as possible and the discussions throughout Bode's books have an honest ring that create immediate connections with readers," writes Hollis Lowrey-Moore in *Twentieth-Century Young Adult Writers.* "Expert interviews which sometimes follow teen's stories are never preachy or arrogant but provide information and differing viewpoints, and offer practical suggestions for help."

Birth and Death

Several of Bode's books have teen pregnancy as their topic. *Kids Having Kids: The Unwed Teenage Parent,* for example, traces the difficulties and responsibilities of teenage parenthood. Bode carefully describes the potential health problems that can arise from unprotected sex (and from birth control, which can have its own separate set of problems), explains the options that are available to sexually active teens, and uses the stories of other teenagers to show how they react to the new responsibilities of caring for an infant. *School Library Journal* contributor Joan Scherer Brewer explains that the book can be read in many different ways, depending on the interests of the reader: it can be used as a guide for teens who think they might be pregnant, and its extensive bibliography directs researchers to other helpful sources. Bode also gives historical perspectives to attitudes on teenage sex and pregnancy, Brewer states, "making this useful for term papers as well as personal guidance."

Kids Still Having Kids: People Talk about Teen Pregnancy, a sequel to *Kids Having Kids,* also confronts issues of sexuality, pregnancy, and parenting. It expands the scope of the earlier book by concentrating on feelings and attitudes toward sexuality. "It touches not only on teenage pregnancy and related issues of abortion and adoption, but also on teenage sex, foster care, and parenting," states *Booklist* contributor Stephanie Zvirin. "For balance and insight Bode includes the perspectives of adults who work with teens." "The discussion of options is generally fair-minded in terms of pros and cons," Libby K. White declares in her *School Library Journal* review of the book; "while Bode appears to be pro-choice, she urges those who believe abortion to be morally wrong to reject it as an option for them." "This book," concludes *Voice of Youth Advocates* reviewer Barbara Flottmeier, "is a compendium of excellent information concerning the facts of teenage pregnancy, the emotional effects of that pregnancy and the help that is available for the pregnant teenage mother and father."

Reviewers comment on Bode's no-nonsense approach to the subject of death in *Death Is Hard to Live With: Teenagers Talk about How They Cope with Loss.* Susan R. Farber states in her *Voice of Youth Advocates* review of the book that the author "goes beyond platitudes and the 'happy, happy, joy, joy' religious approach to dealing with the aftermath of death." "She interviews teenagers about the deaths of friends or relatives," explains a *Publishers Weekly* reviewer, "and she also calls on professionals (doctors, funeral directors, clergymen as well as therapists)." *School Library Journal* contributor Celia A. Huffman calls the volume "a thorough approach to the topic that encourages readers to talk about their personal experiences involving death, let go of the pain, grieve, and move on, allowing it to be a lesson about life." "*Death Is Hard to Live With* has its flaws," Farber concludes, ". . . but overall it's an important book, a book to help teens survive a traumatic time in their lives."

Violence

Bode has also written several books about the subject of rape and how it affects both victims and perpetrators. The earliest of these were *Fighting Back: How to Cope with the Medical, Emotional and Legal Consequences of Rape* and *Rape: Preventing It; Coping with the Legal, Medical and Emotional Aftermath. Fighting Back* was intended for adult women, but *Rape* was directed specifically at teenagers and other young adults. In the latter book, explains a *Kirkus Reviews* contributor, "she emphasizes that the decision to report or prosecute is up to the victim (though a medical exam is a must) and points out the variety of problems—from finding the guy to finding a non-sexist jury—which frequently stand in the way of conviction." "Laced with colloquialisms and street adjectives," states *School Library Journal* reviewer Denise L. Moll, "Bode's book strives to break down the myths and misconceptions that surround the topic of rape."

The book that broke new ground on the topic, however, was *The Voices of Rape*, in which Bode allowed victims and perpetrators of the crime to speak for themselves. "In an effort 'to educate, to help, and to bring the human element to the issue,' she turns most of her platform over to a carefully chosen group of teenagers and specialists," writes Stephanie Zvirin in *Booklist*, "each of whom views rape from a different vantage point—rapist, survivor, police officer, mental health professional, lawyer, nurse." Carolyn Polese, writing in *School Library Journal*, notes that several points of view have been omitted, including male victims of rape "(although the author does address male victims in several passages), discussion of incest or child sexual abuse is negligible, and some of the most disturbing and ambiguous monologues—such as one by a boy who casually participated in several 'gang bangs'—are presented without interpretation or comment." Several reviewers, however, praised Bode's work for just such editorial restraint. Bode, states *Voice of Youth Advocates* contributor Judy Sasges, "survived a robbery and gang rape. Her reassuring yet realistic tone will appeal to readers. Some sentences are choppy and poorly constructed, but Bode acknowledges that 'the language you read is the language I heard—not always perfect . . . but always clear.'" "Choosing not to intrude in the interviews," Zvirin explains, "she lays the burden of interpretation on her reading audience, and while that's a lot to demand from some teens, she gives them honesty and respect in return."

In *Hard Time: A Real Life Look at Juvenile Crime and Violence*, Bode examines the problems faced by young people who commit crimes. She cites Georges Benjamin, M.D., chairman of the trauma care, violence and injury control committee of the American College of Emergency Physicians in Washington, D.C. Dr. Benjamin compares modern hospital emergency rooms to "MASH units in war zones." "We're treating gunshot violence, domestic violence, drug- and alcohol-related violence,"

In this 1993 work, Bode shares advice given by teenagers who have experienced the death of a friend or relative.

the doctor continues. "And the victims of violence I see are younger and younger. Many of you teenagers know this. You've been going to more funerals than proms. It's the adults who often don't seem to understand that everyone's kid is at risk. Even theirs." Dr. Benjamin recommends learning mediation and anger-management skills to counter some of the worst problems. "Violence-free is a goal," the doctor concludes. "If you don't know where you're going, you won't get there."

"Through poems, narrative prose, and cartoon strips," writes a reviewer for *Bulletin of the Center for Children's Books*, "we hear a diversity of voices, including those of Sean, a seventeen-year-old who killed his mother; Randall Watson, the project coordinator who teaches writing workshops to teens in prison; and Tanya, the fifteen-year-old whose letter to the author describes her decision to lead a straight life." "One 17-year-old girl is in [prison] for 'participating in the murder of my best friend. She said she was going to steal my boyfriend,'" explains Carolyn Noah in *School Library Journal*. "*Hard Time* both shocks the reader and provides a glimmer of hope," declares Anne O'Malley in *Booklist*, "stemming from the few success stories inside the grim walls." "That people from urban, suburban, poor, and middle-class environments are represented," Noah concludes, "reinforces the validity of the book." "Bode says the book is a 'wake-up call'; it is not for the faint-hearted," states a *Kirkus Reviews* contributor, "but it should be available to all those in similar situations— whether perpetrators or victims."

Love

Heartbreak and Roses: Real Life Stories of Troubled Love is one of the few nonfiction books aimed at young adults that deals with the subject of romance. "All of the young people in Bode's stories are trying to come to grips with their sexuality," states Evelyn Carter Walker in *School Library Journal*, "and each one portrays a troubled relationship." Bode explains in her introduction to the book that it is a series of twelve short stories that tell of love and pain and the relationship between the two. "Some tell of love gone wrong—violent love, obsessive love, tormented love leading to suicide attempts," Bode writes. "Others speak of bittersweet love—battles for love fought against outside forces." She reminds readers that these are true stories of real teenagers. "As in life, and especially life in the teen years, the course of love in these stories is turbulent. They may upset you. They may comfort you. They may also help you see your own love problems more clearly." She hopes that the stories and the interspersed fact boxes "may give you a little more insight into your own love life."

Like the rest of Bode's work, *Heartbreak and Roses* lets young men and women speak for themselves. "While sex is a concern common to many of the stories," a *Publishers Weekly* contributor says, "the collection explores a wide variety of other issues— coping with a disability, violence, interracial dating, self-acceptance, co-dependence and breaking up among them. Unobtrusive onlookers who offer neither answers nor judgments, Bode and Mack relay each story as if merely transcribing the words of its narrator." "Whether it's a disabled teen talking about the practicalities of having sex, someone involved in an abusive relationship, or a gay youth whose first lover pretends their intimacy never happened, the stories are candid—about love, about pain, and about sex," states Stephanie Zvirin in *Booklist*. "And as in real life, they often have no satisfying conclusion."

All of Bode's books are rooted in the idea that young adults, armed with appropriate information and knowledge, will be able to find their own ways to gain control over their lives. "Bode's abili-

This ALA Best Book for Young Adults features teenagers talking about their experiences with love with the hopes that others will learn from their situations.

If you enjoy the works of Janet Bode, you may want to check out the following books:

Berlie Doherty, *Dear Nobody*, 1992.
Virginia Hamilton, *Cousins*, 1990.
Walter Dean Myers, *Scorpions*, 1988.
Colby Rodowsky, *Lucy Peale*, 1992.

---

ties to communicate honestly with young adults," writes Lowery-Moore, "and to provide information and help in a way that teens find palatable make her books a valuable tool for teens, parents, teachers, and librarians. Bode's works also provide snapshots and insights into some of society's most pressing issues and impart a sense of certainty that today's teens will find solutions to many of the ills they have inherited."

■ **Works Cited**

Bode, Janet, *Death Is Hard to Live With: Teenagers Talk about How They Cope with Loss*, Delacorte, 1993.

Bode, Janet, *Heartbreak and Roses: Real Life Stories of Troubled Love*, Delacorte, 1994.

Bode, Janet, and Stan Mack, *Hard Time: A Real Life Look at Juvenile Crime and Violence*, Delacorte, 1996.

Brewer, Joan Scherer, review of *Kids Having Kids: The Unwed Teenage Parent*, School Library Journal, February, 1981, p. 73.

Review of *Death Is Hard to Live With: Teenagers Talk about How They Cope with Loss*, Publishers Weekly, August 9, 1993, p. 480.

Farber, Susan R., review of *Death Is Hard to Live With: Teenagers Talk about How They Cope with Loss*, Voice of Youth Advocates, April, 1994, p. 43.

Flottmeier, Barbara, review of *Kids Still Having Kids: The Unwed Teenage Parent*, Voice of Youth Advocates, February, 1993, p. 364.

Review of *Hard Time: A Real Life Look at Juvenile Crime and Violence*, Bulletin of the Center for Children's Books, May, 1996, pp. 293-94.

Review of *Hard Time: A Real Life Look at Juvenile Crime and Violence*, Kirkus Reviews, December 15, 1995, p. 1767.

Review of *Heartbreak and Roses: Real Life Stories of Troubled Love*, Publishers Weekly, June 27, 1994, p. 79.

Huffman, Celia A., review of *Death Is Hard to Live With: Teenagers Talk about How They Cope with Loss*, School Library Journal, August, 1993, p. 192.

Lowrey-Moore, Hollis, "Janet Bode," *Twentieth-Century Young Adult Writers*, St. James Press, 1994, pp. 62-63.

Moll, Denise L., review of *Rape: Preventing It; Coping with the Legal, Medical and Emotional Aftermath*, School Library Journal, February, 1980, p. 63.

Noah, Carolyn, review of *Hard Time: A Real Life Look at Juvenile Crime and Violence*, School Library Journal, April, 1996, p. 161.

O'Malley, Anne, review of *Hard Time: A Real Life Look at Juvenile Crime and Violence*, Booklist, April 1, 1996, p. 1351.

Polese, Carolyn, review of *The Voices of Rape*, School Library Journal, October, 1990, p. 146.

Review of *Rape: Preventing It; Coping with the Legal, Medical and Emotional Aftermath*, Kirkus Reviews, November 1, 1979, p. 1268.

Sasges, Judy, review of *The Voices of Rape*, Voice of Youth Advocates, February, 1991, pp. 371-72.

Walker, Evelyn Carter, review of *Heartbreak and Roses: Real Life Stories of Troubled Love*, School Library Journal, July, 1994, p. 116.

White, Libby K., review of *Kids Still Having Kids: People Talk about Teen Pregnancy*, School Library Journal, March, 1993, p. 226.

Zvirin, Stephanie, review of *The Voices of Rape*, Booklist, October 1, 1990.

Zvirin, Stephanie, review of *Kids Still Having Kids: People Talk about Teen Pregnancy*, Booklist, January 1, 1993.

Zvirin, Stephanie, review of *Heartbreak and Roses: Real Life Stories of Troubled Love*, Booklist, October 1, 1994, p. 315.

■ **For More Information See**

PERIODICALS

ALAN Review, winter, 1996.

Booklist, March 15, 1991, p. 462; September 15, 1991.

Bulletin of the Center for Children's Books, February, 1991, p. 138; June, 1995, pp. 538-39.

Kirkus Reviews, April 15, 1980, p. 517; March 15, 1989, p. 458; September 1, 1991, p. 1158; February 15, 1995, p. 221; May 15, 1997, p. 797.

Publishers Weekly, January 2, 1995, p. 78.

School Library Journal, June, 1989, p. 126; October, 1989, p. 139; June, 1991, p. 129; November, 1991,

p. 138; July, 1994, p. 116; February, 1995, p. 115; April, 1996, p. 161.

Voice of Youth Advocates, October, 1989, p. 230; February, 1990, p. 351; June, 1991, pp. 118-19; October, 1991, p. 254; August, 1994, pp. 162-63.

Wilson Library Bulletin, April, 1991, pp. 102-3, 129.

—Sketch by Kenneth R. Shepherd

David Brin

■ Personal

Born October 6, 1950, in Glendale, CA; son of Herbert (an editor) and Selma (a teacher) Brin; married Cheryl Ann Brigham (a doctor of cosmochemistry), March, 1991; children: Benjamin, Ariana. *Education:* California Institute of Technology, B.S., 1972; University of California, San Diego, M.S., 1979; Ph.D., 1981. *Hobbies and other interests:* Backpacking, music, public speaking, environmental activism, science, general eclecticism.

■ Addresses

Office—Heritage Press, 2130 South Vermont Ave., Los Angeles, CA 90007. *Agent*—Ralph Vicinanza, 111 Eighth Ave., New York, NY 10011.

■ Career

Writer. Hughes Aircraft Research Laboratories, Newport Beach and Carlsbad, CA, electrical engineer in semiconductor device development, 1973-77; *Journal of the Laboratory of Comparative Human Cognition,* managing editor, 1979-1980; Heritage Press, Los Angeles, CA, book reviewer and science editor, 1980—. San Diego State University, teacher of physics and writing, 1982-85; postdoctoral research fellow, California Space Institute, 1983-86; Westfield College, University of London, visiting artist, 1986-87. *Member:* Science Fiction Writers of America (secretary, 1982-84), Planetary Society, British Interplanetary Society.

■ Awards, Honors

John W. Campbell Award nomination for best new author of 1982; Locus Award, Locus Publications, Nebula Award, Science Fiction Writers of America, and Hugo Award, World Science Fiction Convention, all 1984, all for *Startide Rising;* Balrog Award, 1984, for *The Practice Effect;* Hugo Award, World Science Fiction Convention, 1985, for short story "The Crystal Spheres"; Hugo Award nomination, World Science Fiction Convention, Nebula Award nomination, Science Fiction Writers of America, Locus Award, Locus Publications, John W. Campbell Memorial Award, and Best Books for Young Adults citation, American Library Association, all 1986, all for *The Postman;* Hugo Award, World Science Fiction Convention, Nebula award nomination, Science Fiction Writers of America, and Locus Award, Locus Publications, all 1988, all for *The Uplift War.*

■ Writings

Sundiver, Bantam, 1980.

Startide Rising, Bantam, 1983, hardcover edition, Phantasia Press, 1985.

The Practice Effect, Bantam, 1984.

The Postman, Bantam, 1985.

(With Gregory Benford) *Heart of the Comet*, Bantam, 1986.

The River of Time (short stories), Dark Harvest, 1986.

The Uplift War, Phantasia Press, 1987.

Dr. Pak's Pre-School (novella), Cheap Street Press, 1988.

Earth, Bantam, 1990.

(Coeditor, with Hans Moravec, Bruce Sterling, R. Bruce Miller, and Milton T. Wolf) *Thinking Robots, an Aware Internet and Cyberpunk Librarians: The 1992 LITA President's Program*, Library and Information Technology Association, 1992.

Glory Season, Bantam, 1993.

Otherness: Collected Stories by a Modern Master of Science Fiction, Bantam, 1994.

Brightness Reef: Book One of the Uplift Trilogy, Bantam Books, 1995.

Infinity's Shore, Bantam, 1996.

OTHER

Contributor to *Far Frontiers*, 1985. Contributor of articles and stories to scientific journals, including *Astrophysical Journal*, and to popular magazines, including *Analog Science Fiction/Science Fact* and *Isaac Asimov's Science Fiction Magazine*.

■ Adaptations

Warner Brothers has purchased the rights to make a film based on *The Postman*; the novella "The Loom of Thessaly" has been recorded on audio cassette by Off-Centaur Press.

■ Sidelights

Few science fiction writers are as well-versed in the facts of science as David Brin; he holds a doctorate in astrophysics and has brought his knowledge to bear on his writing. Of particular interest to Brin is the notion of interspecies genetic mutation, that is, the conversion of dolphins (to use one of his examples) to higher, human forms of thinking. As he once told Jean W. Ross in *Contemporary Authors* (*CA*), "all of the best writers play with reality. They ask the questions that are normally asked, inefficiently, by college sophomores and they do it in a manner that illuminates a self or a world. Maybe someday I will be able to do that." With his large-scale novels that deal with ethical questions and problems beyond the limits of science fiction—and that happen to be very popular—Brin has accomplished that goal.

Brin became interested in writing while an undergraduate in astronomy at Cal Tech. In an interview with Ross, Brin was casual about writing: "I would have liked very much to have been a better scientist, but at least I can take part in the adventure. And certainly my education has helped in my writing career. . . . Perhaps I tried so hard to become a scientist was because it was difficult, whereas I always figured I'd get around to writing sooner or later." His first novel, *Sundiver*, combined a futuristic setting with a murder mystery. Sally A. Lodge, writing in *Publishers Weekly*, described the story as "complex and well-constructed," her only difficulty being with the "all-too-human aliens."

By the time he published *Startide Rising* in 1983, Brin had completed his doctorate degree in Applied Physics and Space Science at the University of California, San Diego. Like *Sundiver*, it is set in the Progenitors universe, whose galaxies are inhabited with various races, some of whom have been "uplifted," their intelligence and understanding increased by a previous, perhaps now-extinct species. In *Startide Rising*, Earth ship Streaker eludes alien enemies but runs aground on the water-planet Kithrup, where it must wait for repairs. The crew, composed of genetically improved dolphins (who speak a language resembling haiku poetry, a touch that Lodge declared "ingenious") and a few humans, are under pressure from their enemies and from mutinous forces within. Critiquing *Startide Rising* in the *Washington Post Book World*, Stephen B. Brown liked that "each of Brin's dolphins is a distinct and unique individual" and found that the descriptions of their relationships "elevates this book into a substantial achievement." Donald M. Hassler, writing in the *Science Fiction and Fantasy Book Review*, praised "Brin's toying with the vision of evolution" as "probably the strongest feature in both books." He goes on to note that the idea of "managed development" as opposed to natural selection gives the author a chance to take on ethical issues, expressed in the ongoing search for the Progenitors and the debt the uplifted feel they owe to them.

Most critics liked *Startide Rising* for its complex but well-resolved plot, lively pace, and striking characterizations (especially the dolphins, whom many found among the strongest personalities). Frank Catalano, writing in *Amazing*, noted that the story was "very complex, with constant action and threat." In the *Minneapolis Tribune*, D. R. Martin

Brin's first book in the "Uplift" series describes the voyage of the Expedition Sundiver into the unknown face of the fiery sun.

noted his disappointment that things had not been "tightened up along the way," declaring the "fuss and heavy sledding" of the novel too slow for him. The novel won both the Hugo and Nebula Awards, among other honors. When Phantasia Press reprinted it in 1985, Brin made massive revisions. The re-issue was termed "an SF event" by *Publishers Weekly*.

Taming the Ego of the Universe Creator

As Brin told *CA* interviewer Ross, he became concerned that creating universes can lead to "self-indulgent" and grandiose writing. "Many scientists get very egotistical, but there are institutions that help them keep it under control. . . . I happen to have a very large ego, but one thing I hope protects me from it is the fact that I very much believe the ego can be the death of an artist's energy," he told her. This belief determined the content of *The Practice Effect*, a gentle send-up of adventure and fantasy books: in Brin's novel, objects are improved by heavy usage rather than worn out. In fact, they can transform themselves from, for example, a zipper into a saw, or a flint knife into a super-saber. The influence of one of Brin's heroes, Mark Twain, is apparent in this book; its fish-out-of-water concept led many reviewers to make favorable comparisons to *A Connecticut Yankee in King Arthur's Court*. Dennis Nuel, the protagonist, enters a strange world in which the skills everyone takes for granted in this world allow him to rescue a princess, to rout an enemy, and to contribute to this new society. "Rollicking" was how Baird Searles described Nuel's adventures in *Isaac Asimov's Science Fiction Magazine*, and, despite some "repetitiveness" and "collegiate humor," he especially liked the off-center references to "great moments in SF history."

Assumed identity has long been a favorite device for many authors to explore how a character perceives himself and is seen in the world. In *The Postman*, Brin used this technique to look at the aftermath of nuclear world war through the eyes of an everyman. As Brin told Ross in *CA*, he sought to capture "the real horror of such a war"—surviving it.

According to Ronald Florence, writing in the *Los Angeles Times Book Review*, "the world Brin draws is terrifying." A post-apocalyptic America is overrun with lawless militias bent on robbing and

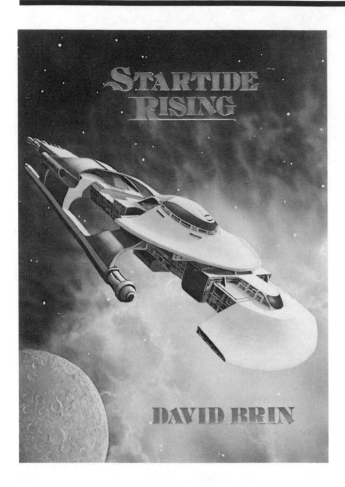

Brin received both the Nebula and Hugo awards in 1984 for this science fiction work in which genetically improved dolphins and humans travel aboard the Earth ship Streaker.

of the passages "false-sounding" and the emotional tone at times "uncertain," he praised *The Postman* as "a highly persuasive, often gripping, and warmly involving odyssey."

Collaborating on his next book with scientific colleague, fellow writer, and friend Gregory Benford, Brin put the emphasis back on the science of his fiction, using hard data and human nature to extrapolate on the implications of meddling with orbits and the galaxy. Written while Brin was still working full-time at NASA, *The Heart of the Comet* details the problems faced by a crew of scientists who ride to the furthest point of the range of Halley's Comet in an attempt to move its path of orbit closer to earth. *Chicago Tribune Book World* reviewers James and Eugene Sloan said that Brin belonged to a select group of writers "who are busy putting the hard science back into science fiction." They hailed the book as perhaps "the masterpiece of [the hard science revival]. . . . Light years ahead of [Carl] Sagan's rival effort, this book is what science fiction is."

Of the actual writing process, Brin said to Ross that it was "a most intriguing, interesting experiment." Living 150 miles apart, Brin and Benford outlined the book in great detail, settling on three points of view expressed by three characters. Benford wrote all the scenes for one character, Brin for another and they wrote alternating scenes for the third. All three characters wound up with distinctive voices, an effort Brin termed "successful" and that he told Ross they might do again.

In a kind of departure, Brin next published a collection of short stories, *The River of Time*, which included "The Crystal Spheres," a Hugo Award winner. Of his shorter work, Brin invoked another author, James Joyce, in his comment to Ross that "the short stories are attempts at epiphanies, at making a ringing note that will hang in the reader's ear." Unlike the novels, the shorter form allows the reader to "take it all in."

Returning once again to the Progenitors universe in *The Uplift War*, Brin concentrated on uplifted chimpanzees and their relations to humans in the efforts to repair ecological damage to their planet and resist invasion by aliens. *Analog's* Tom Easton lauded Brin for his expansion of the Uplift idea, noting that "humans and neochimps and Tymbrini [a race of alien pranksters] together defeat [their attackers] and score massive points in the Uplift

destroying the unprotected encampments of other survivors. Stumbling on the remains of a letter carrier, narrator Gordon Krantz slips into his postal uniform becoming, in the words of Gregory Frost of the *Washington Post Book World*, "a symbol of civilization." Eventually, Krantz re-invents society through his postman persona, literally setting up a series of post offices, postal routes, thereby offering his fellow survivors the inspiring goal of making a civilization rather than merely enduring. Frost did point to "weaknesses" but termed them "minor," giving Brin full marks for the "mythic dimension" he creates throughout the narrative. In *Voice of Youth Advocates*, John O. Christensen took Brin to task for "somewhat mundane" characters, drama, and dialogue, but termed the plot "imaginative and quite well thought out." Although a *Kirkus Reviews* contributor found a few culture with the aid of one of the grandest jokes in galactic history." This humorous streak accounts in part for Brin's quick rise from little-known author to "Favorite Science Fiction Writer of the 80s" in a poll by *Locus* magazine. He used it to great advantage when accepting the Hugo Award for *The Uplift War*, delivering his speech in Chimpanzee.

"Big" and "ambitious" were the terms Gerald Jonas, of the *New York Times Book Review*, used to describe *Earth*, Brin's look at the destruction wrought by a runaway man-made black hole. Though Joan Lewis Reynolds wrote in *School Library Journal* that she found *Earth* "less engaging" than Brin's previous novels, she liked the "element of suspense and intrigue" and noted the "timely" examination of current ecological issues. Several reviewers praised Brin's ability to convey important information in a clear way that included an annotated bibliography and a list of environmental organizations.

Exploring Otherness

In a different spin on his evolutionary speculations, Brin chose to concentrate on efforts to eliminate violence, to increase stability that permeate not only society but also some science fiction. He pressed this pastoralism to its most extreme position, postulating a society in *Glory Season* in which women rule. On planet Stratos, cloning has freed women from virtually any reproductive dependence on men. They are only useful in the production of "variants," the source of new combinations of genes. Protagonist Maia belongs to the "vars" and aims to found her own clone community until she runs into an unexpected male visitor from another planet.

Such a feminist-driven story is unusual for a male science fiction writer to dream up, but, as Brin said in *Waldenbooks Hailing Frequencies*, he wanted to "tell an interesting adventure story about a bright, reflective, and . . . resourceful young woman." As to getting the details about women right, Brin stresses that his wife's advice was invaluable. Writing in *Publishers Weekly*, Sybil Steinberg faulted Brin for "an inconclusive ending and some slow pacing," but found the book offered a "provocative and intriguing new perspective on gender issues." Randy Brough of *Voice of Youth Advocates* praised the book for its excitement

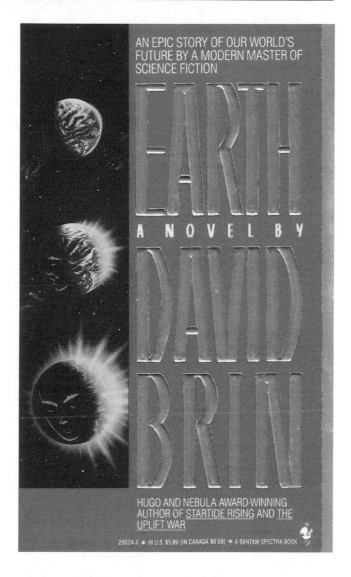

After a microscopic black hole falls into the Earth's core, a team of scientists searches frantically for a way to prevent the Earth's destruction.

and eloquence, concluding that "this is a big novel that vigorously tackles big ideas." A *Kirkus Reviews* contributor, however, found the ideas too big, stating that "Brin has simply overreached himself." And although Gerald Jonas in the *New York Times Book Review* felt that "the one challenge that Mr. Brin seems to have dodged is to get inside the heads of the powerful females who are trying to maintain the status quo," he admired the "considerable ingenuity" with which the author worked out life on Stratos.

In *Otherness*, Brin gathered twelve short stories, four essays, and an excerpt from *Earth* to present a diverse picture of his concerns and ideas. In one essay, "The Commonwealth of Wonder," the author observes that every other civilization looked back in time to a utopic past and that ours is the first to put our hopes in the future for a better life. In another essay, "The Dogma of Otherness," Brin states: "Relativity tells us that there is no absolute frame of reference. . . . Truth—it has been proved mathematically—is a thing with fuzzy outlines when you look up close." The short story "Those Eyes" speculates that elves and fairies may be UFO visitors; "Ambiguity" questions whether scientists may have tampered with creation in

Maia, a young var (gene-mixed girl) who lives in a world of female clones on the planet Stratos, sets forth to earn her place like her foremothers.

their decision to rid the universe of a micro black hole.

Voice of Youth Advocates reviewer Diane G. Yates posited that "the best science fiction writing stimulates our thinking, stretches our imagination, and opens us up to endless possibilities. . . . In this collection . . . Brin does all of that." Writing in *Locus*, Faren Miller found that Brin provoked readers to "an active involvement" in his worlds and ideas and did so "adroitly." And *Analog*'s Easton not only described the collection as "enticing," but praised Brin especially for his meditations on Otherness, a concept the author states may have already had its time.

After several years' absence, Brin took his readers once again to the Progenitors universe in *Brightness Reef: Book One of the Uplift Trilogy*. Characters from six diverse cultures that live on the banned planet Jijo, an ecologically sensitive planet where they are, in effect, squatting, relate the events that follow the arrival of humans eager to "uplift" other species to their level of knowledge. The civilization on Jijo is tranquil and pleasant until the humans wreak havoc. In an review of *Brightness Reef*, *Analog*'s Easton opined that "David Brin created a future both with immense potential for fiction and with such sheer biological and historical *likeliness* that it is easy to believe."

Jackie Cassada, writing in *Library Journal*, noted the author's "flair for spinning a good yarn . . . in this compelling and thought-provoking series opener." For a *Kirkus Reviews* contributor, *Brightness Reef* was "typical Brin . . . tremendously inventive, ambitious work undercut by excess verbiage, one-dimensional characters, and drably unevocative writing." In *Publishers Weekly* Steinberg felt the ending "does not so much conclude as stop in midstream," yet she found the fictional universe "immensely appealing, leaving readers hungry for more of this exciting, epic adventure." Her enthusiasm was echoed by *Voice of Youth Advocates*'s Ann Welton, who recommended the novel to "those who like their science fiction in large, complex doses. . . ." Easton deemed Brin "a master of plot and character and incident, of sheer story-telling, while he is also thoughtful enough to satisfy anyone's craving for meat on those literary bones."

Readers did not have to wait long for the sequel, which Brin produced later in 1996. *Infinity's Shore*

If you enjoy the works of David Brin, you may also want to check out the following books and films:

Greg Bear, *The Forge of God*, 1987.
Emma Bull, *Bone Dance*, 1991.
Arthur C. Clarke, *Rendezvous with Rama*, 1973.
Blade Runner, Warner Brothers, 1982.

---

is also set on Jijo, which is once again threatened by space visitors, in this case the dolphin crew of the Streaker from *Startide Rising* and Rothen, the race who may have done the "uplifting" of all but the human race. Jijo undergoes profound changes in the course of the novel, its peaceful haven as a refuge for those fed up with the machinations of the Progenitors universe most probably gone forever. A reviewer in *Publishers Weekly* noted Brin's "extraordinary capacity to handle a wide-ranging narrative and to create convincingly complex alien races," adding that "undeniably, this is demanding SF; but just as undeniably, it is superior SF as well."

Aside from garnering much praise for choosing to weave plenty of hard science in his work, Brin has also been cited by several reviewers for addressing social and ethical questions. Though categorized as a science fiction writer, his ambitions exceed such specific designations. As Brin told *CA*, "Personally, I don't even like being categorized as strictly a science fiction writer. I write what I want to write and what I think will both entertain the reader and get some ideas across. . . . I think that's the value of extrapolative or speculative fiction, whether you call it science fiction or not."

■ **Works Cited**

Brin, David, *Otherness: Collected Stories by a Modern Master of Science Fiction*, Bantam, 1994.

Brough, Randy, review of *Glory Season, Voice of Youth Advocates*, December, 1993, p. 306.

Brown, Stephen B., review of *Startide Rising, Washington Post Book World*, April 22, 1984, p. 11.

Cassada, Jackie, review of *Brightness Reef: Book One of the Uplife Trilogy, Library Journal*, October 15, 1995, p. 91.

Catalano, Frank, review of *Startide Rising, Amazing*, January, 1984, p. 10.

Christensen, John O., review of *The Postman, Voice of Youth Advocates*, February, 1986, p. 392-93.

Easton, Tom, review of *The Uplift War, Analog Science Fiction/Science Fact*, November, 1987.

Easton, Tom, review of *Otherness, Analog Science Fiction/Science Fact*, January, 1995, pp. 306-7.

Easton, Tom, review of *Brightness Reef: Book One of the Uplife Trilogy, Analog Science Fiction/Science Fact*, February, 1996, pp. 159-61.

Florence, Ronald, review of *The Postman, Los Angeles Times Book Review*, December 15, 1985.

Frost, Gregory, review of *The Postman, Washington Post Book World*, December 22, 1985.

Review of *Glory Season, Kirkus Reviews*, March 15, 1993, p. 338.

Hassler, Donald M., review of *Startide Rising, Science Fiction and Fantasy Book Review*, November, 1983, p. 23.

Review of *Infinity's Shore, Publishers Weekly*, November 18, 1996, p. 65.

Jonas, Gerald, review of *Earth, New York Times Book Review*, July 8, 1990, p. 22.

Jonas, Gerald, review of *Glory Season, New York Times Book Review*, June 13, 1993, p. 22.

Lodge, Sally A., review of *Sundiver, Publishers Weekly*, January 11, 1980, p. 86.

Lodge, Sally A., review of *Startide Rising, Publishers Weekly*, August 12, 1983, p. 63.

Martin, D. R., review of *Startide Rising, Minneapolis Tribune*, December 25, 1983.

Miller, Faren, review of *Otherness, Locus*, October, 1994, p. 19.

Review of *The Postman, Kirkus Reviews*, September 1, 1985, pp. 908-9.

Reynolds, Joan Lewis, review of *Earth, School Library Journal*, December, 1990, p. 135.

Ross, Jean W., interview with David Brin in *Contemporary Authors New Revision Series*, Volume 24, Gale, 1988.

Searles, Baird, review of *The Practice Effect, Isaac Asimov's Science Fiction Magazine*, July, 1984.

Sloan, James and Eugene, review of *The Heart of the Comet, Chicago Tribune Book World*, March 23, 1986.

Review of *Startide Rising, Publishers Weekly*, October 11, 1985.

Steinberg, Sybil, review of *Glory Season, Publishers Weekly*, April 12, 1993, p. 50.

Steinberg, Sybil, review of *Brightness Reef: Book One of the Uplife Trilogy, Publishers Weekly*, September 4, 1995, p. 50.

Waldenbooks Hailing Frequencies, Issue 7, 1993, pp. 3-6, 20.

Welton, Ann, review of *Brightness Reef: Book One of the Uplife Trilogy, Voice of Youth Advocates,* April, 1996, p. 35.

Yates, Diane G., review of *Otherness, Voice of Youth Advocates,* February, 1995, p. 344.

■ **For More Information See**

BOOKS

Contemporary Literary Criticism, Volume 34, Gale, 1985.

St. James Guide to Science Fiction Writers, edited by Jay P. Pederson, 4th Edition, St. James Press, 1996.

PERIODICALS

Booklist, September 1, 1987.

Los Angeles Times, December 16, 1985; January 12, 1986.

Science Fiction Chronicle, December, 1985; March, 1987; June, 1987.

Washington Post Book World, April 22, 1984.*

—Sketch by C. M. Ratner

Stephen Crane

■ Personal

Full name, Stephen Townley Crane; also wrote under pseudonym Johnston Smith; born November 1, 1871, in Newark, NJ; died of tuberculosis, June 5, 1900, in Badenweiler, Germany; buried at Hillside, NJ; son of Jonathan Townley (a minister) and Mary Helen (Peck) Crane. *Education:* Attended Lafayette College, 1890; attended Syracuse University, 1891.

■ Career

Historian, journalist, poet, and author of short stories and novels. Affiliated with New York *Tribune*, New York *Herald*, and New York *Journal*.

■ Writings

(Under pseudonym Johnston Smith) *Maggie: A Girl of the Streets* (novella), privately printed, 1893; revised edition published under the name Stephen Crane, Appleton, 1896.

The Black Riders, and Other Lines (poetry), Copeland & Day, 1895.
The Red Badge of Courage: An Episode of the American Civil War (novella), Appleton, 1895.
George's Mother (novel), Edward Arnold, 1896.
The Little Regiment, and Other Episodes of the American Civil War (short stories; includes "The Veteran"), Appleton, 1896, published in England as *Pictures of War*, Heinemann, 1898.
The Third Violet (novel), Appleton, 1897.
The Open Boat, and Other Tales of Adventure (short stories; also contains "The Bride Comes to Yellow Sky," "A Man and Some Others," "One Dash—Horses," "Flanagan," "The Wise Men," "Death and the Child," and "The Five White Mice"), Doubleday & McClure, 1898.
Active Service (novel), Stokes, 1899.
The Monster, and Other Stories (short stories; includes "The Blue Hotel" and "His New Mittens"), Harper, 1899.
War Is Kind (poetry), illustrated by Will Bradley, Stokes, 1899.
Whilomville Stories (short stories), illustrated by Peter Newell, Harper, 1900.
Wounds in the Rain: A Collection of Stories Relating to the Spanish-American War of 1898 (short stories), Stokes, 1900.
Great Battles of the World, illustrated by John Sloan, Lippincott, 1901.
Last Words (short stories; contains "The Reluctant Voyagers," "Spitzbergen Tales," "Wyoming Valley Tales," "London Impressions," "New York Sketches," "The Assassins in Modern Battles,"

"Irish Notes," and "Sullivan County Sketches"), Digby, Long, 1902.

(With Robert Barr) *The O'Ruddy* (novel), Stokes, 1903.

Men, Women and Boats (contains "Stephen Crane: An Estimate," "The Open Boat," "The Reluctant Voyagers," "The End of the Battle," "The Upturned Face," "An Episode of War," "An Experiment in Misery," "The Duel That Was Not Fought," "A Desertion," "A Dark-Brown Dog," "The Pace of Youth," "Sullivan County Sketches: A Tent in Agony, Four Men in a Cave, The Mesmeric Mountain, The Snake, London Impressions, and The Scotch Express"), edited and introduced by Vincent Starrett, Boni and Liveright, 1921.

The Works of Stephen Crane, twelve volumes, edited by Wilson Follett, Knopf, 1925-26.

The Collected Poems of Stephen Crane (poetry), edited by Follett, Knopf, 1930.

A Battle in Greece (nonfiction), illustrated by Valenti Angelo, Peter Pauper Press, 1936.

The Sullivan County Sketches of Stephen Crane (sketches; originally serialized in New York Tribune and The Cosmopolitan, 1892), edited by Melvin Schoberlin, Syracuse University Press, 1949.

Stephen Crane: An Omnibus, edited and introduced with notes by R. W. Stallman, Knopf, 1952.

Love Letters to Nellie Crouse, edited and introduced by Edwin H. Cady and Lester G. Wells, Syracuse University Press, 1954.

Stephen Crane: Letters, edited by Stallman and Lillian Gilkes, New York University Press, 1960.

An Illusion in Red and White, edited by Don Honig, Avon, 1962.

The Complete Short Stories and Sketches, edited and introduced by Thomas A. Gullason, Doubleday, 1963.

Stephen Crane: Uncollected Writings, edited by Olov W. Fryckstedt, Studia Anglistica Upsaliensia, 1963.

Poems, edited by Gerald D. McDonald, illustrated by Nonny Hogrogian, Crowell, 1964.

The War Dispatches of Stephen Crane, edited by Stallman and E. R. Hagemann, New York University Press, 1966.

The New York City Sketches of Stephen Crane, and Related Pieces, edited by Stallman and Hagemann, New York University Press, 1966.

A Critical Edition, edited by Joseph Katz, Cooper Square Publishers, 1966.

The Complete Novels, edited and introduced by Gullason, Doubleday, 1967.

Sullivan County Tales and Sketches, edited with an introduction by Stallman, Iowa State University Press, 1968.

The Notebook of Stephen Crane, edited by Donald and Ellen Greiner, John Cook Wyllie Memorial Publication, 1969.

The Blue Hotel (contains criticism), edited by Katz, C. E. Merrill, 1969.

The Portable Stephen Crane, edited and introduced by Katz, Viking, 1969.

The Works of Stephen Crane, edited by Fredson Bowers, University Press of Virginia, Volume I: *Bowery Tales: Maggie [and] George's Mother*, 1969, Volume II: *The Red Badge of Courage*, 1975, Volume IV: *The O'Ruddy*, 1971, Volume V: *Tales of Adventure*, 1970, Volume VI: *Tales of War*, 1970, Volume VII: *Tales of Whilomville*, 1969, Volume VIII: *Tales, Sketches, and Reports*, 1973, Volume IX: *Reports of War*, 1971, Volume X: *Poems and Literary Remains*, 1975.

Stephen Crane in the West and Mexico, edited by Katz, Kent State University Press, 1970.

The Complete Poems of Stephen Crane, edited and introduced by Katz, Cornell University Press, 1972.

The Stephen Crane Reader, edited by Stallman, Scott, Foresman, 1972.

The Correspondence of Stephen Crane, edited by Paul Sorrentino and Stanley Wertheim, Columbia University Press, 1988.

Stephen Crane: Prose and Poetry, Library of America, 1988.

■ Adaptations

The Red Badge of Courage was adapted for films of the same name by director John Huston for Metro-Goldwyn-Mayer, 1951, starring Audie Murphy and Bill Mauldin, and by Richard Slote for Universal Education and Visual Arts, 1970. The story was refilmed under its original title for a television movie, featuring Richard Thomas and Michael Brandon, for NBC-TV, 1974. *The Red Badge of Courage* was also adapted for filmstrip by Bruns-wick Productions, 1967, Educational Dimensions Corp., 1968, Popular Science Publishing, 1968, and by Thomas S. Klise Co., 1973. Passages of *The Red Badge of Courage* were featured in the motion picture *Reading Out Loud: Jackie Robinson*, West-inghouse Broadcasting in association with the American Library Association.

"The Bride Comes to Yellow Sky" was adapted for dramatizations by Paul T. Nolan, Pioneer

Drama Service, 1963, and by Frank Crocitto, Dramatists Play Service, 1970. "The Bride Comes to Yellow Sky" was used along with The Secret Sharer by Joseph Conrad as the basis for the film *Face to Face,* Theasquare Productions, 1952. *The Monster* was adapted for the motion picture *Face of Fire,* starring Cameron Mitchell and James Whitmore, Allied Artists, 1959. "The Upturned Face" was filmed under its original title for Changeling Productions, 1973. James Agee adapted "The Blue Hotel" into a screenplay.

Crane's work has also been used in other filmstrips, including: "The Civil War in Prose and Poetry" (includes *The Red Badge of Courage;* series of six filmstrips, color, silent), Miller-Brody Productions; "The Great Novel of the Civil War: The Red Badge of Courage" (seventeen minutes with sound cassette, color), Educational Dimensions Group; "The Vision of Stephen Crane" (two filmstrips, sound, record or cassette, color), Guidance Associates, 1972.

Recordings include: *The Red Badge of Courage,* read by Edmond O'Brien (record or cassette), Caedmon; *Stephen Crane's The Red Badge of Courage,* read by Jack Dahlby (five records or four cassettes, text), Miller-Brody Productions; *Stories of War,* CMS Records.

■ Sidelights

Stephen Crane is considered to be one of the most talented and influential writers of the late 1800s. He is known for his innovative style of writing, his vivid sense of irony, and his penetrating and sometimes disturbing psychological realism. He is considered a pioneer of the new form of literary realism that was seen in the 1920s. He wrote his first novel, *Maggie: A Girl of the Streets,* when he was only twenty-one years old, and his masterpiece, *The Red Badge of Courage: An Episode of the American Civil War,* at the age of twenty-four. When he died at the age of twenty-eight, he had worked as a reporter and war correspondent and had written volumes of war reports and feature stories, six novels, over 100 short stories and sketches, and two books of poetry. Crane's complete works make up ten large volumes in a collection published by the University of Virginia Press, and his writings are studied in American literature classes in high schools, colleges, and universities.

Crane was born on November 1, 1871, in Newark, New Jersey. He was the last of fourteen children (nine of whom survived) of Reverend Doctor Jonathan Townley Crane and Mary Helen Peck Crane. Reverend Crane was a well-known Methodist minister and Mrs. Crane, a descendant of a long line of Methodist preachers, was active in church and reform work and wrote articles on religious topics. As a child, Crane was looked after primarily by his sister Agnes, who was fifteen years older than he.

The family moved every year or so as his father struggled to support his ever-increasing family. He served as pastor at churches in several small villages in New York and New Jersey until his final move to rural Port Jervis, New York, a small town on the Delaware River. It was there that Crane, who was eight, attended school for the first time. However, he was a bright student and had no trouble making up two grades in six weeks. "[That] sounds like the lie of a fond mother at a teaparty," Crane added, "but I do remember that I got ahead very fast and that my father was pleased with me." The setting of fifteen of his short stories, including "The Monster" and "His New Mittens," is Whilomville, a fictional town that is said to be modeled on Port Jervis.

Reverend Crane loved animals, especially dogs and horses, and he passed that love to his son Stephen. However, Crane did not inherit his parents' love of the Christian religion. His religious poems and some of his other writings reflect the spiritual struggle that haunted him until the end of his life. In 1880, when Crane was nine, his father died of pulmonary complications. After two years, Mrs. Crane moved the family to Asbury Park, New Jersey, a popular resort town on the Atlantic Ocean where one of Crane's brothers operated a news agency for the New York *Tribune.* In *Stephen Crane: A Biography,* R. W. Stallman relates that two years later, Crane's sister Agnes, who he described as his "best friend and teacher," also died. "The night of Agnes' death, crashes of thunder lit the sky as if God was trying to say something," Crane said.

Because Mrs. Crane was often busy with church and reform projects, Crane was now left to his own devices, and he roamed the beaches, discovered baseball—a sport that his father had cautioned against in his book *Popular Amusements,* and helped his brother Townley gather news and gos-

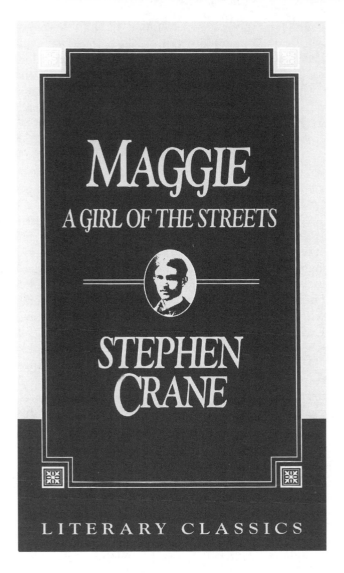

Crane's 1893 work describes the hapless story of Maggie—a girl who struggles to survive the slums of New York at the turn of the century.

sip for his *Tribune* column entitled "On the Jersey Coast." His brothers Townley and Will encouraged him to ignore the harsh sermons of their preacher uncles who frequently visited, and Crane began to develop his own secular point of view. In 1888, when he enrolled in Claverick College and Hudson River Institute, a military prep school in Claverick, New York. In the *Concise Dictionary of American Literary Biography 1865-1917*, James Colvert reports that Crane was described by one of his classmates as "bohemian in dress and manner, aloof and taciturn except on the baseball field." At this time, Crane's two greatest passions were writing and baseball.

In 1890, Crane attended Lafayette College in Easton, Pennsylvania, but he was asked to leave after one semester because he had failed to complete any coursework. He transferred to Syracuse University for the spring semester of 1891; there, he played baseball and worked as a part-time reporter for the *Tribune*, finding his news in the Syracuse slums and police courts. He preferred his own study of "humanity" to the lessons of the classroom, and he spent his afternoons reading and writing in the cupola of his fraternity house. His classmates remembered that he was working on the first draft of a story about a prostitute (*Maggie: A Girl of the Streets*) based on his observations in the Syracuse slums. His writing interfered with his classwork; at the end of the semester, only one grade—an A in English—had been reported for him, and he decided to leave Syracuse University.

Early Writing Career

Crane returned to Asbury Park and took charge of his brother Townley's *Tribune* column, acting as a reporter at religious conferences at nearby Ocean Grove and attending seminars on the arts and sciences in Avon-by-the-Sea. He had little supervision when writing these columns—his brother Townley, it seemed, was more interested in gambling at the local hotels than in anything Crane was writing about. These columns helped to sharpen his literary skills and helped him develop the satirical style that later became his trademark. Colvert recounts a column written by Crane that addresses a seminar in Avon. In the column, he describes students and faculty from the School of Biology who "are constantly engaged in inspecting great glass jars filled with strange floating growths," and "they vary this exciting pursuit by taking a boat and going to dig ecstatically for singular things in the mud flats. . . ." He also wrote fictional sketches in the *Tribune* based on his Sullivan County hunting and fishing trips with his friends. However, in August 1892, Crane's satirical style got the brothers fired when he wrote a graphic and ironic description of a labor union parade in Asbury Park and aroused the anger of politically influential unionists.

In addition to studying resort life, Crane also began studying city life in the summer of 1891. Crane met Hamlin Garland when the critic was delivering a series of lectures at Avon. Garland was impressed with the accuracy of Crane's summary of his lecture, and the two became friends. It is believed that Garland suggested that Crane experience city life firsthand by going into the Bowery and studying the people there. Crane would disappear for days in the Bowery; disguised as a derelict, he would gather materials for sketches and stories, including additional material for *Maggie*. In the *Dictionary of Literary Biography*, Peter Quartermain points out that, in a conversation with Helen Trent in 1891, Crane described the Bowery as "the most exciting place in New York." He believed what Rudyard Kipling had written in *The Light That Failed* in 1891—that poverty was necessary for the production of art. So Crane, dressed in rags, was malnourished and embraced the life of the poor by living in overcrowded dormitories and boarding houses. In addition to working on *Maggie*, Crane wrote sketches about Bowery life and sometimes sold them to the New York *Herald*.

In March of 1892, Crane showed his novel *Maggie: A Girl of the Streets* to Richard Watson Gilder, the editor of *Century* magazine. In the *Concise Dictionary of American Literary Biography*, Colvert recounts how Gilder described the novel as "too honest" and "cruel" in its depiction of life in the slums. Crane revised the novel several times, but editor after editor continued to reject it. In February or March of 1893, Crane published the novel himself using the pseudonym Johnston Smith.

Maggie is the story of a girl from the slums who is abused by her drunken parents and seduced by her brother's best friend. She becomes a prostitute and later commits suicide. *Maggie* received little attention when it was first published. After the success of *The Red Badge of Courage*, Crane released the novel using his own name, and it met with acclaim. The stark descriptions of immorality and squalor depicted in *Maggie* have led to its description as the first naturalistic novel written by an American.

The year 1893 was an exciting one for Crane because it marked the beginning of a vastly creative two-year period. During this time, Crane wrote *The Red Badge of Courage*, *The Black Riders*, a book of poetry, and the book *George's Mother*. He continued, apparently by choice, to live in poverty, still convinced that this state would help to spur his creativity. Colvert describes Crane's views on poverty: "There are few things more edifying unto

Crane, age twenty-six, sat for this photo three years before this death in 1900.

Art," he once said, "than the belly-pinch of hunger." He later described *The Red Badge of Courage* as "an effort born of pain, despair" that made it "a better piece of literature than it otherwise would have been." In the sketches "An Experiment in Misery" and "The Men in the Storm," Crane recounts his experiences when he slept in a flophouse in a tenement district and stood on a bread line in a blizzard.

Crane's Masterpiece

The Red Badge of Courage the novel that made Crane famous, was published in 1895. Ironically, the author who based so much of his writing on his own life received his greatest acclaim when he wrote about something he had not experienced—the horrors of war. Crane claimed that he based some of the novel on his experiences on the football field and on the numerous memoirs of veterans of the Civil War that he read before writing the novel. In *Yesterday's Authors of Books for Children,* Crane is quoted as saying: "I have never been in a battle, of course, and I believe I got my sense of the rage of conflict on the football field. The psychology is the same. The opposing team is an enemy tribe." In an essay entitled "The Casual Brilliance of Stephen Crane," the poet James Dickey describes *The Red Badge of Courage* as "among the most striking examples of works of pure imagination."

The novel, which became successful in England and then in the United States, took the reading public by storm. Critics in the United States and Great Britain praised the novel's realism and descriptive power. In 1896, in an essay entitled "A Remarkable Book," George Wyndham, a critic for the British *New Review,* praised the novel's power of description: "The sights flashed indelibly on the retina of the eye; the sounds that after long silences suddenly cypher; the stenches that sicken in after-life at any chance allusion to decay; or, stirred by these, the storms of passion that force yells of defiance out of inarticulate clowns; the winds of fear that sweep by night along prostrate ranks, with the acceleration of trains and the noise as a whole town waking from nightmare with stertorous, indrawn grasps—these colossal facts of the senses and the souls are the only [colors] in which the very image of war can be painted." In 1900, H. G. Wells, the father of science fiction and a close friend of Crane, described the book's "freshness of method, its vigor of imagination, its force of color and its essential freedom from many traditions that dominate this side of the Atlantic . . . with a positive effect of impact" in an essay entitled "Stephen Crane from an English Standpoint."

The Red Badge of Courage is the story of Henry Fleming, a young soldier who enlists to fight on the Union side in the Civil War. Having heard about the glories of war, Fleming thinks that he is about to embark on a wonderful adventure. Instead, he finds that war means waiting for days on end for battle adventure to actually take place. This waiting causes Fleming to fear that he will lose control and run when a battle finally occurs. He does, in fact, run, seeking shelter in a pristine forest. He finds the body of a dead soldier in the forest and returns to fight. This time, he is as steady in battle as any of the other soldiers.

The Red Badge of Courage is essentially a plotless novel, and it is often compared to an impressionistic painting. Henry Fleming experiences so many emotions, including humility, pride, fear, and courage, as he waits for battle, runs from battle, and later fights. The novel has been described as Impressionistic, Realistic, Naturalistic, and Symbolistic. Crane's consistent use of color imagery throughout *The Red Badge* are indicative of the Impressionistic movement, and proponents of Realism point to the fact that *The Red Badge of Cour-*

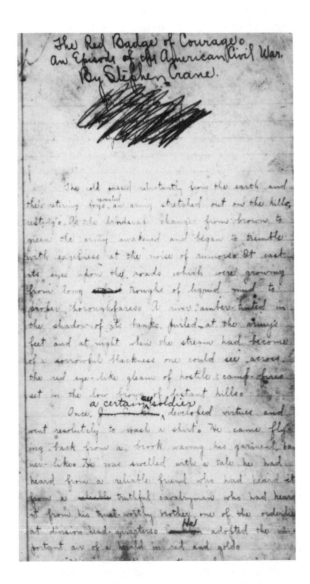

The hand-written opening page of the final manuscript of Crane's most famous novel, *The Red Badge of Courage.*

age represents the first unromanticized account of the Civil War. Fleming's actions and experiences throughout the novel are shaped by biological, social, and psychological forces outside of his control, which points to the novel as Naturalistic. Some critics also claim that the novel is laden with symbolism. Edwin H. Cady, in his biography entitled *Stephen Crane*, described *The Red Badge of Courage* as "a unique work of psychological realism deeply affected in style by the fact that the author was an ironic, imagistic, metaphysical poet."

Crane's Poems

Although Crane didn't think of himself as a poet, there are over 136 poems in the University of Virginia edition of his work. He started writing poems after he was exposed to the work of Emily Dickinson. In 1924, Amy Lowell, who has been described as a leading proponent of the use of images in American poetry, called Crane "an important link in the chain of American poetry" because of his influence on many of the poets who were her contemporaries. *The Black Riders* is a collection of poems that Crane wrote during this period of intense creativity. In March 1894, while Crane was living in New York City, he arrived at Hamlin Garland's home with a bundle of poems. In the *Dictionary of Literary Biography*, Peter Quartermain describes Garland's recollection of the event:

"I can see the initial poem now, exactly as it was written, without a blot or erasure—almost without punctuation—in blue ink. It was beautifully legible and clear of outline. It was a poem which begins thus:

'God fashioned the ship of the world carefully.'"

Garland noted that he read about thirty of Crane's poems with a growing sense of wonder and amazement:

"I could not believe they were the work of the pale, reticent boy moving restlessly around the room. 'Have you any more?' I asked. 'I've got five or six in a little row up here,' he quaintly replied, pointing to his temple. 'That's the way they come—in little rows, all made up, ready to be put down on paper. . . . I've been writing five or six every day. I wrote nine yesterday.'"

The poems were published in *The Black Riders* in May 1895. The collection has two themes: the futility of hope and the cruelty of universal law. It is a collection of short and caustic poems written in free verse that talk about the absurdity of the human condition. In the *Concise Dictionary of American Literary Biography*, Colvert points out that "more than half of the sixty-eight poems" that make up *The Black Riders* "are on religious themes." Colvert describes the topics of these poems as "the inscrutability of God, man's futile quest for God, God's wrath, the terrors of a Godless universe, and man's pride and impotence."

When Crane was writing *The Red Badge of Courage* and *The Black Riders*, he was also working on *George's Mother*, a realistic novel about a young man growing up in the slums. It is the story of the relationship between the spoiled, self-indulgent George and Mrs. Kelcey, a widow who is devoted to her son and her religion. Despite her surroundings, Mrs. Kelcey struggles to maintain a decent, respectable home. In the beginning, George is dependable in providing for himself and his mother, but later he becomes involved with a group of friends at the local saloon. He begins to openly express his contempt for his mother's religion and abuses her when she tries to persuade him to attend prayer meetings. Things become worse when George joins a local gang and loses his job. His mother remains convinced that he will change his ways; when she finally realizes that he will not, she loses her will to live and dies of a stroke. Meanwhile, George is preparing to fight a member of the gang.

Many critics have said that Crane drew on his personal experiences when he wrote *George's Mother*, modeling Mrs. Kelcey after his mother and George after himself. One of Crane's nieces, who was quoted by Colvert, put it this way: "His mother's memory was dear to him, and although he never questioned her ways when he was outside the family portals, he did marvel always that such an intellectual woman, a university graduate . . . could have wrapped herself so completely in the vacuous, futile, psalm-singing that passed for worship in those days." Edward Garnett, a prominent editor for several London publishing houses in the 1920s, describes *George's Mother* this way: "In method it is a masterpiece. . . . The rare thing about Mr. Crane's art is that he keeps closer to the surface than any living writer, and, like the great portrait painters, to a great extent makes the surface betray the depths." In "Stephen Crane's Stories of Life in the Slums: 'Maggie' and 'George's Mother,'" the author Frank Norris wrote: "*George's Mother* seems to me better than *Maggie*. For a short novel it is less pretentious, has fewer characters and more unity, conveying one distinct impression. . . . There is something about [the] death of 'the little old woman' that rings surprisingly true."

Despite the success of *Maggie* and *George's Mother*, Crane's fans and the critics demanded that he write more war stories. Crane was embarrassed because his readers preferred his writing on something that he had not experienced to his carefully studied slum stories. In 1896, he wrote a collection of short stories called *The Little Regiment*. One of the stories in this collection is entitled "The Veteran." In this story, Henry Fleming of *The Red Badge of Courage* is depicted as an old man who attempts to save two colts from a burning barn.

The Travelling Reporter

Although *The Red Badge of Courage* achieved worldwide recognition, Crane was plagued by money problems. This remained true throughout his life, as there always seemed to be more bills than funds. Compounding the problem was his open-handed generosity toward friends, acquaintances, and even down-trodden strangers. Although Crane thought a lot about money, he was never able to actually save it.

At this time, Crane accepted a position as a reporter for a newspaper syndicate, and he travelled to the American West, Mexico, and Florida. He had been pressured to leave New York City because he had defended Dora Clark, a reputed prostitute, from police persecution. When he was asked to cover Cuba's revolt against Spain, he jumped at the chance to observe war firsthand. On the way to Cuba, in Jacksonville, Florida, Crane met Cora Taylor, a woman who had left her husband to become the proprietress of a discreet brothel, the Hotel de Dream. Taylor later became his wife.

In Florida, Crane boarded the *Commodore*, a ship that was carrying guns and ammunition to Cuba. The ship sank at sea, and Crane, the ships' captain, and two other crew members spent thirty hours out at sea in a small dinghy. This event

The Red Badge of Courage by Stephen Crane

First published in 1895, this American classic realistically describes the horrors of the Civil War through the eyes of a young soldier.

was said to be the inspiration for "The Open Boat," Crane's most famous short story. Although he was physically exhausted from the ordeal, he began work on "The Open Boat" almost immediately. The critic R. W. Stallman explains that in *The Red Badge of Courage* and "The Open Boat". . . "that flawless construct of paradox and symbol, Crane established himself as one of the foremost technicians in American fiction. 'The Open Boat' is a perfect fusion of the impressionism of *Maggie* and the symbolism of *The Red Badge of Courage*. The two main technical movements in modern American fiction—realism and symbolism—have their beginnings here in these early achievements of Stephen Crane."

Crane's exposure to the elements marked the beginning of his physical problems, which led to his death at twenty-eight from tuberculosis. He was nursed back to health by Cora Taylor in Florida, but he was never very strong again. Crane and Taylor went to Greece in 1897 for Crane's next reporting assignment for the New York *Journal*—to cover the fighting between the Greeks and the Turks. He was disappointed by Greece and the war; Colvert writes that Crane later told Joseph Conrad that observing the battle at Velestino was like "trying to see a bum vaudeville show from behind a fat man who wiggles." The chance to view these battles led him to say *The Red Badge*

is all right. I have found [war] as I imagined it." His short story entitled "The Death and the Child" draws on his experiences in Greece.

When the fighting was over, Crane and Taylor went to London, England, to live. There, Crane became friends with many of England's literary giants, including Joseph Conrad and Bernard Shaw. He also plunged into his work, writing "The Monster," "Death and the Child," "The Bride Comes to Yellow Sky," and "The Blue Hotel."

Successful Short Tales

"The Monster" is the first of a number of stories that take place in Whilomville, the fictional town

Director John Huston's adaptation of *The Red Badge of Courage* (1951) features sweeping Civil War battle scenes and intense personal drama.

If you enjoy the works of Stephen Crane, you may also want to check out the following books and films:

Philip Caputo, *A Rumor of War,* 1977.
Tim O'Brien, *The Things They Carried,* 1990.
Erich Maria Remarque, *All Quiet on the Western Front,* 1928.
Shane, Paramount, 1953.

that resembled Port Jervis. It is the story of Henry Johnson, a black servant who becomes maimed when he rescues his young friend Jimmie Trescott from a house fire. Jimmie's father, Dr. Trescott, tries to help Henry, but gradually the town turns on him for helping this person who they see as a monster. Although "The Monster" is a story with a moral outlook, it is successful because Crane uses a flatly objective tone that does not condemn the people of Whilomville. The other stories that are set in Whilomville (*The Whilomville Stories*) mainly focus on the town's children.

"Death and the Child," a war story, is the only significant piece of fiction based on Crane's experience covering the Greco-Turkish War. The story involves two characters—Peza, an Italian war correspondent of Greek extraction, and a child who is abandoned by his peasant parents as war rages around them. Peza is moved by a sense of patriotism to fight against the Turks, but he later experiences misgivings when he is called to battle. The story bears a strong resemblance to *The Red Badge of Courage* in its description of panic-driven flight and in its imagery of the psychological distress that afflicts the hero.

"The Bride Comes to Yellow Sky" and "The Blue Hotel" are the best stories based on Crane's western adventure. "The Bride Comes to Yellow Sky" introduced a theme that later became popular in the plots of Western stories and movie scripts—the conflict between the lawman and the gunman, the climactic showdown, and the intolerance of the West to civilization. However, Crane's story had a twist—Sheriff Potter breaks the frontier code by getting married and being gunless, and Scratchy Wilson, the drunken outlaw, cannot bring himself to live in a town with a married sheriff. With his unique sense of humor, Crane creates two memorable characters in this story. The critic Eric

Solomon, writing in *Stephen Crane: From Parody to Realism,* describes "The Bride Comes to Yellow Sky" as "the triumphant example of Stephen Crane's mixture of parody and realism in his fiction." He further describes the story as "a beautifully balanced combination of humor and pathos, tightly, almost rigidly organized; it is perhaps Stephen Crane's finest example of the creative uses of parody."

"The Blue Hotel," which takes place at Fort Rompers, Nebraska, is one of Crane's finest short stories. The hero of the story is a Swede from the East who comes to town expecting violence and ultimately finds it. The theme of "The Blue Hotel" is similar to that of *The Red Badge of Courage* and some of Crane's Sullivan County stories; like Henry Fleming, the Swede is at war against nature but can imagine achieving personal victory over it. The critic Bettina L. Knapp states that "The Blue Hotel" "deals with the theme of brotherhood as well as that of hostility. The Swede is given shelter from the storm, and is invited into a community of friendly people. But because they failed to understand the meaning behind the Swede's hostile behavior, the other characters are as blind and set in their ways as the Swede. As Crane suggested, 'The Blue Hotel' is 'a whirling, fire-smitten, ice-locked, disease-stricken space-lost bulb'—a microcosm of society and the world."

By the time "The Blue Hotel" was completed in 1898, Crane was in poor health and had a burden of debts because of his lifestyle in England. When the U.S. ship *Maine* exploded in 1898, triggering the Spanish-American War, Crane dragged his friend Conrad around London to help him borrow passage money to New York, where he planned to join the United States Navy. He was rejected by the Navy for Spanish-American War service but went to Cuba as a correspondent for the New York *World* and later for the New York *Journal.* After several months in Cuba, his health grew worse. He was sent back to the United States, where it was confirmed that he had tuberculosis.

In 1899, Crane returned to England and rejoined Taylor at Brede Place, an ancient manor house in Sussex that she had rented in his absence. Crane became friends with Henry James and renewed his friendships with Conrad, H. G. Wells, and Edward Garnett. He wrote three pieces that year: *War is Kind,* a book of verse; the Greek war novel

Active Service; and "The Monster," a short story that looks at the problem of community malice. In December 1899, he suffered a tubercular hemorrhage, and was no longer able to do any major work. He began writing the romance *The O'Ruddy* in the early months of 1900, but when he became too ill to continue he turned the manuscript over to Robert Barr, who completed the story based on Crane's outline. By this time, he was hemorrhaging regularly. Cora Taylor took him to Dover and then, in desperation, to a sanatorium in Badenweiler in the Black Forest of Germany. He died in June of that year at the age of twenty-eight.

The poet John Berryman noted how regrettable it was that Crane ruined his health by driving himself to "boring false wars, away from the passionate private real war in his mind." According to Berryman, who was quoted by Colvert in the *Concise Dictionary of American Literary Biography,* Crane was ill and disconsolate in Cuba and exposed himself needlessly to Spanish fire in Guantanamo and San Juan. However, Crane has been described as one of the most successful of war correspondents.

In a letter described in C. K. Linson's *My Stephen Crane,* Crane wrote: "The one thing that deeply pleases me is the fact that men of sense invariably believe me to be sincere. . . . I understand that a man is born into this world with his own pair of eyes, and he is not at all responsible for his vision—he is merely responsible for his quality of personal honesty. To keep close to this personal honesty is my supreme ambition." Perhaps it is this quality of personal honesty that best describes what Crane brought to American fiction. He pioneered a new brand of literary realism and through the use of irony allows the reader to scrutinize his illusions and see the disparity that exists between one's expectations and the events that make up one's life.

■ Works Cited

Cady, Edwin H., *Stephen Crane,* Twayne Publishers, 1980.
Colvert, James, "Stephen Crane," in *Concise Dictionary of American Literary Biography 1865-1917,* Gale, pp. 86-109.
Dickey, James, "The Casual Brilliance of Stephen Crane," in *Washington Post Book World,* August 19, 1984, pp. 1, 9.

Garnett, Edward, "Stephen Crane and His Work" in his *Friday Nights: Literary Criticism and Appreciation,* Albert Knopf, 1922, pp. 201-17.
Linson, C. K., *My Stephen Crane,* Syracuse University Press, 1958.
Knapp, Bettina L., *Stephen Crane,* Ungar, 1987, p. 98.
Lowell, Amy, in an introduction to *The Work of Stephen Crane: 'The Black Riders and Other Lines,' Vol VI,* by Stephen Crane, edited by Wilson Follett, 1926.
Norris, Frank, "Stephen Crane's Stories of Life in the Slums: 'Maggie' and 'George's Mother,'" *Wave,* July 4, 1896.
Quartermain, Peter, "Stephen Crane," in *Dictionary of Literary Biography,* Volume 54: *American Poets, 1800-1945, Third Series,* Gale, pp. 48-57.
Solomon, Eric, *Stephen Crane: From Parody to Realism,* Harvard University Press, 1966.
Stallman, R. W., "Stephen Crane: A Revaluation," in *Critiques and Essays on Modern Fiction, 1920-1951: Representing the Achievements of Modern American and British Critics,* edited by John W. Aldridge, The Ronald Press Company, 1952, pp. 244-69.
Stallman, R. W., *Stephen Crane: A Biography,* Brazillier, 1968.
Wells, H. G., "Stephen Crane from an English Standpoint," *North American Review,* August, 1900.
Wyndham, George, "A Remarkable Book," in *New Review,* January, 1896, pp. 30-40.
Yesterday's Authors of Books for Children, Volume 2, Gale, 1978, pp. 84-95.

■ For More Information See

BOOKS

Beer, Thomas, *Stephen Crane: A Study in American Letters,* Knopf, 1923.
Bergon, Frank, *Stephen Crane's Artistry,* Columbia University Press, 1975.
Berryman, John, *Stephen Crane,* Sloane, 1950.
Bettencourt, Michael, *Stephen Crane,* Creative Education, 1995.
Bloom, Harold, editor, *Modern Critical Views: Stephen Crane,* Chelsea House Publishers, 1987.
Cazemajou, Jean, *Stephen Crane in Transition: Centenary Essays,* Northern Illinois University Press, 1972.
Colvert, James B., *Stephen Crane,* Harcourt, 1984.

Delbanco, Nicholas, *Group Portrait: Joseph Conrad, Stephen Crane, Ford Maddox Ford, Henry James, and H. G. Wells*, William Morrow and Co., 1982, 224 p.

Dictionary of Literary Biography, Gale, Volume 12: *American Realists and Naturalists*, 1982, Volume 78: *American Short Story Writers, 1880-1910*, 1989.

Dooley, Patrick K., *The Pluralistic Philosophy of Stephen Crane*, University of Illinois Press, 1993.

Gibson, Donald B., *The Fiction of Stephen Crane*, Southern Illinois University Press, 1968.

Gullason, Thomas A., editor, *Stephen Crane's Career: Perspectives and Evaluations*, New York University Press, 1972.

Hoffman, Daniel G., *The Poetry of Stephen Crane*, Columbia University Press, 1957.

Holton, Milne, *Cylinder of Vision: The Fiction and Journalistic Writing of Stephen Crane*, Louisiana State University Press, 1972.

Katz, Joseph, editor, *Stephen Crane in Transition: Centenary Essays*, Northern Illinois University Press, 1972.

LaFrance, Marston, *A Reading of Stephen Crane*, Oxford University Press, 1971.

Nagel, James, *Stephen Crane and Literary Impressionism*, Pennsylvania State University Press, 1980.

Mitchell, Lee Clark, editor, *New Essays on "The Red Badge of Courage,"* Cambridge University Press, 1986, 150 p.

Sedycias, Joao, *The Naturalistic Novel of the New World: A Comparative Study of Stephen Crane, Aluisio Azevedo, and Federico Gamboa*, University Press of America, 1993.

Slotkin, Alan Robert, *The Language of Stephen Crane's Bowery Tales: Developing Mastery of Character Diction*, Garland Publishers, 1993.

Solomon, Eric, *Stephen Crane in England: A Portrait of the Artist*, Ohio State University Press, 1964, 136 p.

Twentieth-Century Literary Criticism, Gale, Volume 11, 1983, Volume 17, 1985, Volume 32, 1989.

Weatherford, R. M., editor, *Stephen Crane, The Critical Heritage*, Routledge & Kegan Paul, 1973.

Wertheim, Stanley, *The Crane Log: A Documentary Life of Stephen Crane*, G.K. Hall, 1994.

PERIODICALS

Academy, February, 1986, pp. 134-35.
Accent, summer, 1959, pp. 159-65.
American Literary Realism: 1870-1910, autumn, 1982, pp. 221-31.
American Literature, March, 1939, pp. 1-10; November, 1951, p. 362; January, 1957, pp. 478-87; November, 1957, pp. 322-26; November, 1976, pp. 372-76; October, 1984, pp. 417-26.
American Mercury, January, 1924, pp. 11-14.
American Quarterly, winter, 1962, pp. 587-96.
Arizona Quarterly, summer, 1974, pp. 111-18; summer, 1982, pp. 147-61.
Bucknell Review, December, 1963, pp. 24-34.
Canadian Review of American Studies, spring, 1981, pp. 1-19.
CLA Journal, June, 1981, pp. 451-64.
Comparative Literature Studies, fall, 1984, pp. 270-81.
Dial, February, 1896, pp. 76-81; April, 1896, pp. 227-28; May 1, 1896, pp. 263-64; May 16, 1896, pp. 297-98.
English Journal, January, 1968, pp. 24-5, 99.
Journal of Modern Literature, June, 1983, pp. 346-52.
Kenyon Review, spring, 1953, pp. 310, 312-14; spring, 1956, pp. 276-99.
Literature and History, spring, 1981, pp. 91-123.
Modern Fiction Studies, summer, 1957, pp. 147-58; autumn, 1959, pp. 195-291; winter, 1962-63, pp. 410-15; winter, 1965-66, pp. 371-80; summer, 1966, pp. 200-12; winter 1981-82, pp. 621-28.
Modern Language Notes, February, 1959, pp. 108-11; February, 1960, pp. 111-13.
New York Times, October 19, 1895, p. 3.
New Republic, September 11, 1915, pp. 148-50.
Nineteenth-Century Fiction, June, 1964, pp. 77-86; December, 1968, pp. 324-31.
PMLA, December, 1958, pp. 562-72.
Poetry, June, 1919, pp. 148-52.
Southern Humanities Review, spring, 1978, pp. 141-48.
Southern Review, January, 1970, pp. 137-48.
Studies in American Fiction, spring, 1981, pp. 65-81.
Studies in Short Fiction, fall, 1981, pp. 447-51.
Studies in the Novel, spring, 1974, pp. 76-87; spring, 1978, pp. 48-63; spring, 1979, pp. 77-81; summer, 1979, pp. 216-23.
Texas Studies in Literature and Language, winter, 1963, pp. 568-82.
Yale Review, winter, 1977, pp. 209-22.*

—*Sketch by Irene Durham*

Sharon Creech

School in Switzerland), Lugano, Switzerland, 1983-85.

■ Awards, Honors

Billee Murray Denny Poetry Award, Lincoln College, IL, 1988, for "Cleansing"; School Library Journal Best Book selection, 1994, American Library Association Notable Children's Book selection, 1995, and Newbery Award, American Library Association, 1995, all for *Walk Two Moons*.

■ Writings

FOR YOUNG ADULTS

Absolutely Normal Chaos, first published in England, 1990, HarperCollins, 1995.
Walk Two Moons, HarperCollins, 1994.
Pleasing the Ghost, illustrated by Stacey Schuett, HarperCollins, 1996.
Chasing Redbird, HarperCollins, 1997.

OTHER

The Center of the Universe: Waiting for the Girl (play), produced in New York City, 1992.

Also author, under name Sharon Rigg, of *The Recital*, published in England, 1990, and *Nickel Malley*.

■ Personal

Also writes under name Sharon Rigg; born July 29, 1945, in Cleveland, OH; divorced once; married Lyle D. Rigg (headmaster at TASIS England American School, Thorpe, Surrey), 1981; children: Rob, Karin. *Education:* Hiram College, B.A.; George Mason University, M.A.

■ Addresses

Home—c/o TASIS England, Coldharbour Lane, Thorpe, Surrey, England; and Chautauqua, NY.
Agent—Carol Smith, and Jonathan Dolger.

■ Career

Federal Theater Project Archives, Fairfax, VA; editorial assistant, *Congressional Quarterly*, Washington, DC; teacher of American and British literature, TASIS England American School, Surrey, England, 1979-82, and 1984-, and TASIS (The American

■ Sidelights

"On February 6th, [1995]" writes Sharon Creech in *Horn Book* magazine, "I was home alone in England and had been wrestling all morning with a manuscript. Feeling ornery and frustrated, I fled to our back yard to vent one of my muffled screams (muffled because I am a headmaster's wife and it isn't seemly for me to scream too loudly. In the midst of that scream, the phone rang.

"A ringing telephone in a headmaster's house often signals a crisis," she continues, "and when it rings, I'm well-trained; I grab pencil and paper. . . . That afternoon, I scribbled: American Library Association and Newbery Med . . .

"The writing trails off there."

Sharon Creech describes herself in the same article as unknown in the United States in field of children's literature. Her previous books had all been published first in England, where she and her husband live and work during the school year. *Walk Two Moons,* the 1995 Newbery Medal Award winner, changed that. "I still don't know how I feel about it," she confesses to Judy Hendershot and Jackie Peck in *Reading Teacher.* "It's like someone has given me this beautiful suit of Armani clothes. They look nice and everyone admires them, but I'm a little uncomfortable in them. I like to wear them for brief periods of time and then change back to my blue jeans."

An American in England

Despite her years living and working in England, Sharon Creech is an American citizen. She was born and raised in Cleveland, Ohio, part of "a big, noisy family . . . with hordes of relatives telling stories around the kitchen table," she explains in the *Seventh Book of Junior Authors & Illustrators.* "Here I learned to exaggerate and embellish, because if you didn't, your story was drowned out by someone else's more exciting one." She was an enthusiastic writer throughout grade school and high school, and she was often captivated by the "instruments of writing: paper, pens, pencils, books. I hoarded them." She was an equally enthusiastic reader. "I don't remember the titles of books I read as a child," she recalls in the *Seventh Book of Junior Authors & Illustrators,* "but I

do remember the *experience* of reading—of drifting into the pages and living in someone else's world." "I loved myths—American Indian myths, Greek myths, and the King Arthur legends," she concludes, "—and I remember the lightning jolt of exhilaration when I read *Ivanhoe* as a teenager."

After receiving her bachelor's degree from Hiram College, Creech went on to George Mason University in Washington, D.C., for her master's. "During graduate school," she states in the *Seventh Book of Junior Authors & Illustrators,* "I worked at the Federal Theater Project Archives and longed to write plays. Next I worked at *Congressional Quarterly,* as an editorial assistant, but this was not pleasant work for me, for it was all politics and facts." Nonetheless Creech spent several years

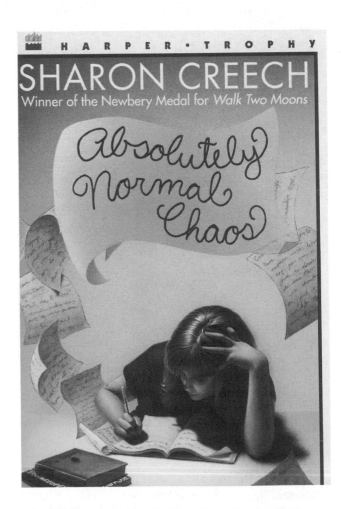

To fulfill her summer homework assignment of keeping a journal, Mary Lou Finney writes about *everything* that happened in her event-filled summer and now fears her teacher will actually read it.

in Washington. She married, had two children, and was divorced. In 1979, she persuaded the headmaster of TASIS (The American School in Switzerland) England School, a grade school for the children of expatriate Americans, in Thorpe, England, to hire her as a teacher of literature. "Before receiving an offer of employment, however," writes Lyle D. Rigg, Creech's husband, in his *Horn Book* appreciation of his wife's work, "Sharon had to convince the headmaster that she, a single parent with two young children, could handle the considerable demands of teaching in an international day/boarding school in the suburbs of London. Although I have never read Sharon's letter to that headmaster, I have heard that it was a masterpiece of persuasion and was instrumental in getting her hired."

Sharon Creech and Lyle D. Rigg were married about three years after they met. "I think it was a combination of our Buckeye roots and ice cubes that drew us together," Rigg recalls. "We met on our first day in England, when Sharon borrowed some ice—that rare commodity in Europe—from me." Rigg had been hired as assistant headmaster—the British equivalent of a school principal—and soon after he and Creech were married, they were transferred to the TASIS branch in Switzerland. In 1984, Rigg returned to Thorpe as headmaster of the English branch, and he and Creech have been there ever since (although they do spend their summers in a cabin in Chatauqua, New York). "As a teacher of American and British literature to American and international teenagers," Rigg writes, "Sharon has shared her love both of literature and of writing. She'd open up Chaucer's world in *The Canterbury Tales* and then head off to Canterbury with her students so that they could make the pilgrimage themselves. She'd offer *Hamlet*, and then off they would all go to Stratford-upon-Avon."

Balancing Teaching and Writing

Creech's teaching took a lot of time away from her writing. For many years she devoted her time almost exclusively to her teaching and her family. "In 1980, when my children and I had been in England for nine months," she recalls in *Horn Book*, "my father had a stroke. Although he lived for six more years, the stroke left him paralyzed and unable to speak . . . Think of all those words locked up for six years . . . " "A month after he

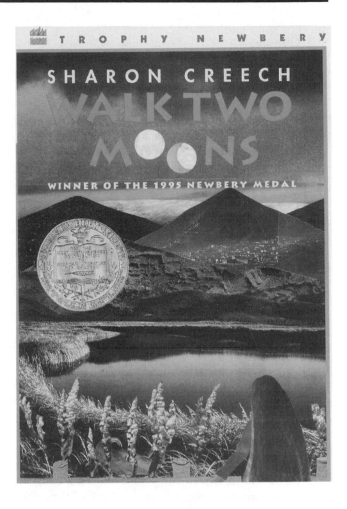

This 1995 Newbery award-winning novel features the young protagonist Sal, a girl driving across country with her grandparents in search of her missing mother.

died in 1986," she concludes, "I started my first novel, and when I finished it, I wrote another, and another, and another. The words rushed out."

Public recognition did not come easily to Creech. The first recognition she got, Rigg explains, was in 1988, when she received the Billee Murray Denny Poetry Award for her poem "Cleansing." She wrote two novels for adults, *The Recital* and *Nickel Malley;* a play, *The Center of the Universe* (which was produced off-off-Broadway); and a young adult novel, *Absolutely Normal Chaos,* before any of her books appeared in the United States. "Sharon wouldn't like for me to suggest that this was all as easy as it might sound," states Rigg. "She'd also spent two years writing an eight-hundred-page manuscript which sits on her closet

---

If you enjoy the works of Sharon Creech, you may want to check out the following books and films:

J. California Cooper, *Family*, 1991.
Will Hobbs, *The Big Wander*, 1992.
Jean Thesman, *The Rain Catchers*, 1991.
The 400 Blows, an award-winning film directed by Francois Truffaut, 1959.

---

shelf, and she received her fair share of rejections along the way." *Absolutely Normal Chaos*, her first book directed at young adults, saw print in England in 1990.

"When I wrote *Absolutely Normal Chaos*," Creech tells Hendershot and Peck, "I didn't know it was a children's book." *Absolutely Normal Chaos* deals with a variety of themes, some specific to adolescence (first love, growing up, schoolwork), and others that can apply to any period in life (dealing with relatives and friends, learning to become compassionate and understanding). The book is the journal of one summer in the life of thirteen-year-old Mary Lou Finney of Easton, Ohio. At the beginning of the book Mary Lou begs her English teacher not to read the remainder of the story. Her summer, it becomes apparent, has been more bizarre than usual. "Her life is disrupted in more ways than one by the arrival of a gangling, uncommunicative cousin, Carl Ray, from West Virginia, by his curious relationship with Charlie Furtz, the genial neighbour from across the road, who subsequently dies of a heart attack, and by her own budding romance with Alex Cheevey," explains Joan Zahnleiter in *Magpies*. These circumstances force Mary Lou to confront issues in her own life and to come to terms with her own family and the way it works.

Throughout her summer, Mary Lou learns to confront such diverse issues as classic literature, death, questionable legitimacy, and family life. "Mary Lou is a typical teen whose acquaintance with the sadder parts of life is cushioned by a warm and energetic family," states Cindy Darling Codell in her *School Library Journal* review. "Her entertaining musings on Homer, Shakespeare, and Robert Frost are drawn in nifty parallels to what is happening in her own life." "Her own hilarious brush with culture shock occurs when she accompanies Carl Ray on a trip to his home," concludes a *Horn Book* reviewer. "This visit also provides Mary Lou with some insights into what her cousin has had to endure at her house. Mary Lou grows in a number of important ways throughout the summer, and the metaphors she now recognizes in the *Odyssey* could, she realizes, very well apply to her own life."

The Impact of *Walk Two Moons*

The same themes of growth and self-recognition appear in Creech's second YA novel (the first published in America), *Walk Two Moons*. It is the story of Salamanca Tree Hiddle, another thirteen-year-old girl like Mary Lou, who relates the tale of her friend Phoebe and how her mother has left home. What makes Phoebe's story particularly relevant to Sal is the fact that Sal's mother Sugar also left home and never returned. Sal is on a trip to Idaho with her grandparents in order to visit her mother. "Sal finds that recounting Phoebe's story helps her understand the desertion of her own mother," explains Deborah Stevenson in the *Bulletin of the Center for Children's Books*. "Creech skillfully keeps these layers separate but makes their interrelationship clear, and the plot moves along amid all this contemplation with the aid of a mysterious noteleaver, a local 'lunatic,' an eccentric English teacher, and Sal's budding romance."

Some of the elements of *Walk Two Moons*, Creech explains, came from her own life and experiences. "In every book I've done," she tells Hendershot and Peck, "the characters are combinations of people. I do draw very much from my family, and so I've speculated that Salamanca and her mother are very much me and my own daughter combined." Creech explains that the idea that originally sparked the writing of *Walk Two Moons* came from a message she found in a fortune cookie: "Don't judge a man until you've walked two moons in his moccasins." The framework of the story was based on a family trip to Lewiston, Idaho that she had made when she was twelve. Sal's Native American ancestry, ideas and concepts, are also taken from the author's own life. "I inhaled Indian myths, and among my favorites were those which involved stories of reincarnation," she states in her *Horn Book* Newbery acceptance speech. "How magnificent and mysterious to be Estsanatlehi, 'the woman who never dies. She grows from baby to mother to old woman and then turns into a baby again, and on and on she goes, living a thousand, thousand lives.' I wanted to be that Navajo woman."

Sal's own name, Salamanca Tree, evokes Creech's connection with her Indianness and the outdoors. "I think I spent half my childhood up a tree," she recalls in *Horn Book.* "You could climb and climb, and you could reach a place where there was only you and the tree and the birds and the sky. And maybe the appeal of trees also lay in the sense that they live 'a thousand, thousand lives,' appearing to die each autumn . . ." "The Indianness is one of the best things about this book," declares *New York Times Book Review* contributor Hazel Rochman, "casual, contemporary and mythic, not an exotic thing apart. Sal is only a small part Indian, and she knows her parents gave her what they thought was the tribe's name but got it wrong. Still, the heritage is a part of her identity. She loves the Indian stories her mother told her, and they get mixed in with Genesis and Pandora's box and Longfellow and with family stories and, above all, with a celebration of the sweeping natural world and our connectedness with it." "For once in a children's book," Rochman concludes, "Indians are people, not reverential figures in a museum diorama. Sal's Indian heritage is a natural part of her finding herself in America."

Despite the many awards *Walk Two Moons* has won, some reviewers objected to some of the elements in the story. *American Spectator* reviewer Diana West complains of "the book's desolate, if prize-winning, theme of dysfunctional family life. Miseries abound." A *Kirkus Reviews* contributor states that "Sal's poignant story would have been stronger without quite so many remarkable coincidences or such a tidy sum of epiphanies at the end." "Creech's surprises," declares Ilene Cooper in *Booklist*, ". . . are obvious in the first case and contrived in the second." Joanna Brod, writing in the Detroit *Metro Times*, explains that "some have found the plot of *Walk Two Moons* too contrived, while others have called it overly realistic. There's a grain of truth in both accusations, but in each case Creech reveals a keen understanding of the age group for which she writes."

Chasing Redbird, a 1997 novel, takes place in Bybanks, Kentucky, the same setting as *Walk Two Moons.* The story concerns thirteen-year-old

Zinnia (Zinny) Taylor, who must come to terms with the death of her beloved Aunt Jessie. When Zinny discovers a twenty-mile path which runs from her parents' farm to Chocton, she takes on the arduous task of clearing weeds and uncovering markers along the length of the trail. Her endeavors lead to an understanding of her family's history. In *Horn Book,* Ethel L. Heins declared that Creech "has written a striking novel, notable for its emotional honesty." A *Publishers Weekly* reviewer termed the work "an affecting tale of love and loss."

One of the most dramatic themes in both *Absolutely Normal Chaos, Walk Two Moons,* and *Chasing Redbird* is that of death. Related to this concept are those of grief and loss. Mary Lou and Carl Ray have to come to terms with the loss of Charlie Furtz. Sal has to deal with death and her own sense of desertion and loss. Zinny has to learn how to cope with her emotions after the death of her Aunt Jessie. These themes are also linked to Creech's life. "When I read Salamanca's story now, with some distance," the author reveals in *Horn Book,* "I hear such longing in her voice—for her mother, for her father, for the land—and I know that her longing is also my longing . . . for my children, my larger family, and for my own country." "Every day my students stared into Pandora's box, rifled with all the evils of the world," the author declares. Yet buried deeply within both stories is an element of hope. "Salamanca and I need to face the evils," Creech states, "but we also need mystery, and we need hope. Maybe you do, too."

■ Works Cited

Brod, Joanna, "Storytelling Sorcery," review of *Walk Two Moons, Metro Times* (Detroit), January 3, 1996, p. 44.
Review of *Chasing Redbird, Publishers Weekly,* January 20, 1997, p. 403.
Codell, Cindy Darling, review of *Absolutely Normal Chaos, School Library Journal,* November, 1995, p. 119.
Cooper, Ilene, review of *Walk Two Moons, Booklist,* November 15, 1994, p. 590.
Creech, Sharon, "Newbery Medal Acceptance," *Horn Book,* July/August, 1995, pp. 418-25.
Creech, Sharon, essay in *Seventh Book of Junior Authors and Illustrators,* edited by Sally Holmes Holtze, H. W. Wilson, 1996, pp. 67-69.

Heins, Ethel L., review of *Chasing Redbird, Horn Book,* May/June, 1997, pp. 316-17.

Hendershot, Judy, and Jackie Peck, "An Interview with Sharon Creech, 1995 Newbery Medal Winner," *Reading Teacher,* February, 1996, pp. 380-82.

Rigg, Lyle D., "Sharon Creech," *Horn Book,* July/August, 1995, pp. 426-29.

Rochman, Hazel, "Salamanca's Journey," review of *Walk Two Moons, New York Times Book Review,* May 21, 1995, p. 24.

Stevenson, Deborah, review of *Walk Two Moons, Bulletin of the Center for Children's Books,* November 15, 1994, p. 590.

Vasilakis, Nancy, review of *Absolutely Normal Chaos, Horn Book,* March/April, 1996, pp. 204-5.

Review of *Walk Two Moons, Kirkus Reviews,* June 15, 1994, p. 842.

West, Diana, "P. C. Mommy Knows Best," *American Spectator,* July, 1995, pp. 64-65.

Zahnleiter, Joan, review of *Absolutely Normal Chaos, Magpies,* September, 1991, p. 32.

■ **For More Information See**

BOOKS

Children's Literature Review, Volume 42, Gale, 1997.

PERIODICALS

Bulletin of the Center for Children's Books, January, 1995, p. 162; November, 1995, p. 87.

Detroit Free Press, February 7, 1995, pp. 1C, 3C.

Fiction, May/June, 1996, pp. 34-35.

New York Times, February 7, 1995.

New York Times Book Review, May 21, 1995, p. 34.

Publishers Weekly, February 13, 1995, p. 16; March 20, 1995, pp. 24-25.

Teaching PreK-8, May, 1996, pp. 48-49.

Top of the News, spring, 1995, pp. 313-14.

Voice of Youth Advocates, February, 1995, pp. 337-38; June, 1996, p. 94.

—Sketch by Kenneth R. Shepherd

Linda Crew

■ Personal

Born April 8, 1951, in Corvallis, OR; daughter of Warren (a photographer) and Marolyn (an administrative assistant; maiden name, Schumacher) Welch; married Herb Crew (a farmer), June 22, 1974; children: Miles, William and Mary (twins). *Education:* Attended Lewis and Clark College, 1969-70; University of Oregon, B.A., 1973. *Politics:* Democrat. *Religion:* Presbyterian.

■ Addresses

Agent—Robin Rue, Anita Diamant Agency, 310 Madison Ave., New York, NY 10017.

■ Career

Farmer and writer. Has worked as a receptionist, florist, and substitute mail deliverer. *Member:* Authors Guild, Society of Children's Book Writers and Illustrators, Phi Beta Kappa.

■ Awards, Honors

Golden Kite Honor Book designation, Michigan Library Association Young Adult Honor Book designation, Best Book For Young Adults citation from American Library Association (ALA), Children's Book Award for older readers, International Reading Association, all 1989, and "Best of the Best" List, Young Adult Library Services Asoociation, 1994, all for *Children of the River*; ALA Notable Book citation, 1991, for *Nekomah Creek*.

■ Writings

FOR CHILDREN

Children of the River, Delacorte, 1989.
Someday I'll Laugh about This, Delacorte, 1990.
Nekomah Creek, illustrated by Charles Robinson, Delacorte, 1991.
Nekomah Creek Christmas, illustrated by Robinson, Delacorte, 1994.
Fire on the Wind, Delacorte, 1995.
Long Time Passing, Delacorte, 1997.

Contributor of articles and stories to periodicals.

FOR ADULTS

Ordinary Miracles (novel), Morrow, 1992.

■ Work in Progress

Screenplay versions of *Long Time Passing* and *Fire on the Wind*.

■ Sidelights

Linda Crew grounds her fiction for young adults firmly in the real world, but also in her own optimistic world view. A native of Corvallis, Oregon, who can boast an ancestor who traveled westward via a wagon train traveling the Oregon Trail in the 1860s, Crew imbues her award-winning novels with a strong sense of place, family and happy endings. "You like to feel that things are going to turn out okay in the end," she maintained in an interview with *Authors and Artists for Young Adults* (AAYA). "Don't you hate to get invested in characters and then realize, 'Oh, this is going to be one of these stories where the author is going to make me love all these people and then kill them all'?" Crew's upbeat fiction is drawn from her own experience of life, defined by her personal attitude. "I don't just *try* to be optimistic. That's the way I look at life. And besides," she adds, "somebody has to write the stories of all the families who have problems but still stay together."

"I'm not one of those who can claim a lifelong determination to be a writer," Crew once admitted, although as a youngster she *was* an avid reader who counted Louisa May Alcott's "Little Women" series, Frances Hodgson Burnett's *The Little Princess*, and classics like *Wuthering Heights* and *The Hunchback of Notre Dame* among her favorite books. She also has always viewed life from a "bookish" perspective. "I don't think that being a writer is just about filling notebooks and notebooks with scribblings all the time," Crew told *AAYA*. "I think it's kind of a way of looking at life and standing back and saying, 'If this is a story, then I am the main character.' In the books I read as a child, the main character might have a lot of problems. But she would triumph in the end. And it was kind of a pattern that I've tried to live my whole life." It's also a pattern that appears throughout her fiction.

The Price of a Glamorous Career

While Crew enjoyed writing assignments in grade school and even won a Jaycee-sponsored essay

Crew's first novel, which features Sundara, a Cambodian refugee adjusting to her new life in America, was inspired by a family of Cambodian immigrants who worked on Crew's family farm.

contest on "What My Country Means to Me" in middle school, she envisioned a future that was far more glamorous. "I wanted to be an artist or maybe a folksinger," the creative Crew recalled. "Peter, Paul, Mary, and Linda is the sort of thing I had in mind. It only took me two or three years of strumming on the old guitar to figure out that I couldn't sing!" By the time she had reached high school, Crew's career goals had made several shifts: from painter to singer, then to actress. She sustained her acting ambition through high school graduation and even into college, where she enrolled at the University of Oregon with the intention of majoring in dramatic arts. "This dream dissolved rather abruptly somewhere around my sophomore year," Crew remembered. "The fall play was *A Midsummer Night's Dream*, and the fairies were to be topless. As a potential fairy, this did not appeal to me! Also, as a fourth-generation Oregonian, it had begun to dawn on me that perhaps I would not be happy living in New York City or Los Angeles. I took the bus home and told my parents I thought I should change my major. Unfortunately, I didn't have a clue as to which program I should pursue.

"'Well,' my mother said, 'how about journalism? You've always been a pretty good writer.'

"I'm not here to argue that moms always necessarily know best, but taking her advice (for lack of any better idea) certainly worked out well for me in this case. I loved journalism. Because I'd never taken any similar classes in high school, it was all fresh and new—interviewing, researching, marketing, saying what you have to say without a lot of fuss. But my assignments always ended up full of dialogue, and I had this compelling urge to make each story a little better than the way it really happened." By the time Crew graduated from college in 1973, she knew she was destined to write fiction.

Small-town Life Yields First Novel

In 1974 the young journalism graduate married a farmer named Herb Crew and settled down on a small farm in the town where she, and her mother as well, had been born and raised. Between helping to manage the farm, raising her family of three—including active twins—and working on home remodeling projects, it wasn't always easy to find the opportunity to write. "But," Crew now realizes, "being a writer has certainly fit into all of this better than being an actress would have!"

Crew's first novel, 1989's *Children of the River*, was inspired by events in her own life. "While we Westerners commonly speak of life as a road with various forks to choose, Asians seem more inclined to see it as a river that sweeps the individual along," Crew once explained as a backdrop to her book. "Thus the title of my book, *Children of the River*, refers not only to the close ties of the Cambodian people to their river, the mighty Mekong, but also to their life philosophy." Crew and her husband first became acquainted with Asian culture in 1980, after a Cambodian family came to help harvest fruit and vegetables on their family farm. They were impressed with the Cambodians'

strong work ethic, their resolve, and their strong sense of family values. "I'm always looking for something that I feel is *my* story, a reason I should be writing it as opposed to somebody else," Crew explained to *AAYA*. "I don't write a book just because there needs to be a book on a certain subject. With the Cambodians, it took a while for me to convince myself that I was the person to tell their story. Finally, I thought, 'Maybe I'm the writer who lives on the farm, who met these people. Maybe I'm in the best position to write it.' And the Cambodians aren't going to write their own stories for a couple of decades, because they're just getting used to living here. Someday, of course, they'll write about this time in their lives, and then *Children of the River* will be old

Illustrated by Charles Robinson

Loosely based on Crew's own family, this ALA Notable Book features Robert Hummer and his warm and wacky family.

hat because of all the things I didn't get right, things they have better insights into."

Uses Journalism Training For First Novel

Even with the realization that this was a story that she was qualified to tell, Crew invested a lot of time in research before she ever set pen to paper. Fortunately, her background in journalism made the process a little less daunting than it otherwise might have been. "I just read everything I could get my hands on for a whole year before I started even thinking in terms of a fictional plot." She also interviewed many Cambodian refugees and their families. In addition, she was helped by the wealth of information then being issued by the U.S. government in its effort to help Americans understand the culture of these new immigrants.

As *Children of the River* opens, thirteen-year-old Sundara Sovann is visiting her Aunt Soka's home in a village on the Gulf of Thailand. It is April of 1975. Suddenly, the political turmoil that had been raging for weeks in the central city of Phnom Phen becomes life-threatening as Khmer Rouge guerilla forces, under communist leadership, overthrow the country's existing government and take political control of Cambodia. From their comfortable, middle-class existence, Sundara and her relatives suddenly find themselves refugees; carrying but few belongings they flee aboard ship, where Soka's newborn baby dies in a wave of sickness and malnutrition that overtakes the hundreds on board during their long journey. Finally, Sundara and her relatives find their way to a small Oregon town, where they are "adopted" by a local parish and begin to make a life for themselves in an alien culture. In the four years since her arrival in Oregon, Sundara has kept her loneliness and her fears as to the whereabouts of her parents and younger sister hidden from everyone except her immediate relatives. Now seventeen, she is still haunted by fear and guilt—especially over the death of her newborn cousin, who had died on the boat while in the young teen's care. She feels torn between the traditions of her Cambodian culture and the less-restrictive social atmosphere and more carefree lifestyle of her new American peers. When she becomes attracted to classmate Jonathan, a handsome football star, the clash between old and new comes to a head; not allowed to date, Cambodian teens follow the wishes of their parents in decisions regarding

marriage, and her aunt and uncle are determined to preserve this tradition even in their new country. Ultimately, Sundara learns that while she may adapt to some American customs, welcoming new ways into her life does not mean that she is rejecting her Cambodian heritage.

Praising Crew's first work of fiction for "its strong storytelling and thorough characterization," Roger Sutton notes in *Bulletin of the Center for Children's Books* that while the character of Jonathan is somewhat idealized, *Children of the River* "is neither sentimental nor sensational: both the horror and the romance are real." Mark Jonathan Harris agrees, writing in the *Los Angeles Times Book Review:* "Sundara's efforts to remain a 'good Cam-

In this 1995 historical novel set in northwestern Oregon, thirteen-year-old Estora Faye and her family battle a raging eighteen-mile-long fire that threatens their community.

bodian girl,' loyal to her past and family and, at the same time, create a new life for herself in this country is a moving story about the immigrant experience that also provides a fresh perspective on our own culture." And commenting on *Children of the River* in *Twentieth-Century Young Adult Writers*, essayist Suzanne M. Valentic praises the book for highlighting "how the struggle for power often results in the senseless destruction of a people, and how we, as Americans, have learned to take freedom for granted, allowing many of the values we once held dear to disappear."

One of the ways in which *Children of the River* illustrates the cultural division between Sundara and her fellow students is through language. "The interviews gave me a good feel for how the Cambodian immigrants spoke English," Crew told *AAYA*. "One girl I spoke to had actually come from Cambodia in the same year, at the same age as Sundara had. She had been well educated. So I figured that any mistakes that she was still making in English were the ones that I should have my character still making." As some readers may realize, Sundara's speech changes when she is in a family setting among her fellow Cambodians. "When the Cambodian characters are speaking within their family, they're speaking Khmer [the language spoken in Cambodia]," the author explained. "Here Sundara's language patterns switch; she doesn't use American idioms or any slang, but she's also not making the grammatical errors she does when speaking to Americans because, of course, she's speaking Khmer." To give an even more vivid sense of the cultural differences, Crew researched short, poetic phrases from a Khmer glossary, which she had her Cambodian characters use in their conversations with each other.

Although the character of Sundara was a composite of many people Crew either met or heard about, she began to quickly take on a life of her own. "There was a girl I was scheduled to interview. . . . I was well into the book and had already made up the character when I found out about her, and I thought she was my character. And I had this portrait of her: really beautiful and smart—she was a Rose Festival Princess in Portland. But when I met her I knew she wasn't Sundara. She was from a more upper-class background and that really changed it. And after that, I realized that I would never actually meet my character. I know that sounds stupid, but you get

so into your writing that you almost begin to believe that this person's out there." Crew hasn't been the only one wishing to meet the real Sundara. "I've even had letters from Cambodian guys, saying 'Please, give me her address!'"

Crew has also received many letters from young Cambodian women, letters saying, "That's just like me." "I have heard from a lot of girls who really identify with the character. *Children of the River* is also used for English as a Second Language classes in high school and college, because the reading level is not that advanced. (I'm not trying to dumb it down, but my journalism background is 'short sentences,' 'don't get too flowery.') Even immigrants from Eastern Europe and Russia have even written to say that they relate to Sundara's plight too."

While many books on the plight of Southeast Asian "boat people" focus on the discrimination these immigrants face upon their arrival in the United States, in Crew's book that element is notably absent. "Maybe I'm missing all the terrible things that are happening to these people," she wonders, "but sometimes I think that people go out and try and make it more dramatic. And I think that *real life*—as it *really* is—is interesting. Maybe that's my journalism background. I don't think that the sort of discrimination that these people encounter is the blatant, people-making-comments sort of thing. I don't honestly see that going on. And the Cambodians I've talked to didn't seem to be reporting these things. I'm not saying they have an easy time of it. I'm saying it's hard enough, without throwing in drama that is not taken from real life."

Turns to Her Own Family for Fiction

Unlike *Children of the River,* which required a great deal of research, Crew's following two books were drawn, for the most part, from her personal experiences. *Someday I'll Laugh about This* has its roots in her childhood and memories of holidays spent at her grandfather's beach cottage in Yachats, on the Oregon coast. In the novel Shelby is looking forward to this year's summer vacation at the family cottage, where she usually spends her time playing with her cousins. Excited about the traditional gathering of aunts, uncles, and assorted other relatives, there is no reason for her to think that this year will be any different than last year, or the year before. But her cousin Kirsten, a year older than Shelby, has reached the transmogrifying age of thirteen; suddenly she is worried about boyfriends, makeup, and keeping the right friends. Rather than spend time with Shelby, Kirsten spends her time with snobby Tanya Dymond, a new girl in the neighborhood. Meanwhile, for some reason, Shelby's boy cousins won't be caught dead playing with a girl this year. And her favorite Uncle Jack is no help either; he spends his time with his new fiancee, whom he has brought to meet the whole family. The beach itself is even changing as a stretch of new condominiums springs up along the waterfront. Over the summer Shelby, who narrates the story, overcomes hurt and jealousy and begins to realize that life is about change; that she herself is changing. She also learns to stand up for herself and be an individual. Praising Crew's ability to "capture the pain of growing up, along with its inherent humor," *Publishers Weekly* calls *Someday I'll Laugh about This* "uplifting."

Nekomah Creek and *Nekomah Creek Christmas* are most closely based on Crew and her family. In fact, she admitted that, by the time 1990 rolled around, *Nekomah Creek*—"the story of a wacky family"—was "the only thing I *could* write, with a nine-year-old, two-year-old twins, and a fun-loving dad underfoot." *Nekomah Creek Christmas* reunites readers with Robby and his rambunctious family. The Holiday season is approaching and Robby is growing both excited and nervous about his acting debut in the school Christmas pageant. In the meantime, his parents mood is shadowed by an impending IRS tax audit, which makes them preoccupied. "The *Nekomah Creek* books were fun," adds Crew; "my family gave me a lot of inspiration and the details came so easily. While I was writing, the dialogue was happening right downstairs!"

Crew's 1997 novel *Long Time Passing* is also partially autobiographical. A love story between two high school students that is set in the free-love era of the 1960s, the novel "isn't just hippies and smoking pot, and the thing about sex; the terror of pregnancy," the author explains. "One of the things that's central to the book is the question, 'Is she going to sleep with him or not?' I'm kind of making a plea to young women for sticking up for yourself and just saying no—you don't *have* to have a great reason. You can just decide, 'I don't want to do this yet.'" Including such per-

If you enjoy the works of Linda Crew, you may also want to check out the following books and films:

Judie Angell, *Don't Rent My Room,* 1990.
Jeanne Betancourt, *More than Meets the Eye,* 1990.
Hadley Irwin, *Kim/Kimi,* 1987.
Avalon, TriStar, 1990.
The Killing Fields, featuring Academy Award winner Haing S. Ngor, 1984.

sonally held beliefs in a published work of fiction can feel very emotionally risky, according to Crew. "In books based on your own stuff, if the reviewer writes, 'This character is a little twerp'—you are going to take it sort of personally. (Luckily, this hasn't happened to me yet, knock wood!) *Children of the River* and *Fire on the Wind* are pretty removed from me. In other books, there are characters that are a lot more a part of me, like Shelby in *Someday I'll Laugh about This,* or the young woman in *Long Time Passing.*"

Oregon History Sparks Novel Idea

Fire on the Wind, a novel set during a huge forest fire called the Tillamook Burn, would be Crew's first historical novel. "I was interested in the trees," she says, explaining how the novel came about. "It was 1990, and I was driving to the [Oregon] coast with my kids. We were going to go to the Tillamook County museum, and talking about the history of the Burn, imagining the fire coming over the ridge, and I said, 'I wonder what that was like to have been there. I don't think I've ever read a book about that, a novel.' And then I thought, 'Hey, maybe I should write it!' And when we got to the museum I bought a stack of books."

1995's *Fire on the Wind* is the story of a thirteen-year-old girl named Estora Faye—"Storie" to her friends—who lives at the Blue Star logging camp in the forests of northwestern Oregon. In the dry heat of August 1933, a fire starts near camp. Although loggers and their families aren't concerned at first, the blaze quickly grows out of control; small fires eventually converge into an eighteen-mile-long wall of flame that threatens both Storie and her entire community. Storie's consuming concerns about school, her future, and a budding romance with the logger Flynn no longer seem important as her father and Flynn join other loggers in their dangerous attempts to battle the raging inferno while she and the other women and children tense for the worst and wait. Based on a true story about the Tillamook Burn, which destroyed a vast area of Oregon forest in 1933, *Fire on the Wind* creates a vivid atmosphere due to Crew's ability to include small realistic details, provide points of view that alternate between the camp and the sites of the approaching fire, and the effective use of conversation as a way to tell the story.

Even before she became a published writer, Crew made a place for writing within her life. "For me, its a way of trying to make sense of life," she told *AAYA*. "I'm just interested in real life, everything people live through, how things *really* feel as opposed to just hearing the party line about how they feel." After she finished *Children of the River*, her writing made even more demands on her time. "*Children of the River* was rejected sixteen times. I kept working on it, so it wasn't like the *same* book got rejected sixteen times, but that's why I believe in persistence. I was running out of publishers and running out of hope, and after *Children* was finally accepted, my husband said, 'Frankly, honey, I wasn't sure how much longer *I* could keep on supporting it.' But the passion that I felt for the story was what sustained me." Unlike more prolific YA authors, Crew doesn't feel pressured to write "just anything. In a way, I feel that too many books are being published. Unless I have something really worth saying, I think the world can probably go without hearing from me."

With an active family putting increasing demands on her time, Crew still finds time for her writing with the help of a supportive spouse. During the winter months, when work around the farm slacks off, her husband punches in as "Parent Number-One" so that Crew can keep to her disciplined schedule. "I really have to keep at it each morning for three hours. It's not a huge chunk of your day, because a lot of working on the story goes on during the rest of the day, when you're doing all sorts of mind-numbing stuff and you need something to think about. But I think you really have to work on it a little every day, or the story's not there." Although she loves what she does, Crew admits that she doesn't find writing all that easy. "But I have a creative nature, and writing has turned out to be something that I can do that I can get paid for. I also like having something that I'm completely in control of. I mean, things have to get cleared with my editor, but I really like having my own thing, my own world. And having that 'thing that I do' is important to me. Just doing the laundry isn't enough. Just being support services is not real satisfying. And besides," she laughs, "I would probably drive my family nutty if I just spent all my energy on trying to make all of them succeed or do stuff or whatever."

■ **Works Cited**

Crew, Linda, interview with Pamela Shelton for *Authors and Artists for Young Adults*, February 10, 1997.

Harris, Mark Jonathan, review of *Children of the River*, *Los Angeles Times Book Review*, February 26, 1989, p. 10.

Review of *Someday I'll Laugh about This*, *Publishers Weekly*, June 8, 1990, p. 55.

Sutton, Roger, review of *Children of the River*, *Bulletin of the Center for Children's Books*, February 1989, pp. 145-46.

Valentic, Suzanne M., "Linda Crew," *Twentieth-Century Young Adult Writers*, St. James Press, 1994, pp. 156-57.

■ **For More Information See**

BOOKS

Gallo, Donald, R., editor, *Speaking for Ourselves, Too*, National Council of Teachers of English, 1993.

PERIODICALS

Booklist, March 1, 1989, p. 1128; October 15, 1991, p. 438; December 1, 1992, p. 660; October 15, 1994, p. 413.

Bulletin of the Center for Children's Books, February, 1989, p. 145; January, 1996, p. 157.

Horn Book, March, 1996, p. 205.

Kirkus Reviews, January 15, 1989; September 15, 1995, p. 1348.

Los Angeles Times Book Review, February 26, 1989, p. 10.

Publishers Weekly, January 13, 1989, pp. 91-92; September 13, 1991, p. 81.

School Library Journal, March, 1989, p. 198; August, 1991, p. 164.

Voice of Youth Advocates, June, 1989, p. 98; June, 1990, p. 101; August, 1991, p. 159.

—Sketch by Pamela L. Shelton

Jenny Davis

■ Personal

Born June 29, 1953, in Louisville, KY; daughter of Marcum Jay (an engineer) and Georgia (a teacher and counselor; maiden name, Ethridge) Schneider; married Dee Davis, August, 1975 (divorced, 1981); married Charlie O'Neill, 1994; children: Boone, Willie; Clair and Rob (stepchildren). *Education:* Allegheny Community College, A.A., 1973; University of Kentucky, B.A., 1976, M.A., 1983. *Politics:* Democrat. *Religion:* "Believer." *Hobbies and other interests:* Walking, reading, art museums, looking at the moon, the ocean, gardening.

■ Addresses

Home—723 Melrose Ave., Lexington, KY 40502-2213.

■ Career

Teacher and writer. Appalachian Regional Hospitals, Hazard, KY, child advocate, 1973-75; Fayette County Health Department, Lexington, KY, sex educator, 1983-85; The Lexington School, Lexington, teacher of English and sex education, 1985—.

■ Awards, Honors

Best Book for Young Adult distinctions, American Library Association, 1987, for *Good-Bye and Keep Cold,* and 1991, for *Checking on the Moon;* novel of the year citation, Michigan Library Association, 1989, for *Sex Education.*

■ Writings

NOVELS FOR YOUNG ADULTS

Good-Bye and Keep Cold, Orchard (New York City), 1987.
Sex Education, Orchard, 1988, published as *If I'd Only Known,* Orchard (London), 1995.
Checking on the Moon, Orchard, 1991.

■ Work in Progress

Notes from the Grave, a novella.

■ Sidelights

Jenny Davis has never been a person to sit on the sidelines. In her writing, teaching, and social activism she has translated her personal experiences—both pleasant and unpleasant—in ways that can help young people survive adolescence. Social concerns such as unemployment, homelessness, illiteracy, and violent crime are shown from the viewpoint of Davis's teen protagonists in such highly praised novels as *Good-Bye and Keep Cold* and *Checking on the Moon*. Growing up involves more than just overcoming one or two obstacles for the young people who inhabit these novels. It means confronting a never-ending succession of challenges. In each of Davis's books, written in an engaging conversational style, teens learn that parents are not always right, and that violence, old age, insecurity, and loneliness are all a part of life, sometimes conquerable, more often accepted and endured to the best of one's ability. "I try very hard not to write down to anyone, myself included," Davis told an *Authors and Artists for Young Adults* (*AAYA*) interviewer. "My protagonists are almost always observers. They're interested in people, they know people, they look at things and they think about them. And I think that's often the kind of kid who reads my books."

Born in Louisville, Kentucky, in 1953, Davis and her family moved to Pittsburgh, Pennsylvania during the 1960s. Despite her enthusiasm for learning, her high school years were not inspiring; because of the youth gangs, racial tensions, and other violence in her urban neighborhood, she frequently cut class. Instead, she went to nearby museums, libraries, or parks to escape the madness of high school and follow her own interests. "It's incredible to me that I'm a schoolteacher now," Davis exclaimed to *AAYA*, reflecting on the contrast between her childhood and her eventual career. "But I think I'm trying to do better than was done to me. Everyday that I'm in the classroom and I'm not crazy or mean, then I'm helping," she explained. Fortunately, college would provide Davis with a more stable environment; she graduated from the University of Kentucky and has since pursued a career in educating young adults, mostly on the middle-school level.

Writes First Novel in Two Weeks

Davis wrote her first novel, 1987's *Good-Bye and Keep Cold*, one summer while her two sons were away on a two-week vacation to California with their father. "It was the first time I had been separated from them for more than just a few days, and it was awful. I remember I said goodbye to

my sons at the door. I shut the door and said, 'I need something to keep me company.'" When she sat down in front of her typewriter to find that companionship in her fiction, Davis didn't intend to write the full-length novel that would become the highly praised *Good-Bye and Keep Cold*. She also didn't consciously write for a YA audience; that was the determination of her editor and the novel's publisher. "I assume this means there's still a lot of teenager in my soul," Davis once commented, "and that's okay by me. There is so much really wonderful writing in the Young Adult category that I feel honored to have a place there."

Twenty-two-year-old Edda Combs, the protagonist and narrator of *Good-Bye and Keep Cold*, recalls her childhood spent in eastern Kentucky, during which time she was the primary caretaker to a mother who was widowed and emotionally troubled. Now a year out of college, Edda reflects on the changes that have occurred in her life since the tragic death of her father in a mining accident when she was eight years old. Edda's mother, Frances, distraught with grief after her husband's death, fell into a love affair with HenryJohn, a kind man guilt-ridden over his ultimate responsibility for the explosion that caused Edda's father's death. Frances finally ended her relationship with HenryJohn and she agreed to raise his infant daughter from a second marriage when her former lover asked her to several years later. Only after she gained knowledge of her deceased husband's past infidelity with a neighbor could Frances begin to take an active part in her own life again. Divorcing her dead husband as a means of breaking with her grief, she relocated her family to Lexington where she attempted to make a new life. Edda, who had been essentially parentless throughout the years of her mom's emotional breakdown, would now be forced to deal with Lexington's urban environment, her only guidance coming from Uncle Banker, an elderly relative who has lived with the family for many years.

"This is a wise book indeed," writes Joyce Reisner Kornblatt of *Good-Bye and Keep Cold* in her review for the *New York Times Book Review*, while noting that Davis sometimes "allows herself those little lectures about sex and social problems to which too many young adult novels succumb." *Bulletin of the Center for Children's Books* reviewer Zena Sutherland praises the author for the "delicate balance" she maintains between delving into the personality of her protagonist and maintaining the

JENNY DAVIS

Checking on the Moon

In this 1991 novel thirteen-year-old Cab Jones must live with her grandmother, whom she barely knows, while her mother is on her honeymoon.

detached, objective viewpoint that allows readers to judge Edda for themselves. Praising *Good-Bye and Keep Cold* for its "purity of . . . writing" in her *Booklist* review, Ilene Cooper calls Davis's first novel "A singular offering with characters and situations that will stick with readers for a long while."

Real Life Becomes the Stuff of Fiction

When she was fifteen years old, Davis spent a year in a psychiatric hospital, trying to make sense of her own difficult adolescence and learning how to cope with the gritty realities of her urban environment. This experience would be mirrored by sixteen-year-old Olivia "Livvy" Sinclair, the narrator of *Sex Education*, published in 1988. Although

the reader immediately learns that Livvy is writing from a psychiatric hospital, the reason for her stay there becomes clear only in the novel's last few pages. Throughout the course of the book the high schooler recounts her experiences in a semester-long sex education class: the teacher's commitment to going beyond mere biology to illustrate the realities of human relationships; Livvy's own deepening romantic involvement with fellow student David Kincaid; and the events surrounding a class project wherein students are assigned simply to care for someone. Livvy and David decide to team up to "care" for some new neighbors, Mr. and Mrs. Parker, who have just moved into the old house on the hill at the end of Livvy's street. However, the two teens soon realize that something is amiss in the Parker's personal life. Attempting to help the obviously distraught and fearful Maggie Parker as she tries to cope with a difficult first pregnancy and the erratic behavior of her husband, Livvy and David are increasingly drawn into ultimately tragic circumstances.

The book's title was daring. But, while her publisher argued against it, Davis has remained convinced that *Sex Education* was "the only title the book could have. And I've heard," she will laugh, "that it holds a record as the book most frequently stolen from library shelves." Interestingly, the novel's title would be changed to *If I'd Only Known* for its 1995 British publication. Despite a somewhat cautious reaction to the title by some librarians and reviewers, the novel was widely lauded. Zena Sutherland has overwhelming praise for *Sex Education*, noting in her review for *Bulletin of the Center for Children's Books* that Davis's second novel is "deftly structured, nicely paced and smoothly written." And Sharleen A. Ober casts another "yes" vote in *Voice of Youth Advocates*, calling the novel "one you will put down only after the final sentence. . . . Teenagers will adore this story of love, mystery, and human pathos." "This is a powerful story . . .," adds a *Junior Bookshelf* reviewer, "particularly interesting for its picture of the possible difficulties of caring for others, whether they are close or not."

Parents Are Only Human . . .

In *Sex Education*, as in *Good-Bye and Keep Cold*, Davis portrays adults and families as oftentimes less than ideal. Edda Combs becomes the parent to her own mother in Davis's first novel, while, in *Sex Education,* Livvy and David's requests for advice regarding their increasingly problematic relationship with Maggie Parker are met by disinterest on the part of their preoccupied parents and lack of comprehension as to its seriousness on the part of their teacher. "This has been my own experience," explains Davis of her decision to paint some adult characters as unreliable. But her novels also frequently contain an elderly adult—like Uncle Banker in *Good-Bye and Keep Cold*—who provides her teen protagonists with advice and emotional stability during otherwise tense moments. The inclusion of older characters is the author's acknowledgment of her own grandparents and the close relationship she was able to share with them while they were alive. "My grandmother, Willie Snow Ethridge, was a writer, and my grandfather Mark Ethridge, a newspaperman," Davis once noted. "They gifted all of us in my family with a love for story and a respect for words. They taught me, too, the difference between fact and fiction."

A Window onto Inner City Life

The foibles of less-than-perfect parents and the wisdom of the elderly both affect the life of Cab Jones, the thirteen-year-old protagonist in Davis's *Checking on the Moon.* This 1991 novel finds Cab (named after the place wherein she was born) wondering, literally, where on earth her future will lead. Forced to leave her quiet Texas hometown after her mother remarries a middle-aged, world-class pianist, she and college-bound brother Bill are deposited at the home of their grandmother on their mom's way to the airport to join her husband on a honeymoon tour of Europe. But "home" doesn't quite describe grandmother Doyle's residence, a small restaurant called EATS that is located in a run-down neighborhood in an industrialized corner of Pittsburgh. Left here, in the care of a relative whom she hardly knows, Cab camps out in a small upstairs bedroom that looks out onto Washco, the area's main street. Helping her grandmother by waiting tables during the day, the curious and outgoing middle-schooler begins to develop friendships with the EATS clientele—long-time residents of the once-homey neighborhood who must now battle an increasing crime rate and watch their once pleasant streets become dilapidated due to the loss of jobs at a local factory. An observant and empathetic young woman, Cab soon becomes drawn into

the lives of her new friend: a young mother staying at a local homeless shelter while she learns to read and write; "Shakespeare," a bookish librarian trying to start an adult education program for Washco residents; and Mr. Johannsen, the elderly victim of a mugging who ponders how to right the violent wrong that has been done to him.

As Cab adjusts to her new surroundings she also finds a close friend in Tracy, a vivacious teen who pursues her dream of becoming a writer with inspiring self-confidence. She also learns to appreciate her grandmother's quiet wisdom, and gains a strengthened sense of herself through her efforts

LAUREL-LEAF CONTEMPORARY FICTION

An unusual high school class

A life-changing lesson

A novel about loving and caring

CAN $3.50

SEX EDUCATION

BY JENNY DAVIS

While fulfilling a term project, sixteen-year-old Livvy Sinclair and her new friend David learn the true meaning of caring for another person in need.

to help organize a block watch system designed to make Washco a safe street once again. Commenting that Davis's themes of growing adolescent self-awareness and the development of one's social responsibility are well-drawn, Nancy Vasilakis notes in her *Horn Book* review that "Davis's story of old people coping with a changing neighborhood alongside young people dealing with their own interior transformations is essentially positive and hopeful." And Judy Silverman agrees in *Voice of Youth Advocates*, remarking that *Checking on the Moon* "is full of real-life situations, with characters we seem to know, and we're eager to see what happens to them."

But *Checking on the Moon* goes beyond the problems of its adolescent protagonist, problems that center on trying to make sense of her place in a changing world. Through its depiction of citizens controlled by an increasing level of day-to-day violence, the novel also directly addresses the problem of crime in the inner cities. In fact, writing the novel was Davis's attempt to work through the traumatizing aftereffects of her own rape, which occurred in the late 1980s and which she fictionalizes through the character of Jessica, Bill's girlfriend. As with Jessica, Davis realizes that the hurt never really goes away. "I wrote something called "The Rape Journal"—I went through this thing where I just wrote it all out," she explained to *AAYA*, describing her method of dealing with the violence done to her, for which the perpetrator was never found. "I spent four months working on that, just putting everything down that I could." The rough draft of *Checking on the Moon* followed: "It was written in the third person. When I finally read it all the way through, I just held it in my arms. It was like a premature birth or something, and I knew it wasn't right."

So Davis put the manuscript away for a while before rewriting it in the first person. "And letting myself meet Cab, which was really helpful." The first time she sent the manuscript to her editor, he didn't like it. "So I really—literally—slept on it for a year; I took it and wrapped it up and put it under my pillow. I just couldn't deal with it; my feelings were hurt. I had always felt that, after being raped, I had not been able to write; that something had happened. And I was trying to fight that. And then when *he* didn't like it. . . ." A year later Davis resubmitted the manuscript with only minor changes. "And this time he *did* like it," she recalls.

If you enjoy the works of Jenny Davis, you may want to check out the following books and films:

Julie Reece Deaver, *Say Goodnight, Gracie*, 1988.
Carolyn Meyer, *The Two Faces of Adam*, 1991.
Erika Tamar, *It Happened at Cecilia's*, 1989.
Gas Food Lodging, Cineville, 1992.

Writing Remains Secondary to Living

A full-time teacher and the mother of four children—including a stepson severely handicapped by cerebral palsy, with whom she has creatively and enthusiastically shared her love of books and writing—Davis doesn't spend a great deal of time fishing around for plots or characters for potential novels. "It seems to me they come and get me," she once explained to *Something about the Author*. "To write, I pay attention—to my ideas, hunches, dreams, memories, to my experiences, all of them, real and imagined." And with her full schedule, the opportunity to write only comes on the weekends. "And you don't really find the time to write; you make it," Davis will add. Although her written work has sometimes been difficult for publishers to classify because its mature subject matter and unique approach tend to cross established genre boundaries, she continues to set aside the time for it. "Writing helps me feel more alive and more aware," the novelist once explained. "It can also make me feel crazy and sad if the story I'm telling is a hard one to get out. Even so, on balance, writing heals me, it amuses me, and most of all—no matter how hard to tell—it makes me wonder. And I love to wonder."

Despite the fact that she has always loved to write, Davis admitted to *AAYA* that she "wasn't prepared to become a writer. It took me by surprise. And actually, it happened because I started teaching writing." Although trained as a sex education teacher, in 1985 a private school in Lexington liked her teaching style so much that they offered Davis a job as an English teacher, just to have her as part of their staff. "My style as a teacher is not to make my students do something I wouldn't do, or wouldn't find value in doing," Davis explained. "So I taught writing for a year, and then the following summer I started writing on my own." She began with short stories; her sons' two-week trip to California would eventually provide the impetus for longer works.

Even before her experiences with writing—and rewriting—*Checking on the Moon*, Davis realized that, because it is so personal, writing can be a very scary thing. "I grew up in a family of embellishers," she once stated. "I took to fiction because it gave me a way to make things up and get away with it. What I found, instead, was that the more I lie, the more I tell the truth. It's scary, but I love it."

■ Works Cited

Cooper, Ilene, review of *Good-Bye and Keep Cold*, in *Booklist*, August, 1987, p. 1736.

Davis, Jenny, interview with Pamela L. Shelton for *Author and Artists for Young Adults*, February 12, 1997.

Kornblatt, Joyce Reisner, review of *Good-Bye and Keep Cold*, in *New York Times Book Review*, November 28, 1987, p. 29.

Ober, Sharleen A., review of *Sex Education*, in *Voice of Youth Advocates*, August, 1988, p. 130.

Review of *Sex Education*, in *Junior Bookshelf*, August, 1995, pp. 152-53.

Silverman, Judy, review of *Checking on the Moon*, in *Voice of Youth Advocates*, December, 1991, p. 309.

Something about the Author, Volume 74, Gale, 1993, pp. 59-60.

Sutherland, Zena, review of *Good-Bye and Keep Cold*, in *Bulletin of the Center for Children's Books*, September, 1987.

Sutherland, Zena, review of *Sex Education*, in *Bulletin of the Center for Children's Books*, September, 1988, p. 5.

Vasilakis, Nancy, review of *Checking on the Moon*, in *Horn Book*, November/December, 1991, pp. 743-44.

■ For More Information See

BOOKS

Davis, Jenny, essay in *Speaking for Ourselves, Too*, edited by Donald R. Gallo, National Council of Teachers of English, 1993.

PERIODICALS

Bulletin of the Center for Children's Books, September, 1987; November, 1991, p. 61.

Publishers Weekly, December 25, 1987, p. 37.

School Library Journal, September, 1988, p. 197; December, 1991, p. 29.

Times Educational Supplement, June 3, 1988, p. 49.

Voice of Youth Advocates, October, 1987, p. 199.

—Sketch by Pamela L. Shelton

Dick Francis

■ Personal

Full name, Richard Stanley Francis; born October 31, 1920, in Tenby, Pembrokeshire, Wales; son of George Vincent (a professional steeplechase rider and stable manager) and Molly (Thomas) Francis; married Mary Brenchley (a teacher and assistant stage manager), June 21, 1947; children: Merrick, Felix. *Education:* Attended Maidenhead County School. *Religion:* Church of England. *Hobbies and other interests:* Boating, fox hunting, tennis.

■ Addresses

Home—P.O. Box 30866, S.M.B., Grand Cayman, British West Indies. *Agent*—Andrew Hewson, John Johnson Authors' Agent, 45/47 Clerkenwell Green, London, EC1R 0HT, England; Sterling Lord Listeristic, Inc., 1 Madison Ave., New York, NY 10010.

■ Career

Novelist. Amateur steeplechase rider, 1946-48; professional steeplechase jockey, 1948-57; *Sunday Express*, London, England, racing correspondent, 1957-73. *Military service:* Royal Air Force, 1940-46; became flying officer (pilot). *Member:* Crime Writers Association (chair, 1973-74), Mystery Writers of America, Crime Writers of Canada, Detection Club.

■ Awards, Honors

Steeplechase jockey championship, 1954; Silver Dagger Award, Crime Writers Association, 1965, for *For Kicks*; Edgar Allan Poe Award, Mystery Writers of America, 1969, for *Forfeit*, 1980, for *Whip Hand*, and 1995, for *Come to Grief*; Gold Dagger Award, Crime Writers Association, 1980, for *Whip Hand*; Order of the British Empire, 1984; Diamond Dagger Award, Crime Writers Association, 1990, for overall achievement in the mystery genre; named Grand Master, Mystery Writers of America, 1996.

■ Writings

MYSTERY NOVELS

Dead Cert, Holt, 1962.
Nerve, Harper, 1964.
For Kicks, Harper, 1965.
Odds Against, Joseph, 1965, Harper, 1966.
Flying Finish, Joseph, 1966, Harper, 1967.
Blood Sport, Joseph, 1967, Harper, 1968.
Forfeit, Harper, 1968.
Enquiry, Harper, 1969.
Rat Race, Joseph, 1970, Harper, 1971.

Bonecrack, Joseph, 1971, Harper, 1972.

Smokescreen, Joseph, 1972, Harper, 1973.

Slay-ride, Joseph, 1973, published as *Slayride*, Harper, 1974.

Knock Down, Joseph, 1974, published as *Knockdown*, Harper, 1975.

High Stakes, Joseph, 1975, Harper, 1976.

In the Frame, Joseph, 1976, Harper, 1977.

Risk, Joseph, 1977, Harper, 1978.

Trial Run, Joseph, 1978, Harper, 1979.

Whip Hand, Joseph, 1979, Harper, 1980.

Reflex, Joseph, 1980, Putnam, 1981.

Twice Shy, Joseph, 1981, Putnam, 1982.

Banker, Joseph, 1982, Putnam, 1983.

The Danger, Joseph, 1983, Putnam, 1984.

Proof, Joseph, 1984, Putnam, 1985.

Break In, Joseph, 1985, Putnam, 1986.

Bolt, Joseph, 1986, Putnam, 1987.

Hot Money, Joseph, 1987, Putnam, 1988.

The Edge, Joseph, 1988, Putnam, 1989.

Straight, Putnam, 1989.

Longshot, Putnam, 1990.

Comeback, Putnam, 1991.

Driving Force, Putnam, 1992.

Decider, Putnam, 1993.

Wild Horses, Putnam, 1994.

Come to Grief, Putnam, 1995.

To the Hilt, Putnam, 1996.

OTHER

The Sport of Queens: The Autobiography of Dick Francis, Joseph, 1957, revised edition, 1968, Harper, 1969, newly revised edition, Joseph, 1974, Macmillan, 1993.

(Editor with John Welcome) *Best Racing and Chasing Stories*, Faber, 1966.

(Editor with John Welcome) *Best Racing and Chasing Stories II*, Faber, 1969.

(Editor with John Welcome) *The Racing Man's Bedside Book*, Faber, 1969.

Lester: The Official Biography, Joseph, 1986, published as *A Jockey's Life: The Biography of Lester Piggott*, Putnam, 1986.

Works have been included in anthologies; contributor to periodicals, including *Horseman's Year*, *Sports Illustrated*, and *Stud and Stable*.

■ Adaptations

Dead Cert was filmed by United Artists in 1973; *Odds Against* was adapted for Yorkshire Television as *The Racing Game*, 1979, and also broadcast on the PBS-TV series "Mystery," 1980-81; Francis's works were adapted for the television series "Dick Frances Mysteries" by Dick Francis Films Ltd., 1989. Many of Francis's books have been recorded on audiocassette.

■ Overview

Mystery writing powerhouse Dick Francis first came to the public eye as a victim in one of the most unusual sports mishaps of the century. The incident happened just after Francis, then a jockey, and his horse headed towards the finish post, after having just cleared the last jump at the Grand National. The Grand National is a British steeplechase race considered by many to be the world's most prestigious horse racing event, and Francis was riding Devon Loch, the Queen Mother's horse. Suddenly and inexplicably, the horse that had seemed destined to win collapsed, and would not complete the race. Francis never figured out what startled his horse that day, but that singular occurrence turned into a triumph than the seasoned jockey could never have imagined the morning of the race. The accident actually marked the beginning of his writing career.

A literary agent's continued interest in Francis's perspective of the race led him to write his autobiography. "The one good thing about an autobiography as a first introduction to writing is that at least you don't have to research the subject: the story is all there in your own head," Francis stated in *The Sport of Queens*. The same year the work was published, 1957, Francis retired as a jockey and began covering horse racing for London's *Sunday Express*.

Economic necessity, more than anything else, made him try his hand at fiction writing. The mystery surrounding his loss at the Grand National seemed to naturally lead him to write a mystery— but this time, one he could solve. His debut novel, *Dead Cert*, sold well enough for him to consider writing another one. Since 1964, with the appearance of his second work, *Nerve*, Francis's fans have been able to read a new novel by their favorite author each year. So rather than looking for Francis in the winner's circle at the race track, his fans on both sides of the Atlantic know to find him on the bestseller lists.

Francis has used his horse racing background to give him the framework on which to hang his fictional material. Sometimes his novels focus on the racing world, and sometimes the horses are kept in the background, as a side note to add color to the story. His reputation for writing about the races has made it something readers expect, however, and the colorful book jackets that grace his most recent offerings always bear the stylized picture of a jockey and a race horse. Born as he was into a family with connections to the sport—Francis's father was a steeplechase jockey and, later, a manager of stables—racing was what Francis lived for thirty-seven years; he couldn't be expected to let it go completely. Reviewers have noted, however, that even those readers not interested in horse racing can find something to love in a Francis mystery. In the *New York Times,* John Leonard noted, "Not to read Dick Francis because you don't like horses is like not reading Dostoyevsky because you don't like God. Baseball, boarding houses, race tracks and God are subcultures. A writer has to have a subculture to stand on."

Critics agree that Francis adeptly describes this subculture. In a *New York Times Book Review* critique of Francis's third novel, *For Kicks,* published in 1965, Anthony Boucher wrote, "The background of life among horses and trainers and stable lads (and criminals) is so real you can smell and taste it." In a *London Magazine* review of Francis's 1979 thriller, *Whip Hand,* John Welcome observed, "Francis can make a race come alive off his pages in thrilling fashion. One can hear the smash of birch, the creak of leather and the rattle of whips." These two volumes won their author recognition from his fellow mystery writers: a Silver Dagger award from the British Crime Writers Association for *For Kicks,* and a Gold Dagger award from the same organization, as well as an Edgar Award from the Mystery Writers of America, for *Whip Hand. For Kicks* is about Australian horse-breeder, Daniel Roke, who is hired to go undercover to figure out how a group of British criminals are managing to fix horse races. The villain, Humber, is an unscrupulous trainer, whom Welcome calls "a living and lasting portrait."

One of Francis's many novels set in the horse racing world, this 1989 work describes Derek Franklin's search for safety and truth after he inherits his brother's fortune as well as his enemies.

The other award winner, *Whip Hand,* marked the first time Francis had ever repeated a character from a previous book. To keep his outlook fresh, Francis had avoided the series characters so popular among other mystery writers, and instead created a unique personality to do the detective work in each novel. Only on rare occasion has Francis deviated from this rule, and his use of Sid Halley in his celebrated novel, *Whip Hand,* is one exception; Halley had already appeared in *Odds Against,* Francis's fourth novel. Speaking of the two books in *The Sport of Queens,* Francis commented, "Sid Halley, in *Odds Against,* lost his left hand, and in *Whip Hand* I set out to explore the mental difficulties of someone coming to terms with such a loss. In the event, it proved a most disturbing book to write, a psychological wringer which gave me insomnia for months." Halley is a former jockey, working as a professional detective. While the main plot line deals with Halley's investigation of a case in which several leading racehorses die from heart problems, a multitude of other plot elements are introduced including a balloon race, Halley's relationships with his ex-wife and his new

In this 1992 novel, ex-jockey Freddie Croft finds himself playing the role of detective to save his horse carrier business when a hitchhiker is found murdered in one of Croft's horse vans.

girlfriend, and a racket involving a sham charity. "All this comes together," writes Marty S. Knepper in *Twelve Englishmen of Mystery*, "under Francis' expert manipulations, to become a well-integrated novel about love and courage."

Besides varying leading characters, Francis also spends an enormous amount of time on research so he can include other topics besides horse racing in his novels. In a *U.S. News & World Report* interview with Alvin P. Sanoff, Francis explains how he and his wife combined his writing business with pleasure while doing research. "[My wife and I] spend a lot of time at the laboratories at UCLA to learn all about pharmacology for *Banker*," Francis noted. "For the book *Proof*, we

spent thirty years researching and drinking wine." Francis's wife, in fact, took flying lessons as background research for the novel *Flying Finish* and took up painting before her husband wrote of the art world in *Frame*. In the novel *Reflex*, Francis explores the world of photography. The book, which sold eighty-five thousand copies in its original hard-cover edition, features jockey and amateur photographer Philip Nore. Much of the action of the novel takes place in the darkroom as Nore painstakingly works to decipher a series of photographic mysteries left him by George Millace before his untimely death . "The portrait of Philip Nore, the mediocre jockey nearing the end of his career," wrote John Welcome in *London Magazine*, "is created with real insight." "In writing scenes of action, not all of them violent, and blending them into a mystery adventure," Julian Symons observed in the *New York Times Book Review*, "[Francis] is now a long way ahead of the rest of the field."

While in *Reflex* readers learned about the world of photography, in *Proof* they get a crash course in the intricacies of the wine-making business. This time, Francis's protagonist is Tony Beach, the son and the grandson of jockeys who were also war heroes. He gets involved in a mystery when he provides wine from his liquor store to a training farm. While there, he witnesses a ten-ton horse trailer plunge into a tent of party-goers. Later, his expertise is sought by both the police and a private detective agency to aid in their investigations of a scam in which lesser grade liquor is substituted for a more expensive brand. Several reviewers discovered the book to be typical Francis fare. Charles Monaghan, in the *Washington Post Book World*, claimed "all the classic Francis elements are there in abundance. There are the protagonist darkened by personal tragedy, beautifully drawn cameos of English eccentrics, the horse-racing background and enough blood and guts spattered about for several books on surgery." Ross Thomas, in the *New York Times Book Review*, wrote that "The style is patented Francis—serviceable, practiced and plain." In the *Armchair Detective*, Mary Frances Grace found Beach a notable leading man. "Tony Beach, like Francis's other protagonists, is an interesting, living-and-breathing character who because he is so carefully and fully developed has earned our concern and our affection."

After emphasizing non-racing themes in his writing, Francis returned full force to racing with *Break*

In and *Bolt.* Both novels feature Kit Fielding, a steeplechase jockey, who in *Break In* attempts to discover the source of a damaging item about his twin sister, Holly, and her horse trainer husband, Bobby Allardeck, in a popular gossip column. While in the *New York Times Book Review* Marilyn Stasio admitted thinking that after twenty-five novels Francis couldn't possibly have anything fresh to say about horse-racing, she confessed that reading the novel changed her mind. "The vigor of the novel's racing-world background, its hero's cocky energy and the absolute lustiness of its horse racing scenes," Stasio conceded, "convey no whiff of ennui but rather the high spirits of a homecoming." In *Bolt*, Fielding helps the Princess

Critics praised Francis for this 1993 novel about architect and builder Lee Morris's struggle to restore an old racecourse partially owned by Morris and the disagreeable heirs of the park's founder.

Casilia de Brescou, whose horses he rides, evade the threats of blackmailers, while a feud between the Fieldings and the Allardecks intensifies. In the *New York Times Book Review* Mel Watkins recognized several key ingredients in the novel, including "an intricately concocted plot, a raft of characters ranging from race track plungers and stable hands to royalty, and a good deal of the gritty ambiance of England's racecourses." A *Booklist* reviewer called the novel "vintage Francis."

The Edge highlights the activities of Tor Kelsey, whom Gina Macdonald in *Concise Dictionary of British Literary Biography* called "another of Francis's quietly competent, resilient heroes." Kelsey is working as an undercover agent for Britain's Jockey Club, traveling on The Great Canadian Transcontinental Mystery Race Train. A master of disguises, during the course of the novel Kelsey appears as a rich horse owner, an actor in a staged murder, and a waiter. On the train along with Kelsey are important figures from the international world of horse racing bound for races in Winnipeg and Vancouver. When the private car of the multimillionaire Lorrimore family disappears from the end of the train, Kelsey must use all his resources to trap Julius Apollo Filmer, the appealing, but violent extortionist. "Like all Dick Francis novels," wrote Margaret Cannon in the Toronto *Globe & Mail*, "this one is thoroughly researched and impeccably constructed. Filmer is as nasty as needs be, and the rest of the characters are skilfully drawn." In the *New York Times Book Review*, Sue Grafton observed, "A series of near misses keeps the story moving, along with the shenanigans of a 'murder mystery' being enacted en route, which are cleverly incorporated into the plot."

According to Macdonald, while Francis's earlier novels included a lot of violence against the hero, his "later books concentrate more specifically on psychological stress—emotional conflict and self-doubt. The hero is less a man who can endure torture than one who has the strength to face self-doubt, fear, and human inadequacy and still survive and thrive." Other critics have noticed the change in Francis's writing. In the *Armchair Detective* Barry Bauska maintained that in the mysteries "physical pain is being supplanted by psychological strain." "The result, of course," continued Bauska, "is that Dick Francis is becoming less a writer of thrillers and more a creator of literature—while remaining, as he always has been, splendidly readable." On the other hand, Newgate Callendar found that readers are enthusiastic about Francis's novels because the author has taught them what to expect, and in each novel he delivers what has been promised. "Perhaps one reason for his reliability, and for his readers' delight in the product," Callendar remarked in the *New York Times Book Review,* "is the fact that he discovered a dependable formula from the very beginning and has relentlessly pursued it."

■ Update

Refusing to slow down even as passed an age at which many people would have retired, Francis continues to publish on a regular basis. In 1990, Francis received the Diamond Dagger award from the Crime Writers Association for overall achievement in the mystery genre. In 1995, his novel *Come to Grief* won for him a third Edgar Award from the Mystery Writers of America, the first time any writer had received three such awards. In 1996, the Mystery Writers of America named him a Grand Master. Not one to rest on his accomplishments, Francis published his thirty-fifth thriller in 1996.

Writing in the *British Book News* nearly a decade earlier, James Melville called Francis "the author who can truthfully say that his best book is the one most recently published." Based on critical response, Francis's most recent books stand up well to Melville's analysis. In *School Library Journal,* for example, Pam Spencer deemed Francis's 1991 novel, *Comeback,* full of "the same storytelling magic as always," and a *Kirkus Reviews* contributor noted that the book showed Francis's "touch with a story as sure as ever." In *Comeback,* race horses are mysteriously dying during or after surgery performed by veterinarian Ken McClure, a friend of British Foreign Service officer Peter Darwin. As Darwin begins his investigation, a fire destroys part of McClure's animal hospital and a body is discovered in the ashes. Then an anesthetist is found dead on the operating table, and Darwin must discover the connections between the series of bizarre events. "All the action, suspicions, and deaths," Jim and Janet Mura observed in *Voice of Youth Advocates,* "make for a fast and exciting read."

Francis's next thriller, *Driving Force,* spent ten weeks on the *Publishers Weekly* bestseller list in

Francis combines horse racing and movie making in this suspenseful tale about a director, Thomas Lyon, determined to solve a mystery partially revealed by his dying friend.

1992, and in *Booklist* Robert Seid called it "one of the best Francis novels in years." The "Driving Force" of the title is the name of the race horse transporting business run by ex-jockey Freddie Croft. When it is discovered that the vans used to haul the horses are also being used for smuggling, and a hitchhiker dies in one of the them, Croft begins investigating. "Clues abound," wrote Carolyn E. Gecan in *School Library Journal,* "with those needed to solve the mystery satisfyingly mixed in with enough red herrings to keep readers happily guessing." In the *New York Times Book Review* Elizabeth Tallent hailed Francis for his story-telling ability, as well as for the vast amount of information included in his novels. While reading a book by Dick Francis, according to Tallent, the reader feels "not only the thrill of vicarious competence imparted by the company of his heroes, but also the lore you collect as you go, feel like a field trip with the perfect guide."

Francis turned to the study of architecture for his next novel, *Decider.* The narrator is Lee Morris, an architect and builder with a special interest in restoring dilapidated buildings and the father of six young sons. Morris has obtained a small interest in Stratton Park racecourse and, when there is talk of tearing the course down to make way for development, he decides to save the place for its architectural merit. Morris only obtained the shares through the divorce settlement of his mother, who was just briefly married to one of Lord Stratton's sons. The heirs of Lord Stratton have been resentful of Morris for a long time, so a confrontation is inevitable when he shows up for a shareholders' meeting held at the track. While he is there, an explosion flattens the grandstands, nearly killing Morris and one of his sons. Immediately, suspicion falls on a member of the Stratton family. "Francis's deft plotting," Sybil S. Steinberg wrote in *Publishers Weekly,* "and sharp characterization are, as usual, on the mark: both Lee and his progeny are realistic and appealing." Christy Tyson in *Voice of Youth Advocates* similarly praised Francis's ability to plot out a novel. She remarks: "Francis is a master storyteller, without a doubt, enhancing his solidly plotted mysteries with deceptively casual prose and fully-fleshed characters."

Such is the interest in Francis's novels that J. P. Donleavy wrote in the *New York Times Book Review,* "Any mention of Dick Francis to one of his readers brings unrestrained eruptions of enthusiasm of every pleasant kind." Such is the enthusiasm of his readers that Francis's 1957 autobiography, *The Sport of Queens,* has been revised and reissued several times. In a review of the 1993 edition of the work, *Los Angeles Times Book Review* critic Dick Roraback stated, "Underscored by genuine and disarming modesty, with honest praise for rivals and colleagues alike, with rare communion with God's noblest beasts, the updated reissue of Francis' autobiography is odds-on to delight." In his autobiography Francis describes the slow process of completing his novels which he writes in only one draft. "My 'first draft' is IT," he explained. "I can't rewrite to any extent: I've tried once again or twice, but I haven't the mental stamina and I feel all the time that

although what I'm attempting may be different, it won't be *better* and may very well be worse, because my heart isn't in it."

In *Wild Horses,* Francis takes advantage of the book's focus on the moviemaking industry to experiment with the novel form. "Francis put his novel together," wrote Sybil S. Steinberg in a *Publisher Weekly* review of the book, "in the same way a movie is constructed, with out-of-sequence scenes, dissolves and brilliant images." *Wild Horses* concerns the making of a movie about the puzzling death by hanging of a horse trainer's young wife. The director, Thomas Lyon, is so intrigued by the unsolved mystery that he begins to put together the pieces of the puzzle he has managed to uncover. A confession from a newspaperman dying of bone cancer, who mistakenly takes Lyon for a priest, followed by a murder and death threats against him, serve only to whet Lyon's appetite for knowing more. He becomes convinced that his film can only have a satisfactory ending if he can reveal the true murderer—if he manages to live that long. Commenting on the novel in her *Booklist* review, Emily Melton concluded, "[Francis's] writing is as unobtrusively smooth and classy as a single-malt scotch. His latest book promises to be another hit." Besides the to-be-expected information about horse racing that the reader finds in the book, in *School Library Journal* Katherine Fitch wrote that *Wild Horses* "offers an in-depth, fascinating behind-the-scenes view of filmmaking."

Sid Halley Returns

One of the issues Francis deals with in his autobiography is the motivation behind his decision to use Sid Halley in another novel, after using him once before. His inspiration to do so came from actor Mike Gwilym's portrayal of Halley in a television version of the first novel the character appeared in, *Odds Against.* Francis wrote: "To Mike Gwilym also I owe the existence of the double award-winner, *Whip Hand,* since it was because the Royal Shakespeare Company actor so incredibly matched my concept of Sid Halley . . . that I became interested in writing a second book about the same man." Brought back by reader demand, Sid Halley reappears in Francis's 1995 best-seller, *Come to Grief.* The novel won for its author his unprecedented third Edgar Award for best novel of the year from the Mystery Writers

If you enjoy the work of Dick Francis, you may want to check out the following books and films:

K. M. Peyton, *Darkling*, 1990.
Agatha Christie, *Murder on the Orient Express*, 1934.
John D. MacDonald, *A Purple Place for Dying*, 1964.
Pharlap, Twentieth Century-Fox, 1983.

of America. In the *New York Times Book Review*, John Mortimer concluded: "What makes [Francis's] books attractive is his sense of decency and honorable behavior," especially when it comes to his heroes. In another *New York Times Book Review* piece, contributor Tobin Harshaw remarked, "What makes [Francis] successful . . . is his ability to create refreshingly likable sleuths." Such is the case with Halley, whom Melton described as "solid, engaging, and true blue."

In *Come to Grief* Sid Halley becomes involved in a mystery when he is called to the home of Linda Ferns after someone cuts off the left front hoof of her daughter Rachel's pony, Silverboy. Rachel has leukemia and now suffers from recurrent nightmares, months after the incident. Halley soon discovers that someone has been mutilating thoroughbreds—some have had their hooves cut off with almost surgical precision, while still others have been blinded. Looking for clues, Halley interviews the owners of the other horses, and questions an old friend, a fellow ex-jockey by the name of Ellis Quint. Now a respected television personality, Quint had once done a story on Rachel. When Halley's investigative work points to Quint as the perpetrator, a public outrage against the investigator ensues.

Critical commentary on the novel, while not totally positive, was favorable. Melton wrote: "Francis' latest is one of his very best, offering a cleverly contrived plot, unforgettable characters, and steadily mounting suspense." In *School Library Journal* Linda A. Vretos recommended the book to young adult readers, concluding, "Francis has once again created a plausible mystery that can't be solved before finishing the book." Harshaw found the subplot concerning Rachel Fern "sappy," but maintained, "Sid Halley has never been better."

Steinberg marveled at the consistency of Francis's work through his many years of writing. Reflecting with pleasure on the subtle humor the author displays in the novel, she wrote, "Francis, who turns 75 later this year, proves himself still at the top of his game."

To the Hilt, Francis's next novel, begins with a brutal confrontation between Alexander Kinloch and four thugs who keep asking, "Where is it?" Kinloch, an artist who prefers to live in his secluded shepherd's hut on a Scottish mountainside where he can paint in solitude, does not even have time to rest up from his wounds before he rushes to London to help his mother after his stepfather has a heart attack. Once there, Kinloch discovers that his stepfather's brewery is on the verge of bankruptcy due to the company's chief financial officer having taken millions from he company's accounts. Kinloch agrees to take over the brewery at least until his stepfather's health improves. In the meantime, he must endure more attacks, help hide Golden Malt, his stepfather's horse scheduled to run in the important King Alfred Gold Cup, and protect the cup itself—a medieval chalice.

"Still at Top Form"

The *New York Times Book Review*'s Marilyn Stasio finds the book "delivers the pleasures people pay for: an exciting story told with great narrative drive and a hero who suffers 'fear and pain and humiliation' for the sake of his honor." The entire novel revolves around Kinloch's ability to confront the many obstacles in his path, including the people who matter most to him. "The diverse plot threads tie up neatly," notes Steinberg in *Publishers Weekly*, "but not before Al achieves an understated emotional breakthrough with his wife and with his undemonstrative mother, endures gruesome torture with hardly a murmur and wins his stepsister's trust." Other commentators put *To the Hilt* in the long line of Francis successes. *Publishers Weekly* contributor Daisy Maryles asserted that the book proved that Francis "is still at top form."

How could a steeplechase jockey become such a popular writer? By way of explanation John Mortimer noted in the *New York Times Book Review*, "What he brought with him from the race track were the crowd-pulling powers of suspense, surprise and the shared enthusiasm to discover who's going to win." Perhaps his best trait is the diversity in character and plot he purposefully brings to his writings. "Despite his standard approach," writes Gina Macdonald in *Concise Dictionary of British Literary Biography*, "Francis's works are never the same. His plots remain fresh, unexpected, solid. They move forward briskly, with an admirable sense of timing, and are lent variety by his interweaving of racing and other concerns." His works have sold more than twenty million copies worldwide and have been translated into close to two dozen languages. Remarkably, he has managed to continue a three-decade long writing career with no noticeable slumps. "The author's notes for Mr. Francis' books often observe that as a jockey he rode for the Queen Mother," Elizabeth Tallent observed in the *New York Times Book Review*. "At this point in his illustrious writing career," the critic continued, "the Queen Mother might wish to note in her *vita* that the writer Dick Francis once rode for her."

■ Works Cited

Bauska, Barry, "Endure and Prevail: The Novels of Dick Francis," *Armchair Detective*, July, 1978, pp. 238-44.

Review of *Bolt*, *Booklist*, December 1, 1986, p. 529.

Boucher, Anthony, "Criminals at Large," *New York Times Book Review*, March 21, 1965, p. 22.

Callendar, Newgate, "Crime: 'Trial Run,'" *New York Times Book Review*, May 20, 1979, pp. 34, 36.

Cannon, Margaret, review of *The Edge*, *Globe & Mail* (Toronto), November 11, 1988.

Review of *Comeback*, *Kirkus Reviews*, August 15, 1991, p. 1047.

Donleavy, J. P., "Racing All the Way to the Bank," *New York Times Book Review*, October 17, 1993, p. 40.

Fitch, Katherine, review of *Wild Horses*, *School Library Journal*, January, 1995, p. 145.

Francis, Dick, *The Sport of Queens: The Autobiography of Dick Francis*, Joseph, 1957.

Gecan, Carolyn E., review of *Driving Forces*, *School Library Journal*, February, 1993, p. 126.

Grace, Mary Frances, *Armchair Detective*, winter, 1986, pp. 77-78.

Grafton, Sue, review of *The Edge*, *New York Times Book Review*, February 12, 1989, p. 9.

Harshaw, Tobin, review of *Come to Grief*, *New York Times Book Review*, October 8, 1995, p. 26.

Knepper, Marty S., "Dick Francis," *Twelve Englishmen of Mystery*, edited by Earl F. Bargainnier,

Bowling Green University Popular Press, 1984, pp. 222-48.

Leonard, John, "Books of the Times: Reflex," *New York Times*, March 20, 1981, p. 21.

Macdonald, Gina, "Dick Francis," in *Concise Dictionary of British Literary Biography*, Volume 8: *Contemporary Writers, 1960 to the Present*, Gale, 1992, pp. 107-27.

Maryles, Daisy, "Behind the Bestsellers: Putnam's Pride," *Publishers Weekly*, October 7, 1996, p. 20.

Melton, Emily, review of *Wild Horses*, *Booklist*, August, 1994, p. 1988.

Melton, Emily, review of *Come to Grief*, *Booklist*, August, 1995, p. 1909.

Melville, James, review of *Proof*, *British Book News*, October, 1984, p. 617.

Monaghan, Charles, "Vintage Dick Francis," *Washington Post Book World*, March 17, 1985, p. 5.

Mortimer, John, "Back in the Saddle Again," *New York Times Book Review*, October 2, 1994, p. 26.

Mura, Jim, and Janet Mura, review of *Comeback*, *Voice of Youth Advocates*, February, 1992, p. 370.

Roraback, Dick, review of "The Sport of Queens," *Los Angeles Times Book Review*, April 17, 1994, p. 6.

Sanoff, Alvin P., "Finding Intrigue Wherever He Goes," *U.S. News & World Report*, March 28, 1988.

Seid, Robert, review of *Driving Force*, *Booklist*, September 15, 1992, p. 100.

Spencer, Pam, review of *Comeback*, *School Library Journal*, March, 1992, p. 266-67.

Stasio, Mary, "Back on the Track," *New York Times Book Review*, March 16, 1986, p. 7.

Stasio, Mary, review of *To the Hilt*, *New York Times Book Review*, October 13, 1996, p. 29.

Steinberg, Sybil S., review of *Decider*, *Publishers Weekly*, August 2, 1993, p. 60.

Steinberg, Sybil S., review of *Wild Horses*, *Publishers Weekly*, August 8, 1994, pp. 368-69.

Steinberg, Sybil S., review of *To the Hilt*, *Publishers Weekly*, August 12, 1996, p. 65.

Symons, Julian, "Argentine Detective & English Jockey," *New York Times Book Review*, March 29, 1981, pp. 3, 45.

Tallent, Elizabeth, "He Gets the Horse Right There," *New York Times Book Review*, October 18, 1992, p. 32.

Thomas, Ross, "Who Watered the Whisky?," *New York Times Book Review*, March 24, 1985, p. 13.

Tyson, Christy, review of *Decider*, *Voice of Youth Advocates*, October, 1994, p. 207.

Vretos, Linda A., review of *Come to Grief*, *School Library Journal*, May, 1996, p. 148.

Watkins, Mel, review of *Bolt*, *New York Times Book Review*, March 29, 1987, p. 22.

Welcome, John, "Under Pressure," *London Magazine*, March, 1980, pp. 95-96.

Welcome, John, "Photo-Finish," *London Magazine*, February-March, 1981, pp. 143-44.

■ For More Information See

BOOKS

Bestsellers 89, Issue 3, Gale, 1989.

Contemporary Literary Criticism, Gale, Volume 2, 1974, Volume 22, 1982, Volume 42, 1987.

St. James Guide to Crime and Mystery Writers, 4th edition, edited by Jay P. Pederson, St. James Press, 1996.

PERIODICALS

Christian Science Monitor, July 17, 1969.

Family Circle, July, 1970.

Globe and Mail (Toronto), November 16, 1985; August 12, 1989.

London Magazine, February-March, 1975.

Los Angeles Times, March 27, 1981; April 9, 1982; September 12, 1984.

Newsweek, April 6, 1981.

New Yorker, March 6, 1969; April 7, 1971; March 20, 1981; December 18, 1989.

New York Times, March 6, 1969; April 7, 1971; December 18, 1989.

New York Times Book Review, March 10, 1968; March 16, 1969; June 8, 1969; July 26, 1970; May 21, 1972; July 27, 1975; September 28, 1975; June 13, 1976; July 10, 1977; April 25, 1982.

Time, March 11, 1974; July 14, 1975; May 31, 1976; July 7, 1978; May 11, 1981.

Times (London), December 18, 1986.

Times Literary Supplement, October 28, 1977; October 10, 1980; December 10, 1982.

Washington Post, October 3, 1986.

Washington Post Book World, April 30, 1972; February 18, 1973; April 19, 1980; April 18, 1982; March 27, 1983; February 21, 1988; February 5, 1989.*

—Sketch by Marian C. Gonsior

Robert Frost

■ Personal

Born March 26, 1874, in San Francisco, CA; died January 29, 1963, in Boston, MA; son of William Prescott (a newspaper reporter and editor) and Isabel (a teacher; maiden name, Moodie) Frost; married Elinor Miriam White, December 19, 1895 (died, 1938); children: Elliott (deceased), Lesley (daughter), Carol (son; deceased), Irma, Marjorie (deceased), Elinor Bettina (deceased). *Education:* Attended Dartmouth College, 1892, and Harvard University 1897-99.

■ Career

Poet. Held various jobs between college studies, including bobbin boy in a Massachusetts mill, cobbler, editor of a country newspaper, school-teacher, and farmer. Tufts College, Medford, MA, Phi Beta Kappa poet, 1915 and 1940; Amherst College, Amherst, MA, professor of English and poet-in-residence, 1916-20, 1923-25, and 1926-28; Harvard University, Cambridge, MA, Phi Beta Kappa poet, 1916 and 1941; Middlebury College, Middlebury, VT, co-founder of the Bread-Loaf

School and Conference of English, 1920, annual lecturer, beginning 1920; University of Michigan, Ann Arbor, professor and poet-in-residence, 1921-23, fellow in letters, 1925-26; Columbia University, New York City, Phi Beta Kappa poet, 1932; Yale University, New Haven, CT, associate fellow, beginning 1933; Harvard University, Charles Eliot Norton Professor of Poetry, 1936, board overseer, 1938-39, Ralph Waldo Emerson Fellow, 1939-41, honorary fellow, 1942-43; associate of Adams House; fellow in American civilization, 1941-42; Dartmouth College, Hanover, NH, George Ticknor Fellow in Humanities, 1943-49, visiting lecturer. *Member:* International PEN, National Institute of Arts and Letters, American Academy of Arts and Letters, American Philosophical Society.

■ Awards, Honors

Levinson Prize, *Poetry* magazine, 1922; Pulitzer Prize for poetry, 1924, for *New Hampshire,* 1931, for *Collected Poems,* 1937, for *A Further Range,* and, 1943, for *A Witness Tree;* Golden Rose Trophy, New England Poetry Club, 1928; Russell Loines Prize for poetry, National Institute of Arts and Letters, 1931; Mark Twain medal, 1937; Gold Medal of the National Institute of Arts and Letters, 1939; Gold Medal of the Poetry Society of America, 1941 and 1958; Gold Medal, Limited Editions Club, 1949; unanimous resolution in his honor and gold medal from the U.S. Senate, March 24, 1950; American Academy of Poets Award, 1953; Medal of Honor, New York University, 1956; Huntington Hartford

Foundation Award, 1958; Emerson-Thoreau Medal, American Academy of Arts and Sciences, 1958; participated in President John F. Kennedy's inauguration ceremonies, 1961, by reading his poems "Dedication" and "The Gift Outright"; Congressional Gold Medal, 1962; Edward MacDowell Medal, 1962; Bollingen Prize in Poetry, 1963; inducted into American Poet's Corner at Cathedral of St. John the Divine, 1986. Chosen poet laureate of Vermont by the State League of Women's Clubs; more than forty honorary degrees from colleges and universities, including Oxford and Cambridge Universities, Amherst College, and the University of Michigan.

■ Writings

POETRY

Twilight [Lawrence, MA], 1894, reprinted, University of Virginia, 1966.
A Boy's Will, D. Nutt, 1913, Holt, 1915.
North of Boston, D. Nutt, 1914, Holt, 1915, reprinted, Dodd, 1977.
Mountain Interval, Holt, 1916.
New Hampshire, Holt, 1923, reprinted, New Dresden Press, 1955.
Selected Poems, Holt, 1923.
Several Short Poems, Holt, 1924.
West-Running Brook, Holt, 1928.
Selected Poems, Holt, 1928.
The Lovely Shall Be Choosers, Random House, 1929.
The Lone Striker, Knopf, 1933.
Two Tramps in Mud-Time, Holt, 1934.
The Gold Hesperidee, Bibliophile Press, 1935.
Three Poems, Baker Library Press, 1935.
A Further Range, Holt, 1936.
From Snow to Snow, Holt, 1936.
A Witness Tree, Holt, 1942.
A Masque of Reason (verse drama), Holt, 1942.
Steeple Bush, Holt, 1947.
A Masque of Mercy (verse drama), Holt, 1947.
Greece, Black Rose Press, 1948.
Hard Not to Be King, House of Books, 1951.
Aforesaid, Holt, 1954.
The Gift Outright, Holt, 1961.
"Dedication" and "The Gift Outright" (poems read at the presidential inaugural, 1961; published with the inaugural address of J. F. Kennedy), Spiral Press, 1961.
In the Clearing, Holt, 1962.
Stopping by Woods on a Snowy Evening, Dutton, 1978.

Early Poems, Crown, 1981.
A Swinger of Birches: Poems of Robert Frost for Young People (with audio cassette), Stemmer House, 1982.
Spring Pools, Lime Rock Press, 1983.
Birches, illustrated by Ed Young, Holt, 1988.

Also author of *And All We Call American*, 1958.

POEMS ISSUED AS CHRISTMAS GREETINGS

Christmas Trees, Spiral Press, 1929.
Neither Out Far Nor In Deep, Holt, 1935.
Everybody's Sanity [Los Angeles], 1936.
To a Young Wretch, Spiral Press, 1937.
Triple Plate, Spiral Press, 1939.
Our Hold on the Planet, Holt, 1940.
An Unstamped Letter in Our Rural Letter Box, Spiral Press, 1944.
On Making Certain Anything Has Happened, Spiral Press, 1945.
One Step Backward Taken, Spiral Press, 1947.
Closed for Good, Spiral Press, 1948.
On a Tree Fallen Across the Road to Hear Us Talk, Spiral Press, 1949.
Doom to Bloom, Holt, 1950.
A Cabin in the Clearing, Spiral Press, 1951.
Does No One but Me at All Ever Feel This Way in the Least, Spiral Press, 1952.
One More Brevity, Holt, 1953.
From a Milkweed Pod, Holt, 1954.
Some Science Fiction, Spiral Press, 1955.
Kitty Hawk, 1894, Holt, 1956.
My Objection to Being Stepped On, Holt, 1957.
Away, Spiral Press, 1958.
A-Wishing Well, Spiral Press, 1959.
Accidentally on Purpose, Holt, 1960.
The Woodpile, Spiral Press, 1961.
The Prophets Really Prophesy as Mystics, the Commentators Merely by Statistics, Spiral Press, 1962.
The Constant Symbol [New York], 1962.

COLLECTIONS

Collected Poems of Robert Frost, Holt, 1930, new edition, 1939, reprinted, Buccaneer Books, 1983.
Selected Poems, Holt, 1934, reprinted, 1963.
Come In, and Other Poems, edited by Louis Untermeyer, Holt, 1943, reprinted, F. Watts, 1967, enlarged edition published as *The Road Not Taken: An Introduction to Robert Frost*, reprinted as *The Pocket Book of Robert Frost's Poems*, Pocket Books, 1956.
The Poems of Robert Frost, Modern Library, 1946.

You Come Too: Favorite Poems for Young Readers, Holt, 1959, reprinted, 1967.

A Remembrance Collection of New Poems by Robert Frost, Holt, 1959.

Poems, Washington Square Press, 1961.

Longer Poems: The Death of the Hired Man, Holt, 1966.

Selected Prose, edited by Hyde Cox and Edward Connery Lathem, Holt, 1966, reprinted, Collier Books, 1968.

Complete Poems of Robert Frost, Holt, 1968.

The Poetry of Robert Frost, edited by Lathem, Holt, 1969.

Robert Frost: Poetry and Prose, edited by Lawrence Thompson and Lathem, Holt, 1972.

Selected Poems, edited by Ian Hamilton, Penguin, 1973.

LETTERS

The Letters of Robert Frost to Louis Untermeyer, Holt, 1963.

Selected Letters, edited by Thompson, Holt, 1964.

OTHER

A Way Out: A One-Act Play, Harbor Press, 1929.

The Cow's in the Corn: A One-Act Irish Play in Rhyme, Slide Mountain Press, 1929.

(Contributor) John Holmes, editor, *Writing Poetry,* Writer, Inc., 1960.

(Contributor) Milton R. Konvitz and Stephen E. Whicher, editors, *Emerson,* Prentice-Hall, 1962.

Robert Frost on "Extravagance" (the text of Frost's last college lecture, Dartmouth College, November 27, 1962) [Hanover, NH], 1963.

Robert Frost: A Living Voice (contains speeches by Frost), edited by Reginald Cook, University of Massachusetts Press, 1974.

(With Caroline Ford) *The Less Travelled Road,* Bern Porter, 1982.

Stories for Lesley, edited by Roger D. Sell, University Press of Virginia, 1984.

Frost's papers are collected at the libraries of the University of Virginia, Amherst College, and Dartmouth College, and the Huntington Library in San Marino, California.

■ **Sidelights**

Robert Frost is considered one of the foremost American poets of the twentieth century. Through his imagery of nature and life in rural New England, Frost explored fundamental questions about man's existence. He became America's favorite and most beloved poet, winning both popular and critical acclaim during his lifetime. Using deceptively simple language he combined the roles of farmer-poet and philosopher to create a memorable body of distinctly American poetry. In addition to winning the Pulitzer Prize four times and receiving countless other honors, Frost received a Congressional Gold Medal for his achievements and also participated in the inauguration of President John F. Kennedy in January, 1961.

Frost lived during a remarkable time of change and development. He was born in 1874, a mere decade after the Civil War, and he died in 1963, the same decade man walked on the moon. Just as his lifetime spanned between two centuries, his poetry too formed a bridge between the traditions of nineteenth century verse and the modern poetry of the twentieth century. Frost wrote poems in verse forms reminiscent of his nineteenth century predecessors, while his contemporaries such as T. S. Eliot and Wallace Stevens experimented with unconventional forms and structures known as free verse. Frost was not impressed with free verse, also known as *vers libre,* which was written without adherence to any metric frame. Rather, he chose to use conventional techniques such as meter, line length, and rhyme scheme to create an unconventional and completely modern effect.

Frost's primary contribution to modern poetic technique is his masterful uniting of iambic meter with the freedom of the spoken voice. Using vivid imagery, Frost describes ordinary rural activity and muses upon the mysteries of life in a simple, accessible language. His finely crafted poems exhibit his command of form and rhythm and his remarkable ability to create the distinct sound of New England speech patterns. He termed this quality "the sounds of sense" or "sentence sounds." Throughout his writing career, Frost experimented with his style of setting traditional meters with natural rhythms of speech. He wrote in a variety of traditional forms, including blank verse, sonnets, lyrics, and a type of dramatic verse known as *masques.*

While some critics view Frost's work as a simple imitation of the New England farmer idiom, most commend his celebration and recreation of the spoken word. In the Introduction to *Selected Po-*

ems of Robert Frost, Robert Graves observed that "Frost was the first American who could be honestly reckoned a master-poet by world standards." Graves went on to remark that Frost "won the title fairly, not by turning his back on ancient European tradition, nor by imitating its success, but by developing it in a way that at last matches the American climate and the American language." When the free verse poetry of other modern poets' work was considered daring and new, Frost's poems were frequently viewed as old-fashioned. Undaunted, Frost continued to reject free verse and, according to Graves, remarked that "writing free verse was like playing tennis without a net."

The literary scholar Randall Jarrell placed Frost along with Stevens and Eliot as the greatest American poets of the twentieth century. In his 1953 book *Poetry and the Age,* Jarrell commented that no other poet "has written so well about the actions of ordinary men; his wonderful dramatic monologues and dramatic scenes come out of a knowledge of people that few poets have had, and they are written in a verse that uses, sometimes with absolute mastery, the rhythms of actual speech." But Frost was not merely interested in capturing the spoken voice, for he explored philosophical matters in his poems, especially about man and the nature of his existence.

Fear, Confusion, and Uncertainty

Frost's greatest subjects were fear, confusion and uncertainty. In "West-Running Brook," he spoke of "The universal cataract of death / That spends to nothingness. . . ." Frost believed that confusion was a natural state of affairs, but he tried not to despair because he felt that humanity could create form out of confusion. He also believed that no man-made form is permanent, which led him to coin the phrase "a momentary stay against confusion" (from "The Figure a Poem Makes"). Frost felt that man's greatness stemmed from his ability to create form out of nothing. Part of his lifelong preoccupation with form was reflected in his adherence to meter, line length, and rhyme scheme.

Frost's use of the natural spoken speech of New England is only one aspect of the regionalism that is seen in his poetry. He referred to New Hampshire as one of the two best states in the Union—the other being Vermont. He was still living in

England when *North of Boston* was published, yet Amy Lowell, reviewing the book in the *New Republic,* wrote, "Indeed, Mr. Frost is only expatriated in the physical sense. . . . not only is his work New England in subject, it is so in technique. . . . Mr. Frost's book is American in the sense that Whittier is American, and not at all in the subtler sense in which Poe ranks as the greatest American poet."

In his essay entitled "Re-Assessments," the English critic C. W. Bowra described Frost's choice of setting for his poetry this way: "His poetry is concerned not only with his mere corner of New England but, strictly and accurately, with what he actually knows of it. Since it deals in the first

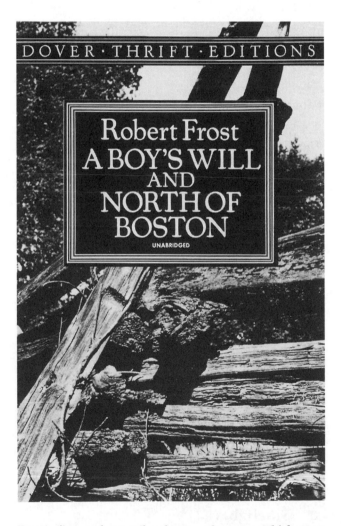

Frost's first and second volumes of poetry, which were first published in England in 1913 and 1914, respectively, are featured in this unabridged republication.

place not with fancies but with facts, it can fairly be called realistic. Its subjects are drawn from country life and often from its most familiar activities, and are presented with an experienced knowledge which proves that the poet is a true countryman."

In "Robert Frost," T. K. Whipple notes, "But to say that Frost is not a New England poet would be like saying that [Robert] Burns is not Scottish or that [John Millington] Synge is not Irish. For good and evil his work is the distilled essence of New England, and from this fact springs both his marked limitations and his unique value."

Although Frost is the quintessential New Englander, he was actually born in San Francisco on March 26, 1874. He was the first child of William Prescott Frost, Jr., of New Hampshire and Isabelle Moodie of Scotland. Frost's father had graduated Phi Beta Kappa from Harvard, but he was also a heavy drinker who moved to California to earn a living in politics and journalism. He died when Frost was eleven, and Frost's mother moved him and his sister (born in June of 1876) to New England, working as a schoolteacher in Massachusetts and New Hampshire. By the time Frost was sixteen, he had decided to be a poet; when he graduated from Lawrence High School in 1892, he was class poet and co-valedictorian with Elinor White, the woman who would later become his wife. In 1894, the *New York Independent* accepted his poem, "My Butterfly," for publication. Frost was elated; not only had he received a payment of $15, but he was now convinced that he could support himself by writing.

To celebrate the publication, Frost had two copies of a book containing this poem and five others privately printed—one he kept for himself and one he gave to his fiancee Elinor. The name of the edition was *Twilight*. When Elinor did not respond as enthusiastically as he had hoped, he destroyed his own copy of the book.

Over the next eight years, only thirteen additional poems were published; during this time, he sporadically attended Dartmouth, worked briefly as a reporter for the *Daily American* and the *Sentinel*, and taught school. In December, 1895, he married Elinor, and in 1896 their first child, Elliot, was born. He began attending Harvard, but left after eighteen months when his second child, Lesley, was born in 1899. The following year Elliot died;

the tragedy became the catalyst for the poem entitled "Home Burial" (published in *North of Boston*, 1914).

Because he realized the stress that their son's death had placed on the Frosts' already tense marriage, Frost's grandfather bought a farm in Derby, New Hampshire, and allowed the couple and their family to live on it. They lived on the farm from 1900 to 1909; these years were intensely creative ones for Frost. However, his work was frequently rejected by the editors at American magazines. In 1912 Frost took his family to England, where he could "write and be poor without further scandal in the family."

Success Abroad

In England, success came quickly to Frost. He arrived in London in September, 1912, and in October of that year *A Boy's Will* was accepted for publication. The book was printed in 1913, and Ezra Pound published the first important American review of *A Boy's Will* in the same year. In this essay, Pound wrote "[*A Boy's Will*] is a little raw, and has in it a number of infelicities; underneath it has the tang of the New Hampshire woods, and it has just this utter sincerity. It is not post-Miltonic or post-Kiplonian. This man has the good sense to speak naturally and paint the thing, the thing as he sees it."

A Boy's Will has been described as Frost's weakest collection. In later editions of the book, Frost omitted three of the poems—"Asking for Roses," "Spoils of the Dead," and "In Equal Sacrifice," because he found them undeserving. However, *A Boy's Will* has its merits. It is basically a collection of love lyrics written to Elinor, but it also looks at the themes of fear and uncertainty in the face of nature's nonhuman otherness.

Several recurring motifs in Frost's work are seen for the first time in *A Boy's Will*. "Mowing," which has been described as the best loved of these early poems, describes a person cultivating a field and thereby imposing their own sense of order on the world. "Storm Fear," often seen as the prize of the collection, describes a man who is awed and subdued by sublime natural forces. The opening poem, "Into My Own," involves a speaker who wants to enter a dark forest, a metaphor for the self and life that is seen in Frost's later works.

Following the success of *A Boy's Will,* Frost relocated to Gloucestershire, England, and directed publication of *North of Boston,* his second collection of poetry. While *North of Boston* is considered Frost's strongest overall collection, it confused many early readers. Donald J. Greiner, in *Dictionary of Literary Biography,* points out that in 1914, when the collection was published, free verse was at the "vanguard of the poetic renaissance." Readers recognized that poems such as "Home Burial" and "A Servant to Servants" were not composed in traditional forms, but they were not free verse either. Those who mistook the poems for free verse were unable to assimilate the unusual merger of the regular pentameter line and what Frost called "sentence sounds," or the irregular rhythms of speech. These poems are actually written in blank verse, a form that represents Frost's major contribution to American poetry.

Amy Lowell, writing in the *New Republic* in 1915, described Frost's use of blank verse in *North of Boston* this way: "The poems are written for the most part in blank verse, blank verse which does not hesitate to leave a syllable out or put one in, whenever it feels like it. To the classicist such liberties would be unendurable. But the method has its advantages. It suggests the hardness and roughness of New England granite. It is halting and maimed, like the life it portrays; unyielding in substance, and broken in effect."

Frost was aware of what he had accomplished with the development of blank verse. He sent letter after letter to his friends in the United States, describing the technique and asking them to publicize his achievement. The most masterful poems in *North of Boston* are "The Wood-Pile," "After Apple-Picking," and "Home Burial."

Frost denied that "Home Burial" was autobiographical. He had written the poem in 1912 or 1913, but did not include it in *North of Boston* because it did not complement the lyrics of that collection. In *Dictionary of Literary Biography* Greiner explains that Frost pointed to the death of his sister-in-law's child as the catalyst for the poem, but that it was impossible to ignore the connection between this remarkable collection and the death of Frost's first son in 1900 at the age of four. Frost also refused to read the poem in public because he was overwhelmed by emotion when he did read it. His biographer Lawrance Thompson reported that Elinor could not over-come her grief when Elliot died, believing that the world was an evil place. The character Amy in "Home Burial" makes the same statement.

Greiner describes "Home Burial" as "a sympathetic contrast of opposing ways to grieve, its skill at jerking the reader's sympathy back and forth between husband and wife, its unblinking understanding that the couple's sex life has also died—the graveyard is 'not so much larger than a bedroom'—indicates that not only a baby but also a home has been irrevocably buried. Alienation is unrelieved in this poem."

In "Robert Frost," T. K. Whipple describes what he sees as the "exaggerated emotionalism" of some of Frost's poems. "The most terrible and tragic illustration of this morbid excess, though the cause is not trivial, is "Home Burial," the story of a woman so sunk in her grief for child, so deliberately and purposely sunk in it, that she has contracted a violent hatred of her husband and is all but outright insane."

"After Apple Picking" also looks at fear; this is one of the poems in which Frost looks at one of mankind's greatest terrors: that our efforts may not be good enough. The poem does not have a regular rhyme scheme; the iambic pentameter line breaks down when the speaker realizes his predicament. Frost unifies technique and theme to illustrate how man is unable to contain the confusion that surrounds him. In "The Themes of Robert Frost," Robert Penn Warren describes "After Apple Picking" this way: "The process [Frost] has employed . . . is to order his literal materials so that, in looking back as the poem proceeds, the reader suddenly realizes that they have been transmuted. . . ."

"Wood-Pile," another noteworthy poem in *North of Boston,* uses a stack of firewood that is left lying outdoors as a metaphor for neglect, disintegration, and waste. In her 1984 essay "Separateness and Solitude in Frost," Patricia Wallace notes: "What other poet could begin a poem, as Frost does in 'The Wood-Pile,' with the decision to walk further into a frozen swamp on a grey day and yet make us feel pleasure in it? One of the things Frost does in 'The Wood-Pile' is explore a form of solitude . . . where the world doesn't bend to the self, but seems to stand apart from it. And he is seeing just how far he can maintain his sense of his own distinctness as he tests out the

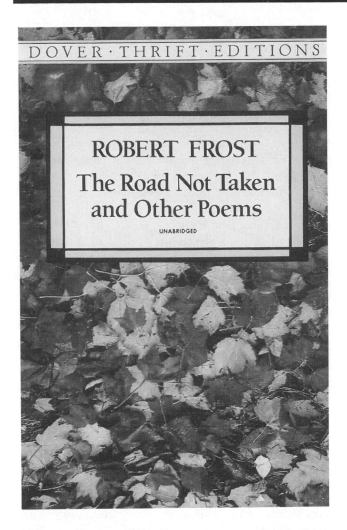

DOVER · THRIFT · EDITIONS

ROBERT FROST
The Road Not Taken
and Other Poems

UNABRIDGED

Originally published in 1916 as *Mountain Interval*, this collection of poems features "An Old Man's Winter Night," "In the Home Stretch," and the well-known "The Road Not Taken."

reaches of the self." In "Searching for Home," Richard Poirier notes "'The Wood-Pile' is like a sequel to 'Home Burial' . . . more a meditation than a dramatic narrative, it offers the soliloquy of a lone figure walking in a winter landscape.

Success in the United States

The triumph of *North of Boston* coincided with the outbreak of World War I. In 1915 Frost and his family returned to the United States to find that the American version of *North of Boston* had already been published by Henry Holt. Within four months, *A Boy's Will* was also published in America, and Frost was seen as a leader of the

new poetry. He was named Phi Beta Kappa at Tufts University. Within four years, he had a third collection of poetry published, was named Phi Beta Kappa poet by Harvard, was elected to the National Institute of Arts and Letters, and was awarded the first of forty-four honorary degrees by Amherst. He was now receiving invitations and recognition from editors and other poets who had once ignored him. But Greiner reports that he was still jealous of the recognition given to other poets. For example, he still referred to Edgar Lee Masters as "my hated rival." He was also distrustful of anyone who disagreed with him. He began to hide behind the mask of the gentle farmer-poet, thereby using art to order his life.

The intense publicity surrounding Frost caused his publisher to rush *Mountain Interval* into print in 1916, before Frost thought it was ready. Frost was disappointed with the collection, but it does contain some of his best poems, including "Birches," "The Road Not Taken," and "The Oven Bird." *Mountain Interval* also contains "An Old Man's Winter Night," described by Greiner in *Dictionary of Literary Biography* as "a superior poem by any standard and one of the best Frost ever wrote." In "Birches," the speaker wonders whether a birch branch was bent by a child at play or by natural elements. In this poem, Frost metaphorically links tree climbing with aspirations for heaven.

In his essay entitled "From Woods to Stars: A Pattern of Imagery in Robert Frost's Poetry," John T. Ogilvie discusses what he sees as the autobiographical nature of "The Road Not Taken." He writes "'The Road Not Taken' . . . can be read as a further commentary on the price of the poet's dedication. The two roads that 'diverged in the yellow wood' represent a critical choice between two ways of life. The poet takes 'the one less traveled by,' the lonelier road, which, we can presume, leads deeper into the wood. . . . The dark woods, though they hold a salutary privacy, impose a stern isolation, an isolation endured not without cost."

In his essay "Robert Frost, or the Spiritual Drifter as Poet," critic Yvor Winters describes "The Road Not Taken" as a poem about a man who could be called a spiritual drifter. Winter adds, "a spiritual drifter is unlikely to have either the intelligence or the energy to become a minor poet. Yet the poem has definite virtues, and these should not be overlooked. In the first place, spiritual drifters exist, they are real, and although their decisions may not be comprehensible, their predicament is comprehensible. The poem renders the experience of such a person, and renders the uncertain melancholy of his plight. Had Frost been a more intelligent man, he might have seen that the plight of the spiritual drifter was not inevitable; he might have judged it in the light of a more comprehensible wisdom. Had he done this, he might have written a greater poem."

"The Oven Bird" is another important poem that appeared in *Mountain Interval*. In "Robert Frost's Solitary Singer," George Monteiro describes the poem this way: "Time has made it evident that 'The Oven Bird' stands at the center of Robert Frost's early poetry. Indeed, this sonnet struck a note that has become central to the themes of many of the major poets of the first quarter of the twentieth century. Anticipating by several years that sorrowful observation of his younger contemporary T. S. Eliot that in our time the ancient song of the nightingale had degenerated into the 'Jug Jug' of dirty ears, Frost focused on the transformation and diminution of Whitman's central symbol for the poet. . . . Like the ovenbird of mid-summer song, the poet that Frost recognized in himself was one who faced the hardest of facts: seasonally, but above all historically, the world has diminished, and 'dust is over all.'"

Many believe that Frost began working on "An Old Man's Winter Night" as early as the winter of 1906 and 1907. Frost himself recognized the extraordinary achievement that this poem represented; according to Greiner in the *Concise Dictionary of Literary Biography*, Frost wrote a letter to Sidney Cox in 1916 describing "An Old Man's Winter Night" as "Probably the best thing in the book." The poem is a sad account of a man's unfortunate fate as he grows old, has nothing to look forward to, and faces the worst: death, the final sleep of night. Frost ends the poem with the memorable lines "One aged man—one man—can't keep a house, / A farm, a countryside. . . ."

Notable American Poet

After the publication of *Mountain Interval*, Frost was accepted as a major poet. In the *Dictionary of Literary Biography*, Greiner writes that Frost described this next period as a time of "barding around." Frost resigned from his position on the

faculty at Amherst University in January, 1920 and accepted a post at the University of Michigan in September, 1921. He returned to Amherst in November, 1923, and stayed there until June, 1925, when he returned to the University of Michigan for the academic year 1925-1926. In September of 1926 he returned to Amherst, and he stayed until June, 1938. During this time, he lectured at the Bread Loaf Writers' Conference in Vermont and served on the faculty of Harvard from 1939 to 1943. He resigned from Harvard in 1943 and accepted a position at Dartmouth College; in 1949, he went back to Amherst where the "barding around" began—and was given a lifetime appointment as a Simpson Lecturer in Literature.

Although Frost was rarely a full-time professor at any of these schools, he did lecture, meet with students, and teach a variety of classes from time to time. The associations were advantageous to the colleges and to Frost and they gave the poet the freedom to write. In 1923, he published *New Hampshire*, a collection of poems that he humorously dedicated to Michigan and Vermont. This collection brought him the first of four Pulitzer Prizes that he was awarded in his lifetime.

In "Frost and Eliot," Jeffrey Hart describes the collection this way: "['*New Hampshire*'] as a whole is immensely rich. Frost fashions the state of New Hampshire before our eyes into a poetic world of many modes and many voices, a poetic quarry from which the subsequent poems are drawn, a quarry of apparently inexhaustible resources." When he wrote the poems that make up *New Hampshire*, Frost was still dedicated to his "sentence sounds" and blank-verse narratives; however, according to Greiner, he was also developing a disturbing tendency—"a proclivity to use certain poems as soapboxes from which he could comment on everything from government interference to psychoanalysis." Despite the politics, *New Hampshire* is a collection of superior lyrics as seen in "A Star in a Stoneboat," "Two Witches," "Fire and Ice," and "Stopping by Woods on a Snowy Evening."

"Stopping by Woods on a Snowy Evening" is one of the most familiar poems in all of American literature. It is frequently studied and often memorized by schoolchildren, and critics continue to debate it even today. According to Greiner, Frost knew that this poem has 'immortality written all over it.' In 1923 Frost wrote to Louis Untermeyer that "Stopping by Woods on a Snowy Evening" was his "best bid for remembrance." At first glance, the poem appears to be a simple one; according to Greiner, Frost embellished the aura of simplicity surrounding the poem by claiming that he wrote it with "one stroke of the pen." However, the truth is that "Stopping by Woods on a Snowy Evening" is a poem that was as difficult to write as it is to interpret. In "The Themes of Robert Frost," Robert Penn Warren writes that the poem, if read literally, looks quite simple: "A man driving by a dark woods stops to admire the scene, to watch the snow falling into the special darkness. He remembers the name of the man who owns the woods and knows that the man . . . cannot begrudge him a look. He is not trespassing. The little horse is restive and shakes the harness bells. The man decides to drive on, because, as he says, he has promises to keep—he has to get home to deliver the groceries for supper—and he has miles to go before he can afford to stop, before he can sleep."

Yet, as Ogilvie points out in "From Woods to Stars: A Pattern of Imagery in Robert Frost's Poetry,": "What appears to be 'simple' is not really simple, what appears to be innocent is not really innocent. . . . The repetition of 'sleep' in the final two lines suggests that he may succumb to the influences that are at work. There is no reason to suppose that these influences are benignant. It is, after all, 'the darkest evening of the year,' and the poet is alone 'between the woods and frozen lake.' . . . The ascription of 'lovely' to this scene . . . complicates rather than alleviates the mood when we consider how pervasive are the connotations of dangerous isolation and menacing death."

Returns to England

In 1928 Frost made a nostalgic return to England and published the collection *West-Running Brook.* Although no one poem stands out in the collection, it is an impressive volume that includes such lyrics as "Spring Pools," "On Going Unnoticed," "Bereft," "Tree at My Window," and "Acquainted with the Night." John Ogilvie describes this time as a midpoint in Frost's career when his orientation seemed to change: "He becomes more the neighborly poet who chats at length with his readers about the issues of the day, and less the objective dramatist and self-absorbed lyricist of the

If you enjoy the works of Robert Frost, you may also want to check out the following:

The poetry of Emily Dickinson ("Because I could not stop for Death"), William Carlos Williams ("The Red Wheelbarrow"), Amy Lowell ("Patterns"), and William Rose Benet (*The Dust Which Is God*).

earlier books. He becomes more outspoken about himself and about the world of men."

West-Running Brook is divided into six sections, one of which is made up of the title poem. This poem describes a brook which flows west to the Atlantic instead of east like all other brooks. Frost uses the brook as a metaphor for eccentric individualism. When she reviewed the collection in the *New York Herald Tribune*, Babette Deutsch wrote: The courage that is bred by a dark sense of Fate, the tenderness that broods over mankind in all its blindness and absurdity, the vision that comes to rest as fully on kitchen smoke and lapsing snow as on mountain and stars—these are his, and in his seemingly casual poetry, he quietly makes them ours."

The 1930s represented a period of severe private loss for Frost. He won Pulitzer Prizes for *Collected Poems of Robert Frost* (1930) and *A Further Range* (1936). He also won the Russell Loines Poetry Prize in 1931 and was appointed Charles Eliot Norton Professor at Harvard in 1936. However, his daughter Marjorie, a favorite child, died of puerperal fever in 1934. Four years later, his wife Elinor died of a heart attack and cancer; when she lingered in a conscious state for days, she refused to admit Frost into her bedroom. In 1940 Frost's son Carol committed suicide, leaving behind a family that Frost took under his protection.

A Further Range, which earned Frost a Pulitzer Prize, is a collection of two groups of poems entitled "Taken Doubly" and "Taken Singly." Although William Rose Benet found the work inspiring, many influential commentators such as R. P. Blackmur, Newton Arvin, and Rolfe Humphries criticized the volume because they disagreed with some of the politics that Frost espoused in his poems. According to Greiner, the negative reviews for *A Further Range* can be explained by the fact that it was written in the "midst of the Great Depression, with fascism about to invade Europe and war about to engulf the world. Stunned by these legitimate signals of disaster, the negative critics rejected what they took to be Frost's casual, conservative politics as expressed in 'A Lone Striker,' 'Build Soil,' 'To a Thinker,' and the famous 'Two Tramps in Mud Time.' . . . The poems are far from Frost's best, but the political climate in 1936 was such that public figures who paraded their conservatism were suspect."

Although *A Further Range* contains some of Frost's finest work, he never again received the nearly unanimous critical approval that he began to see when he returned from England in 1915. He experienced problems in his personal life as well; the personal tragedies in his family caused him to suffer from guilt and depression. Some of his adult children accused him of sacrificing his family to art. His days were disorganized and his future looked bleak. However, Kathleen Morrison, a wife of a Harvard professor, helped him to reorder his life at this time. He dedicated *A Witness Tree* to Mrs. Morrison.

A Witness Tree was the fourth collection of Frost's to win a Pulitzer Prize. Although he continued to write great poems during the last twenty years of his life, this is the last totally satisfying volume of his work. Poems included in this collection include "Beech," "All Revelation," "The Most of It," "November," "The Silken Tent," "The Subverted Flower," and "The Rabbit Hunter." The collection also includes "The Gift Outright," a poem about the heritage and responsibilities of American citizens which Frost would read twenty years later at President Kennedy's inauguration. Frost claimed that he wrote "The Subverted Flower" before the publication of *A Boy's Will* in 1913. The poem, which is autobiographical in nature, describes a sexual crisis that occurred when Frost was dating Elinor. If it is true that the poem was written before *A Boy's Will*, then Frost withheld publication for thirty years until after Elinor's death, probably for fear that offering this frank poem to the public would damage their already unstable marriage.

Frost now had his life back in order, and he published three volumes in the 1940s: *A Masque of Reason* (1945), *A Masque of Mercy* (1947), and *Steeple Bush* (1947). These final three collections received less than enthusiastic reviews. However, *Steeple Bush* contains the poem "Directive," which is considered one of Frost's best works. In this poem, Frost begins with a line of ten monosyllables and ends with the word "confusion." In *Dictionary of Literary Biography*, Greiner points out that Frost's "sense that poetry was a 'momentary stay against confusion' sustained him through many decades, and it is significant that the last notable poem in his canon explores the notion in a religious context."

American Diplomat

During the last fifteen years of his life, Frost was showered with public honors. The Nobel Prize, the award that he coveted most, eluded him, but he won almost everything else. In 1949 *The Complete Poems of Robert Frost* was published, and the Limited Edition Club awarded him the Gold Medal. The United States Senate wished him a happy birthday on March 24, 1950. In 1954 the State Department sent him to Brazil as a delegate to the World Congress of Writers. In 1955 the state of Vermont named a mountain after him. In 1960 Congress authorized a Congressional Gold Medal for Frost, and President Kennedy awarded it to him in 1962. In 1961 he participated in the inauguration of President Kennedy and said "The Gift Outright" from memory because his failing eyesight prevented him from reading some lines that were prepared especially for the occasion. In 1962 when Frost was nearly eight-nine years old, he was sent on an official mission to the Soviet Union. Upon his return, he made some thoughtless remarks to reporters about America's liberalism, thereby unintentionally misrepresenting President Kennedy and Premier Nikita Kruschev. The President never spoke to him again.

Frost published *In the Clearing,* his final book, in March, 1962. Taken as a collection, critics felt that the book was disappointing. However, two of the poems in the volume, "The Draft Horse," and "In Winter in the Woods," are considered a dramatic conclusion to Frost's career because they allow him to wrap up the theme and metaphor of the dark woods that Frost had been writing about for his whole life.

Frost died on January 29, 1963, twenty-four days after winning the Bollingen Prize for poetry. In October, 1963, President Kennedy summed up the life of this American poet in a speech he delivered at the dedication of the Robert Frost Library in Amherst, Massachusetts: "In honoring Robert Frost," he said, "we therefore can pay honor to the deepest source of our national strength. That strength takes many forms and the most obvious forms are not always the most significant. . . . Our national strength matters; but the spirit which informs and controls our strength matters just as much. This was the special significance of Robert Frost."

■ Works Cited

Bowra, C. M., "Re-Assessments," *Adelphi*, November, 1950, pp. 46-64.

Deutsch, Babette, *New York Herald Tribune*, November 18, 1928.

Graves, Robert, in the "Introduction" to *Robert Frost's Selected Poems of Robert Frost*, Frost, Holt, Rinehart and Winston, 1963, pp. ix-xiv.

Greiner, Donald J., "Robert Frost," *Dictionary of Literary Biography*, Volume 54: *American Poets, 1880-1945*, Gale, 1987, pp. 93-121.

Greiner, Donald J., "Robert Frost," *Concise Dictionary of Literary Biography: The Twenties, 1917-1929*, Gale, 1989, pp. 68-87.

Hart, Jeffrey, "Frost and Eliot," *Sewanee Review*, Summer, 1976, pp. 425-47.

Jarrell, Randall, "The Other Frost," *Poetry and the Age*, Alfred A. Knopf, 1953, pp. 26-33.

Kennedy, John F., "Poetry and Power," *Atlantic Monthly*, February, 1964.

Lowell, Amy, review of "North of Boston," *New Republic*, February 20, 1915, pp. 81-82.

Monteiro, George, "Robert Frost's Solitary Singer," *New England Quarterly*, March, 1971, pp. 134-140.

Ogilvie, John T., "From Woods to Stars: A Pattern of Imagery in Robert Frost's Poetry," *South Atlantic Quarterly*, Winter, 1959, pp. 64-76.

Poirier, Richard, "Soundings for Home," (originally published in the *Georgia Review*, Summer, 1977), *Robert Frost: The Work of Knowing*, Oxford University Press, 1977.

Pound, Ezra, review of *A Boy's Will*, *Poetry*, May, 1913 (and reprinted in *Robert Frost: The Critical Reception*, edited by Linda W. Wagner, Burt Franklin and Co., Inc., 1977, pp. 1-2).

Wallace, Patricia, "Separateness and Solitude in Frost," *Kenyon Review*, Winter, 1984, pp. 1-2.

Warren, Robert Penn, "The Themes of Robert Frost" (1948), *Selected Essays*, Random House, 1958, pp. 118-36.

Whipple, T. K., "Robert Frost," *Spokesmen—Modern Writers and American Life*, Appleton, 1928, pp. 94-114.

Winters, Yvor, "Robert Frost, or the Spiritual Drifter as Poet," *The Function of Criticism: Problems and Exercises*, Alan Swallow, 1957.

■ For More Information See

BOOKS

Anderson, Margaret, *Robert Frost and John Bartlett: The Record of a Friendship*, Holt, 1963.

Barry, Elaine, compiler, *Robert Frost on Writing*, Rutgers University Press, 1973.

Barry, Elaine, *Robert Frost*, Ungar, 1973.

Breit, Harvey, *The Writer Observed*, World Publishing, 1956.

Contemporary Literary Criticism, Gale, Volume 1, 1973, Volume 3, 1975, Volume 4, 1975, Volume 9, 1978, Volume 10, 1979, Volume 13, 1980, Volume 15, 1980, Volume 26, 1983, Volume 34, 1985, Volume 44, 1987.

Cook, Reginald L., *The Dimensions of Robert Frost*, Rinehart, 1958.

Cook, Reginald L., *Robert Frost: A Living Voice*, University of Massachusetts Press, 1974.

Cox, James M., *Robert Frost: A Collection of Critical Essays*, Prentice-Hall, 1962.

Cox, Sidney, *Swinger of Birches: A Portrait of Robert Frost*, New York University Press, 1957.

Dodd, Loring Holmes, *Celebrities at Our Hearthside*, Dresser, 1959.

Doyle, John R., Jr., *Poetry of Robert Frost: An Analysis*, Hallier, 1965.

Evans, William R., editor, *Robert Frost and Sidney Cox: Forty Years of Friendship*, University Press of New England, 1981.

Francis, Robert, recorder, *A Time to Talk: Conversations and Indiscretions*, University of Massachusetts Press, 1972.

Frost, Lesley, *New Hampshire's Child: Derry Journals of Lesley Frost*, State University of New York Press, 1969.

Gerber, Philip L., *Robert Frost*, Twayne, 1966.

Gould, Jean, *Robert Frost: The Aim Was Song*, Dodd, 1964.

Grade, Arnold, editor, *Family Letters of Robert and Elinor Frost*, State University of New York Press, 1972.

Greiner, Donald J., *Checklist of Robert Frost*, Charles E. Merrill, 1969.

Greiner, Donald J. and Charles Sanders, *Robert*

Frost: The Poet and His Critics, American Library Association, 1974.

Hall, Donald, *Remembering Poets,* Hater, 1977.

Isaacs, Emily Elizabeth, *Introduction to Robert Frost,* A. Swallow, 1962, reprinted, Haskell House, 1972.

Jarrell, Randall, *Poetry and the Age,* Vintage, 1955.

Jennings, Elizabeth, *Frost,* Barnes & Noble, 1966.

Lathem, Edward C. and Lawrance Thompson, editors, *Robert Frost: Farm Poultryman; The Story of Robert Frost's Career As a Breeder and Fancier of Hens,* Dartmouth Publishers, 1963.

Lathem, Edward C., editor, *Interviews with Robert Frost,* Rinehart, 1966.

Lathem, Edward C., editor, *A Concordance to the Poetry of Robert Frost,* Holt Information Systems, 1971.

Lentriccia, Frank, *Robert Frost: Modern Poetics and the Landscapes of Self,* Duke University Press, 1975.

Lowell, Amy, *Tendencies in Modern American Poetry,* Macmillan, 1917.

Mertins, Marshall Louis and Esther Mertins, *Intervals of Robert Frost: A Critical Bibliography,* University of California Press, 1947, reprinted, Russell, 1975.

Mertins, Marshall Louis, *Robert Frost: Life and Talks—Walking,* University of Oklahoma Press, 1965.

Munson, Gorham B., *Robert Frost: A Study in Sensibility and Good Sense,* G. H. Doran, 1927, reprinted, Haskell House, 1969.

Newdick, Robert Spangler, *Newdick's Season of Frost: An Interrupted Biography of Robert Frost,* edited by William A. Sutton, State University of New York Press, 1976.

Orton, Vrest, *Vermont Afternoons with Robert Frost,* Tuttle, 1971.

Pearce, Roy Harvey, *The Continuity of American Poetry,* Princeton, 1961.

Poirier, Richard, *Robert Frost,* Oxford University Press, 1977.

Pound, Ezra, *The Literary Essays of Ezra Pound,* New Directions, 1954.

Pritchard, William H., *Frost: A Literary Life Reconsidered,* Oxford University Press, 1984.

Reeve, Franklin D., *Robert Frost in Russia,* Little, Brown, 1964.

Rosenthal, M. L., *The Modern Poets,* Oxford University Press, 1965.

Shepley, Elizabeth, *Robert Frost: The Trial by Existence,* Holt, 1960.

Sohn, David A. and Richard Tyre, *Frost: The Poet and His Poetry,* Holt, 1967.

Spiller, Robert E. and others, *Literary History of the United States,* 4th revised edition, Macmillan, 1974.

Squires, Radcliffe, *Major Themes of Robert Frost,* University of Michigan Press, 1969.

Tharpe, Jac, editor, *Frost: Centennial Essays II,* University Press of Mississippi, 1976.

Thompson, Lawrence, *Fire and Ice: The Art and Thought of Robert Frost,* Holt, 1942, reprinted, Russell, 1975.

Thompson, Lawrence, *Robert Frost,* University of Minnesota Press, 1959.

Thompson, Lawrence, editor, *Selected Letters of Robert Frost,* Holt, 1964.

Thompson, Lawrence, *Robert Frost: The Early Years, 1874-1915,* Holt, 1966.

Thompson, Lawrence, *Robert Frost: The Years of Triumph, 1915-1938,* Holt, 1970.

Thompson, Lawrence and R. H. Winnick, *Robert Frost: The Later Years, 1938-1963,* Holt, 1976.

Unger, Leonard and William Van O'Connor, *Poems for Study,* Holt, 1953.

Untermeyer, Louis, *Makers of the Modern World,* Simon & Schuster, 1955.

Untermeyer, Louis, *Lives of the Poets,* Simon & Schuster, 1959.

Untermeyer, Louis, *Robert Frost: A Backward Look,* U.S. Government Printing Office, 1964.

PERIODICALS

America, December 24, 1977.

American Literature, January, 1948.

Atlantic, November, 1966.

Bookman, January, 1924.

Books, May 10, 1942.

Boston Transcript, December 2, 1916.

Commonweal, May 4, 1962, April 1, 1977.

New Republic, February 20, 1915.

New York Herald Tribune, November 18, 1928.

New York Times, October 19, 1986.

New York Times Book Review, July 17, 1988.

New York Times Magazine, June 11, 1972; August 18, 1974.

Poetry, May, 1913.

Saturday Review of Literature, May 30, 1936; April 25, 1942.

South Atlantic Quarterly, summer, 1958.

Times Literary Supplement, December 14, 1967.

Virginia Quarterly Review, summer, 1957.

Wisconsin Library Bulletin, July, 1962.

Yale Review, spring, 1934, summer, 1948.

Obituaries

PERIODICALS

Current Biography, March, 1963.
Illustrated London News, February 9, 1963.
Newsweek, February 11, 1963.
New York Times, January 30, 1963.
Publishers Weekly, February 11, 1963.*

—Sketch by Irene Durham

Barbara Hall

Association (ALA) Notable Book and Best Books of 1990 citations, all 1990, for *Dixie Storms*; ALA Notable Book and Best Books citations, 1992, for *Fool's Hill*; ALA Books for Reluctant Readers citation, 1996, for *The House across the Cove*.

■ Personal

Born July 17, 1960, in Danville, VA; daughter of Ervis Harvard (a company manager) and Florine Hardie (a homemaker) Hall. *Education:* James Madison University, B.A., 1982. *Politics:* Liberal. *Religion:* Protestant. *Hobbies and other interests:* Guitar, skiing, pro- basketball ("Lakers especially"), travel.

■ Addresses

Home—10720 Le Conte Ave., Los Angeles, CA 90024. *Agent*—Cynthia Manson, 444 East 86th St., New York, NY 10028.

■ Career

Screenwriter and producer for television, 1982—; writer. *Member:* Writers Guild of America West, Academy of Television and Motion Pictures.

■ Awards, Honors

Booklist editors list citation, *School Library Journal's* Ten Best Books of 1990 citation, American Library

■ Writings

NOVELS FOR YOUNG ADULTS

Skeeball and the Secret of the Universe, Orchard Books, 1987.
Dixie Storms, Harcourt, 1990.
Fool's Hill, Bantam, 1992.
The House across the Cove, Bantam, 1996.

NOVELS FOR ADULTS

A Better Place, Simon and Schuster, 1994.
Close to Home, Simon and Schuster, 1997.

OTHER

Also story editor for episodes of television series *Newhart*, CBS-TV, 1982-83; executive story editor for episodes of series *A Year in the Life*, NBC-TV, 1986-87; screenwriter and producer of episodes of series *Moonlighting*, 1989, and *Anything But Love*, 1990, both ABC-TV; co-executive producer of series *I'll Fly Away*, NBC-TV, 1990-92; writer and producer of episodes of series *Northern Exposure*, CBS-TV, 1993; screenwriter and producer for episodes of *New York News*, CBS-TV, 1995-96; screenwriter for "Young Again," a *Disney Movie of the Week*.

■ Work in Progress

Adult novel about two sisters attempting to find a missing sibling, set in North Carolina and New York; producer for *The Doyles*, a pilot for an ABC-TV series.

■ Sidelights

Barbara Hall's novels for young adults and adults are evocations of the small-town South where she grew up. Most of her books are set in the South, "a very special microcosm," as Hall described the locale in an interview with *Authors and Artists for Young Adults (AAYA)*, "I am not one of those charmed by the South," Hall noted. "But there is an intriguing atmosphere to the place—very gothic—with a heightened sense of drama to everyday things. It's this idea of small town gossip with a constant telling and re-telling of stories." In the award-winning story, *Dixie Storms*, that gothic setting is "lovingly detailed," according to Betsy Hearne in *Bulletin of the Center for Children's Books*. And into such settings, Hall introduces characters in search of their true identity, in search of a meaning and belonging; adolescents, they are in the midst of quiet crises. Additionally, Hall deals with domestic life, of the many long arms of the family, another theme central to her work. She told *AAYA*, "That is the sort of family I grew up in, extended with aunts and uncles and cousins in abundance."

Hall was born in one small town near another small town. "Chatham, Virginia is near Danville," Hall recalled for *AAYA*. "Chatham's population was about 2,000 at the time, and we were miles away from anything resembling a city. As a result, I learned very young to enjoy my own company and that of my sister and brother. I can't remember a time when I didn't consider myself a writer. My sister and I made up stories, sometimes together, sometimes independently. We thought of ourselves as the Bronte sisters." By age eight Hall was already "dabbling in poetry," as she once commented. At age fifteen she had her first poem published in a national magazine, 'Teen, and earned $10 for it. All the while she was absorbing the sights, sounds, and smells of the world around her: of rural Virginia and its tobacco economy, of the lives of farmers and shopkeepers and housewives. She continued writing throughout her high school years, "volumes of long stories," as she once noted, "though I rarely finished them." Her high school years were not her happiest. "High school is a moral test for everyone concerned," Hall told *AAYA*. "But the very fact that it was so alienating was a contributing factor to me becoming a writer. Writing was the only place I felt safe."

Hall attended college in Virginia, at James Madison University where she continued writing, and

Tyler Crane and Abby Winston, two teenagers from opposite sides of the track become involved in a mystery that is dangerous for them both.

"began to take the whole business very seriously," as she once noted. "I tried everything from free verse poetry to rock music criticism. The only forms I never experimented with were ones I ultimately settled down with—screen writing and novel writing. For a long time I was a truly uninspired writer, but my saving grace was that I was always serious about it. I had great respect for good writing and never balked at constructive criticism." College, for Hall, was the antithesis of high school. "It was an inclusive, intellectual experience for me," Hall recalled for *AAYA*. "And it was my first experience of getting out of the restrictions of a small town environment." Hall graduated with a B.A. in English in 1982. Two days after graduation, she left the hills and small towns of Virginia behind for the bright lights of Los Angeles.

From Poet to Screenwriter

Hall's sister, Karen, was already established in Los Angeles at the time, working in television. She had no other connections in the city and at first spent a fair amount of time playing skeeball on the Santa Monica pier. Soon she had the idea for a novel, a book inspired by a Bruce Springsteen song and her time on the pier. "Skeeball was fading in popularity then, as was a lot of the music that I loved," she once reported, "and I wanted to write about a character who was watching many of the things he valued becoming a part of the past. I also wanted to write about an adolescent boy because I had more in common with boys than girls when I was growing up (I liked football, hard rock music, stereo equipment and motorcycles, and I had lofty ambitions)."

The ensuing novel, *Skeeball and the Secret of the Universe*, earned rejections for the next five years, though it did win her an introduction to a Los Angeles agent who queried her interest in screen writing. "I was twenty-two," Hall told *AAYA*. "I would have written for cereal boxes." The young poet and novelist from Virginia proved a quick study in the world of screen writing. "You learn as you go along with script writing," Hall told *AAYA*. "But you don't have a whole lot of time to learn. On most series you've got twenty-two scripts a year and seven days for a shoot. Three weeks is a nice chunk of time to research and write an episode, but I was writing scripts in ten days before shooting began."

Initially, Hall looked at writing for television simply as a means of supporting herself before she made it big with her novel. "I wanted to write serious novels full of well-meaning, angst-ridden, soul-searching adults," she once commented. Novels that "would change the face of contemporary society." Soon, writing for television took more and more of her time and talent. "I've been lucky in that I've always been able to do good television," Hall said in her interview with *AAYA*. "The medium is writer-driven; the writer is very much involved in the process with television. Producers are in actuality often the writers as well; you are not cut out of the production loop as writers are in movies." As she moved from comedy with the *Newhart* show, to drama with such popular series as *Moonlighting, I'll Fly Away*, and *Northern Exposure*, she had to learn different tricks of the trade, changing for example from three-camera comedy format to the dramatic format which more resembles movie production. "Everyone seemed to think that the writers for *Northern Exposure* were all Ph.D.'s or something, because the scripts were so detailed. In truth you had three weeks to become an expert on, say dog-sledding, and then three weeks for writing and shooting." All the while Hall was honing her literary skills with this deadline-writing: learning to pace action; to draw characters economically. Meanwhile, Hall made different contacts, including a New York agent who placed her first novel. No one was more surprised than Hall when the book was taken on as a young adult title.

Chronicles of Adolescence

Hall's preconceived notions about the writer's life—the Bronte equation—had already taken a few revisions with her television work. With publication of *Skeeball and the Secret of the Universe*, she made further adjustments. "I was as surprised as anyone when my first novel turned out to be a somewhat funny story about a teenager," Hall once noted. "From that moment on I realized I was drawn in the direction of young adult fiction. Kids make such great protagonists. They are asked to cope, even thrive, in circumstances not of their own choosing. They are not autonomous, and because of that they come with a built-in set of conflicts." In a biographical comment for *Twentieth-Century Young Adult Writers*, Hall expanded on this theme: "I've heard that a writer keeps writing about any part of his or, her life which is unresolved," Hall noted. "That certainly has something to do with why I write about adolescence. Every time I explore that age, I have an opportunity to go back and fix something that never got fixed, confront someone I never confronted, or reaffirm a desire or conviction that I possessed back then, and might be in danger of losing."

The protagonist, seventeen-year-old Matty Collier, is in danger of losing his dreams in *Skeeball and the Secret of the Universe*. Matty is a self-styled rebel; in fact his favorite actor is the brooding James Dean, his favorite movie *Rebel Without a Cause*. It's the summer before his senior year, and Matty is desperately seeking "the Thing" that will set him apart from the people he sees all around him. Matty's best friend, Cal, is busy with a summer job, something that Matty is determined to avoid. His parents are disappointed at his moping condition, yet Matty is driven by the search for the secret out there that will transform him: "I was all the time praying to something that had no name, that had no real definition in my mind at all. More than anything else, I prayed to this feeling I had that there was some kind of great pattern . . . the one that kept kids like me from working in a hot-dog joint."

Matty hangs out at the arcade of his coastal resort town, playing skeeball—a game rejected by video-crazed younger kids. Encouraged by an old man named Finch, Matty becomes something of a skeeball whiz, but this skill is not enough to impress the teasing Jennifer, a beautiful summer visitor for whom Matty develops a crush. But Matty wins consolation from his best friend's sister and from the old man, who lets him know that there are always goals worth attaining. "Skeeball becomes a metaphor for life in [Matty's] mind," Hall once explained, "and he mistakenly believes that if he can master it, he can master his future." A *Horn Book* review of *Skeeball and the Secret of the Universe* noted: "It has been a long while since we had a good, old-fashioned novel of adolescent angst and teenage rebellion. . . . The story rings true and is a worthy addition to a classic genre." Judith M. Beckman and Elizabeth A. Belden, writing in *English Journal*, commented that Matty speaks "with exceptional sensitivity" about the "confusion, insecurity, idealism, loneliness, and frustration of many adolescents. . . . Barbara Hall writes with humor and grace." *Publishers Weekly* also noted that Matty was a "genuinely likable character" who learns "that growing up doesn't have to mean abandoning his hopes and dreams."

Skeeball and the Secret of the Universe is something of an anomaly in Hall's works, for its setting is not the rural South of most of her novels; additionally, Matty is one of the few male protagonists in her books. Her second novel, *Dixie Storms*, was Hall's "journey back home," as she once characterized it. "Though it really isn't very autobiographical, the setting is a familiar one to me. I spent a great deal of time on my grandfather's farm, and many of the kids I went to school with were children of tobacco growers."

In *Dixie Storms*, fourteen-year-old Dutch Peyton narrates the action. She is faced with difficult circumstances, situations that she must learn to cope with. The summer seems interminably long, and there is no rain in sight, either physically or emotionally. Her father is beset by financial woes caused by the drought; her brother holds a permanent grudge for the woman who abandoned him and their son; this boy, Dutch's nephew, is in danger of becoming infected with his father's hatred. Dutch involves herself in all these family conflicts—perhaps too much—and in her growing fondness for Ethan Cole. The arrival of a city cousin promises to bring relief, but in the event Norma is a sophisticated urbanite, the sort of girl who "could trip on the sidewalk, laugh all the way down, and make you feel stupid for standing up." Barbara Flottmeier, writing in *Voice of Youth Advocates*, noted that "This is a 'slice of life' novel with characters that are well drawn and dialogue that rings with sincerity and truth," and concluded that the story "is full of humor and humanity and is delightful to read." Betsy Hearne, in her *Bulletin of the Center for Children's Books* review, dubbed the book a "seamless novel of family encounter," while *School Library Journal*, in its Best Books citation, noted particularly the "fully realized tempestuous characters," as well as the lesson the book provides, that you "cannot manipulate the lives of others."

Family Ties

Hall stayed with the South for her third YA novel, *Fool's Hill*, and with an adolescent female protagonist, *and* with a summertime setting. "A friend of mine once told me that there really is more than one season," Hall quipped in her *AAYA* interview.

From 1982 to 1983, Hall served as a story editor for various episodes of the television series *Newhart*, which ran on CBS-TV.

"I realize that I do use the summer in many of my books, but it's an important time. There is no school there to organize your life, and kids are thrust back into the family and its structures. That's an important theme for me to work on." As Hall once noted, the combination of family and the South "always results in something colorful, humorous, and larger than life."

Fool's Hill employs all these ingredients: a small Virginia town in the summer and a tightly knit family, "Though this book was my third publication," Hall explained to *AAYA*, "it was actually the second novel I wrote, so it is more autobiographical than others. I wanted to show what it is like to grow up in a small town in the South with the difficulties inherent of fitting in to such

a restricted environment." For fourteen-year-old Libby, the family is constricting; her parents' rules for proper behavior seemingly keep her out of the in-crowd. Eager-to-please Libby is beginning to see that the world is made up of two types; those who fall down and those who laugh at them. Libby's perfect older sister Gloria is one of the "laughers," and with Gloria away for the summer, Libby figures it's her turn to join the laughers for once. But the price she must pay is a large one. A couple of new girls come to town in a red convertible, the sisters Rosalyn and Linda. They include Libby in their society and together the trio infiltrates the laughers. But soon Rosalyn sets her sights on Libby's crush, and Libby begins to see that maybe the in-group is not so likable after all. Along the way Libby learns "about the importance of true friendship and family values," according to Kathy Elmore in *Voice of Youth Advocates*. In fact, Libby learns the truth of her mother's favorite saying: "It's not how you go over fool's hill, it's how you come down it." *Kirkus Reviews* called this novel of self-identity a "tender, appealing growing-up story," and Hearne, in *Bulletin of the Center for Children's Books*, noted that the book "tackles a large cast with energy," and that the "family dynamics are subtle, and the theme of maturation is realized through credible storytelling." *Publishers Weekly* concluded that "Libby's discoveries about the difference between being good and looking good are on target."

Hall's fourth YA title, *The House across the Cove*, was something of a departure in terms of plot. There is the familiar setting—the South and summer—but this time a mystery forms the backdrop for a story of teen romance. "I'd always wanted to write a mystery," Hall told *AAYA*. "And I decided to blend it with a sort of Romeo-and-Juliet style love story; to explore the socio-economic differences between a young girl and boy who fall in love. And I also wanted to take a look at a troubled family and at a boy who is forced to grow old before his time." What resulted is a "fast-paced page-turner guaranteed to engage the imagination and interest of its intended audience," according to Joanne Kelleher writing in *School Library Journal*.

The two teenage protagonists are Tyler and Abbey, who meet one summer at a lake resort in western Virginia. Tyler, whose father has apparently just killed himself and whose mother is mentally unstable, is staying with friends for the summer, while Abby, daughter of a wealthy family and of a congressman, is spending the summer with her well-off cousins. Tyler is on his own, forced into maturity by the dissolution of his family. Tyler and Abby fall in love, but are warned about the hopelessness of their love—they come from two separate worlds. Soon, however, the two are involved in more than a beleaguered love: mysterious lights from a supposedly unoccupied house across the cove sets the two investigating. But when their investigations lead to the disappearance of Tyler, Abby is forced to go it alone. Soon the murder of an alcoholic writer thickens the plot. Hall employs a dual narrative technique—from the point of view of both Tyler and of Abby—that "allows for multiple clues, or perhaps red herrings, to clarify and then confuse the

---

If you enjoy the works of Barbara Hall, you may want to check out the following books and films:

Sue Ellen Bridgers, *All Together Now,* 1979.
Alden R. Carter, *Growing Season,* 1984.
Richard Peck, *Princess Ashley,* 1987.
The Man in the Moon, MGM, 1991.

---

readers," according to *School Library Journal*'s Kelleher. Hall creates characters who are "searching for identity and a sense of belonging," according to Anne Liebst in *Voice of Youth Advocates*, who concluded: "This skillfully written suspense novel will appeal to mystery lovers."

Using Different Muscles

Hall continues to conduct a dual, if not triple, writing life, as a script writer and producer for television and as a novelist, both for young adults and adults. Two examples of the latter are *A Better Place* and *Close to Home*, both set in the South and with family problems at the center of the plot. "A troubled family is at the center of much of my fiction," Hall told *AAYA*. "It's something that everyone has, a family, and everyone can relate to it. And a small town is a mirror-image of the family: it's got rules and can be nurturing or strangling, just like a family. Families keep secrets, just like small towns, and that's how they can become unhealthy. Families as well as small towns can be threatened by a bid for independence in the young. It doesn't have to be that way, but when it is, the kid needs to get out of that restricting environment. I find the subject endlessly interesting."

Hall has now managed to balance the two facets of her writing life. "Writing for television is not less or more interesting than writing books," Hall told *AAYA*. "The two are essentially different activities. You use different muscles for each. I don't think I'd ever give up screen writing, not even if my books became bestsellers. And I don't think I'd ever want to be a full-time author, either. I tried it with my last book, and it was just too solitary for me. I need interaction with people, and I need activity." Hard at work on both a pilot for television as well as her next adult book,

Hall is also contemplating another YA title. "I want to write a book about the death penalty, and the YA market is perfect for that. That's the great thing about young readers—they are open to all sorts of ideas."

Hall does not subscribe to the notion of a writer's 'message.' "I don't think any of us sit down with a conscious theme in mind, with symbols all neatly lined up. At least I don't think a writer should do that; it makes the writing flat. But I know I do want to talk to kids, to address their problems, to let them know that it's okay not to be perfect and that other people are having a hard time, too. That's where good or bad emotional health all starts. If a kid grows up unempowered, then he or she is going to have a hard time of it as an adult. Just listening to someone and letting them know they are not a freak is a help. . . . In the end, I don't have any answers with my books, but I do try to ask the right questions." One thing is certain, however. Dreams can come true. Hall and her sister Karen, who grew up fantasizing themselves as the Bronte's, have realized a piece of that fantasy. In addition to Hall's success, her sister has also become a well known author of adult novels. Not bad for a couple of small-town girls.

■ Works Cited

Beckman, Judith M., and Elizabeth A. Belden, review of Skeeball and the Secret of the Universe, English Journal, February, 1988, p. 85.

Review of Dixie Storms, School Library Journal, December, 1990, p. 22.

Elmore, Kathy, review of Fool's Hill, Voice of Youth Advocates, December, 1992, p. 278.

Flottmeier, Barbara, review of Dixie Storms, Voice of Youth Advocates, December, 1990, p. 281.

Review of Fool's Hill, Kirkus Reviews, September 15, 1992, p. 1187.

Review of Fool's Hill, Publishers Weekly, September 14, 1992, p. 126.

Hall, Barbara, Skeeball and the Secret of the Universe, Orchard Books, 1987.

Hall, Barbara, Dixie Storms, Harcourt, 1990.

Hall, Barbara, Fool's Hill, Bantam, 1992.

Hall, Barbara, interview with J. Sydney Jones for Authors and Artists for Young Adults, conducted March, 1997.

Hearne, Betsy, review of Dixie Storms, Bulletin of the Center for Children's Books, July, 1990, p. 265.

Hearne, Betsy, review of Fool's Hill, Bulletin of the Center for Children's Books, September, 1992, p. 12.

Kelleher, Joanne, review of The House across the Cove, School Library Journal, February, 1996, p. 112.

Liebst, Anne, review of The House across the Cove, Voice of Youth Advocates, February, 1996, p. 371.

Review of Skeeball and the Secret of the Universe, Horn Book, March-April, 1988, pp. 206-7.

Review of Skeeball and the Secret of the Universe, Publishers Weekly, August 28, 1987, p. 82.

Sukraw, Tracy, "Barbara Hall," Twentieth-Century Young Adult Writers, St. James Press, 1994, pp. 264-65.

■ For More Information See

BOOKS

Contemporary Authors, Volume 135, Gale, 1992, pp. 193-94.

PERIODICALS

Booklist, May 1, 1990, p. 1693; March 15, 1991, p. 1488; March 15, 1993, pp. 1342, 1345; July 1, 1993, p. 1864; September 15, 1995, p. 152; March 15, 1996, p. 1294.

Kirkus Reviews, May 15, 1997, p. 740.

Kliatt, November, 1995, p. 8.

Publishers Weekly, July 4, 1994, p. 53; August 28, 1995, p. 114.

Voice of Youth Advocates, October, 1987, p. 200.

—Sketch by J. Sydney Jones

Virginia Hamilton

■ Personal

Born March 12, 1936, in Yellow Springs, OH; daughter of Kenneth James (a musician) and Etta Belle (Perry) Hamilton; married Arnold Adoff (an anthologist and author), March 19, 1960; children: Leigh Hamilton (daughter), Jamie Levi (son). *Education*: Antioch College, B.A., 1955, attended Ohio State University, 1957-58, and New School for Social Research, 1959.

■ Addresses

Home—Box 293, Yellow Springs, OH 45387. *Agent*—Arnold Adoff Agency, Box 293, Yellow Springs, OH 45387. *Electronic*—bodeep @ aol.com.

■ Career

"Every source of occupation imaginable, from singer to bookkeeper"; author of books for young people. Whittall Lecturer, Library of Congress, Washington, DC, 1957; Distinguished Visiting Professor, Queens College, New York, 1986-88, and Ohio State University, 1988-89; Mary Hill Arbuthnot Honor lecturer, 1993.

■ Awards, Honors

Notable Children's Book citation, American Library Association (ALA), 1967, and Nancy Block Memorial Award, New York City downtown community school awards committee, both for *Zeely*; Edgar Allan Poe Award for best juvenile mystery, Mystery Writers of America, 1969, for *The House of Dies Drear*; Ohioana Literary Award, 1969, award for body of work, 1984, and Career Medal, 1991; John Newbery Honor Book Award, 1971, for *The Planet of Junior Brown*, 1983, for *Sweet Whispers, Brother Rush*, and 1989, for *In the Beginning: Creation Stories from around the World*; Lewis Carroll Shelf Award, *Boston Globe-Horn Book* Award, 1974, John Newbery Medal, and National Book Award, both 1975, and Gustav-Heinemann-Friedinspreis fur kinder und Lugendbucher (Dusseldorf, Germany), 1991, all for *M. C. Higgins, the Great*; Coretta Scott King Award, *Boston Globe-Horn Book* Award, and American Book Award nomination, all 1983, all for *Sweet Whispers, Brother Rush*; *Horn Book* Fanfare Award in fiction, 1985, for *A Little Love*; Coretta Scott King Award, *New York Times* Best Illustrated Children's Book citation, *Children's Book Bulletin* award, and *Horn Book* Honor List selection, all 1986, all for *The People Could Fly: American Black Folktales*; *Boston Globe-Horn Book* Award, 1988, and Coretta Scott King Award, 1989, both for *Anthony Burns: The Defeat and Triumph of a Fugitive Slave*; Regina Medal, Catholic Library Association, 1990, for lifetime achievement; Hans Christian Andersen Award nomination, 1992, for body of work; Laura Ingalls Wilder Award for body of work, ALA, 1995; John D. and Catherine C. MacArthur fellowship, 1995; Best Books citations from *Publishers Weekly* and *School Library Journal,* both 1996, both for *When Birds Could Talk and Bats Could Sing;* Coretta Scott King Award, and Honor Titles Storytelling World Award, both 1996, both for *Her Stories: African American Folktales, Fairy Tales and True Tales;* L.L.D., Wright State University; D.H.L., Bank Street College, 1990, and Ohio State University.

■ Writings

FICTION

Zeely, illustrated by Symeon Shimin, Macmillan, 1967, recorded by the author as *Virginia Hamilton Reads "Zeely"* (cassette), Caedmon, 1974.

The House of Dies Drear, illustrated by Eros Keith, Macmillan, 1968.

The Time-Ago Tales of Jahdu, Macmillan, 1969.

The Planet of Junior Brown, Macmillan, 1971.

Time-Ago Lost: More Tales of Jahdu, illustrated by Ray Prather, Macmillan, 1973.

M. C. Higgins, the Great, Macmillan, 1974, published with teacher's guide by Lou Stanek, Dell, 1986.

Arilla Sun Down, Greenwillow, 1976.

Justice and Her Brothers (first novel in "Justice" trilogy), Greenwillow, 1978.

Jahdu, pictures by Jerry Pinkney, Greenwillow, 1980.

Dustland (second novel in "Justice" trilogy), Greenwillow, 1980.

The Gathering (third novel in "Justice" trilogy), Greenwillow, 1981.

Sweet Whispers, Brother Rush, Philomel, 1982.

The Magical Adventures of Pretty Pearl, Harper, 1983.

Willie Bea and the Time the Martians Landed, Greenwillow, 1983.

A Little Love, Philomel, 1984.

Junius over Far, Harper, 1985.

The People Could Fly: American Black Folktales, illustrated by Leo and Diane Dillon, Knopf, 1985, published with cassette, 1987.

The Mystery of Drear House: The Conclusion of the Dies Drear Chronicle, Greenwillow, 1987.

A White Romance, Philomel, 1987.

In the Beginning: Creation Stories from around the World, Harcourt, 1988.

Anthony Burns: The Defeat and Triumph of a Fugitive Slave (an historical reconstruction based on fact), Knopf, 1988.

Bells of Christmas, illustrated by Lambert Davis, Harcourt, 1989.

The Dark Way: Stories from the Spirit World, illustrated by Lambert Davis, Harcourt, 1990.

Cousins, Putnam, 1990.

The All Jahdu Storybook (revision of *Time-ago Tales of Jahdu, Time-ago Lost,* and *Jahdu*), illustrated by Barry Moser, Harcourt, 1991.

Drylongso, illustrated by Jerry Pinkney, Harcourt, 1992.

Plain City, Scholastic, Inc., 1993.

Her Stories: African American Folktales, Fairy Tales and True Tales, Scholastic, Inc., 1995.

Jaguarundi, Blue Sky Press (New York City), 1995.

When Birds Could Talk and Bats Could Sing: The Adventures of Bruh Sparrow, Sis Wren, and Their Friends, illustrated by Barry Moser, Blue Sky Press, 1995.

OTHER

W. E. B. Du Bois: A Biography, Crowell, 1972.

Paul Robeson: The Life and Times of a Free Black Man, Harper, 1974.

(Editor) W. E. B. Du Bois, *The Writings of W. E. B. Du Bois,* Crowell, 1975.

(Author of introduction) Martin Greenberg, editor, *The Newbery Award Reader,* Harcourt, 1984.

Many Thousand Gone, illustrated by Leo Dillon and Diane Dillon, Knopf, 1992.

■ Adaptations

Several books by Hamilton have been adapted as a filmstrip with cassette, including *Sweet Whispers, Brother Rush,* Miller-Brody, 1974; *M. C. Higgins, the Great,* Listening Post, 1975; and *The Planet of Junior Brown,* Miller-Brody, 1976. *The House of Dies Drear, M. C. Higgins, the Great, Paul Robeson, The Time-Ago Tales of Jahdu, The People Could Fly,* and *W. E. B. Du Bois* have been recorded on audio cassette. *The House of Dies Drear* was translated into Braille and was adapted for the Public Broadcasting Service series *Wonderworks* in 1984.

■ Overview

One of the most respected and prolific contemporary authors of books for children and young adults, Virginia Hamilton was the first African American writer to win the prestigious John Newbery Medal, in recognition of *M. C. Higgins, the Great,* a novel she published in 1974. In addition to its Newbery honor, *M. C. Higgins* also garnered the National Book Award; its multi-award winning status would be characteristic of many of Hamilton's works. Considered challenging, literary, and thematically complex, Hamilton's books are often credited by critics with having raised the standards of American children's literature. "Few writers of fiction for young people are as daring, inventive, and challenging to read . . . ," commented Ethel L. Heins in *Horn Book.* "Frankly making demands on her readers, she nevertheless expresses herself in a style essentially simple and concise."

Much of Hamilton's writing is inspired by her childhood experiences of the Great Depression in her hometown of Yellow Springs, Ohio. "What personal self I have is in my books," Hamilton once Marguerite Feitlowitz in an interview for *Authors and Artists for Young Adults (AAYA).* "Everything that might become neurotic or personally problematic I put into a narrative. My stories are little pieces of me." In addition to her personal memories, Hamilton draws from the well of family history. She is descended from farmers who once were fugitives from slavery, men and women for whom the attainment of land and homes was a symbol of their freedom. "My fictions for young people derive from the progress of Black adults and their children across the American hope-scape," the author explained in *Horn Book.* "Occasionally, they are light-hearted; often they are speculative, symbolic and dark, and brooding. The people are always uneasy because the ideological difference they feel from the majority is directly derived from heritage. In the background of much of my writing is the dream of freedom tantalizingly out of reach."

Hamilton was raised in a traditional household, where the men—both her father and her two older brothers—dominated. Her father, a musician, performed classical mandolin at clubs throughout the United States. Because his race prevented him from joining either the musician's union or established orchestras, he formed his own musical groups, performing on radio and in dance halls, working hard to keep his family together through the years of the Great Depression. "My father was also a great reader," Hamilton recalled to *AAYA.* "He loved Wendell Wilkie, whose *One World* was one of his favorite books. He knew W. E. B. Du Bois, and subscribed to *Crisis* magazine, which Du

Bois edited under the auspices of the [National Association for the Advancement of Colored Persons]. Du Bois and Franklin Delano Roosevelt were my father's heroes. He subscribed to the *New Yorker,* and talked about what he read. Books were an important part of our lives—Poe, de Maupassant, many of the classics. I didn't realize then how unusual it was for a man like my father to have such a library. It was an important factor in my education."

Hamilton attended a small country school, where she was the only black girl in her class until her early teens. Even with her school's limited facili-

This 1968 work, which revolves around a house that was once a station on the Underground Railroad and contains the ghosts of two fugitive slaves and an abolitionist, ensured Hamilton's status as a high ranking writer for young adults.

ties, Hamilton excelled at her studies, and after high school one of her teachers arranged for her to attend nearby Antioch College. While at Antioch, Hamilton took advantage of the school's writing program and was encouraged by her instructors to go to New York and try to become published. Throughout college, Hamilton spent her summers in New York City, working as a bookkeeper and earning far more money than she could in Ohio. Finally the lure of the city became so much that Hamilton left school before graduation and moved there to live. A part-time clerical job and a low-rent apartment in New York's East Village allowed her the freedom to write. "New York was such a different scene in the fifties," she remembered of those years. "The East Village was a mix of Polish and Ukrainian immigrants, young writers and artists. It was easy to meet people. The painters Raphael and Moses Soyer held a weekly salon, attended by everyone who was anyone. Today, I get the feeling that writers, artists and musicians operate pretty much in separate spheres. It wasn't like that then. We were all together. It was a completely integrated scene."

Shortly after arriving in New York City, Hamilton met author Arnold Adoff, whom she later married; the couple's travels to Europe and northern Africa would provide inspiration for many of Hamilton's later books. Meanwhile, working at her writing, she submitted several stories to the *New Yorker*, but had yet to have anything published. In 1950, on the advice of a friend, Hamilton enrolled in a class at the New School for Social Research. With encouragement from her teacher, she eventually submitted a children's story she had written while at Antioch to Macmillan. That story became *Zeely*, her first published book.

Zeely is a coming of age story that revolves around twelve-year-old Elizabeth "Geeder" Perry, who, along with younger brother John, spends the summer on a farm owned by her Uncle Ross. While there, Geeder becomes fascinated by a woman named Zeely Tayber. The beautiful, six-and-a-half-foot tall, ebony-skinned woman, the daughter of a tenant farmer renting land on the farm, becomes a Watusi queen in Geeder's active imagination. After Geeder spreads a fantastic story about Zeely's royal heritage around town, the tale ultimately comes back to Zeely. Reminded of her own childhood, the woman tells Geeder a story about the origins of her people that helps the

young teen to balance reality with her "most fine way of dreaming." Zeely's creation story also instills in Geeder an appreciation for her African American ancestry. "*Zeely* looks to Africa," explained Hamilton in *AAYA*, recalling her trip to the continent. "For years, I had kept a scrapbook on Africa, and a map that I was constantly revising as nations won their independence from European powers. A lot of the material became part of *Zeely*."

Zeely garnered very good reviews, eventually moving into the ranks of a children's classic. Critics praised the author's storytelling abilities, her apt descriptions, and her unique characters. Elinore Standard's assessment, which appeared in the *Washington Post Book Week*, was typical: "*Zeely* is a fresh, sensitive story, with a lingering, serene, misty quality about it which the reader can save and savor." According to Rudine Sims Bishop, *Zeely* was more than an entertaining first novel. "At a time when most of the books featuring African-American characters were focusing on segregation, integration, or discrimination, *Zeely* presented the summer experience of an everyday, but extraordinary, young African-American girl," Bishop wrote in *Horn Book*. "It concerned itself neither with overcoming racism, nor pretending to be color-blind, but with identity, heritage, and the importance of imagination."

Hamilton's next book, *The House of Dies Drear*, was awarded the Edgar Allan Poe Award for the best juvenile mystery of 1969 and was generally lauded by critics. The novel, which would be followed in 1987 by *The Mystery of Drear House*, abounds with elements of ghost stories and gothic novels, as well as points of U.S. history. After thirteen-year-old Thomas Small and his family move from North Carolina to a large, forbidding house in a college town in Ohio, strange things begin to happen. Soon Thomas finds himself confronted by ghostly apparitions and the possibility of a treasure hidden somewhere within the ancient house's maze of secret passages. As the mystery unfolds, Thomas learns through the history of the house and its former owner, Dies Drear, the story of the Underground Railroad, an organized route along which abolitionists aided fugitive slaves escaping the plantations of the south, slowly moving them north to freedom. As Dorothy Sterling of the *New York Times Book Review* wrote, "*The House of Dies Drear* is written with poetic precision. Miss Hamilton polishes her sentences with care, devel-

Various myths about the origins of the universe from cultures around the world are presented by Hamilton in this 1988 work.

ops her characters with imagination and love. . . . [It] is not an angry book—although there is a need for anger too. Instead, Miss Hamilton has found her own way of saying 'Black is beautiful.'"

Hamilton's multi-award-winning *M. C. Higgins, the Great,* published in 1974, would feature another thirteen-year-old protagonist in Mayo Cornelius Higgins. M. C.'s favorite perch is a bicycle seat attached to the top of a forty-foot pole on the side of Sarah's Mountain, from which he can keep watch over his younger brothers while also taking in the beauty of the surrounding Ohio countryside. Watching the rural homestead that has been in his family for generations gradually being encroached upon by the ravages of strip miners, M. C. tries to find a way whereby he can convince his family to escape from their unsafe conditions near the miner's growing spoil heap, yet preserve their close-knit home. "*M. C. Higgins, the Great* is not an adorable book, not a lived-happily-ever-after kind of story," explained Nikki

Giovanni in her review of the novel in the *New York Times Book Review.* "It is warm, humane and hopeful and does what every book should do—creates characters with whom we can identify and for whom we care."

Other themes run through *M. C. Higgins,* including a young boy's coming of age and the battle for supremacy between father and son. M. C.'s father, Jones, feels helpless and despondent in the face of the changes occurring near his home, and his helplessness turns to anger. Meanwhile, M. C. demands action, and his energy threatens his father, resulting in contests of strength, including Jones' failed attempt to climb to the top of M. C.'s pole. Peter Neumeyer notes of the novel in an article for *Bookbird* that *M. C. Higgins* is both "one of our most sensitive probings of the inextricable and contradictory fluxes of love and hate," and "a convincing, vital affirmation of birth, of healing, of sexual awakening, and of the fluid pulsing livingness of the whole world."

Justice and Her Brothers, Dustland, and *The Gathering* form Hamilton's "Justice" trilogy. In the novels, protagonists Justice Douglass, twin brothers Thomas and Levi, and friend Dorian Jefferson have special extrasensory abilities, such as telepathy and telekinesis, that allow them to "mind-jump" a million years into the future. In this future place, they discover an Earth that has been converted into a hot, desert wasteland ruled by a creature known as "Mal." Language has been replaced by musical tones and chants in this futuristic world, a reflection of the author's own interest in music. In *Dustland,* the second novel in the series, the four children find themselves able to physically inhabit this dust-covered future land where they discover a series of strange beings, creatures that have adapted to the altered earthscape. Survival in this harsh alien environment forces the four to draw upon their separate strengths: Justice, the most powerful, leads the group, while Thomas and Levi provide a magical balance, leaving compassionate Dorian to cure the group's ills. Only when all four children work together as a unit, joining hands and channelling their psychic strength, can they travel back through time and reach their home.

In 1981's *The Gathering,* the group once again enters Dustland, this time through the dream of one of the future land's strange inhabitants. Their travels around the future planet allow them to understand the reasons for Earth's environmental collapse into heat and dust; they return without their psychic powers but with a more mature, responsible outlook on society and the environment. In *The Gathering,* the main theme is once again survival and the ability to adapt to change. "Hamilton's imaginative creations seem natural to the landscape," wrote a *Dictionary of Literary Biography* essayist in praise of Hamilton's futuristic vision, "believable adaptations of earlier forms of life transmuted by nature and radiation."

Hamilton's "Justice" trilogy has often been referred to as science fiction, a classification that its author never intended. "I don't think of those books as science fiction, at all," she told *AAYA.* "They fall into the category of fantasy, and have elements of the cautionary tale. Science fiction is based on scientific fact; fantasy need not be. Someone did say that these books start with reality, turn into fantasy and end in science fiction. This may be true. I certainly did a lot of research for the third book. . . . Twins and clairvoyance are themes that have long fascinated me. So, too, has the theme of the alien, and the possibility of global disaster. I feel less involved with my own heritage and more preoccupied with survivors of all kinds: Will the few who survive the cataclysm do so because they are genetically different? Is it possible that telepathy, prophecy, and genius are genetic mutations? Could the striking talents of a few be the means of survival for many? These are the questions I explore in *The Justice Cycle.*"

One of Hamilton's favorite books is *The People Could Fly: American Black Folktales,* an award-winning volume featuring illustrations by Leo and Diane Dillon. The twenty-four short stories included in the 1985 volume are representative of the wealth of black folklore created by first- and second-generation African Americans, bringing readers a greater understanding and respect for the thoughts and beliefs of these people. Many of the stories in *The People Could Fly* feature sections of Gullah, a creole dialect spoken by the blacks that inhabited the sea island near the coast of South Carolina, which the author explains in detail in a glossary. The work is divided into four sections: animal stories, stories of the supernatural, stories of realistic content, and tales about the quest for freedom.

"You see, the slaves—those former Africans—brought, chained, to this continent, had no power,

no weapons to aid them in overcoming their oppressors," the author explained in her Coretta Scott King Award acceptance speech, reprinted in *Horn Book.* "So it was that they used the folklore they created here to comment on their lives of servitude and to give themselves comfort and strength through endless hard times." African American folk stories "allow us to share in the known, the remembered, and the imagined together as Americans sharing the same history . . . ," Hamilton continued. "From teller to reader is the unbroken circle of communication. We all contribute to a construction of mere words. We are all together. That is what language does for us. That is what *The People Could Fly* may do for us. To say from one of us handed down to the other, you are not alone."

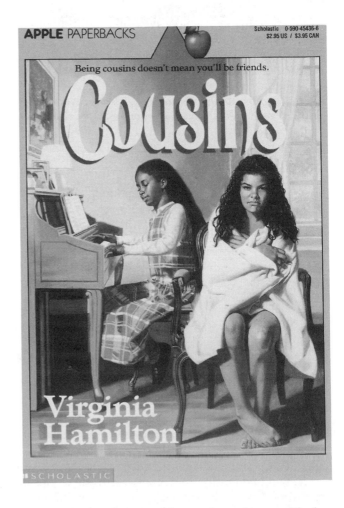

Cammy, who has trouble getting along with her cousin Patty Ann, learns the hard way about the importance of family, love, and forgiveness.

Throughout her career, Hamilton has developed strong feelings about the YA genre as it has been shaped by mainstream publishing houses. "Ask most editors, and they will talk about novels for young adults as 'problem books,'" she once told *AAYA.* "Supposedly, adolescents should be able to read them for the answers to the questions that typically plague them at that time of their life. Of course books can, and do, help us to live; and some may even change our lives, but it is not a good thing to put sociological/didactic considerations before literary ones. Besides, kids are very knowing. I tend to treat sexuality as a given, as something almost commonplace, in the lives of my characters. This leaves me—and my readers—free to concentrate on other things. I think about my story, characters, images, symbolism—the dynamics that hold those elements together in a pleasing sort of tension.

"There are certain technical advantages for writing for YA," the author added. "You're allowed to linger over descriptions—words, rather than actions, may be in the forefront. I love setting up scenes, starting with a wide view and then gradually moving in for the close-up. You can develop characters in a more sophisticated way. I consider most of the novels I've written for adolescents to be classical romances, but there are other, equally important, themes. The protagonist [in my books] is made to undertake a journey—physical, psychic or both. As a result of that journey, she grows and changes, a complicated, usually painful, process."

■ Update

Virginia Hamilton's later books have continued to challenge readers with their use of symbolism and vivid characterization, while also continuing to reflect the author's love of history, close family ties, and strong spiritual sense. Increasingly sophisticated themes of the development of self-knowledge, love of family, and breaking boundaries have become characteristics of her novels and nonfiction, both for young adults and junior readers. Her works, many of which are quickly hailed as classics of modern children's literature, continue to draw praise for their author's lucid style. "If her ability to create subtle impressions with a few simple strokes is exceptional, even more extraordinary is Ms. Hamilton's use of language," gushed Gloria Jacobs in the *New York Times Book Review.*

"Like the gift of perfect pitch, she has an ear for the cadences of everyday conversations and internal debates. She re-creates the language of African-American children in prose as smooth and liquid as poetry."

Hamilton's 1990 novel, *Cousins,* takes place over the course of one summer, as three female cousins enroll in a day camp where rivalries and deep hostilities develop. As her parents go through the throes of a divorce, the first cousin, eleven-year-old Cammy, grows close to her ninety-four-year-old grandmother, whom she frequently visits at a nearby nursing home. Disgruntled over her parent's breakup, the outgoing preteen becomes caught up in a secret battle with cousin Patty Ann, whose abundance of material possessions, good looks, intelligence, and talents make Cammy feel inferior. The added presence of shy Elodie, a poor distant cousin by adoption, does not help; Cammy rejects Elodie's attempts at striking up a friendship. Jealous of Patty Ann's successes—including her friendliness towards Elodie—Cammy wishes her "perfect" cousin would just go away, and she looks for reasons, such as Patty Ann's physical frailty, to put her rival down. Tragically, during a nature walk near a quickly rushing stream, Elodie falls into the water. While Cammy stands by, shocked, Patty Ann bravely attempts to rescue Elodie, saving her cousin but drowning in the effort. With the understanding of her wise Gram, Cammy eventually copes with her feelings of guilt and sadness over Patty Ann's death, and begins to see her late cousin in a new light. Cammy learns that Patty Ann's seeming perfection had covered her own insecurities and pressures from family members to be perfect, personal problems that had manifested themselves in the bulimia that had caused her physical weakness.

"Hamilton encases the story in family tradition," maintained Ethel L. Heins in her discussion of *Cousins* in *Horn Book,* "which offsets the instabilities of contemporary life, and she beautifully counterpoises superstition and rationality, separation and reconciliation, love and death." While noting that the novel is a demanding read for its intended preteen audience, Peter Hollindale called *Cousins* "a strong, richly imagined, emotionally truthful story" in his review in the *Times Educational Supplement,* adding that Hamilton's novel is "a book that will 'grow the mind a size larger', and we should be grateful for it."

Harkening back to her first novel, *Zeely*, Hamilton's *Plain City* is also a coming of age story. Twelve-year-old Buhlaire-Marie Sims has reached the age where she has started to look at her life through new eyes—the eyes of friends and people outside her small family. She is dissatisfied with their humble home on stilts standing astride the city's flood plain, and also with the fact that her mother, a nightclub dancer, is hardly ever home. But most of all, she is dissatisfied with the explanations for why she looks different than the rest of her family, with her hair's golden highlights and her light complexion. Raised believing that her father had died during the Vietnam War, Buhlaire now studies the dates and realizes that this explanation just does not add up. This knowledge lessens her shock only slightly, however, when a homeless street person who rescues her from a blinding winter storm turns out to be her father. At first viewing his entrance into her life as a chance to escape her surroundings, Buhlaire gradually realizes that her dad—homeless, destitute, and mentally ill—could never provide for her what her mother has worked so hard to achieve.

In the independent-minded Buhlaire, "Hamilton creates a complex, introspective character," noted Cathryn M. Mercier in *Five Owls*, "a loved child who feels forgotten, a forlorn adolescent emerging from the protective cocoon of family." Hazel Rochman lauded the author's use of setting as a reflection of her young protagonist, writing in *Booklist* that "Much of the story takes place outdoors, and the changes in the winter landscape—from frozen stillness to transforming flood—mirror Buhlaire's inner experience." And a *Publishers Weekly* reviewer had high praise for the novel, calling *Plain City* "Richly textured with a cast of unforgettable characters," and commending it for providing "a rare glimpse of unconditional love, family loyalty and compassion."

Finds New Outlet in Story Collections

In recent years, Hamilton has begun compiling collections of stories or nonfiction accounts, among these *The People Could Fly, In the Beginning: Creation Stories from around the World*, and *The Dark Way: Stories from the Spirit World*. She finds the work of adapting old stories satisfying because, as she wrote in *Horn Book*, "past and present, the known and remembered are invented anew," and the work actually becomes a collaboration between the author and "the words of long-past authors and storytellers" as those words are "delivered down through time." Collections also illustrate the fact that, as Hamilton noted in an interview with Hazel Rochman in *Booklist*, "people have the same mind about certain things. They have the same fears and the same need for order. Creation stories [like those in *In the Beginning*] come out of the need for making sense of the universe, and *The Dark Way* . . . is attempting to bring us from an outside chaotic place into the place of safety where stories can be told."

In the Beginning: Creation Stories from around the World, published in 1988, collects twenty-five myths and legends surrounding the origins of the earth and those creatures who inhabit it. Gods and devils, heroes and heroines all figure prominently. Named as a Newbery Honor Book—the third of Hamilton's titles to achieve that honor—*In the Beginning* contains stories ranging from Egypt to Guatemala, from Babylonia to the Russian steppe, many of which Hamilton researched in the New York Public Library and the Museum of Natural History while she was teaching at nearby Queens College. "The most striking purpose of a creation myth," Hamilton writes in her introduction to the book, "is to explain something. Yet it also asks questions and gives reasons why groups of people perform certain rituals and live a particular way. . . . People everywhere have creation myths, revealing how they view themselves *to themselves* in ways that are movingly personal." In an effort to put each of these stories into a context for young readers, Hamilton includes information on its origins and significance within the panorama of creation folklore.

Included are such diverse offerings as the classic Greek myth story of Pandora's box; "Ulgen the Creator," a Russian tale that explains why dogs have fur; a Blackfoot Indian legend of an old man who assembles the world gradually during a walk through time; and "The Frost Giant," a section of the Icelandic *Prose Edda* epic that explains how the separation between the earth and sky came about through the body of a terrible giant. Profusely illustrated by artist Barry Moser, the collection was highly praised by reviewers. Hamilton's efforts to retain the simple style of the original creation myths "results in some brilliant retellings, complete with the clarity of vision and fluidity of language synonymous with her work," noted Janice Del Negro in *School Library Journal*.

And Rosemary L. Bray added in the *New York Times Book Review* that "there are flights of imagination and hours of conversation for children and adults in *In the Beginning.* In her evocative retelling of these creation stories, Virginia Hamilton has created worlds of wonder all her own."

The Dark Way: Stories from the Spirit World is a collection of twenty-four scary stories from around the world, augmented by an original story by reteller Hamilton. Spanning cultures and races, the stories show that human fear is universal, transcending political and social boundaries. Vampires, goblins, genies, elves, giants, and trickster characters are just some of the creatures readers meet in a collection that Wendy Martin described in the *New York Times Book Review* as "a tribute to the limitless imagination common to all people." Despite the shadowed images called forth by the volume's title, some of the tales contain themes of transformation and renewal—witches change into horses and cats, trickster characters disguise themselves as a gust of wind, and a lump of clay comes to life as a benevolent giant. "In ingenious and varied ways, the stories in this collection demonstrate the extraordinary connections between all living forms, as well as between animate and inanimate matter," added Martin. However, others are chilling examples of ancient folklore; the fright value of facing the Irish Banshee, Medusa, and the Flying Dutchman is enhanced by the illustrations provided by artist Lambert Davis. "This is a twilight zone where gods and tricksters mingle, the human and the supernatural overlap, and reality mixes freely with superstition," noted Betsy Hearne in a *Bulletin of the Center for Children's Books* review in praise of Hamilton's deft retellings.

Bringing Historic Figures Back to Life

In addition to novels and short story collections, Hamilton has also authored several works of nonfiction, including biographies of African American singer and athlete Paul Robeson and fugitive slave Anthony Burns. Her *Many Thousand Gone: African Americans from Slavery to Freedom* collects individual histories from the Old South, as slaves fled the injustices and hardships of plantation life and journeyed towards freedom. Chronicling the lives of African Americans from the docking of the first slave ships in the early 1600s through the end of the Civil War, the book is organized chronologi-

After being treated strangely for sometime by her friends and family, twelve-year-old Buhlaire Sims starts to question her past.

cally, with each chapter devoted to a particular person. Some are famous, others less so, but all led lives of bravery in their quest for freedom. One chapter details the life of Henry "Box" Brown, a slave who escaped captivity by convincing a carpenter to build a box in which he could be mailed north to Philadelphia and to freedom. In another, the story of a Virginia slave named Gabriel Prosser is related, followed by chapters on the life and times of rebel leader Nat Turner, distinguished black orator Frederick Douglass, Underground Railroad conductor Harriet Tubman, and former slave Sojourner Truth. "Each [chapter] speaks for thousands silenced," noted Betsy Hearne in *Bulletin of the Center for Children's Books*, commenting on Hamilton's ability to tell the stories of a multitude.

If you enjoy the works of Virginia Hamilton, you may also want to check out the following books and films:

Rosa Guy, *The Music of Summer*, 1992.
Sharon Bell Mathis, *The Sidewalk Story*, 1971.
Patricia C. McKissack, *The Dark-Thirty: Southern Tales of the Supernatural*, 1992.
Sounder, directed by Martin Ritt, 1972.

Beyond a mere collage of biographies, *Many Thousand Gone* is a book about transformation. The narrators in *Many Thousand Gone* "through acts of will and courage determine the outcome of their own lives," Hamilton explained in *Horn Book*. "By their actions, the runaways touched the lives of all they encountered. Indeed, they did finally, literally, change their society by their deeds, by rallying the Abolition Movement to their cause." Citing the book as must reading in any lesson on slavery, *New York Times Book Review* critic David Haward Bain wrote that "all of these profiles drive home the sickening realities of slavery in a personal way. . . . These are powerful stories eloquently told." Citing the work as a "heartfelt and ultimately heartening chronicle," a *Publishers Weekly* reviewer maintained that "Hamilton's narrative deftly peels back time's layers and lends an unusual immediacy to this critical chapter in American history."

Painting a Panorama of Black Experience

In an essay in *Elementary English*, Hamilton explained the philosophy underlying her writing. "I attempt in each book to take hold of one single theme of the black experience and present it as clearly as I can," she wrote. "The black experience in America is deep like the rivers of this country," she continued. "At times through our history it became submerged only to emerge again and again. Each time it emerges, it seems strong, more explicit and insistent." "Perhaps," she concluded, "some day when I've written my last book, there will stand the whole of the black experience in white America as I see it." As critic David L. Russell observed in an article in *Children's Literature in Education*, Hamilton's oeuvre is a study of survival, of how young protagonists

learn to deal with the complexities of the adult world. "Her fiction is not so much a vehicle of social protest, like that of many African-American writers," noted Russell; "rather, it is the impassioned portrayal of individuals engaged in the difficult process of getting along in the world, of persevering, and, occasionally, winning out. [To Hamilton,] the African-American experience is strikingly different from the white American experience. Through her use of symbolism, this process [of becoming a unique individual while retaining racial and cultural roots] unfolds as an almost mythic enactment of the African-American will and means for survival."

■ Works Cited

Bain, David Haward, review of *Many Thousand Gone: African Americans from Slavery to Freedom*, *New York Times Book Review*, February 21, 1993, p. 23.

Dictionary of Literary Biography, Volume 52: *American Writers for Children since 1960: Fiction*, Gale, 1986, pp. 174-84.

Bishop, Rudine Sims, "Books from Parallel Cultures: Celebrating a Silver Anniversary," *Horn Book*, March/April, 1993, pp. 175-80.

Bray, Rosemary L., review of *In the Beginning: Creation Stories from around the World*, *New York Times Book Review*, November 13, 1988, p. 52.

Del Negro, Janice, review of *In the Beginning: Creation Stories from around the World*, *School Library Journal*, December, 1988, p. 127.

Giovanni, Nikki, review of *M. C. Higgins, the Great*, *New York Times Book Review*, September 22, 1974, p. 8.

Hamilton, Virginia, "Portrait of the Author as a Working Writer," *Elementary English*, April, 1971, pp. 237-40.

Hamilton, Virginia, "Ah, Sweet Rememory!," *Horn Book*, December, 1981, pp. 633-40.

Hamilton, Virginia, "Coretta Scott King Award Acceptance Speech," *Horn Book*, November/December, 1986.

Hamilton, Virginia, *In the Beginning: Creation Stories from around the World*, Harcourt, 1988.

Hamilton, Virginia, in an interview with Marguerite Feitlowitz for *Authors and Artists for Young Adults*, Volume 2, Gale, 1989.

Hamilton, Virginia, interview with Hazel Rochman in *Booklist*, February 1, 1992, pp. 1020-21.

Hamilton, Virginia, "Planting Seeds," *Horn Book*, November/December, 1992, pp. 674-80.

Hearne, Betsy, review of *The Dark Way: Stories from the Spirit World, Bulletin of the Center for Children's Books,* December, 1990, p. 85.

Hearne, Betsy, review of *Many Thousand Gone, Bulletin of the Center for Children's Books,* March, 1993, p. 212.

Heins, Ethel L., *Horn Book,* October, 1982, p. 505-6.

Heins, Ethel L., review of *Cousins, Horn Book,* January/February, 1991, p. 69.

Hollindale, Peter, review of *Cousins, Times Educational Supplement,* October 4, 1991, p. 30.

Jacobs, Gloria, "When Children Hate," *New York Times Book Review,* November 11, 1990, p. 34.

Review of *Many Thousand Gone: African Americans from Slavery to Freedom, Publishers Weekly,* January 18, 1993.

Martin, Wendy, review of *The Dark Way: Stories from the Spirit World, New York Times Book Review,* August 11, 1991, p. 16.

Mercier, Cathryn M., review of *Plain City, Five Owls,* January/February, 1994, p. 66.

Neumeyer, Peter, "'Touch My Pole Again, and You Won't Ever Stand Up,'" *Bookbird,* summer, 1994, pp. 33-34.

Review of *Plain City, Publishers Weekly,* August 30, 1993, p. 97.

Rochman, Hazel, review of *Plain City, Booklist,* September 15, 1993, p. 151.

Russell, David L., "Cultural Identity and Individual Triumph in Virginia Hamilton's *M. C. Higgins, the Great,*" *Children's Literature in Education,* December, 1990, pp. 253-59.

Standard, Elinore, review of *Zeely, Washington Post Book Week,* June 25, 1967, p. 12.

Sterling, Dorothy, review of *The House of Dies Drear, New York Times Book Review,* October 13, 1968, p. 26.

■ For More Information See

BOOKS

Children's Literature Review, Gale, Volume 1, 1976, Volume 11, 1986, Volume 40, 1996.

Contemporary Literary Criticism, Volume 26, Gale, 1983.

Dictionary of Literary Biography, Volume 33: *Afro-American Fiction Writers after 1955,* Gale, 1984.

Mikkelsen, Nina, *Virginia Hamilton,* Twayne, 1994.

Twentieth-Century Young Adult Writers, 1st edition, St. James Press, 1994.

PERIODICALS

Booklist, November 1, 1990, p. 519; December 1, 1992, p. 665.

Bulletin of the Center for Children's Books, June, 1988; November, 1990, p. 60; November, 1993, p. 83.

Five Owls, March/April, 1989, pp. 54-55.

Growing Point, November, 1991, p. 5595.

Horn Book, March/April, 1989, pp. 183-85; November/December, 1990, p. 753; September/October, 1993, p. 621; April, 1994, pp. 204-5; July/August, 1995, pp. 436-45.

Junior Bookshelf, October, 1991, pp. 224-25.

Kirkus Reviews, September 15, 1988, p. 1403; August 1, 1990, p. 1085; September 1, 1990, p. 1250; September 1, 1993, p. 1144.

Language Arts, October, 1994, pp. 453-59.

Lion and the Unicorn, Volume 9, 1985, pp. 50-57.

New Advocate, spring, 1995, pp. 67-82.

New York Times Book Review, October 16, 1988, p. 46; December 17, 1989, p. 29; November 11, 1990, p. 6.

Publishers Weekly, August 30, 1993, p. 97; February 19, 1996, p. 214.

School Library Journal, December, 1990, p. 117; May, 1993, p. 116; November, 1993, p. 125.

Tribune Books (Chicago), February 26, 1989, p. 8; November 11, 1990.

Voice of Youth Advocates, February, 1991, p. 350; February, 1994, p. 367.

Washington Post Book World, April 8, 1990, p. 8; November 4, 1990, p. 19; December 9, 1990, p. 14.

WEBSITE

The Virginia Hamilton home page is located at http://www.virginiahamilton.com.*

—*Sketch by Pamela L. Shelton*

Keith Haring

■ Personal

Born May 4, 1958, in Kutztown, PA; died of AIDS-related illness, February 16, 1990, in New York, NY; son of Allen (an electricity plant foreman) and Joan Haring. *Education:* Attended an art school in Pittsburgh, PA; attended School of Visual Arts, New York City, 1979-80; studied with Joseph Kosuth, Keith Sonnier, and Barbara Schwartz.

■ Career

Artist, beginning 1980. Also worked as a clothing and stage set designer. Teacher, Fort Greene Day Care Center, Brooklyn, New York, 1982; artist-in-residence, Montreux Jazz Festival, Montreux, Switzerland, 1983; founder and owner, the Pop Shop, New York City, 1986-90, and Pop Shop Tokyo, Tokyo, Japan, 1988. Founder, Keith Haring Foundation, 1989. *Exhibitions:* At numerous galleries, including Westbeth Gallery, New York City, 1981; Annina Nosei Gallery, New York City, 1981; Club 57, New York City, 1982; Rotterdam Arts Council, 1982; Tony Shafrazi Gallery, New York City, 1982, 1983, 1985, 1987, 1988, 1990; Fun Gallery, New

York City, 1983; Wadsworth Athenaeum, Hartford, CT, 1984; Leo Castelli Gallery, New York City, 1985, 1986; Kutztown New Arts Program, Kutztown, PA, 1987; Michael Kohn Gallery, Los Angeles, 1988; Hokin Gallery, Bay Harbor Island, FL, 1988; Charles Lucien Gallery, New York City, 1990; Philip Samuels Fine Art, St. Louis, MO, 1990; and Andre Emmerich Gallery, New York City, 1995; works also exhibited in Tokyo, Paris, Milan, Turin, Basel, Munich, and Amsterdam; works included in numerous group exhibitions, both in the United States and abroad. Works included in permanent collections at Dag Hammarskjold Plaza Sculpture Garden, United Nations Headquarters, New York City; Museum of Modern Art, New York City; Whitney Museum of American Art, New York City; Casino Knokke-le-Zoute, Belgium; Stedelijk Museum, Amsterdam; and the Museum of Modern Art, Rio de Janeiro, among others.

■ Awards, Honors

Granted Chevalier de l'Ordre du Merite Culturel by Princess Caroline of Monaco, c. 1987.

■ Writings

Art in Transit: Subway Drawings by Keith Haring, photographs by Tseng Kwong Chi, Harmony Books (New York City), 1984.
(And illustrator) *Against All Odds,* Bebert (Rotterdam), 1990.

Nina's Book of Little Things, te Neus, 1995.
Keith Haring Journals, introduction by Robert Farris Thompson, preface by David Hockney, Viking (New York City), 1996.

ILLUSTRATOR

The Keith Haring Coloring Book, FotoFolio, 1992.
Keith Haring: Complete Editions on Paper, 1982-1990, Cantz (Stuttgart), 1993.
My First Coloring Book, FotoFolio, 1993.

OTHER

Keith Haring (collected art works), text by Robert Pincus-Witten, Jeffrey Deitch, and David Shapiro, Appearances Press, 1982.

Works photographed and collected in numerous museum catalogues.

■ Sidelights

In February 1989, as the news spread that Keith Haring had died of complications resulting from AIDS, he was mourned around the world. The thirty-one-year-old artist had been known worldwide as the high-spirited and creative talent behind a vast body of work consisting of cartoon-like images that he set down with deft pen and brush-strokes, often spontaneously. Noted as a muralist and graffiti artist, much of Haring's work could almost be considered performance art due to its creation in front of audiences of passersby. Glorifying the street culture of the inner city, Haring's work held a vast appeal; his graphic images transcended race, culture, and geography, joining the "high" art of the exclusive galleries with the mass art of the common people. Representing the common character of humanity through his cartoon renderings, Haring's political and social activism became increasingly visible throughout his brief career. The posthumous publication of *Keith Haring Journals,* the artist's personal diaries, would reveal, even more than his artwork, the inner vision of an artist dedicated, as Haring wrote, to "live my life my way."

Haring's lean, graphic drawings, paintings, and sculptures are considered by many critics to mirror the popular culture of the 1980s in the United States. From designs sketched out in chalk on the walls of New York City subway stations to large-scale murals painted for churches, hospitals, and other public sites, Haring sensed a need for new means of visual communication that reflected the advances in human technology. He squarely addressed the issues of the era: from nuclear annihilation to apartheid, while also reflecting the socio-emotional needs of many of his contemporaries: human interaction, the need for stability amid large-scale social change, and a fresh perception of the world. Through their ubiquitous presence in the cultural mainstream—especially within New York City—Haring's images were transformed into icons of popular culture, recognizable symbols of the decade. While some critics would criticize Haring's work as entertaining but without lasting significance, others viewed him as one of the decade's most important artists. As friend and fellow artist Kenny Scharf recalled of Haring in *People,* "He was definitely the quintessential 1980s artist. He started with nothing but a lot of ideas, devised a plan of getting his message out into the world and was relentless until he succeeded."

Populism—believing in the virtues and wisdom of average men and women—is readily apparent in Haring's work: his use of bold, uncluttered line drawings make his works easily interpreted and unambiguous to even the artistically unsophisticated. Social messages are clear: the dangers of crack cocaine and other drugs, the importance of safe sex, and the condemnation of apartheid policies can easily be discerned in many of his works. During his brief life, Haring remained dedicated to his art and committed to use his talent for the betterment of society; he traveled to numerous communities throughout the world, involving both adults and children in the creation of murals, posters, and other large-scale works of art.

From Small Town Rebel to Big City Iconoclast

Haring was born in the small town of Kutztown, Pennsylvania, on May 4, 1958. As a child, he made up wildly imaginative stories, inspired by the cartoons of the era. With the encouragement of his father, Allen Haring, a foreman at a local Western Electric power plant, Haring illustrated his stories with simple line drawings similar to those he saw in the funny papers. Like many teens of his generation, he became rebellious in

Many of Haring's works are displayed in public places, like this sculpture in New York City's Riverside Park.

high school, drinking and experimenting with drugs. After graduation, inspired by his wish to channel his creativity and ambition into art, nineteen-year-old Haring enrolled in an art school in nearby Pittsburgh. Unfortunately, he soon became disillusioned by the uninspired work of the students in the school's graphic and commercial arts program and decided to move to New York. Arriving in the city in 1979, the twenty-year-old art student attended classes at the School of Visual Arts, while surveying the works of many noted artists that were constantly on exhibit throughout the city. An ambitious, restless individual, Haring caught the energy of New York and channelled it into his work, synthesizing ideas about change, evolution, and individuality that would form his future artistic perspective. Among his projects during his first year in New York City was *Video Clones,* a video/dance performance which Haring and friend Molissa Fenley staged at Manhattan's popular Club 57.

Haring rejected the imposition of what he considered to be artificial "movements," set down as "official" pigeonholes by the art world's elite. Art, he felt, was created by all individuals and manifested itself through countless creative, individual acts rather than by only those persons self-designated as "artists." As he would write in his diary in October 1978: "it seems like it is high time for the realization that art is everything and everywhere. That the conception of art occurs in *every* individual in day-to-day life in endless forms and ideas and is undefinable *because* it is different for each individual. . . . That everybody on every level identifies with art. . . . That the importance of the 'individual idea' in a society of this size and mentality is the only reality." Eschewing the formal galleries, Haring found his inspiration in the graffiti adorning much of the city, the work of city kids who created "moveable art" using the mediums of spray-paints and advertising boards attached to the sides of buses.

Haring quickly joined the ranks of the graffiti artists, although he used a brush rather than an aerosol can and his canvas was black paper, which he mounted over the blank advertising panels he found dotting the walls of Manhattan's subway stations. His impromptu artistry attracted interested spectators, and his notoriety among subway passengers quickly grew. Between 1980 and 1985 Haring estimated creating five thousand subway "installations" drawings, meanwhile developing alternative methods for mass-distributing his art, such as button pins, which he gave to interested onlookers.

The Evolution of Haring's Art

Haring listed several individuals as strongly influencing his early subway work, among them writers William S. Burroughs, Gertrude Stein, and the poet John Giorno; musician John Cage; and artists Jean-Michel Basquiat, Jenny Holzer, Walt Disney, and Andy Warhol, who would eventually become a close friend. Haring's evolving "cave cartoons," as they were dubbed, although unsigned, became widely recognized throughout New York City; although their creator would be arrested numerous times for defacing public property—on occasion Haring even spent a night in jail—bemused N.Y.P.D. officers even began to ask the local celebrity for his autograph.

Through his public creative displays, Haring attempted to create an art form that was accessible to all New York residents, no matter what their economic or cultural station in life. Such "democratic" art, Haring maintained, was closer to that of primitive cultures, where art was woven into all aspects of daily life. This was to become Haring's artistic credo: to remove art from the studios and art galleries and bring it into the open, into the streets of the city via advertising boards and walls, using the mediums of modern society. Gouache, water color, and oils were replaced by indelible marking pens, four-inch paintbrushes and rollers, and commercial paint. But behind Haring's effort to "simplify" art was a sophisticated knowledge of the field, from folk art, cartooning, and graffiti to the works of European and American modernists. "The role of the artist has to be different from what it was 50, or even 20 years ago," Haring maintained during a 1984

This 1989 drawing surrounding an exhibition announcement was on display at the Sidney Janis Gallery in New York City.

interview in *Flash Art* magazine. "I am continually amazed at the number of artists who continue working as if the camera were never invented, as if Andy Warhol never existed, as if airplanes and computers and videotape were never heard of."

Eclectic Imagery

Haring created a fresh array of icons for the 1980s: uncomplicated figures and rhythmic patterns that included barking dogs, mysterious beasts, and dancing figures; spaceships, robots, and rayguns; crosses, lightbulbs, computers, and television sets. His human caricatures are androgynous, ageless, and without an identifiable race. They are universal and ambiguous, no one in particular and yet signifying everyone. Although shades of Warhol's pop portraits and the large-scale cartoon imagery of artist Roy Lichtenstein could be discerned, Haring's work remained unique: he added to the pop culture mix the African American and Latino images that he saw evolving within New York's ethnic urban neighborhoods. While Haring's graphics at first appear childish—his famous "Radiant Baby" is a simply drawn, crawling baby with short lines radiating from its body—critics maintain that they contain a clear artistic sensibility, as well as political undertones reflective of the artist's position as a child of the 1950s ("the first generation of the Space Age," as he would dub it in his *Journals*) born to a world of television, the Vietnam War, race riots, and instant gratification. "Things are beyond my control and beyond comprehension," he wrote in March 1982. "I do not have dreams of changing the world. I do not have dreams of saving the world. However, I am in the world and I am a human being. In 1982, with telephones and radio, computers and airplanes, world news and video tape, satellites and automobiles, human beings are still frighteningly similar to human beings 2,000 years ago. I am scared to death."

Although appearing visually lighthearted and fun-loving on the surface, Haring's underlying message was usually far from inconsequential: his art was employed against the use of nuclear weapons, drugs, racism, consumerism-spawning advertising, and discrimination on the basis of sex or sexual preference. While some critics dismissed them as simplistic, David Galloway explained Haring's significance in universal terms: "Haring

argued that 'the contemporary artist has a responsibility to continue celebrating humanity,'" Galloway wrote in *Art in America.* "But 'celebration' does not merely imply a carefree festival; it also means, as in the eucharistic rites, a solemn, reflective occasion. That implicit duality, present in Haring's work from the start, is the reason why we look again at even his simplest ideograms, and it is why they strike a seemingly universal chord." Galloway dismissed the criticism set forth by some that the appeal of Haring's work to children is that his art is immature, stating that "One might as well raise the same myopic objection to Mark Twain and Huckleberry Finn."

As the 1980s ran their course, Haring's subject matter shifted from the streetside portrayal of joyous babies and hip-hop dancers toward more somber, thoughtful images: Christian symbols, television set-headed humanoids in the process of self-electrocution, and fantastic creatures with deformed genitals. Indeed, sexuality played a dominant role in many of the works Haring created for private, gallery viewing. While his message in both public and private art forums grew increasingly darker in nature, Haring's work also gained in popularity as more and more collectors recognized his politically reactionary position within the conservative 1980s.

Aboveground and Uptown

Shortly after his graffiti became the talk of New York, Haring switched from creating spontaneous underground "performance" art to being commissioned to complete above-ground murals and gallery installations. The first organized "showings" of his work were in abandoned buildings in New York's East Village, but Haring's art soon moved to more prestigious SoHo addresses, including the galleries of Tony Shafrazi and Annina Nosei. A large-scale painting on the wall of a Houston Street handball court done in fluorescent colors brought him attention from local Bowery residents and became one of the first of the artist's many outdoor murals. In 1982 Haring used the eye-catching Spectacolor billboard hanging high over New York City's Times Square to flash a half-minute animated drawing, which broke the billboard's steady chain of crass advertising messages by its repetition at twenty-minute intervals over the course of an entire month. As his work became more popular, Haring gained such highly visible commissions as decorating Manhattan's Palladium discotheque, MTV sets for rock bands, and props for theater, ballet, and performance art works. 1984 marked one of Haring's most unusual works: he used a living canvas—the body of supermodel and actress Grace Jones—which was afterwards photographed by Robert Maplethorpe. Murals for such causes as anti-nuclear rallies and anti-liter campaigns that featured Haring's unique graphics became a common sight papering walls along the streets of the Big Apple.

In 1983 Haring travelled to Switzerland to serve as the artist-in-residence at that year's Montreux Jazz Festival. Outside installations of his work during the early 1980s caused him to travel further, as he created large-scale murals at Marquette University in Milwaukee, Wisconsin, on a building in Tokyo, and for the Museum of Modern Art in Rio de Janeiro, the National Gallery of Victoria in Melbourne, Australia, and several other installations around the globe. In 1986, without the use of preliminary sketches or notes, Haring painted a three hundred-fifty foot long mural on West Germany's Berlin Wall, laying a background in the colors of the German flags with a chain of human figures interwoven upon its surface. "It is a humanistic gesture, a political and subversive act," Haring commented at the time, "an attempt to psychologically destroy the wall by painting it." Three years after he completed his mural on its surface, the Berlin Wall finally came down.

Known for His Generosity of Spirit

Much of Haring's work focused on young people, both as inspiration and as participants in his creative vision. The innate purity of children was, for the artist, a refuge against the cynicism he perceived in adult society. As he would write in his diary, "The reason that the 'baby' has become my logo or signature is that it is the purest and most positive experience of human existence. Children are the bearers of life in its simplest and most joyous form. Children are color-blind and still free of all the complications, greed, and hatred that will slowly be instilled in them through life." Haring was well known for his generosity in giving both his time and his talent to causes involving young people. In 1985, at the first annual Children's Worlds Fair in Asphalt Green Park, New York, Haring hosted a painting workshop and gave away free coloring books; he de-

This 1996 publication follows Haring's progression as an artist from his teenage years until his death from AIDS in 1990.

signed the cover illustration and centerfold for an issue of *Scholastic News,* a popular elementary school publication distributed nationwide; he was involved in activities for young people at Dobbs Ferry, New York's Children's Village, which sponsored a "Keith Haring Day" in 1985 during which the artist, in characteristic fashion, distributed drawings, buttons, and other tokens to the many young people in attendance; and the 1986 "City Kids Speak on Liberty" banner, which was six stories tall, found Haring at work with almost a thousand New York City youths. He continued to participate in numerous other youth-focused public activities, both in the U.S. and abroad, up until his death.

Commercial Enterprise Disturbs Critics

By the mid-1980s, Haring's easily recognizable graphics had become well known even beyond Manhattan; they now appeared on Swatch watches, T-shirts, and in Absolut vodka ads. This fact irritated many elitists who felt that a legitimate "artist" should only exhibit his or her work in established art galleries. Nevertheless, Haring's images continued to permeate pop culture through the remainder of the decade: on buttons, billboards, textiles, and album covers; on ghetto murals painted in collaboration with groups of teens; and in more traditional venues such as museum and gallery exhibitions in both Europe and the United States. Criticism particularly surrounded the 1986 opening of Haring's Pop Shop, a retail store located at 292 Lafayette Street, New York City, which the artist founded sell to objects embellished with his art. Two years later, he would open Pop Shop Tokyo, in Japan. "I could earn more money if I just painted a few things and jacked up the price," Haring explained to Paula Span in the *Washington Post* in response to his critics, "but my shop is an extension of what I was doing in the subway stations, breaking down the barriers between high and low art."

Despite criticism from certain members of the art community, the graffiti-like nature of Haring's oil and acrylic paintings, the high-profile exposure provided by the artist's many public works, and his commercial successes only enhanced his appeal; he would hold more than forty one-man shows during the second half of the 1980s. Haring's works would also be acquired for permanent collections of several museums, including the Stedelijk in Amsterdam, the Whitney in New York City, and the Beaubourg at the Pompidou Center in Paris. Mural installations were undertaken for the Schneider Children's Hospital of New Hyde Park, New York, the Cranbrook Academy of Art Museum in Bloomfield Hills, Michigan, and Grace Hospital, in Atlanta, Georgia, among many others. Haring's works became increasingly refined as the artist sought to meld his street style to the technicalities of "fine art." Although his work for gallery showings and private clients made increasing demands on Haring's time during the late 1980s—his period of greatest popularity—he continued to create art for the public, on the walls of hospitals, in schoolyards, and in his own Pop Shop.

Some of Haring's later projects included sets for ballets, murals for New York's Mount Sinai Hospital, a "Subway Show" at Lehman College in the Bronx, sculptures exhibited by gallery owner Leo Castelli, and a mural of the Ten Commandments for the Musee d'Art Contemporain de Bourdeaux.

If you enjoy the works of Keith Haring, you may also want to check out the following:

The works of Andy Warhol, a close friend of Haring's.
The art of Jean-Michel Basquiat, whom Haring cited as an early influence.
The writings of Williams S. Burroughs and Gertrude Stein.

Proof that money was not a motivating factor—despite the fact that his artworks had by now earned him a small fortune—Haring continued to initiate art projects with inner-city children, including a mural for the Boys Club of New York, and created posters and did public service announcements for the New York Public Library Association's 1988 literacy campaign. He also contributed to *Live AID* in 1985 and the Campaign for Nuclear Disarmament, and made a series of images on the plight of Blacks in South Africa and the United States for use in various social awareness campaigns.

Diagnosed with AIDS

In 1988, at the height of his success, Haring was diagnosed with AIDS, a disease to which he was no stranger, having lost many friends to its deadly affects. For a man consumed by a sense how much there was to do and how little time there was to do it, the knowledge of his imminent death was cathartic. Haring "went down to Houston Street, in Manhattan, until he reached the East River," explained Robert Farris Thompson in his introduction to Haring's *Journals*. "There, before the water, and its own sweet song, he let himself weep for the longest time. Purified by this, he went on to complete a life to the last full moment."

In a 1989 *Rolling Stone* interview, Haring expressed what it was like knowing that his life was limited. "The hardest thing is just knowing that there's so much more stuff to do," he said. "I'm a complete workaholic. I'm so scared that one day I'll wake up and I won't be able to do it." He managed to keep working, despite the degenerative effects of his illness, until several months before his death. Among his final works was the mural titled *Once upon a Time*, which he contributed to the ACT UP—Stop the Church campaign held in New York City near the end of 1989, a protest against the homophobic religious fever sweeping the nation in the wake of the AIDS scare.

Keith Haring Journals would be Haring's final creative gift to the many people who supported his art. Written "on planes, on the bullet train to Nagoya, [Japan], waiting in airports, in a strange, dragon-shaped guesthouse of patrons in Belgium," according to Thompson, the handwritten and illustrated diaries were a deliberate effort by the artist to reflect on the development of his personal creative vision. While covering the period between 1977 and late 1989, the *Journals* contain many lapses, some of many months in duration. Constant travel, emotional interludes, and a life dedicated to furthering his art sometimes got in the way of Haring's writing. "But most of the time [he] wrote with responsibility to the future," added Thompson, "demonstrating, in turn, the intellectual underpinning to the flow and substance of his art. Chance, he loved to say, favors the prepared mind."

Haring's diaries comprise two separate pieces of his life: the period between 1977 and 1980, as he was studying the works of other modernists, such as French cubist Fernand Leger, and Americans Warhol and the minimalist painter Frank Stella; and 1982 through September 22, 1989, the years of his international travels and greatest renown. Praising the artist as a visionary possessing a "natural-born gallantry," Calvin Tomkins would comment in the *New Yorker* after the artist's death that Keith Haring "never lost his initial certainty— naive, but essential to his own later achievement— that art was for everybody."

■ Works Cited

Galloway, David, "Keith Haring: Made in Germany," in *Art in America*, March, 1991, p. 163.
Haring, Keith, interview in *Flash Art*, March, 1984.
Haring, Keith, interview with Paula Span, "The Rich Young New York Artist as Pop Star," in *Washington Post*, December 10, 1985.
Haring, Keith, interview in *Rolling Stone*, August 10, 1989.
Haring, Keith, *Keith Haring Journals*, Viking, 1996.

People, March 5, 1990.
Thompson, Robert Farris, introduction to *Keith Haring Journals*, Viking, 1996.
Tomkins, Calvin, "The Time of His Life," *New Yorker*, July 8, 1996, p. 66.

■ For More Information See

BOOKS

Gruen, John, *Keith Haring: The Authorized Biography*, Simon & Schuster, 1991.
Hager, Steven, *Art after Midnight: The East Village Scene*, St. Martin's Press, 1986.
In a Different Light: Visual Culture, Sexual Identity, Queer Practice, City Light Books (San Francisco), 1995.
Kurtz, Bruce K., editor, *Keith Haring, Andy Warhol, and Walt Disney*, Prestel-Verlag (Munich), 1992.

PERIODICALS

Art Forum, February, 1986; May, 1990, p. 137.
Art News, February, 1986; December, 1986.
Booklist, July, 1996, p. 1793.
Boston Globe, July 3, 1986.
Chicago Tribune, May 18, 1989, p. 1.
Heavy Metal, August, 1983.
Interview, October, 1982; November, 1983; December, 1984.
Los Angeles Times, May 13, 1984.
Newsweek, October 15, 1984; May 20, 1985; April 11, 1988.
New York Times, January 29, 1984; November 8, 1985; April 18, 1986; February 20, 1987; March 8, 1996.
Publishers Weekly, May 6, 1996, p. 59.
Rolling Stone, August 10, 1989.
Time, November 3, 1986.
U.S. News & World Report, March 9, 1997.
Village Voice, January 8, 1985; May 6, 1986; December 27, 1988; spring, 1990 (special art issue), p. 3; October, 1990.
Vogue, November, 1988.

■ Obituaries

BOOKS

Annual Obituary, 1990, St. James Press, 1991.
Newsmakers 1990, Gale, 1991.

PERIODICALS

Los Angeles Times, February 17, 1990.
New York Times, February 17, 1990.
Washington Post, February 17, 1990.*

—*Sketch by Pamela L. Shelton*

Frank Herbert

■ Personal

Full name Frank Patrick Herbert; born October 8, 1920, in Tacoma, WA; died of complications following cancer surgery, February 11 (some sources say February 12), 1986, in Madison, WI; son of Frank and Eileen Marie (maiden name, McCarthy) Herbert; married Flora Parkinson, March, 1941 (divorced, 1945); married Beverly Ann Stuart, June 23, 1946 (marriage ended); married Theresa; children: Penny (Mrs. D. R. Merrit), Brian Patrick, Bruce Calvin. *Education:* Attended University of Washington, 1946-47.

■ Career

Novelist. Worked as a reporter, photographer, and editor for newspapers, including the *Glendale Star* (California), the *Oregon Statesman*, the *Seattle Star*, and the *San Francisco Examiner*, 1939-69; *Seattle Post-Intelligence*, Seattle, WA, educational writer, 1969-72; director and photographer of television show, *The Tillers*, 1973; technical advisor for the motion picture, *Dune*, 1984. University of Washington, Seattle, WA, lecturer in general and inter-

disciplinary studies, 1970-72; Lincoln Foundation, and governments of Vietnam and Pakistan, consultant in social and ecological studies, 1971. Also worked as an oyster diver and jungle survival instructor.

■ Awards, Honors

Co-winner, International Fantasy Award, 1956, for *The Dragon in the Sea*; Nebula Award for best novel, Science Fiction Writers of America, 1965, and co-winner, Hugo Award for best novel, World Science Fiction Convention, 1966, both for *Dune*; Prix Apollo, 1978; Doctor of Humanities, Seattle University, 1980.

■ Writings

THE "DUNE CHRONICLES"

Dune (originally serialized in *Analog*; also see below), Chilton, 1965, twenty-fifth anniversary edition, Ace Books, 1990.

Dune Messiah (originally serialized in *Galaxy*; also see below), Berkley Publishing, 1970.

Children of Dune (also see below), Berkley Publishing, 1976.

The Illustrated Dune, Berkley Publishing, 1978.

The Great Dune Trilogy (contains *Dune, Dune Messiah*, and *Children of Dune*), Gollancz, 1979.

God Emperor of Dune (excerpt appeared in *Playboy*), Berkley Publishing, 1981.

Heretics of Dune, Putnam, 1984.
Chapterhouse: Dune, Putnam, 1985.

SCIENCE FICTION NOVELS

The Dragon in the Sea (originally serialized in *Amazing Science Fiction* as "Under Pressure"), Doubleday, 1956, published as *Twenty-First Century Sub*, Avon, 1956, published as *Under Pressure*, Ballantine, 1974.

The Green Brain (originally serialized in *Amazing Stories*), Berkley Publishing, 1966.

Destination: Void (originally serialized in *Galaxy*; also see below), Berkley Publishing, 1966, revised edition, 1978.

The Eyes of Heisenberg (originally serialized in *Galaxy*), Berkley Publishing, 1966.

The Heaven Makers (originally serialized in *Amazing Stories*), Avon, 1968.

The Santaroga Barrier (originally serialized in *Amazing Stories*), Berkley Publishing, 1968.

Whipping Star (originally serialized in *If*; also see below), Berkley Publishing, 1970.

The God Makers (also see below), Berkley Publishing, 1971.

Hellstroms' Hive (based on the film *The Hellstrom Chronicle*; originally serialized in *Galaxy* as "Project 40"), Doubleday, 1973.

The Dosadi Experiment (sequel to *Whipping Star*; also see below), Berkley Publishing, 1977.

(With Bill Ransom) *The Jesus Incident* (also see below), Berkley Publishing, 1979.

Direct Descent, Ace Books, 1980.

Priests of Psi (also see below), Gollancz, 1980.

The White Plague, Putnam, 1982.

(With Ransom) *The Lazarus Effect*, Putnam, 1983.

Worlds Beyond Dune: The Best of Frank Herbert (contains *The Jesus Incident*, *Whipping Star*, *Destination: Void*, *The God Makers*, and *The Dosadi Experiment*), Berkley Publishing, 1987.

(With son, Brian Herbert) *Man of Two Worlds*, Ace Books, 1987.

(With Ransom) *The Ascension Factor*, Ace Books, 1989.

SHORT STORIES

(With others) *Five Fates*, Doubleday, 1970.

The Worlds of Frank Herbert, Ace Books, 1970.

The Book of Frank Herbert, DAW Books, 1972.

The Best of Frank Herbert, Sphere Books, 1974.

The Priests of Psi, and Other Stories, Gollancz, 1980.

Eye ("Masterworks of Science Fiction and Fantasy" series), edited by Byron Preiss, illustrated by Jim Burns, Berkley Publishing, 1985.

OTHER

(Editor) *New World or No World* (interviews), Ace Books, 1970.

Soul Catcher (fiction), Berkley Publishing, 1972.

Threshold: The Blue Angels Experience (nonfiction), Ballantine, 1973.

(Editor with others) *Tomorrow, and Tomorrow, and Tomorrow. . . .*, Holt, 1974.

Sandworms of Dune (recording), Caedmon, 1978.

The Truths of Dune (recording), Caedmon, 1979.

The Battles of Dune (recording), Caedmon, 1979.

(With Max Barnard) *Without Me You're Nothing: The Essential Guide to Home Computers* (nonfiction), Simon & Schuster, 1981.

(Editor) *Nebula Awards Fifteen* (anthology), Harper, 1981.

The Dune Encyclopedia, edited by Willis E. McNelly, Putnam, 1984.

The Maker of Dune, edited by Timothy O'Reilly, Berkeley Publishing, 1987.

(Author of foreword) Bryan Brewer, editor, *Eclipse*, second edition, Earth View, 1991.

The Songs of Muad'Dib: The Poetry of Frank Herbert, edited by B. Herbert, Ace Books, 1992.

Contributor of fiction to *Esquire*, *Galaxy*, *Amazing Stories*, *Analog*, and other magazines. *Dune* has been translated into over fourteen languages. Some of Herbert's papers are kept in a collection at The Library of the California State University at Fullerton.

■ Adaptations

Dune was adapted for the screen and directed by David Lynch, produced by Raffaella De Laurentiis, and released by Universal in 1984. Film products include: *The Dune Coloring Book*; *Dune Storybook* (adapted from the screenplay by David Lynch for the motion picture *Dune*), by Joan Vinge, Putnam, 1984; *The Dune Activity Book* and *The Dune Pop-Up Panorama Book*; "The World of Dune" (teaching kits based on the film for junior and high school teachers), Life-time Learning Systems, Inc., 1984; *Dune: The Making of Dune* (based on the making of the movie *Dune*, reported by Ed Naha), Berkley, 1984; *The Art of Dune* (includes artwork from the film and the complete screenplay), Berkley, 1984. The film rights for *The White Plague* were sold in 1987.

■ Sidelights

Paul Atreides, the young renegade Duke, and his mother, Jessica, were fleeing across the desert when they got their first good look at a maker. "Where the dunes began . . . a silver-gray curve broached from the desert, sending rivers of sand and dust cascading all around. It lifted higher, resolved into a giant, questing mouth. It was a round, black hole with edges glistening in the moonlight." The enormous creature, which had heard the surface-sounds of their footsteps from deep below, had pushed up through the sand to devour them. "The mouth snaked toward the yellow crack were Paul and Jessica huddled. Cinnamon yelled in their nostrils. Moonlight flashed from crystal teeth."

Paul, the hero of Frank Herbert's most popular novel, *Dune,* did not fear the giant worm. Neither did he find himself in the middle of a waking-dream, viewing a potential future, as he had been since the death of his father days before. Instead, Paul began "registering every available aspect of the thing that lifted from the sand there seeking him. Its mouth was some eighty meters in diameter . . . crystal teeth with the curved shape of crysknives glinting around the rim . . . the bellows breath of cinnamon, subtle aldehydes . . . acids. . . ."

For imagining a desert planet, where men with eyes of blue-within-blue drink their own recycled fluids and ride giant worms across cinnamon-scented sands, for envisioning a universe in which messiahs can see the varied paths of possible futures, and make their own predictions come true, Frank Herbert is himself remembered as a hero of sorts. *Dune,* which is considered a science fiction masterpiece and has sold over twelve million copies since it was first published in 1965, has greatly influenced the literary realm in which Herbert worked.

Dune, in the words of Bob Collins in *Fantasy Review,* "may indeed be one of the very best science fiction novels ever produced." The novel not only brought Herbert the status of famous authors C. S. Lewis and Isaac Asimov, it directed the fu-

ture of science fiction. "Together with such books as [Robert] Heinlein's *Stranger in a Strange Land* (1961) and [J. R. R.] Tolkien's *Lord of the Rings* (1954-55)," commented Robert A. Foster in the *Dictionary of Literary Biography,* "*Dune* helped establish two traditions in contemporary science fiction: the long novel and the invented-world novel, in which details of history, languages, customs, geography, and ecology . . . are combined with a rich complexity that pleases the reader by its verisimilitude and imaginative scope. "

Herbert, who, according to Bob Collins in an obituary in *Fantasy Review,* "was an ecologist long before it was fashionable," is still recognized as one of the first science fiction writers to take up ecological themes. In the words of John Leonard of the *New York Times,* Herbert was "in the business of producing what might as well be called eco novels." Given the popularity of these novels among young people, one may argue that, just like the fictional heroes of *Dune,* Herbert played an irreversible role in the unfolding future of his planet. "Herbert has said that the function of science fiction is not always to predict the future but sometimes to prevent it. . . . By increasing our awareness of a problem, science fiction can be a powerful tool for change," recalled Timothy O'Reilly in *Critical Encounters.*

Despite Herbert's popularity and cult-figure status, he refused to take up a leadership role in politics, religion, or the environmental movement. One of Herbert's major themes warned that heroes eventually destroyed themselves—and their followers. Still, as John Leonard remarked in the *New York Times,* the fact that he wrote so many sequels to the original *Dune* novel suggested that "Mr. Herbert is the prisoner of a cult, his own Leto. I suspect he would prefer to branch out and risk something else," and write something different. "His cult won't let him."

The Development of the Novelist

Herbert spent his childhood in the semi-isolation of rural America, in Kitsap County, Washington. There, he performed the daily tasks required of farmers' children: he milked cows, fed pigs, and raised chickens. "I developed all of my basic ideas during my childhood years on" the farm, Herbert explained in a *Mother Earth News* interview. According to Herbert in a 1980 interview with Jean

W. Ross of *Contemporary Authors,* he told his parents when he was just eight years old that he intended to become a writer. "I cut my teeth on Poe, Guy de Maupassant, Pope, Will James. Ezra Pound really blew my mind when I discovered him. . . ."

Herbert did not immediately began to write fiction when he reached adulthood. He served in the United States Navy during World War II, and worked odd, yet interesting jobs (which included oyster diving and jungle survival instruction). When Herbert began to write professionally, it was as a journalist and not a novelist. He gained experience in communications and media as a correspondent in Vietnam, and later as a photographer, a television cameraman, and a radio news commentator. During this time, Herbert understood that work in this field would help prepare him for his career as a novelist. In an interview with Ellen M. Kozak in *Writer's Digest,* Herbert explained that his work as a journalist influenced the creation of *Dune.* "Journalism is the entertainment business. You have to realize that, or your message is going to be lost. *Dune* is just journalism cast as fiction."

Although Herbert never finished college (he attended courses at the University of Washington), he read a great deal to educate himself about the many subjects that interested him. When Herbert was especially intrigued by a particular subject, he could work, in his spare time, as a diligent student. The knowledge he gained, on subjects from science, social science, and the humanities, emerged in his novels. For one example—many scholars have noted the importance of psychological symbols and themes in Herbert's work. This was no accident. Herbert revealed to Ross Stagner in *Psychology Today* that he was a dedicated student of psychology before he wrote *Dune.* According to Herbert, he'd met a "pair of psychologist-psychoanalysts" who "influenced my thinking a great deal. . . . [They] directed my reading and thinking and gave me the equivalent of a doctorate in psychology in 3 1/2 years."

While working in the newspaper business, Herbert wrote articles and short stories, and had some success publishing them. In 1950, he deliberately selected the genre of science fiction as the one in which he would concentrate his efforts, and by 1952 he had published his first piece of science fiction, a short story. *The Dragon in the Sea,*

Herbert's first novel (and one of his favorites), was published in 1956. In this underwater adventure, Herbert explored the psychological limits of sanity as his characters, riding in an atomic submarine, attempted to steal oil in enemy waters. In the opinion of Willis E. McNelly, writing after Herbert's death in *Extrapolation, The Dragon in the Sea* "is a fully developed, serious novel that still rates as one of his best. In it Herbert shows the same control of ideas, concepts, characters, and psychological insights combined with action-adventure that made *Dune* a masterpiece." *The Dragon in the Sea* won Herbert an International Fantasy Award.

The Birth of a Planet: Dune

Despite his initial success in science fiction in the late 1950s, Herbert continued to make his living as a journalist. In 1958, he found himself working on a news story about Oregon's coastal sand dunes and human ecological intervention. As Herbert explained to Ellen M. Kozak in *Writer's Digest,* he "became fascinated by the way we inflict ourselves on the planet." Around the same time, Herbert also began to seriously ponder another problem: how power "attracts the corruptible" and has the potential to generate a "power-structure" in which "the corruptible begin to congregate."

Herbert began to write a story which addressed the themes of human intervention in nature and power. He wrote with his knowledge and understanding of ancient mythology, biblical stories and characters, ecology, medieval history, Arabic, psychology, and comparative linguistics. The result— his second novel—was serialized in *Analog.* Later, Herbert sent it to twenty-two publishers, each of whom rejected it. *Dune* was finally accepted and published by Chilton in 1965.

If *Dune* is a difficult novel to describe, it is in part because so much of the story depends on an understanding of the world that Herbert created. The vocabulary, relationships, and plans of *Dune*'s characters would make little sense if read out of context. Yet "excerpts" from the writings of a fictional character (whose importance, as David M. Miller in *Frank Herbert,* noted, is unknown at the beginning of the book) help the reader understand why the characters are important, and give her clues about the plot's development. In Miller's

WORLD-FAMOUS CREATOR OF **DUNE**
AND **THE JESUS INCIDENT**

FRANK HERBERT
DESTINATION:
VOID

This 1966 novel tells the story of a scientific crew that has been sent on an experimental starship mission to test the crew's innovative solutions of previously planned emergencies.

words, these "head-notes to each section tip the hand." The "world" of *Dune* unfolds with each page, and readers learn about it as the novel's main characters do. *Dune* comes complete with helpful appendixes, a glossary, a map, and cartographic notes.

The world of *Dune* is located in the future, in some universe in which travel from planet to planet is possible and frequent, but not easy. It is on travel, or transportation, provided by the "Space Guild" from planet to planet that the economic and political systems of this universe depend. "Great Houses," each with its own feudalistic power and resources, trade with one another, and support one another formally in the "Lands-

raat" against the Emperor and his forces (the "Imperium"). Yet they compete with each other for money and power, both of which are determined by stock in CHOAM, which Herbert describes in the glossary of *Dune* as "Combine Honnete Ober Advancer Mercantiles—the universal development corporation."

The story in *Dune* begins as one of the royal families—the Atreides—prepare to leave their home planet of Caladan for another planet, Arrakis. Arrakis is an inhospitable desert planet, but the Atreides are moving upon the orders of the Emperor, and Arrakis is the only source of spice, the geriatric and addictive substance that allows the Space Guild pilots to navigate through space. The protagonist of *Dune*, young Paul Atreides, is just fifteen years old when readers meet him, but he has the concerns of an adult. He is warned that life on Arrakis will be difficult for him, and worries about an attack on his father's life.

Throughout his childhood, Paul understood that he was not an ordinary boy. As a son of a Duke, he has noble lineage, and he has received training for his future role as a politician, leader, and warrior. Yet Paul soon learns that he was trained, without his knowledge, as a Mentat. Mentats are very powerful figures in the *Dune* world, for they are the only humans able to perform the work that computers would do, if they had not been outlawed. Paul also begins to realize that her mother's training is a part of her effort to give him skills she learned as a select member of the Bene Gesserit, a class of women who can control their bodies, their minds—and even the bodies and minds of others. Finally, Paul begins to suspect that, as his mother ignored the orders of the Bene Gesserit and bore him as a male, and not a female, he may be the Kwisatz Haderach, the one "who can be in many places at once." (The Bene Gesserit had been breeding its members with certain males of the Great Houses for ages, all in an attempt to produce a male Bene Gesserit).

Not too long after the Atreides' arrival on Arrakis, the terrible predictions of the Duke Leto's death are realized, and the Harkonnen House attacks the Atreides with the secret help of the Emperor. Wearing his dead father's ducal signet, Paul flees with his mother from the Harkonnens into the desert. It is in this deadly environment, where they may be desiccated by the heat of the sun, devoured by sandworms, or buried in a sandstorm

Director David Lynch adapted Herbert's award-winning novel *Dune* to a film of the same name in 1983, which starred Sting (left) and Kyle MacLachlan.

that Paul, ingesting quantities of the mysterious spice, begins to have visions of the future.

The renegades are saved by the Fremen, the people of the desert, who have adapted to make the most of their environment. Rather than merely fear the sandworms (which they call "makers"), the Fremen respect, ride, and worship them; they alone understand how the melange spice is related to the life cycle of the sandworms. Wearing special suits that recycle bodily fluids, and harvesting the little moisture the desert ecosystem provides, the Fremen dream of a day when water flows freely across the land and plants are plentiful. Paul and his mother, who is pregnant with a girl-child, ritually join the Fremen. They capitalize on the myths implanted among the Fremen

by the Bene Gesserit long ago to become leaders among them. Although he fears he will ultimately lead the Fremen into a terrible holy war, Paul embarks upon a plan: to regain his rightful place as Duke and to turn Arrakis from a desert into a paradise.

Around the dream of transforming Arrakis into a bountiful planet moves one of Herbert's most important themes: thinking about the consequences of intervening in natural systems before one acts, if one acts. The fictional planet of Arrakis is supposed to be, naturally, a closed ecological system in which each living thing has a function related to the others. As Herbert explained in *Mother Earth News*, when "one change was *made*" in the environment of Arrakis, "it had a regular 'domino theory' series of consequences that hadn't been anticipated."

The second major message, or lesson, in Herbert's *Dune* is generally recognized to be a warning against heroes, leaders, and messiahs. Natural systems depend upon the collective wisdom—the genetic memories—of a people or species. They can only be disrupted when they are manipulated by the ideas, whims, and actions of one individual. And as a natural system is harmed by one leader, so are the people who live within it. Yet humans, faced with crisis, are continually faced with the temptation to call upon heroes. "In Herbert's analysis," wrote Timothy O'Reilly in *Frank Herbert*, "the messianic hunger is an example of a pervasive human need for security and stability in a universe that continually calls on people to improvise and adapt to new situations." We "must question our leaders," and leaders should refuse to be made messiahs, asserted Herbert in an interview with Ross Stagner of *Psychology Today*.

In *Dune*, the idea of intervention in natural systems is not limited to ecology. Herbert believed, as he remarked in *Mother Earth News* that psychology, religion, ecology, and economics were "interrelated." He explained, "I feel that the historical interrelationship between the native Fremen and their desert planet had created what amounted to a religion. They had learned not to question the way to behave in their environment, but to act in certain ways on faith." In Herbert's work, social, economic, and political systems resemble and parallel natural ones. Even the "power structure" of *Dune*, noted David M. Miller in *Frank Herbert*, is a "closed ecology, in unstable equilibrium. The Imperium depends upon the Landsraat, the Landsraat upon the Imperium. Both draw economic power from CHOAM. CHOAM cannot function without the Space Guild, but the Space Guild is dependent upon spice. Since spice comes only from his majesty's desert planet, the emperor remains in charge but only by playing Machiavelli on a tightrope."

The Success of *Dune*

It was not long before *Dune*, initially rejected by so many publishers, became recognized as a science-fiction classic. While, as Bob Collins noted in *Fantasy Review*, "professional critics gave it bad reviews," "word-of-mouth praise largely on college campuses . . . soon made [*Dune*] a best-seller. . . . Herbert's imaginary world, the desert planet of Arrakis, reminded many fans of J. R. R. Tolkien's Middle Earth, and *Dune* soon drew a cult of admirers." According to Burt A. Folkart in a *Los Angeles Times* obituary, "Herbert credited the successes of *Dune* to timing, for his tales of transforming the face of a barren land touched the heart of the ecology movement." *Dune* was the first novel ever to win both of science fiction's coveted awards, the Hugo and the Nebula.

Critics, too, gradually began to appreciate *Dune*. In the years following its publication, the novel was appraised primarily as a work of science fiction and fantasy, and compared with other novels of this type, even though many acknowledged the difficulty of categorizing the work. Many critics marveled at the integration of science and fantasy in the creation of Dune. "The ecological cycle which connects melange and the giant sandworms is one of the best examples of true scientific imagination in science fiction," wrote Robert A. Foster in the *Dictionary of Literary Biography*. Others appreciated the interplay of philosophy and fiction, and the way Herbert embedded meaningful messages in the structure of his work as well as the dialogue. In any case, the richness of the work gave critics much to discuss.

The success of *Dune* changed Herbert's life in three ways. First, it eventually gave him the income he needed to devote himself entirely to his career as a novelist. He worked on sequels to *Dune* and began to write or revise other science fiction novels. Second, Herbert also had enough time and money to develop a lifestyle which corresponded to his ecological philosophy. He turned property on Mercer Island, Washington, into a scientifically planned, uniquely constructed, ecologically-sound home environment, complete with solar power and a wind machine. (This demonstrated his assertion that technology was *not* "bad in and of itself." "Everything depends on how we use it," explained Herbert in *Mother Earth News*.)

Finally, as he was so well known among science fiction fans, environmentalists, and college students, Herbert's services—as an environmentalist, as a consultant, and as a lecturer on topics from writing to ecology—were in demand. From 1970 to 1973, he was a member of the national council of the World Without War Council. He lectured at the University of Washington, Seattle from 1970 to 1972. He served as a consultant on social and ecological studies at the Lincoln Foundation, and on land reclamation and reform for Vietnam and Pakistan in 1971.

The Story of Dune Continues

Among the novels that Herbert published after *Dune* in the late 1960s and 1970s, the most anticipated were its sequels. Yet the last two novels in the "Dune Trilogy" were not as well received as the original *Dune*; according to Don D'Ammassa in *Science Fiction Chronicle*, "as novels, they were considerably weaker." *Dune Messiah* (1970) demonstrates the trouble power can bring: the Fremen, given access to water, maintain a religion empty of significance. When Paul realizes that his prescience has brought him evil, he blinds himself and abandons himself to die in the desert. Meanwhile, Paul's twin children, a boy and a girl, carry on his mission for power. While still in the womb, they learn the past and the future of their people.

As the story of the twins, Leto and Ghanima, continues in *Children of Dune* (1976), so proceeds an evaluation of Paul's effect on the environment of Arrakis and its people. Leto attempts to restore the planet by cultivating the ancient Fremen traditions that had been developed centuries ago. Merging with the form of a sandtrout, he becomes superhuman. While Timothy O'Reilly in *Frank Herbert* wrote that *Children of Dune* "creates an uncanny sense of reality," and "frustrates the reader's hunger for a single point of view that will sum up the rest," he explained: "To Herbert, the hero mystique is symptomatic of a deadly pathology in contemporary society, a compulsive yearning for easy answers. As long as men are looking for simple solutions to their problems, they will give over their ability to think for themselves to the first person who comes along and promises a solution. The *Dune* trilogy is an attempt to unveil that pattern and, in some small part, to change it."

God Emperor of Dune (1981) continues the "Dune" story; it is set millennia after the birth of Paul, and, as some critics have noted, the narrative indulges philosophy. It is Leto (in the process of turning himself into a half-human, half-sandworm monster) who recalls the past for the reader, and who shares his various thoughts, beliefs and attitudes; the reader witnesses his gradual preference for tyranny and progress. Also, as a *Kirkus Reviews* critic noted, "the ecological transformation of Dune is complete"—green plants grow where the desert once was, the sandworms are gone, and regular crops replace melange. Leto eventually sacrifices himself by dividing himself into sandfish, the ancestors of Arrakis' future giant worms, for the good of his people. While the *Kirkus Reviews* critic described the book as "fatalistic" and "somber," the critic wrote that the novel is "ultimately profound, poignant, and powerful." "Although this novel is a pale reflection when compared to *Dune*, Lord Leto himself is one of the more original and awe-inspiring creations in science fiction . . .," argued D. Douglas Fratz in the *Washington Post Book World*.

In *Heretics of Dune* (1984), Arrakis is a desert, and its people struggle to contend with their environment. At the same time, they must deal with invaders from other colonies and a ghola—a reincarnated warrior-servant of the first Duke Leto—named Duncan Idaho. The final "Dune Chronicles" novel, *Chapterhouse: Dune* was published in 1985, the year before Herbert's death. This novel moves even further ahead in time, 15,000 years after Leto II, when his prophecies have been fulfilled. The Bene Gesserit Mother Superior and Duncan Idaho are main characters in this work.

Given the popularity of the "Dune Chronicles" series, many expected the movie *Dune*, directed by David Lynch, to be a hit when it came out at the end of 1984. Herbert seemed pleased with the project. He told Ross Stagner during a *Psychology Today* interview that "The movie begins as *Dune* begins. It ends as *Dune* ends . . . and I hear my dialogue all the way through it." Despite Frank's optimism, the motion picture *Dune* was generally greeted with disappointment. A critic for *Variety* described it as a "huge, imaginative, and cold sci-fi epic" which "won't . . . create the sort of fanaticism which has made Frank Herbert's 1965 novel one of the all-time favorites in its genre." The critic suggested that, perhaps, the director had "been too faithful to his source material; in striving to retain as much of as possible, he has overloaded the film with so many elements that many of them ultimately get lost in the shuffle." Although the movie *Dune* did not succeed in 1984, in late 1996, Paul Nathan of *Publishers Weekly* reported talk of filming the material from *Dune* and its sequels "as a miniseries."

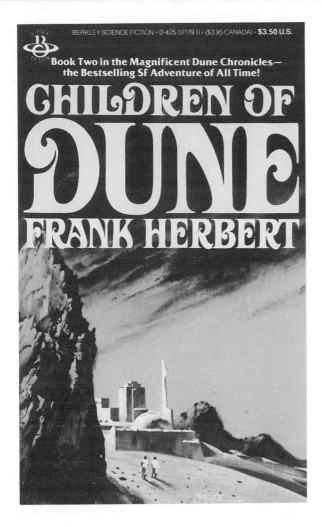

BERKLEY SCIENCE FICTION · 0·425·07179·0 · ($3.95 CANADA) · $3.50 U.S.

The story of the twins, Leto and Ghanima, continues in this 1976 sequel to *Dune Messiah*, with Leto trying to restore the planet by cultivating ancient Fremen traditions.

Herbert's Other Works

Throughout his career, Herbert published a number of short stories and novels which did not take place in the imagined world of *Dune*. According to Don D'Ammassa of *Science Fiction Chronicle*, "the most notable" of his short stories are "Try to Remember," "A-W-F Unlimited," "'The Mary Celeste Move," "The Tactful Saboteur," and "Committee of the Whole." Some critics assert that many of Herbert's other novels—which explore themes involving psychology, politics, religion, ecology, and man's relationship to machines—deserve as much attention, if not more, than most of the novels in the "Dune Chronicles."

The Green Brain (1966), set in Brazil, carries an ecological message. When humans intervene in the natural systems of the Earth to improve their food output, a giant brain attempts a warning by sending insects (grouped together in human form) to them. The humans, of course, cannot or will not heed the warning; they are too busy fighting amongst themselves to come up with a solution. *Destination Void* (1966), which Patricia S. Warrick in *The Cybernetic Imagination in Science Fiction* called "very underrated," tells the story of a scientific crew that has been sent on a starship mission with previously planned emergencies in order to force them to innovate. Unaware that their situation is an experimental one created by design, the scientists work as an interdisciplinary team to save the thousands of humans on their ship and bring their computer consciousness. Although the computer saves the ship's occupants by finding them a planet they can live on, the computer insists that they worship it as a god in exchange. *The Eyes of Heisenberg* (1966) is set in a future Earth; it takes up the subject of genetic manipulation.

In *The Heaven Makers* (1968), an alien movie producer finds Earth a rich source of material for the filming of terrible situations that his bored viewers can actually feel. The producer, however, greedily attempts to make his movies more entertaining by interfering in human affairs. *The Santaroga Barrier* (1968) is about a small community that, through mass drug consumption, develops a shared consciousness and begins to reject the interference of the larger society in which it is embedded. According to Leon E. Stover in *Extrapolation*, the "Santarogan utopia turns out to be a totalitarian utopia, in which men are domesticated for community life at the sacrifice of their souls"; the story is a critique of the "theory of mass society." *The God Makers* (1971) features a character who attempts to detect the signs of future wars on planets throughout the space system.

Whipping Star (1970) and *The Dosadi Experiment* (1977) are set in a world developed first in Herbert's 1968 short story, "The Tactful Saboteur," and follow the adventures of secret agent Jorj X. McKie. According to Robert A. Foster in the *Dictionary of Literary Biography*, the strongpoint of the series "lies in its numerous alien races, whose strange customs and abilities provide a satisfying richness of detail to fill out otherwise thin plots."

In *Whipping Star,* McKie must save his world's primary method of transportation—the jump-doors—and also the lives of those who have used a jumpdoor in the past. McKie finds himself fighting to survive on a mission on Dosadi in *The Dosadi Experiment.* Doing so is complicated, because the planet is populated by humans and aliens specially bred for fighting. Foster described the work as "pleasing adventure science fiction, with a tightly organized plot, characters who are distinguishable at least because of their racial differences, plenty of action and intrigue, and some fairly original ideas. . . ."

The Jesus Incident and *The Lazarus Effect,* which Herbert wrote with poet Bill Ransom, continue the story of *Destination Void.* In the first novel, which carries an ecological message as well as a philosophical one, the space-shipwrecked scientists and crew of *Destination Void* are forced to contend with life on a hostile water planet, Pandora. They must also deal with their own differences: some of these humans are clones grown in test tubes and some are naturally bred and born. The colonists set a precedent for their people by attempting to destroy the alien forms of life that present dangers to them, instead of living with and learning from them. *The Lazarus Effect* continues the story of the colonists, but much time has passed. Two groups have developed their own methods of inhabiting Pandora: the merman who live in the sea and cultivate sentient kelp, and the fisherfolk who float on enormous organic rafts. When the kelp generates a child with miraculous powers, the inhabitant's lives change forever. In *The Ascension Factor,* both mermen and fisherfolk must work together.

The protagonist in *The White Plague* (1982) is a biologist who has lost his wits after the violent deaths of his wife and children in an Irish Republican Army bombing. John O'Neill is determined to get revenge by spreading a virus he is developed. The virus, which kills women and girls only, threatens to destroy civilization. Governments from around the world must cooperate to save the remaining women.

Herbert's Legacy and Lessons

By the late 1970s and early 1980s, Herbert's success allowed him to write full-time, whether in Washington or at his home in Hawaii. Herbert

also wrote with his son, Brian. He was working on the seventh novel in the "Dune Chronicles" when he went to the University of Wisconsin Hospital for cancer surgery and died of complications. In the words of Willis E. McNelly, writing in *Extrapolation,* "It is something of the measure of his success as a writer that virtually every major paper in the country printed an extensive obituary" after Herbert's death.

Herbert's legacy to the future includes over twenty books, and critics continue to ponder their significance. Increasingly, *Dune* is not just seen as a science fiction novel. Some scholars, like Michael R. Collings in *Aspects of Fantasy,* have analyzed *Dune* in comparison with other epic stories and novels. Still others began to assess *Dune* and Herbert's other works as cultural products.

"*Dune* reflects the turmoil and political chaos which have characterized the twentieth century. Mans' weaponry has outstripped his moral development, and instruments of destruction are turned against his fellow beings," explained Collings. In *Extrapolation,* Juan A. Prieto-Pablos asserted that the thematical roots of *Dune* are specific to a decade in America: "*Dune* is imbued with references extrapolated from life in the sixties. . . . It is in fact easy to find parallels in the major conflicts at work in *Dune* and in the ones that were upsetting the America of that decade. . . . Paul and Leto show the inadequacy of the old romantic heroes to appeal to a reading public that had lost its belief in America as a world of dreams and innocence. The result is a kind of hero in whom the readers' fears are projected more intensely than their desires."

While "Jessica remains one of the very best science fiction portraits of a woman," as Willis E. McNelly asserted in *Extrapolation,* some critics call attention to the *role* of women in Herbert's work. Susan McLean treated this subject with a psychological approach in *Extrapolation:* "One of the most important of the buried themes of the *Dune* series is the theme of Oedipal conflict. . . . Fear of sexuality is accompanied by fear of women, yet the most frightening women are seen not in their roles as wives or lovers but as mothers." McLean further noted, "Most of the major enemies of Paul and Leto that are not female are feminized in some way. . . . A preference for the masculine over the feminine plays a key role in Herbert's depiction of the world of the *Dune* series." Ac-

If you enjoy the works of Frank Herbert, you may also want to check out the following books and films:

Lois McMaster Bujold, *Barrayar*, 1991.
Ursula Le Guin, *The Earthsea Trilogy*, 1968-1972.
Larry Niven, *Ringworld*, 1977.
The Star Wars Trilogy (*Star Wars, The Empire Strikes Back, Return of the Jedi*) directed by George Lucas, 1996.

cording to Jack Hand in the same journal, "all the important women of *Dune* act within the traditional areas of female activity. . . . If the Fremen women sometimes fight beside their men, they are also property which can be lost in a duel. . . ."

Young writers interested in emulating Herbert do not have to read all of his works to glean an understanding of Herbert's writers' craft. Herbert often explained that his novels were not just "written"—each required research, or the application of specific knowledge, scientific or otherwise. In addition, the meticulous author ensured the consistent portrayal of his characters through a method he developed. As he revealed in *Psychology Today*, after he "sketched" a plot, he began work on his characters. For each important character, he developed a case history that charted the character's "heredity, early development, traumatic experiences, successes, unusual abilities, vocational interests and skills." If he found a photo that resembled the character he had in mind, he would attach it to the file. Given this method, Herbert had "the basis for a consistent and psychologically congruent mode of speech and action."

When he was alive, Herbert refused to read stories people sent him, and explained in a *Contemporary Authors* interview, "I actually don't think you can teach writing. People learn to write by writing." Yet Herbert was generous in the provision of expert practical and technical advice. Herbert was quoted in *Something about the Author* that he would "like to see more young writers coming on," and he encouraged them to try to publish in "the magazine market" and "the regional press market. A lot of young writers don't know about that, and I think it would help if they

got the word." Herbert also offered a piece of advice: "I don't like to talk about work in progress, because you use the same energy to talk about it as you do to write it. I would give that advice to anybody who wants to write. Don't talk about it, write it. That's the best single piece of advice I had as a young writer."

■ Works Cited

Collings, Michael R., "The Epic of *Dune*: Epic Traditions in Modern Science Fiction," *Aspects of Fantasy: Selected Essays from the Second International Conference on the Fantastic in Literature and Film*, edited by William Coyle, Greenwood Press, 1986, pp. 131-39.

Collins, Bob, "Death of a Prophet," *Fantasy Review*, February, 1986, pp. 6, 14.

D'Ammassa, Don, "Frank Herbert," *Science Fiction Chronicle*, April, 1986, p. 24.

Review of *Dune* (motion picture), *Variety*, Wednesday, December 5, 1984, p. 16.

Folkart, Burt A., "Frank Herbert, Author of *Dune* Series, Dies," *Los Angeles Times*, February 13, 1986, pp. 3, 39.

Foster, Robert A., "Frank Herbert," *Dictionary of Literary Biography*, Volume 8: *Twentieth-Century American Science-Fiction Writers, Part 1: A-L*, Gale, 1981, pp. 232-39.

Fratz, D. Douglas, "It's a Man! It's an Emperor! It's a Giant Sandworm!," *Washington Post Book World*, May 24, 1981, p. 8.

Review of *God Emperor of Dune*, *Kirkus Reviews*, March 15, 1981, p. 363.

Hand, Jack, "The Traditionalism of Women's Roles in Frank Herbert's *Dune*," *Extrapolation*, Spring, 1985, pp. 24-28.

Herbert, Frank, "Plowboy Interviews: Frank Herbert: Science Fiction's 'Yellow Journalist' is a Homesteading 'Technopeasant'," *Mother Earth News*, May/June, 1981.

Herbert, Frank, interview with Jean W. Ross in *Contemporary Authors New Revision Series*, Volume 5, Gale, 1982, pp. 261-65.

Herbert, Frank, interview with Ross Stagner in *Psychology Today*, October, 1984, pp. 69-74.

Herbert, Frank, comments in *Something about the Author*, Volume 37, Gale, 1985, pp. 68-75.

Herbert, Frank, *Dune*, Ace, 1987.

Kozak, Ellen M., "The Writing Life," *Writer's Digest*, pp. 6-7.

Leonard, John, "Two Novels," *New York Times*, June 1, 1979, pp. 262-63.

Leonard, John, "Books of the Times," *New York Times*, April 27, 1981, p. 17.

McLean, Susan, "A Psychological Approach to Fantasy in the *Dune* Series," *Extrapolation*, Summer, 1982, pp. 150-58.

McNelly, Willis E., "In Memoriam: Frank Herbert, 1920-86," *Extrapolation*, Winter, 1986, pp. 352-55.

Miller, David M., *"Dune," Frank Herbert*, Starmont House, 1985, pp. 15-26.

Nathan, Paul, "A New 'Dune,'" *Publishers Weekly*, October 21, 1996, p. 31.

O'Reilly, Timothy, "From Concept to Fable: The Evolution of Frank Herbert's *Dune*," *Critical Encounters: Writers and Themes in Science Fiction*, edited by Dick Riley, Ungar, 1978, pp. 41-55.

O'Reilly, Timothy, *Frank Herbert*, Ungar, 1981.

Prieto-Pablos, Juan A., "The Ambivalent Hero of Contemporary Fantasy and Science Fiction," *Extrapolation*, Spring, 1991, pp. 64-80.

Stover, Leon E., "Is Jaspers Beer Good for You? Mass Society and Counter Culture in Herbert's *Santaroga Barrier*," *Extrapolation*, May, 1976, pp. 160-67.

Warrick, Patricia S., "The Open-System Model," in *The Cybernetic Imagination in Science Fiction*, MIT Press, 1980, pp. 161-202.

■ For More Information See

BOOKS

Platt, Charles, *Dream Makers: The Uncommon Men & Women Who Write Science Fiction*, Berkley, 1980.

Scholes, Robert, *Structural Fabulation: An Essay on Fiction of the Future*, University of Notre Dame Press, 1975.

Yoke, Carl B., and Donald M. Hassler, editors, *Death and the Serpent: Immortality in Science Fiction and Fantasy*, Greenwood Press, 1985.

PERIODICALS

America, June 10, 1972.

Analog, March, 1983, p. 160.

Book World, May 24, 1981, p. 8.

Fantasy Review, June, 1987, p. 45.

Kirkus Reviews, August 15, 1965, p. 847; December 1, 1987, p. 657.

Library Journal, January 15, 1970, p. 259.

Locus, November, 1990, p. 58.

Los Angeles Times Book Review, August 28, 1983, p. 4.

Newsweek, April 30, 1984.

New York Times Book Review, August 1, 1976, p. 18.

Publishers Weekly, March 20, 1972, p. 61; July 4, 1977, p. 69; December 26, 1980, p. 53.

School Library Journal, May, 1976, p. 82; October, 1977, p. 128; September, 1979, p. 167.

Science Fiction Studies, July, 1981, pp. 149-155.

Time, March 29, 1971.

Voice of Youth Advocates, October, 1984, p. 206; August, 1992, p. 189; December, 1993, p. 277.

■ Obituaries

Chicago Tribune, February 14, 1986.

Detroit Free Press, February 13, 1986.

Newsweek, February 24, 1986.

Time, February 24, 1986.*

—Sketch by R. Garcia-Johnson

Kristin Hunter

■ Personal

Born September 12, 1931, in Philadelphia, PA; daughter of George Lorenzo (a principal and U.S. Army colonel) and Mabel (a pharmacist and teacher; maiden name, Manigault) Eggleston; married Joseph Hunter (a journalist), 1952 (divorced, 1962); married John I. Lattany, June 22, 1968. *Education:* University of Pennsylvania, B.S. (education), 1951.

■ Addresses

Office—Department of English, University of Pennsylvania, Philadelphia, PA 19104. *Agent*—Don Congdon Associates, 156 Fifth Ave., Suite 625, New York, NY 10010.

■ Career

Writer. Columnist and feature writer for Philadelphia, PA, edition of *Pittsburgh Courier*, 1946-52; copywriter for Lavenson Bureau of Advertising, Philadelphia, 1952-59, and Werman & Schorr, Inc., Philadelphia, 1962-63; research assistant, University of Pennsylvania, 1961-62; City of Philadelphia, information officer, 1963-64, 1965-66; University of Pennsylvania, Philadelphia, lecturer in English, 1972-79, adjunct associate professor of English, 1981-83, senior lecturer in English, 1983—. Writer-in-residence, Emory University, 1979. *Member:* National Council of Teachers of English, University of Pennsylvania Alumnae Association (director, 1970-73).

■ Awards, Honors

Fund for the Republic Prize, 1955, for television documentary, *Minority of One;* John Hay Whitney fellowship, 1959-60; Philadelphia Athenaeum Award, 1964; National Council on Interracial Books for Children award, 1968, Mass Media Brotherhood Award form National Conference of Christians and Jews, 1969, and Lewis Carroll Shelf Award, 1971, all for *The Soul Brothers and Sister Lou;* Sigma Delta Chi reporting award, 1968; Spring Book Festival Award, 1973, Christopher Award, and National Book Award finalist, both 1974, all for *Guests in the Promised Land;* Drexel Children's Literature Citation, 1981; New Jersey State Council on the Arts prose fellowship, 1981-82, 1985-86; Pennsylvania State Council on the Arts literature fellowship, 1983-84.

■ **Writings**

YOUNG ADULT FICTION

The Soul Brothers and Sister Lou, Scribner, 1968.
Boss Cat, Scribner, 1971.
The Pool Table War, Houghton, 1972.
Uncle Daniel and the Raccoon, Houghton, 1972.
Guests in the Promised Land (story collection), Scribner, 1973.
Lou in the Limelight, Scribner, 1981.

OTHER

Minority of One (documentary), Columbia Broadcasting System, 1956.
God Bless the Child, Scribner, 1964.
The Double Edge (play), first produced in Philadelphia, 1965.
The Landlord, Scribner, 1966.
(Contributor) Langston Hughes, editor, *The Best Short Stories by Negro Writers*, Little, Brown, 1967.
The Survivors, Scribner, 1975.
The Lakestown Rebellion, Scribner, 1978.

■ **Sidelights**

There was never any question that Kristin Hunter would be a writer. "I believe in Ralph (Waldo) Ellison's theory of names influencing destiny; with a name like that, he had to be an intellectual and a philosopher. I was named for the heroine of Sigrid Undset's trilogy *Kristin Lavransdatter*, so I, too, had to be a writer—either that, or a tragic heroine, which was never an attractive option," she related in an autobiographical essay for *Something about the Author Autobiography Series (SAAS)*.

A pioneer in the field of young adult fiction, Hunter has won critical accolades for her realistic and optimistic depictions of the African American experience. The author of a series of novels and a collection of short stories, she was awarded both the 1968 Council on Interracial Books for Children Award and the 1971 Lewis Carroll Shelf Award. Her stories, which often portray black ghetto life, owe much to the acquaintances she made as a youngster as well as to the vibrant culture she encountered as a teenager working in Philadelphia's South Street area.

Hunter was born in Philadelphia, Pennsylvania, in 1931. Although she grew up in a comfortable, middle-class neighborhood near Camden, New Jersey, her early years were not untroubled. Her father, George L. Eggleston, a military man and school principal, showed little affection for his child. "My father was an aloof, unapproachable man who advised, and lived by, the British slogan, 'Keep a stiff upper lip,' and everyone except my mother was terrified of him," Hunter recalled in *SAAS*. A graduate from Howard University with an ROTC commission, Eggleston was rapidly promoted to lieutenant colonel, commanding a battalion and, at one point, an entire base—a rare honor for an African-American officer at the time. Although her father's military career ended in a medical discharge before the end of World War II, Hunter remembers her father as a man in uniform: "Military images dominate my memories of my father from first to last," she explained in *SAAS*.

An only child, Hunter was keenly aware that her mother had made "sacrifices" on her behalf—although she never fully explained those sacrifices to her daughter. She later discovered that Mabel Eggleston had been appointed to a public school teaching position in New Jersey just two months before her daughter was born. At that place and time, however, the law prohibited women with children from teaching; Hunter's birth had effectively terminated her mother's career. She described her reaction upon reading the letter appointing her mother to a teaching post in *SAAS*: "Studying it, I finally understood why my birth had been a disaster for her." Hunter found no playmates among her parents' friends: since many of the Egglestons' female friends were teachers, most were childless. In fact, children were so rare among her parents' friends that Hunter believed that childless couples were the norm until she reached her late twenties.

A Voracious Reader

Hunter learned to read before she entered kindergarten. "My mother . . . had me reading at the age of four, and once I was started, there was no stopping me. I read the books in my parents' bedroom (Havelock Ellis and Boccaccio's *Decameron*) as soon as I knew that I was forbidden to read them, which makes me think that prohibiting books might be an excellent way of getting youngsters to read," she explained in *SAAS*. As a child, she devoured everything from Charles

KRISTIN HUNTER

THE SOUL BROTHERS AND SISTER LOU

After joining a local band made up of members from the Hawks street gang, Louretta Hawkins learns to express her feelings through music.

Kingsley's *The Water Babies* to Richard Henry Dana, Jr.'s *Two Years Before the Mast*. Richard Halliburton's travel books were also among her childhood favorites, as was any story that took place on or near water.

Hunter never remembers a time when she did not want to become a writer. "I really cannot say when I *didn't* want to be a writer," she told Jean W. Ross in an interview in *Contemporary Authors*. "It probably started shortly after I became a reader, which was when I was four. I found books very exciting, and it was my biggest ambition to produce something myself that would be in books." As the only child among adults, she found that writing provided her with an imaginative

outlet—and a medium through which she could voice her thoughts. "I believe these circumstances—onliness, loneliness and resultant fantasizing and omnivorous reading—are the most favorable for producing writers (when they do not produce hopeless schizophrenics)," she reflected in *SATA*. What's more, the women on Hunter's mother's side of the family (her Grandma Manigault; her aunts Edna and Bertha; and her mother, Mabel) were blunt and straightforward—and sometimes made it difficult for the young writer to express herself. "One reason I turned to writing was that I never got to finish a sentence around these loud, vocal women," she remembered in *SAAS*.

With the help of her Aunt Myrtle, who encouraged her niece in a variety of cultural activities, Hunter landed her first writing job as a teenager. For six years, as a high school and college student, she wrote a teen column for the Philadelphia edition of the *Pittsburgh Courier*. Even more importantly, however, she spent hours taking in the sights and getting to know the people of Philadelphia's South Street, a center of African American culture and publishing—and the wellspring of much of her fiction.

Having graduated from high school when she was only fifteen, Hunter was younger than most of her classmates at the University of Pennsylvania. What's more, she was one of only a handful of African American students. She graduated in 1951 with a bachelor's degree in elementary education, and set out to pursue a career as a teacher. But pedagogy was not her niche. "I endured only four ghastly months of teaching in a third grade where I was literally terrorized by thirty-eight undisciplined children. Arriving early, I would fill the blackboards with busywork, then listen, trembling, to the roar of the youngsters in the schoolyard. They sounded like hungry lions, and I felt like an early Christian martyr," she recounted in *SAAS*.

Hunter broke her contract with the Camden school board and resigned from her post. Although she resented her parents for forcing her into teaching—one of few career options available to African American women of their generation—she eventually came to terms with their intentions. "A principalship in Camden was a hard-won triumph for my father who, like most black men of his time, had been forced to begin his teaching in the poorly paid, segregated schools of the rural South.

And I can hardly blame my mother for wanting me to have the career she had been denied," she explained in *SAAS*.

A Writer for Better or Worse

Without a look backward, Hunter left teaching and set out to earn her living as a writer, quickly discovering that the racial barriers her parents had encountered were not entirely a matter of history. "I tried several interviews with publishing and advertising companies on my own, only to be flattened each time by what I called the 'double whammy'—initial enthusiasm over me and my portfolio of newspaper writing, followed by sud-

When plans to build a massive highway threatens a small black town, the older and younger members of the community invent ways to sabotage the project.

den embarrassment and total rejection when the interviewer got a better look at me in a brighter light," she continued in *SAAS*. Eventually, however, with the aid of the Armstrong Association, a group which helped African Americans find "non-traditional" employment, she was hired by the Lavenson Bureau of Advertising. After six months' probation in a clerical position, she was promoted to copywriter. That same year, Hunter married her first husband, Joseph Hunter, a journalist; they divorced ten years later, in 1962.

During her seven years at the agency, Hunter wrote advertisements and promotional materials for clients ranging from toy manufacturers to pickle-makers. Although overworked, she enjoyed the job, with the exception of one assignment that required her to write a food column that focused *exclusively* on recipes that included mayonnaise. "I began with my own meager stock of recipes, for barbecued pork chops and chocolate cake, then went on to plagiarize recipes from popular cookbooks, adding only a dollop of mayonnaise to each one. There was no kitchen on our premises for testing these formulas, nor did I have time for such testing. I dreaded hearing from people who had been made ill by my recipes, but over the years the ads appeared, there was never any such reaction," she recounted in *SAAS*.

When the Lavenson Bureau changed management, Hunter and several other employees resigned. Shortly thereafter, she was awarded a year's stipend from the John Hay Whitney Foundation, which provided support to minority artists and scholars. Although she took various jobs in subsequent years, including speech writer and research assistant, Hunter began to view writing as her true vocation. "My real work from then on was writing, to which earning a living, as my frequent resignations show, would now take second place," she explained in *SAAS*.

Selling Soul

Although written for adults, Hunter's first book, *God Bless the Child*, published in 1964, introduced themes the author explores in later works. Set in a community similar to the one Hunter encountered on Philadelphia's South Street, it tells the story of a young African American girl who fights desperately to overcome poverty, only to find herself embroiled in the gambling underworld.

"Hunter does not miss a sight or a sound of humor, pain, or vulgarity. Her eye is sharp, her ear true," Henrietta Buckmaster, writing in the *Christian Science Monitor,* declared. Hunter's next novel, *The Landlord,* returns to the theme of poverty in the African American community, this time with a satirical twist, as a wealthy young man tries to earn his father's respect by purchasing a ghetto apartment building. Gwendolyn Brooks, writing in *Book Week,* proclaimed, "The characters [in *The Landlord*] are not lovable or loathable. . . . They are lookable—due to the inventiveness and earnestly exercised power of Miss Hunter's talent."

With the publication of *The Soul Brothers and Sister Lou* in 1968, Hunter made her first foray into juvenile fiction. "Oddly enough, I never intended to write for children," she recalled in *Something about the Author.* "*Soul Brothers and Sister Lou* came about only because my publisher's juvenile editor asked me to consider writing a children's book. I considered this an outlandish suggestion at first, but something in the back of my mind filed it away, then went to work on it without my conscious knowledge," she continued.

South Street resurfaced as the author's muse. Having returned to the area to live with her second husband, John Lattany, Hunter transformed the South Street of Philadelphia to the Avenue in her fictional tale. "From the rooftop sundeck of that apartment I heard, on long summer nights, the magnificent *a cappella* group singing by young people that inspired *The Soul Brothers and Sister Lou,*" she wrote in *SAAS.* The story revolves around Louretta Hawkins, a light-skinned African American girl who joins some friends who have formed a singing group. As the group's pianist, Louretta learns how to compose music from Blind Eddie Bell, a blues musician. After one of her friends is killed by a white policeman who mistakes an epileptic seizure for an act of aggression, Lou finds herself seething with racial hatred. Ultimately, however, she discourages her peers from retaliating. At the story's end, "The Soul Brothers and Sister Lou" have been offered a recording contract on the basis of their song "Lament for Jethro"—the eulogy they dedicated to their slain friend at his funeral.

The Soul Brothers and Sister Lou garnered the Lewis Carroll Shelf Award, among others, and won praise from a contributor to the *Kirkus Reviews* for its depiction of the "misery and sweetness of

In this 1981 sequel to *The Soul Brothers and Sister Lou,* Hunter depicts the pitfalls that can accompany sudden success in the entertainment industry.

growing up black." "And if it sells *soul,*" the reviewer concludes, "it also talks sense." Soul, the author explained in *Publishers Weekly,* is exactly what her story is about: "I have tried to show some of the positive values existing in the so-called ghetto—the closeness and warmth of family life, the willingness to extend help to strangers in trouble . . . the natural acceptance of life's problems and joys—and there is a great deal of joy in the ghetto—and the strong tradition of religious faith. All of these attitudes have combined to create the quality called 'soul,' which is central to the theme of the book." *New York Times Book Review* contributor John Neufeld found the book's ending to be overly simplistic: "Hunter writes too well—of revivalism, of revolt, of de-

If you enjoy the works of Kristin Hunter, you may also want to check out the following books and films:

Mildred D. Taylor, *The Road to Memphis*, 1990.
Alice Walker, *Meridian*, 1976.
Virginia Euwer Wolff, *The Mozart Season*, 1991.
The Color Purple, Warner Brothers, 1985.

spairing blacks hanging onto church, or a crowbar, with equal determination—to have settled for a false solution, when honest ones exist."

Promised Lands and Forbidden Things

Hunter's next work, *Boss Cat*, published in 1971, was aimed at a younger audience. Lauded by a *Booklist* reviewer as "a winning story of a proud-to-be-black family," it describes a family's gradual acceptance—in spite of superstition and other obstacles—of a black cat named Pharaoh. Pamela Bragg, writing in *Publishers Weekly*, called the story "A welcome addition to the growing list of books for black children," while a reviewer for *Bulletin of the Center for Children's Books* faulted Hunter's story for "a tendency to stereotype," citing the mother's fear of mice and superstition of black cats.

Paramount to Hunter's storytelling is the ability to portray African American characters, especially African American children. She once commented in *Top of the News* that black children were noticeably absent from the books she read as a child, though she did recall a racist situation in one book that angered her. "I haven't seen any of today's books about black children except my own, but I hope they're peopled with three-dimensional characters, not just black-faced Dicks and Janes."

Next among Hunter's publications was *Guests in the Promised Land*, a collection of short stories. Comprised of realistic portrayals of the problems African American adolescents encounter as they try to make their way in a white-dominated world, Hunter's collection garnered a Christopher

Award and was a finalist for the National Book Award. Writing in *Horn Book,* Paul Heins called the stories "superb" for their depiction of the African American experience "as well as for their art." He added that the pieces "present various facets of lives that have been warped by a frustrating racial milieu and—at the same time—have gone beyond it into universal humanity." A contributor to *Kirkus Reviews,* however, argued that "Hunter seems to be sniping at everyone: the whites who try so complacently to "help," the brothers and sisters who enforce conformity to a soul lifestyle, the striving oreos who lock their children out of both worlds."

The title story in Hunter's collection relates what happens when a young African American boy is treated to a day at an all-white country club—an outing that quickly sours when the boy oversteps invisible boundaries and is ousted. Praising Hunter's deft characterization, Huel Perkins wrote in *Black World*, "One may even be led to sympathize with the small Black lad who plunges his pocket-knife into a beautiful piano at an all-white country club. Especially when the explanation lies in the fact that 'it ain't no Promised Land at all if some people are always guests and others are always members.'"

As a child, Hunter was keenly aware of racial boundaries that relegated African Americans to "guest" status in a segregated nation. Writing in *SAAS,* she described "a solitary crusade" to integrate Washington, D.C., in the mid-1940s, at a time when racial segregation was the norm. "I knew this in an abstract way, but was nevertheless appalled to hear a pair of teen girls my age describe the limitations under which they lived," she explained. The girls, because of their race, were not allowed to eat at some restaurants, drink at soda fountains, or try on hats at department stores. Hunter went on: "I queried them closely—'What else can't you do?'—and made a written list of all the prohibitions. I then dressed with quiet determination, went downtown and, trembling inwardly, proceeded to do all of the forbidden things."

With *The Survivors*, published in 1975, Hunter returned to adult fiction. The story of a lonely middle-aged woman who eventually forms a bond with a street-wise boy, *The Survivors* attracted critical accolades for its urban insight. "Portraits, often remarkable, of major and minor characters, avoid much of tragic realism as the roughest edges of urban violence are smoothed off just enough to let a cheerful atmosphere shine through all the trouble," a *Booklist* reviewer asserted. Other critics' praise was qualified: a contributor to *Kirkus Reviews,* for instance, proclaimed that "In spite of the heavy hand of coincidence, and the Valentine ending (admittedly with a wry twist), the author saves a damp tale from mawkishness with some grainy inner-city insights." Not all of the novel's critics were so forgiving of Hunter's reliance on coincidence. One such reviewer Aurora Simms, complained in *Library Journal* of "a plot leaning so heavily on the long arm of coincidence that it almost pulls it out of its socket."

Self-Doubt and Self-Acceptance

Hunter, who has no children of her own, believes that her stories have brought her an extended surrogate family. She wrote in *SATA*: "It has often seemed to me that I have hundreds of children—thousands, if I count the young readers of my books, especially *The Soul Brothers and Sister Lou,* who have formed intense personal bonds with my characters, and then with me through their letters. This responsive audience, the fans and the critics alike, is one of the greatest rewards I have gained from writing for children." This audience is also responsible for urging Hunter to continue the saga of Louretta Hawkins. In *Lou in the Limelight,* a sequel to the author's earlier work, Hunter vividly depicts the pitfalls that can accompany sudden success in the entertainment industry.

Exploited by a dishonest manager, Lou and her band members succumb to the temptations of celebrity. Drugs and gambling dominate their lives until the aunt of their slain friend helps them find their way back to a better life. Writing in the *New York Times Book Review,* Marilyn Kaye calls *Lou in the Limelight* an "ambitious indictment of the entertainment industry." Becky Johnson of the *Voice of Youth Advocates* referred to the tale as "a highly readable depiction of talented young performers and the difficulty of their rise from ghetto poverty," although she points out that Hunter's characters are sometimes "two-dimensional."

Although the story takes place in the entertainment milieu, *Lou in the Limelight* is, above all, the story of an African American girl's struggle to come to terms with race and identity as a young adult. Writing in the *Saturday Book Review,* Zena Sutherland suggested that the success of the Sister Lou stories lies in Hunter's thoughtful, sensitive depiction of a young girl "who learns to appreciate her racial heritage during those years when self-acceptance and self-identity are problems for all adolescents."

Self-acceptance and self-identity are at the core of much of Hunter's fiction. Referring to *The Soul Brothers and Sister Lou,* the author commented in *Publishers Weekly:* "by writing about a lonely little light-skinned girl named Louretta Hawkins and the growth of her self-confidence and pride in her black identity, I feel I've been able to exorcise some of my own adolescent demons, some of which have persisted unconsciously into adulthood."

Hunter admits to a certain degree of self-doubt as a writer. In *SAAS,* she confessed: "I have been, and still am, hard on myself about many things. One of my harshest self-indictments has been the judgment that I lacked the courage to go anywhere; that I was unwilling to relocate far from this Delaware Valley area in which I was born. After my books began to appear, people frequently made remarks like 'When are you moving to New York?' or 'Why aren't you in Paris?' which I could only answer with vague, shamed mumblings." By not straying far from her roots, however, Hunter has managed to maintain ties with the "nourishing sources" of a writer's inspiration—friends and family. Ultimately, she concluded in *SAAS,* the "dreadful rut" of living in the house she grew up in and teaching at the university she attended may, in fact, be the wellspring of her inspiration. She continued: "And so I am still here, still experiencing life and still writing about it, which may mean that the faithful guardian angel who sits on my shoulder has deliberately kept me close to home. And I see that the rut may be a reason for gratitude and even celebration, not complaining and self-criticism, and that it may not even be a rut at all."

■ Works Cited

Review of *Boss Cat, Booklist,* February 15, 1972, p. 506.
Review of *Boss Cat, Bulletin of the Center for Children's Books,* May, 1972, p. 140.

Bragg, Pamela, review of *Boss Cat, Publishers Weekly,* December 15, 1971, p. 43.

Brooks, Gwendolyn, review of *God Bless the Child, Book Week,* May 8, 1966.

Buckmaster, Henrietta, review of *God Bless the Child, Christian Science Monitor,* September 10, 1964.

Review of *Guests in the Promised Land, Kirkus Reviews,* May 15, 1973.

Heins, Paul, review of *Guests in the Promised Land, Horn Book,* August, 1973, p. 386.

Hunter, Kristin, "'The Soul Brothers': Background of a Juvenile," *Publishers Weekly,* May 27, 1968, pp. 30-31.

Hunter, Kristin, comments in *Something about the Author,* Volume 12, Gale, 1977.

Hunter, Kristin, in an interview with Jean W. Ross, *Contemporary Authors New Revision Series,* Volume 13, Gale, 1984.

Hunter, Kristin, essay in *Something about the Author Autobiography Series,* Volume 10, Gale, 1990, pp. 119-33.

Johnson, Becky, review of *Lou in the Limelight, Voice of Youth Advocates,* February 1982, p. 33.

Kaye, Marilyn, review of *Lou in the Limelight, New York Times Book Review,* February 21, 1982, p. 35.

"Kristin Hunter—Profile of an Author," *Top of the News,* January, 1970.

Neufeld, John, review of *The Soul Brothers and Sister Lou, New York Times Book Review,* January 26, 1969, p. 26.

Perkins, Huel, review of *Guests in the Promised Land, Black World,* September, 1974, p. 91.

Simms, Aurora, review of *The Survivors, Library Journal,* June 15, 1975, p. 1240.

Review of *The Soul Brothers and Sister Lou, Kirkus Reviews,* July 15, 1968, p. 765.

Review of *The Survivors, Booklist,* May 15, 1975, p. 941.

Review of *The Survivors, Kirkus Reviews,* March 15, 1975, p. 322.

Sutherland, Zena, *Saturday Review,* October 19, 1968, p. 37.

■ For More Information See

BOOKS

Carpenter, Humphrey, and Mari Prichard, *Oxford Companion to Children's Literature,* Oxford University Press, 1984.

Children's Literature Review, Volume 3, Gale, 1978, pp. 97-101.

Foremost Women in Communications, Foremost Americans Publishing Corp., 1970.

Green, Carol Hurd, and Mary Grimley Mason, editors, *American Women Writers,* Continuum Publishing Co., 1994.

O'Neale, Sondra, "Kristin Hunter," *Dictionary of Literary Biography,* Volume 33: *Afro-American Fiction Writers After 1955,* Gale, 1984, pp. 119-24.

Page, James A., and Jae Min Roh, editors, *Selected Black American, African and Caribbean Authors,* Libraries Unlimited, 1985.

Rush, Theressa Gunnels, Carol Fairbanks Myers, and Esther Spring Arata, *Black American Writers Past and Present,* Scarecrow Press, 1975.

Ward, Martha, et al, *Authors of Books for Young People,* Scarecrow Press, 1990.

PERIODICALS

Bulletin of the Center for Children's Books, June, 1973; February, 1982.

Childhood Education, October, 1972, p. 28.

Horn Book, April, 1969.

Kirkus Reviews, November 15, 1971; May 15, 1973; February 1, 1982.*

—*Sketch by Marie J. MacNee*

Robin Klein

■ Personal

Born February 28, 1936, in Kempsey, New South Wales, Australia; daughter of Leslie Macquarie (a farmer) and Mary (a homemaker; maiden name, Cleaver) McMaugh; married Karl Klein, August 18, 1956 (divorced April, 1978); children: Michael, Peter, Ingrid, Rosalind. *Education:* Attended schools in New South Wales, Australia.

■ Addresses

Home—Belgrave, Victoria 3160, Australia. *Agent*—Curtis Brown, P.O. Box 19, Paddington, Sydney NSW 2021, Australia.

■ Career

Writer, 1981—. Worked as a "tea lady" at a warehouse, and as a bookshop assistant, nurse, copper enamelist, and program aide at a school for disadvantaged children.

■ Awards, Honors

Special Mention, Critici in Erba Awards, Bologna Children's Book Fair, 1979, for *The Giraffe in Pepperell Street*; Australian Junior Book of the Year Award, Children's Book Council of Australia, 1983, for *Thing*; Book of the Year Award Highly Commended Citation, Children's Book Council of Australia, 1984, for *Penny Pollard's Diary*; senior fellowship grant, Arts Council of Australia Literature Board, 1985; West Australian Young Readers' Book Award and KOALA (Kids Own Australian Literature Award) Award, both 1987, both for *Hating Allison Ashley*; Australian Human Rights Award for Literature, 1989, and Australian Book of the Year Award for older readers, Children's Book Council of Australia, 1990, for *Came Back to Show You I Could Fly*; Honour Book, Children's Book Council of Australia, 1991, for *Boris and Borsch*; Dromkeen Medal, 1992, for significant contribution to the appreciation and development of children's literature in Australia; New South Wales's Premier's Award for Literature (Children's Books), 1992, for *All in the Blue Unclouded Weather.*

■ Writings

FICTION

Honoured Guest, illustrated by Margaret Power, Macmillan, 1979.
Sprung!, illustrated by Margaret Power, Rigby, 1982.

Thing (also see below), illustrated by Alison Lester, Oxford University Press, 1982.

Oodoolay, illustrated by Vivienne Goodman, Era Publications, 1983.

Junk Castle, illustrated by Rolf Heimann, Oxford University Press, 1983.

Penny Pollard's Diary, illustrated by Ann James, Oxford University Press, 1983.

People Might Hear You, Penguin, 1983, Viking Kestrel, 1987.

The Tomb Comb, illustrated by Heather Potter, Oxford University Press, 1984.

Brock and the Dragon, illustrated by Rodney McRae, Hodder & Stoughton, 1984.

Hating Allison Ashley, Penguin (Melbourne and London), 1984, Penguin (New York), 1985.

Ratbags and Rascals, illustrated by Alison Lester, Dent (Melbourne), 1984.

Thalia the Failure, illustrated by Rhyll Plant, Ashton Scholastic, 1984.

Thingnapped! (sequel to *Thing*), illustrated by Alison Lester, Oxford University Press, 1984.

The Enemies, illustrated by Noela Young, Angus & Robertson, 1985, published as *Enemies,* Dutton, 1989.

Halfway across the Galaxy and Turn Left, Viking Kestrel, 1985, Viking, 1986.

Separate Places, illustrated by Anna Lacis, Kangaroo Press (Kenthurst, New South Wales), 1985.

Annabel's Ghost (stories), Oxford University Press, 1985.

Boss of the Pool, illustrated by H. Panagopoulos, Omnibus Books (Adelaide), 1986, illustrated by Paul Geraghty, Viking Kestrel, 1987.

Games . . . , illustrated by Melissa Webb, Viking Kestrel, 1986.

Penny Pollard in Print, illustrated by Ann James, Oxford University Press, 1986.

The Princess Who Hated It, illustrated by Marie Smith, Omnibus books, 1986.

Birk the Berserker, illustrated by Alison Lester, Omnibus Books, 1987.

I Shot an Arrow, illustrated by Geoff Hocking, Viking Kestrel, 1987.

Get Lost, illustrated by June Joubert, Macmillan (Melbourne), 1987.

The Last Pirate, illustrated by Rick Armor, Rigby (Melbourne), 1987.

(With Max Dunn) *The Lonely Hearts Club,* Oxford University Press (Melbourne), 1987, Oxford University Press (New York), 1988.

Parker-Hamilton, illustrated by Gaston Vanzet, Rigby, 1987.

Laurie Loved Me Best, Viking Kestrel, 1988.

Penny Pollard's Passport, illustrated by Ann James, Oxford University Press, 1988.

Against the Odds, illustrated by Bill Wood, Viking Kestrel, 1989.

Boris and Borsch, Allen & Unwin, 1990.

Came Back to Show You I Could Fly, Viking, 1990.

Tearaways: Stories to Make You Think Twice (stories), Viking, 1991.

All in the Blue Unclouded Weather, Viking, 1992.

Dresses of Red and Gold, Viking Kestrel, 1993.

Seeing Things, Viking, 1993.

The Sky in Silver Lace, Penguin Books Australia, 1995, Viking, 1996.

Also author of *The Ghost in Abigail Terrace,* 1989, *Penny Pollard's Guide to Modern Manners,* 1989, *Amy's Bed,* 1992, and *Turn Right for Zyrgon,* 1994.

OTHER

The Giraffe in Pepperell Street (poetry), illustrated by Gill Tomblin, Hodder & Stoughton, 1978.

Snakes and Ladders: Poems about the Ups and Downs of Life (poetry), illustrated by Ann James, Dent, 1985.

Christmas, illustrated by Kristen Hilliard, Methuen (Sydney), 1987.

Don't Tell Lucy (miscellany), illustrated by Kristen Hilliard, Methuen, 1987.

Robin Klein's Crookbook, illustrated by Kristen Hilliard, Methuen, 1987.

Dear Robin . . . : Letters to Robin Klein, Allen & Unwin, 1988.

■ Adaptations

Thing was adapted into a cartoon by Australian Children's Television Foundation, Kaboodle Series, 1987; *Penny Pollard's Diary* was adapted for television by Australian Children's Television Foundation, Kaboodle Series, 1987; *Hating Alison Ashley* was adapted for stage by Richard Tulloch and published by Puffin Books, 1988; *Boss of the Pool* was adapted for stage by Mary Morris, 1990; *Halfway across the Galaxy and Turn Left* was adapted for television by Crawford Productions, 1992.

■ Sidelights

"Miranda wasn't paying much attention to Mr Nancarrow reading aloud to the class. Her own thoughts, tinged with habitual anxieties of one kind or another, were still more interesting than hearing about Captain Cook sailing up the coast of Australia and complaining because he didn't fancy the look of the place. Probably he'd been a gentlemanly wimp, too scared to land in case natives jumped out at him from behind a rock, she thought. Usually she liked history, but Mr Nancarrow, reading aloud, could make anyone in a book sound wimpy. His vowels were as plump as chocolates in a box and he had a habit of looking up and catching someone's eye, then smiling cosily to draw them into the story."

Miranda Palgrave, the eleven-year-old girl introduced in this excerpt from Robin Klein's novel *Seeing Things* has a lot in common with many of the characters in the Australian author's popular books for young adults. She is one of those "awkward misfits that still manage to achieve goals" that Klein once discussed in her comments to *Contemporary Authors*. In *Seeing Things*, Miranda's grades have been dropping and she has become somewhat of an outcast at school, when she suddenly appears to have developed psychic abilities and becomes the center of attention. Like many of the characters in Klein's novels, Miranda comes from a troubled family, as does Frances in *People Might Hear You* and the Melling sisters who appear in Klein's series of books about growing up in Australia in the 1940s. Lastly, Miranda's story is told with Klein's characteristic ironic humor found throughout her work. Miranda, and the other out-of-the-ordinary characters found in Klein's novels, have made the Australian author popular with young readers in her own country—where she has received numerous honors, including several children's choice awards—and in the United States.

First Success

Nearly as soon as she learned to write, Klein began putting words together to form poems and stories. Playing with words was an inexpensive form of amusement for Klein and her eight brothers and sisters growing up on a rural Australia farm in the thirties and forties. Their poverty did not keep the children from enjoying assembling a family newspaper and putting on backyard play productions to pass the time. Following in the footsteps of her mother, who contributed short stories to the Australian magazine *Women's Jour-*

nal, Klein published her first short story at the age of sixteen. Klein explored a variety of professions as she grew older and, after her marriage in 1956, was the full-time mom to her four children as they grew up. Later, she began contributing short stories, poems, and plays to *New South Wales School Magazine*, published in the Australian states of New South Wales and Victoria. Klein didn't publish her first book, however, until 1978 when *The Giraffe in Pepperell Street* appeared. This humorous children's book in verse was her first big success. In 1981, Klein became a full-time author.

Among her most popular characters is Penny Pollard, who has starred in several Klein books, including *Penny Pollard's Diary*, *Penny Pollard's Letters*, and *Penny Pollard in Print*. Klein introduced the independent ten-year-old Penny to her readers in the 1983 book, *Penny Pollard's Diary*. The book was written as if it actually contained Penny's diary entries describing her love of horses and her unlikely friendship with eighty-year-old Edith Bettany. The tomboy became a quick favorite with Klein's readers. "All the little boys in Australia are in love with her," Klein told Stephanie Nettell in a 1985 *Books for Keeps* interview, "and write to her as if she exists." In the next installment of Penny's escapades, *Penny Pollard's Letters*, readers were treated to a collection of Penny's letters to her friends and enemies. The letters were dubbed "hilarious" by a *Learning* reviewer, and were soon followed by the third installment in the Penny Pollard series, *Penny Pollard in Print*, Penny offers her peculiar take on life in a collection of articles about cannibal plants and methods of chicken hypnosis, written for the Kurringa *Gazette*. Reviewing the book in *Reading Time*, Margot Nelmes detected a subtle change in the lead character. "But something tells me that Penny," she wrote, "while still as stubborn and rebellious as ever, might be softening just a little around the edges."

"Stubborn and rebellious" are two adjectives that might be used to describe quite a few of the author's protagonists. Klein herself noted in *Contemporary Authors* that "most of my books seem to have a strong female character, capable or dealing with any problem that arises." In *Hating Alison Ashley* and *People Might Hear You*, both published in the mid-1980s, Klein presented two such strong characters. Reviewing the two books in the *Times Literary Supplement*, Deborah Singmaster wrote:

"The plots move rapidly; the spare style is peppered with snappy dialogue; and the main characters are misunderstood rebels guaranteed to evoke teenage sympathies." *Hating Alison Ashley* features Erika Yurken, known as "Yuk," who impulsively hates the pretty and rich new girl at school, Alison Ashley. Yuk learns that appearances can be deceiving. As Leonie Margaret Rutherford noted in *Twentieth-Century Young Adult Writers,* "Alison Ashley is a beautifully dressed, beautifully behaved interloper in the deprived world of Barringa East Primary School: she is also a lonely latchkey child whose high-powered executive mother has no time to give her the love she craves." Eventually, Yuk and Alison solve their differences and become best friends.

While Yuk must break through her feelings of hatred in order to experience friendship, orphaned Frances in *People Might Hear You* must break through more literal barriers that surround the home where she is forced to live. The teenager does not mind having her Aunt Loris as her guardian, but her life becomes unbearable when her aunt marries Finely Tyrell, a follower of a religion that frowns on contact with the outside world. Frances and her aunt move into Tyrell's house along with his three daughters. There Frances's personal belongings—even her clothes— are taken away, and she must remain hidden from school officials as Tyrell and his followers wait for the start of what they feel is an inevitable nuclear war. When any hint of rebellion is threatened with strict punishment, Frances searches desperately for a way to escape from behind the locked doors and barbed-wire covered fences of the house. Her discovery that Helen, not yet fully convinced of the cult's mission, also wants to escape, makes hatching her plan a little easier. "The evil of religious fanaticism, as great as that of any enslaving political doctrine," wrote Margery Fisher in *Growing Point,* "has seldom been more clearly demonstrated than in this bitter look behind one colourless dwelling in an Australian city." Stephanie Netell in *Books for Keeps* found the novel possessed "a controlled simplicity that heightens both the emotion and the suspense."

Klein likes to vary her method of writing just as much as her plots; this can be seen in *The Lonely Hearts Club,* written with Max Dunn, and *Laurie Loved Me Best.* The former is about two boys eager to attract girls; the latter, about two girls in love with the same boy. *The Lonely Hearts Club*

follows the story of Donovan and Scuff, two boarders at a school run by a group of religious brothers. Each chapter begins with an epigraph reportedly drawn from the school's etiquette manual. The short excerpts prove to be ironic commentary on the activities of Donovan and Scuff. Told with great humor, the book also includes letters written by fictional counterparts of Klein and her co-author, commenting on their progress in the writing of the novel. A *Magpies* reviewer noted that because of the letters the authors are actually "dramatic participants in their own work." Commenting further, the reviewer

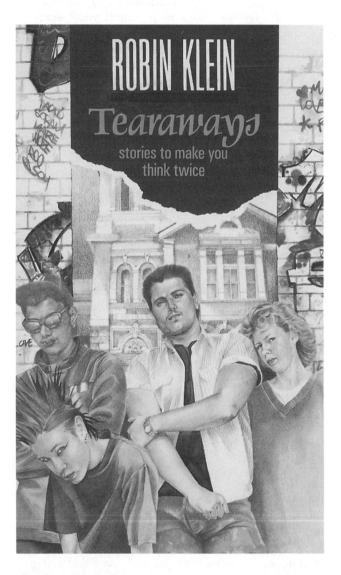

The Australian author's 1990 collection of short stories features conniving characters who wreak havoc on their unsuspecting victims.

added: "The story has, given the writing team, the expected vivacity in plot, language, broad characterization and insight into the sense of humour of the young adolescent." Equally experimental is *Laurie Loved Me Best*, which is narrated by Julia and Andre, two fourteen-year-olds who are best friends. In alternating chapters, the pair discuss their relationship with Laurie, an eighteen-year-old stranger who suddenly appears at their cottage. A *Kirkus Reviews* critic found the book "well told and entertaining," and Cindy Darling Codell wrote in *School Library Journal* that the "story transcends its Australian setting to make universal statements about friendship and love at all ages."

In Klein's 1990 novel *Came Back to Show You I Could Fly*, Klein demonstrates her ability to portray a male protagonist. Like so many of Klein's other characters, eleven-year-old Seymour has trouble fitting in. During the summer, his mother takes him to a friend's house, in hopes that Seymour's father—from whom his mother is separated—will not find him. When the friend forbids Seymour from leaving the house, he rebels and wanders out into the surrounding neighborhood looking for something to ease his boredom. On one of his excursions he meets Angie, a colorful eighteen-year-old. The two become friends and only later does Seymour discover his older friend takes drugs and is pregnant. The two seem to need each other: Angie helps Seymour develop confidence in himself, while Seymour's interest in Angie makes her seek out help to end her drug use. Reviewers were generally taken by the pair, finding them engagingly drawn. In *School Library Journal*, Libby K. White described Angie and Seymour as "wonderful creations," while in the *Bulletin of the Center for Children's Books* Roger Sutton judged them "a pair of protagonists readers will be pleased to meet." In *Voice of Youth Advocates* James E. Cook lauded Klein's creation of Angie. "Angie, in particular," he wrote, "will catch the interest of YA readers. Her beginning bravado slowly gives way to an underlying vulnerability." The book received the Australian Children's Book of the Year award.

Sisters Growing Up

While *Came Back to Show You I Could Fly* touched on the very contemporary issue of drug use among adolescents, some of Klein's most successful work has been set in the past. Beginning with

Eleven-year-old Miranda Palgrave is an outcast at school until she suddenly appears to have developed psychic abilities.

All in the Blue Unclouded Weather, and continuing with *Dresses of Red and Gold* and *The Sky in Silver Lace*, she has drawn on personal memories to create stories about growing up in Australia during the late 1940s. Each chapter in the novels offers an episode in the life of the four Melling girls: Grace, Heather, Cathy, and Vivienne. Always humorous, sometimes heart-rending, the stories follow the girls from their home in the small fictional town of Wilgawa to the suburb of the small city where the girls' mother grew up. The girls are particularly close-knit because they must look out for each other; their mother neglects the house so she can write poetic obituaries for the local newspaper, and their father is often away hoping to strike it rich.

All in the Blue Unclouded Weather includes scenes of the eldest daughter, Grace, getting ready to leave home, Cathy's efforts to win a schoolmate's attentions, and Vivenne's hatred of the hand-me-downs she, as the youngest, has to endure. Their days are enlivened by the antics of cousin Isobel, who Roger Sutton in *Bulletin of the Center for Children's Books* describes as "a breathtakingly imaginative troublemaker." Other reviewers also praised the lively group of characters Klein developed in the novel. In *School Library Journal*, Sara Miller remarked on the "youthful characters at once unique and undeniably creatures of their age group." In *Booklist* Chris Sherman called the girls "scrappy, conniving, and refreshingly normal." Klein's ability to recreate the world of her youth was honored when the book received the New South Wales Premier's Award for Literature in the children's books category.

In the series' second installment, *Dresses of Red and Gold*, Grace has moved away from home to study dressmaking, and Klein focuses on Cathy and Vivenne. Cathy, the tomboy in the group, dreads the day she has to stand up in her cousin's wedding as a bridesmaid, preferring instead to work on her treehouse. When a mishap keeps Cathy from wearing the beautiful red and gold bridesmaid dress, Vivenne is only too happy to step in as a substitute, but she first makes sure that Cathy squirms a little. Dad, usually an embarrassment to the girls, comes up with a wild solution to Cathy's problem when some of her friends show up for a non-existent birthday party. Again, reviewers were appreciative of Klein's portrait of this group of girls. "By turns touching, raucously funny, and realistic," wrote Ann A. Flowers in *Horn Book*, "each episode is a small gem, making a whole far beyond the sum of its parts." Sutton commented in the *Bulletin of the Center for Children's Books*, "The postwar rural Australian setting is easy to get settled into, and the girls each have their distinctly bratty idiosyncrasies that make them an entertaining group to get to know." A *Kirkus Reviews* critic found the book a worthy sequel. "The schemes and shenanigans of these vibrant, tenacious characters," he wrote, "are as lively and funny as ever, their more poignant feelings as skillfully suggested."

The third book in the series, *The Sky in Silver Lace*, brought a change in setting from rural Australia—where the girls had been living—to the suburbs of an unnamed city. Told with good humor, the

If you enjoy the works of Robin Klein, you may also want to check out the following books:

Caroline Cooney, *Among Friends*, 1987.
Chris Crutcher, *Athletic Shorts: Six Short Stories*, 1991.
Lynn Hall, *Fair Maiden*, 1990.
Sharon Bell Mathis, *A Teacup Full of Roses*, 1972.

book nevertheless confronts serious subjects as the girls must deal with poverty, the possibility of homelessness, and the chance that their father might not return from his last trip away from the family. Klein is able to show how the girls triumph over their circumstances. Critics, again, singled out for praise the author's ability to create believable characters. "Klein excels," remarked Connie Tyrrell Burns in *School Library Journal*, "at drawing unique characterizations and sibling relationships." In *Horn Book*, Flowers observed that the book's best features were "the carefully observed and solid setting, and . . . the perceptively delineated, realistic relationships between the girls and their mother." In the *Bulletin of the Center for Children's Books*, Sutton faulted the novelist for her "penchant for neat endings," but conceded the book "does offer a chance to visit a likeably obstreperous bunch."

With Klein's 1994 novel *Seeing Things*, she again returned to a contemporary setting. Like Frances in *People Might Hear You*, Miranda, the protagonist of this novel, is also an orphan. After Miranda's parents die, she goes to live with her grandmother and her great-uncle Bernie. While Grandma tries to give Miranda the love she needs, she is too busy helping Miranda's older sister, Yvette, raise her three-month-old baby, Regan, and looking after Miranda's withdrawn younger brother, Jimmy. Since her parents died, Miranda cannot stand going to school, but when she suddenly begins to see images from the past, everyone seems interested in her. Uncle Bernie wants to cash in on her talents, and Yvette's tough ex-boyfriend, Dave, wants Miranda to help him find one of his unsavory companions. According to Sutton in *Bulletin of the Center for Children's Books*, the working out of the plot is "a tribute to Klein's powers of storytelling." In *School Library Journal* Melissa Yurechko similarly praised Klein's ability to bring together all the elements of the story. "Suspense, drama, and snappy dialogue," she wrote, "are skillfully interwoven into the well-paced plot."

From psychic powers to poverty, Klein is a novelist who is known, in the words of a *Kirkus Reviews* commentator, "for incisive realistic portrayals and original plots." Along with realistic novels she has also published science fiction, including *Halfway across the Galaxy and Turn Left*, about aliens from the planet Zyrgon. She is also the accomplished author of numerous short stories, including those in *Tearaways: Tales to Make You Think Twice*, which Gail Richmond in *School Library Journal* called "a nice modern contrast to the stories of O. Henry." She has even published a collection of some of the letters she has received from her fans. In 1992, she was awarded the coveted Dromkeen Medal for her significant contribution to the appreciation and development of children's literature in Australia, but her works seem to speak to young adult readers on either side of the Pacific. "Her writing," noted Sophie Masson in *Magpies*, " is . . . an example of how good writing can also be popular writing, how books which are not mere social handbooks can speak to us deeply of our social experiences."

■ Works Cited

Burns, Connie Tyrrell, review of *The Sky in Silver Lace*, *School Library Journal*, February, 1996, p. 100.

Codell, Cindy Darling, review of *Laurie Loved Me Best*, *School Library Journal*, January, 1989, p. 94.

Cook, James E., review of *Came Back to Show You I Could Fly*, *Voice of Youth Advocates*, February, 1991, pp. 352-53.

Review of *Dresses of Red and Gold*, *Kirkus Reviews*, June 1, 1993, p. 723.

Fisher, Margery, review of *People Might Hear You*, *Growing Point*, March, 1984, p. 4208.

Flowers, Ann A., review of *Dresses of Red and Gold*, *Horn Book*, July/August, 1993, p. 467.

Flowers, Ann A., review of *The Sky in Silver Lace*, *Horn Book*, April, 1996, p. 340.

Klein, Robin, *Seeing Things*, Viking, 1993.

Klein, Robin, comments in *Contemporary Authors*, *New Revision Series*, Volume 40, Gale, 1993, pp. 236-38.

Review of *Laurie Loved Me Best*, *Kirkus Reviews*, December 1, 1988, p. 1740.

Review of *The Lonely Hearts Club*, *Magpies*, September, 1987, p. 26.

Masson, Sophie, review of *All in the Blue Unclouded Weather*, *Magpies*, September, 1993, p. 22.

Miller, Sara, review of *All in the Blue Unclouded Weather*, *School Library Journal*, September, 1992, p. 254.

Nelmes, Margot, review of *Penny Pollard in Print*, *Reading Time*, Volume 31, number 2, 1987, p. 50.

Nettell, Stephanie, "Stephanie Netell Introduces Robin Klein," *Books for Keeps*, September, 1985, p. 26.

Review of *Penny Pollard's Letters*, *Learning*, November-December, 1986, p. 56.

Richmond, Gail, review of *Tearaways: Stories to Make You Think Twice*, *School Library Journal*, June, 1991, p. 110.

Rutherford, Leonie Margaret, "Robin Klein," *Twentieth-Century Young Adult Writers*, St. James Press, 1994, pp. 357-58.

Review of *Seeing Things*, *Kirkus Reviews*, February 1, 1994, p. 145.

Sherman, Chris, review of *All in the Blue Unclouded Weather*, *Booklist*, March 15, 1992, p. 1349.

Singmaster, Deborah, "Cold Confinement," *Times Literary Supplement*, May 29, 1987, p. 589.

Sutton, Roger, review of *Came Back to Show You I Could Fly*, *Bulletin of the Center for Children's Books*, November, 1990, p. 64.

Sutton, Roger, review of *All in the Blue Unclouded Weather*, *Bulletin of the Center for Children's Books*, April, 1992, p. 211.

Sutton, Roger, review of *Dresses of Red and Gold*, *Bulletin of the Center for Children's Books*, May, 1993, p. 286.

Sutton, Roger, review of *Seeing Things*, *Bulletin of the Center for Children's Books*, April, 1994, p. 263.

Sutton, Roger, review of *The Sky in Silver Lace*, *Bulletin of the Center for Children's Books*, February, 1996, p. 194.

White, Libby K., review of *Came Back to Show You I Could Fly*, *School Library Journal*, February, 1991, pp. 81-82.

Yurechko, Melissa, review of *Seeing Things*, *School Library Journal*, August, 1994, p. 156.

■ For More Information See

BOOKS

Children's Literature Review, Volume 21, Gale, 1990.

PERIODICALS

Booklist, June 15, 1991, p. 1956; February 15, 1996, p. 1021.
Junior Bookshelf, June, 1984, pp. 129-30; April, 1990, pp. 100-101; June, 1993, p. 105.
Horn Book, May/June, 1992, pp. 341-42.
Reading Time, January, 1987, pp. 49-50; Volume 33, number 1, 1989, p. 34.
Times Educational Supplement, June 5, 1987, p. 56.
Voice of Youth Advocates, August, 1991, pp. 172-73; June, 1994, pp. 85-86.*

—Sketch by Marian C. Gonsior

Katherine Kurtz

■ Personal

Full name, Katherine Irene Kurtz; born October 18, 1944, in Coral Gables, FL; daughter of Fredrick Harry (an electronics technician) and Margaret Frances (an educator/paralegal; maiden name, Carter) Kurtz; married Scott Roderick MacMillan (an author and producer), March 9, 1983; children: Cameron Alexander Stewart. *Education:* University of Miami—Coral Gables, B.S., 1966; University of California, Los Angeles, M.A., 1971. *Religion:* Christian: Church of Ireland (Anglican). *Hobbies and other interests:* Reading, needlework, costuming, calligraphy, protocol and heraldry, restoration of period architecture, riding, hypnosis.

■ Addresses

Home—Holybrooke Hall, Kilmacanogue, Bray, County Wicklow, Ireland. *Agent*—Russell Galen, Scott Meredith Literary Agency, 845 Third Ave., New York, NY 10022.

■ Career

Los Angeles Police Department, Los Angeles, CA, junior administrative assistant, 1969-71, training technician, 1971-74, senior training technician, 1974-81; full-time writer, 1981—. *Member:* Authors Guild, Science Fiction Writers of America, Order of St. Lazarus of Jerusalem (Dame of the Military and Hospitaller Order), Temple of Jerusalem (Dame Grand Officer, Supreme Military Order), Order of St. John of Jerusalem (Dame of Honor of the Hospitaller Order), Noble Company of the Rose (Dame); Royal House of O'Conor (companion); Augustan Society (fellow) and Octavian Society (fellow), Phi Alpha Theta, Alpha Epsilon Delta, Pi Kappa Phi, Mortar Board.

■ Awards, Honors

Edmund Hamilton Memorial Award, 1977, for *Camber of Culdi*; Gandalf Award nomination for best book-length fantasy, World Science Fiction Convention, 1978, for *Saint Camber*; Balrog Award, 1982, for *Camber the Heretic*; Best Science Fiction Titles of 1986 citation, *Voice of Youth Advocates,* for *The Legacy of Lehr.*

■ Writings

"CHRONICLES OF THE DERYNI" SERIES

Deryni Rising, Ballantine, 1970.
Deryni Checkmate, Ballantine, 1972.
High Deryni, Ballantine, 1973.
The Chronicles of the Deryni (contains *Deryni Rising, Deryni Checkmate,* and *High Deryni*), Science Fiction Book Club, 1985.

"LEGENDS OF SAINT CAMBER" TRILOGY

Camber of Culdi, Ballantine, 1976.
Saint Camber, Del Rey, 1978.
Camber the Heretic, Del Rey, 1981.

"HISTORIES OF KING KELSON" TRILOGY

The Bishop's Heir, Del Rey, 1984.
The King's Justice, Del Rey, 1985.
The Quest for Saint Camber, Del Rey, 1986.

"HEIRS OF SAINT CAMBER" TRILOGY

The Harrowing of Gwynedd, Del Rey, 1989.
King Javan's Year, Del Rey, 1992.
The Bastard Prince, Del Rey, 1994.

"ADEPT" SERIES; WITH DEBORAH TURNER HARRIS

The Adept, Ace, 1991.
Adept II: The Lodge of the Lynx, Ace, 1992.
Adept III: The Templar Treasure, Ace, 1993.
Adept IV: Dagger Magic, Ace, 1995.
Adept V: Death of an Adept, Ace, 1996.

OTHER

Deryni Magic: A Grimoire, Del Rey, 1981.
Lammas Night (historical thriller), Ballantine, 1983.
The Legacy of Lehr (science fiction), Walker & Co., 1986.
The Deryni Archives (short stories), Del Rey, 1986.
(Editor) *Tales of the Knights Templar*, Warner, 1995.
Two Crowns for America, Bantam, 1996.
(With Robert Reginald) *Codex Derynianus*, Borgo, 1997.
King Kelson's Bride, Del Rey, 1997.

Contributor to anthologies, including *Flashing Swords #4: Warriors and Wizards*, edited by Lin Carter, Dell, 1977; *Hecate's Cauldron*, edited by Susan Schwartz, DAW, 1982; *Nine Visions*, edited by Andrea LaSonde Melrose, Seabury Press, 1983; *Moonsinger's Friends*, edited by Schwartz, Bluejay, 1985; *Once Upon a Time*, edited by Lester Del Rey and Risa Kessler, Del Rey, 1991; *Crafter I*, edited by Bill Fawcett and Christopher Stasheff, Ace, 1991; *The Gods of War*, edited by Fawcett and Stasheff, Baen Books, 1992; *Battlestation Book II: Vanguard*, edited by Fawcett and Stasheff, Ace, 1992. Kurtz's work has been translated into Dutch, French, German, Italian, Japanese, Polish, Romanian, Spanish, and Swedish.

■ **Sidelights**

The tyrannical young King Imre, hated by many in the medieval kingdom of Gwynedd for his injustices against the people, has just murdered courtier Cathan MacRorie, who has been like a brother to him and truly had no knowledge of a treasonous plot afoot in the kingdom. Now that his body has been returned home and the suspicious circumstances of his death left officially unexplained, the MacRories know the time has come for decisive action against the crown. A company of the king's soldiers is keeping a close watch on the family's movements, and there is no time to

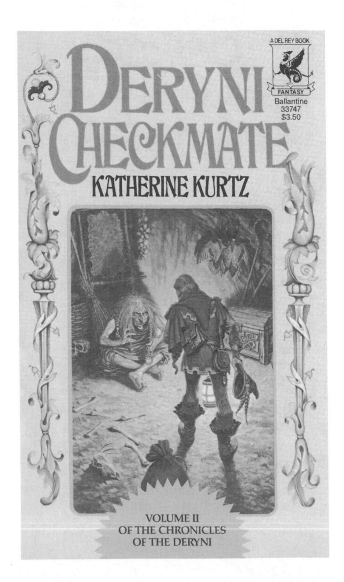

In this 1972 novel from the first "Deryni" trilogy, Duke Alaric Morgan fears for his life as the priests of Gwynedd detest his magical powers.

lose. Nobleman Camber MacRorie sets aside his grief for his lost son, and, drawing on the arcane mental powers that are his as a member of the Deryni race, casts a shape-changing spell that enables his other two sons to escape without notice. They will make a wintery journey to a remote monastery in order to abduct the cloistered monk, Brother Benedict, who is really Prince Cinhil Donal Ifor Haldane, the last of his royal line, and the rebellion's only hope. . . .

For readers who love historical fantasy fiction about long-ago, faraway places, where detailed pageants of kings, nobles, damsels, soldiers, monks, and peasants alike are caught up in tempestuous plots full of magic and intrigue, feasts and family trees, battles and romance—then Gwynedd is the place to go and author Katherine Kurtz is the one to take them there.

In recent years, Kurtz has written several modern-day science fiction and historical novels and co-authored a detective mystery series. But she is best known for her "Deryni" novels, published over the last two decades. There are four trilogies—the "Chronicles of the Deryni"; the "Legends of Saint Camber"; the "Histories of King Kelson"; and the "Heirs of Saint Camber"—as well as the novel, *King Kelson's Bride*; a short story collection, *The Deryni Archives*; a book about Deryni rituals titled *Deryni Magic: A Grimoire*; and, last but not least, an encyclopedia of the people and places in the Deryni universe, co-written with Robert Reginald, titled *Codex Derynianus*.

Together these record the life and times of the people of imaginary Gwynedd and its neighboring kingdoms, all of which are based largely on the culture, technology, social structure, and religious practices of tenth, eleventh, and twelfth century Wales, Scotland, and England. A major difference, as Kurtz has noted in her introduction to *The Deryni Archives*, is the existence of real magic, and indeed, driving the plots of these fantasy tales is the ongoing high conflict between two races: ordinary humans and the Deryni, a people with magical ESP-like powers that include healing, mind reading and mind influence, changeable identities, and the ability to transport themselves telepathically via special portals. As Robert Reginald stated in *Twentieth-Century Science-Fiction Writers*, "Politics and religion are inextricably intertwined in Kurtz's creation, as they were in our own history, with state and church constantly vy-

This 1976 novel features Cinhil, a cloistered monk who is really the sole-surviving grandson of the Haldanes, who were slaughtered by the Festils, the current and hated rulers.

ing with each other and the Deryni minority for power and authority. The key players of these historical fantasies recognize that the price of failure is disgrace—or more likely death. What sustains them is faith, an abiding and sincere belief in God, his Church, the King, and friends and family as the key structures of society. . . . Kurtz champions intelligence, duty, sensitivity, love, faith, truth, all the finer virtues. Man makes of his world what he will, she seems to be saying, a heaven or a hell, a condition which clearly presages what he (or she) will become in the after-life."

"Obviously, one of the important themes that runs through most of [my] books is the reality of spiritual dimensions to one's life, and examples of how various characters handle this element in their day to day living," Kurtz once told *Contemporary Authors.* "I like to think that we all have a little Deryni in us, that could be developed to make us better human beings. In a way, perhaps the Deryni are an archetype for the perfected human being—what we would all be like, if we have the courage to stand by our convictions and actively enlist on the side of the Light. And also, I obviously have a lot to say about the stupidity and destructiveness of blind prejudice. There's a lot happening, on many different levels. Mostly, though, I want to tell stories about interesting, multi-dimensional characters who will get my readers involved. If those readers get something in addition to a good read, then that's best of all!"

Genevieve Stuttaford, writing in *Publishers Weekly* about *The Quest for Saint Camber,* summarized Kurtz's work as "teeming with distinctive characters, fascinated by theology and genealogy, her weakness for cliches and homilies is surmounted by a rare craftsmanship with narrative exposition that is also dramatic and moving." Indeed, most reviewers of Kurtz's work, whether they be Deryni fans or not, commonly cite such story-telling mastery as a particular strength of the author. Her ability to imaginatively chink together, brick by brick, whole sections of time into a complete monument to the history of a world has drawn praise, as have the strong characters who prevail despite complicated plots that, some critics say, get bogged down in Kurtz's cataloging of historical and ritualistic detail. They are real-seeming people, heroes and heroines with whom one can celebrate and suffer, and enemies that one loves to hate.

Born In A Hurricane

For Kurtz, it all started with a storm and some good library books. She was born in Coral Gables, Florida, during a hurricane, and as the biographical note to *Camber of Culdi* points out, she "has led a somewhat whirlwind existence ever since," dabbling in everything from marine science, anthropology, and the cataloging of Chinese painting to educational and commercial television, police science, and hypnotism. Recalling her childhood, she once told *Something About the Author*

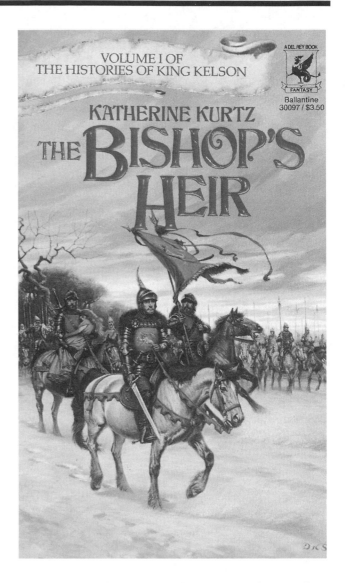

While King Kelson realizes he must produce an heir to his throne, ex-Archbishop Loris, now free from prison, is sowing the seeds of unrest in Gwynedd by proclaiming as evil all Deryni magic.

(*SATA*) that "I can barely remember a time when I couldn't read. None of elementary school was particularly challenging to me, so I used to take library books to school and hide them in my lift-top desk or under the book I was supposed to be reading. I also read under the covers at night by flashlight." She was especially fond of science fiction.

Her high school aptitude for science led her to the University of Miami, from which she received a degree in chemistry in 1966. But by then she had discovered a passion for history, and, after one year of medical school, she abandoned hard science for the humanities. She wrote her first two novels, *Deryni Rising* (1970) and *Deryni Checkmate* (1972) while pursuing a master's degree in medieval English history from the University of California, Los Angeles, which she received in 1971. (A third novel, *High Deryni*, published in 1973, completes the first of her trilogies, the "Chronicles of the Deryni.") She once commented in *SATA* that more important than the degree itself "was the formal knowledge of the medieval and renaissance world that I gained and the sharpening of research skills which would stand me in good stead as I continued writing medievally-set fantasy." For more than a decade, Kurtz worked for the Los Angeles Police Department, writing and designing instructional materials, still turning out her Deryni novels all the while. In 1980, she devoted herself full-time to her career as a novelist.

A World's Winding History

The Deryni novels follow each other chronologically within the trilogies, but the trilogies themselves were not written in "historical" order. Readers new to the series can spend some time with a bibliography to figure out how to begin at the beginning, or better yet, they might just pick up Gwynedd's history in midstream and let it take them, as it will, forward and backward in time. The first trilogy, the "Chronicles of the Deryni," focuses on the early reign of King Kelson Haldane. His father's assassination catapults him onto the throne while he is still a teenager, in the year 1120 (according to one of several lineage charts that, along with hand-drawn maps and lengthy glossaries of character and place names, help give these fantasies the heft of historical reality). The Haldanes have a capacity for developing special powers like those of the Deryni, making them potentially capable of ruling with empathy over both races. (In fact, Kelson's mother is Deryni, though she doesn't know it.) Kelson makes way for the Deryni to return to power by defeating challengers from the Festil dynasty, and by acting on his idealism, too. According to Edward James in the *St. James Guide to Fantasy Writers*, the early Chronicles grouping is "the most tightly written" of Kurtz's trilogies.

Kurtz's next trilogy, the "Legends of Saint Camber," takes readers back about 200 years, chronicling history's changing view of a nobleman's life,

casting him first as a political victor, then as a saint, and finally, as a heretic. In *Camber of Culdi*, Gwynedd is under the reign of the hated Festils, who usurped the throne five generations before by slaughtering the ruling Haldanes. But one Haldane escaped, and his grandson, Cinhil, becomes the cloistered monk that the MacRories discover. With the help of their allies, the knight-priests of the Michaeline order, the Haldanes bring him to power after a successful coup against King Imre. Camber MacRorie is himself a Deryni, but he recognizes that if magic is not anchored by morality, it will harm rather than help his race. In *Saint Camber*, ill will has developed between Camber and King Cinhil at a time when Ariella, sister of the late King Imre, is staging a comeback. For the sake of the kingdom, Camber decides to exchange shapes with Alister Cullen when that knightly priest is killed in battle. Still inhabiting Cullen's body, he is made a bishop in his friend's place and can only watch as his "dead self"—Camber—is declared a saint. As Barbara A. Bannon explained in *Publishers Weekly*, "This is a gripping novel, dignified by serious moral issues and brightened with all the color of an imaginary world." And, while a *Kirkus Reviews* contributor found "that this ingeniously developed situation is hampered by such plodding characterization and uncertain prose," he concluded that Kurtz's chronicles as a whole "have more to them than most of the ilk."

The author concludes the trilogy with *Camber the Heretic*, which details an angry turn in the political tide. King Cinhil has tried to mend the rift between humans and Deryni, appointing the latter to high government posts. But when Cinhil dies, the magical powers of the Deryni are not enough to counter the human backlash, and Camber loses his life in the ensuing violence. "The first part of the book drags somewhat, as Kurtz fills in all the fine nuances of her large cast of characters and indulges in a scholar's passion for the minutiae of medieval existence. The last third of the book—the stark tale of the persecutions—is the finest writing yet to come from this gifted storyteller," a *Booklist* contributor declared.

The third trilogy, the "Histories of King Kelson"— *The Bishop's Heir*, *The King's Justice*, and *The Quest for Saint Camber*—returns readers to where the original Chronicles left off. In the first two novels, King Kelson, now a young adult, is trying to grow into his role as leader while facing troubled times. A marriage must be arranged because he needs to produce an heir. There is a challenge to his sovereignty by a princess in the neighboring province of Meara, and a fanatical bishop is sowing the seeds of unrest at home by proclaiming as evil all Deryni magic. Having squelched rebellion at last, Kelson, in *The Quest for Saint Camber*, is determined to re-elevate the Deryni and the memory of Saint Camber to their former prestige and he embarks on a religious quest for relics. Following an accident during their journey, he and his companion are declared dead, which opens the door for a scheming cousin to make a play for the throne and Kelson's wife-to-be.

Noting Kurtz's "ear for language and an eye for detail," Dale F. Martin wrote in *Fantasy Review* that although "the quest of the title, in fact, is almost overlooked in the political maneuverings of church and state," and "the melodrama takes on the flavor of 12th century soap opera in spots," Kurtz "spins a good tale, and the trio of trilogies is a significant contribution to fantasy literature." Of *The Bishop's Heir*, Michael J. Ducharme stated in *Fantasy Review*, "This latest has the ingredients that Deryni fans have come to love: political, religious, and magical maneuverings, hidden motives and anguish. Kurtz is one of those writers you either love or hate; there is no middle ground."

In this volume from the final "Deryni" trilogy, dead King Cinhil's son Alroy sits on the throne, and the remaining Deryni attempt to save their people by magically nullifying Deryni powers, taking the risk that those powers will re-emerge in a safer future.

Heirs Open A Dark Chapter

Finally, the "Heirs of Saint Camber" trilogy looks at the time between the Camber legends and King Kelson's rule. It is the darkest of the Deryni trilogies, and more than one reviewer concluded that it suffers from a preponderance of gloom. First, in *The Harrowing of Gwynedd*, dead King Cinhil's son Alroy, a weak boy-king, sits on the throne, with the real power in the hands of cunning regents. Those Deryni who survived the attempted genocide against them begun in Camber's day are now in hiding. They attempt to save their people by magically nullifying Deryni powers so that they can pass as humans, taking the risk that those powers will re-emerge in a future generation when the climate is again safe for them.

In *King Javan's Year*, the sickly Alroy dies, and his more independent twin brother, sixteen-year-old Javan, succeeds him to throne, to the dismay of the regents. Javan has some Deryni-like powers, and with the help of the Deryni underground, he gives his enemies a fight. But evil wins out, making this a dark chapter in Gwyneddian history. A contributor in *Kirkus Reviews* called it a "grim, brutal installment, but well up to Kurtz's usual standard: layer upon layer of patient detail, life-sized characters, and controlled, intricate plotting." Warning away newcomers to the series, though, Carolyn Cushman, writing in *Locus*, said that *King Javan's Year* "suffers both from being a middle book . . . and from its pervasive sense of doom" and that, since the book's title removes all doubt about who will reign, and for how long, "the only mystery is how Javan dies, and how much he can accomplish in the meantime. The answer is not enough; his few small accomplishments do little to pierce the abiding gloom, much less abate it." Similarly, *Voice of Youth Advocates* reviewer Diane G. Yates remarked, "It remains to be seen whether readers of these wonderfully crafted fantasies can stand the emotional strain of having so many of the characters that they have grown to love, lose their lives in an unceasing struggle with the forces of evil." She concludes, however, that the novel "is up to Kurtz's usual high standards, is beautifully written, and should appeal to teens as well as adults."

Those who *can* stand the sorrow will read on to find that the struggle continues on various fronts in the trilogy's concluding novel, *The Bastard Prince*. "With strong characterizations and sustained tension, this volume once again reflects the atmospheric gloom of a dark and secret land, full of treachery and cruelty but shot through with light and a promise of hope," wrote Sybil S. Steinberg in *Publishers Weekly*. The last of Cinhil's sons, Rhys Michael, is now the human regents' puppet king, but he is able to assert his independence when he must fight a Deryni threat to his throne, mounted by old enemies: the long-dead King Imre's bastard son, Marek of Festil, and his forces. Meanwhile, a group of sympathetic Deryni attempt to reawaken the king's mental powers. "His actions, and his growing realization of his own innate gifts initiate a chain of circumstances that heralds the beginning of a new age for a beleaguered land," wrote Jackie Cassada in *Library Journal*, adding that "Kurtz portrays credible characters caught in a struggle to remain true both to themselves and their faith amid a tangle of betrayal and intrigue."

Meanwhile, Outside The Kingdom . . .

Kurtz has stepped outside the realm of her imaginary medieval kingdoms to write several novels set in more recent times, but her penchant for creating stories involving tradition, magic, and intrigue persists. Her first such attempt was *Lammas Night*, a World War II thriller published in 1983. "British folk tradition has it that England has been saved from invasion more than once by the magical intervention of those appointed to guard her, Napoleonic and Armada times being

---

If you enjoy the works of Katherine Kurtz, you may also want to check out the following books and films:

Marion Zimmer Bradley, *The Mists of Avalon*, 1983.
C. J. Cherryh, *The Dreamstone*, 1983.
Frank Herbert, *The Dune Series*, 1965-1985.
Robert Jordan, *The Dragon Reborn*, 1991.
Labyrinth, TriStar, 1986.

---

cited as two specific examples," Kurtz explained in *SATA*. "Less well-known tradition has it that similar measures were employed to keep Hitler from invading Britain during that fateful summer of 1940. . . . *Lammas Night* is the story of how and why that might have been." Then in 1986, her science fiction novel, *The Legacy of Lehr*, was published as the first entry in the "Millennium" series of illustrated science fiction for young adults. In the work, she concocts a murder mystery on board a starship in which imperial agents are transporting a politically important load of ferocious wild cats, which seem to be responsible for the vampire-style killings of passengers and crew. Stuttaford in *Publishers Weekly* called it "an SF version of a gothic shipboard tale," which she concluded was "slight" in comparison to Kurtz's Deryni books, but "lively" nonetheless.

Kurtz has co-authored, with Deborah Turner Harris, a series of "modern Scottish detective novels with an occult twist," as Kurtz described them in *SATA*, known as the "Adept" novels. With her husband, Scott MacMillan, she created the murder mystery *Knights of the Blood*, about Nazi vampires who have come into being through contact with an ancient order of sequestered vampire knights. In a more recent book, the historical novel *Two Crowns for America*, Kurtz explores occult influences during America's Revolutionary War. Sybil S. Steinberg wrote in *Publishers Weekly* that "Kurtz depicts a believable alternate American Revolution" that "rightly emphasizes the more human characters, likeable and three-dimensional in their political and personal struggles as she fleshes out historical figures from George Washington and Benjamin Franklin to the exiled Jacobites" who hope Prince Charles will be enthroned in America. "Readers are left with some provocative questions about our national values," Steinberg concluded.

Kurtz once told *SATA* that she "can't imagine a more satisfying life than to be making a living doing what I love. Far too few people get the opportunity to do that, and especially at a relatively young age." The author pursues an eclectic mix of hobbies that both stem from and feed her writing interests. Still an avid reader, she is also a professionally trained hypnotist and is accomplished at various kinds of needlework, ceremonial calligraphy, and manuscript illumination. For many years she was active in the Society for Creative Anachronism, an organization devoted to elaborate medieval dramatizations. These days, Kurtz continues to live her writing life, appropriately, from a historical country home in County Wicklow, Ireland, where she moved with her husband and son from California in 1986. There, they belong to a number of chivalric orders and are involved in Scottish clan activities. Kurtz has promised to write more Deryni novels—in particular, a "Childe Morgan" trilogy pre-dating the initial Chronicles of Deryni—and, indeed, with so much scenic, cultural, and historical inspiration at the author's hand, and with so many loose ends waiting to be woven into the fantasy tapestry that is Gwynedd, it's hard not to imagine a good many Kurtz novels yet to come.

■ Works Cited

Bannon, Barbara A., review of *Saint Camber, Publishers Weekly*, September 11, 1978.

Review of *Camber the Heretic, Booklist*, November 1, 1981.

Cassada, Jackie, review of *The Bastard Prince, Library Journal*, April 15, 1994.

Cushman, Carolyn, review of *King Javan's Year, Locus*, November, 1992.

Ducharme, Michael J., "Dandy New Deryni," *Fantasy Review*, January, 1986.

James, Edward, "Katherine Kurtz," *St. James Guide to Fantasy Writers*, 1st edition, St. James Press, 1996.

Review of *King Javan's Year, Kirkus Reviews*, October 1, 1992.

Kurtz, Katherine, biographical note in *Camber of Culdi*, Del Rey/Ballantine, 1976.

Kurtz, Katherine, comments in *Something About the Author*, Volume 76, Gale, 1994.

Kurtz, Katherine, comments in *Contemporary Authors, New Revision Series*, Volume 50, Gale, 1996.

Martin, Dale F., "Third Trilogy Ends," *Fantasy Review*, December, 1986.

Reginald, Robert, "Katherine Kurtz," *Twentieth-Century Science Fiction Writers*, 3rd edition, St. James Press, 1991.

Review of *Saint Camber, Kirkus Reviews*, August 15, 1978.

Steinberg, Sybil S., review of *The Bastard Prince, Publishers Weekly*, May 23, 1994.

Steinberg, Sybil S., review of *Two Crowns for America, Publishers Weekly*, November 27, 1995.

Stuttaford, Genevieve, review of *The Quest for Saint Camber, Publishers Weekly*, August 8, 1986.

Stuttaford, Genevieve, review of *The Legacy of Lehr, Publishers Weekly*, September 26, 1986.

Yates, Diane G., review of *King Javan's Year, Voice of Youth Advocates*, April, 1993.

■ For More Information See

BOOKS

Clarke, Boden, and Mary A. Burgess, *The Work of Katherine Kurtz: An Annotated Bibliography and Guide*, Borgo Press, 1993.

Spivack, Charlotte, *Merlin's Daughters: Contemporary Women Writers of Fantasy*, Greenwood Press, 1987.

PERIODICALS

Booklist, October 1, 1985, p. 153; August, 1986, p. 1667; November 15, 1986, p. 502; January 1, 1990, p. 905; March 1, 1991, p. 1322; May 15, 1992, p. 1670; May 1, 1994, p. 1583; February 1, 1996, p. 920.

Fantasy Review, March, 1985, p. 23.

Kirkus Reviews, October, 1985, p. 1049; August 1, 1986, p. 1161; December 15, 1988, p. 1781; April 1, 1994, p. 442; December 1, 1995, p. 1672.

Kliatt, April, 1991, p. 20; November, 1992, p. 16; November, 1993, p. 8.

Library Journal, November 15, 1984, p. 2162; September 15, 1986, p. 102; November 15, 1986, p. 113; February 15, 1989, p. 179; March 15, 1991, p. 119; August, 1994, p. 139.

Locus, February, 1989, p. 17; November, 1989, p. 56; December, 1990, p. 25; February, 1991, pp. 27, 57; April, 1991, p. 43; July, 1992, pp. 31, 50; June, 1993, p. 31; August, 1993, p. 46; February, 1994, p. 75; June, 1994, p. 58.

Publishers Weekly, July 23, 1979, p. 158; September 25, 1981, p. 87; July 5, 1985, p. 66; December 2, 1988, p. 48; December 21, 1990, p. 50; February 8, 1991, p. 54; October 12, 1992, p. 68.

School Library Journal, January, 1985, p. 92; February, 1986, p. 103; November, 1986, p. 116; January, 1990, p. 128; September, 1992, p. 291.

Science Fiction Chronicle, May, 1987, p. 48; August, 1988, p. 52; May, 1993, p. 32; June, 1995, p. 38.

Voice of Youth Advocates, April, 1985, p. 55; December, 1986, p. 238; April, 1987, p. 38; August, 1989, p. 166; June, 1991, p. 110; October, 1992, p. 240; October, 1993, p. 230; October, 1994, p. 224; April, 1995, p. 8; October, 1995, p. 234; April, 1996, p. 18.

—Sketch by Tracy J. Sukraw

David Macaulay

■ Personal

Full name, David Alexander Macaulay; born December 2, 1946, in Burton-on-Trent, England; came to the United States in 1957; son of James (a textile machine technician) and Joan (Lowe) Macaulay; married Janice Elizabeth Michel, 1970 (divorced), married Ruth Marris, 1978 (divorced), married Ruth Ellen Murray, 1997; children: (first marriage) Elizabeth Alexandra, (second marriage) Charlotte Valerie. *Education:* Rhode Island School of Design, B.Arch., 1969.

■ Addresses

Studio—146 Water St., Warren, RI 02885.

■ Career

Freelance illustrator and writer, 1979—. Rhode Island School of Design, Providence, instructor in interior design, 1969-73, instructor in two-dimensional design, 1974-76, adjunct faculty, department of illustration, 1976-90, chairman, department of illustration, 1977-79. Public school teacher of art in Central Falls, RI, 1969-70, and Newton, MA, 1972-74; designer, Morris Nathanson Design, 1969-72. Visiting lecturer, Yale University, 1978-79, Simmons College, 1989-90; visiting professor of art, Wellesley College, 1985-87; visiting instructor, Brown University, 1982-86. Worked as a consultant and presenter for television shows produced by Unicorn Projects, Washington, DC, including "Castle," 1982, "Cathedral," 1985, and "Pyramid," 1987; presenter of television show "Sense of Place," WJAR-TV, Providence, RI, 1988. Trustee, Partners for Livable Places, Washington, DC, Slater Mill Historic Site, Pawtucket, RI, and Community Preparatory School, Providence. Macaulay's works are in the permanent collections of Cooper Hewitt Museum, Toledo Museum of Art, and Museum of Art, Rhode Island School of Design.

■ Awards, Honors

New York Times Ten Best Illustrated Books citation, 1973, American Institute of Graphic Arts Children's Book Show citation, 1973-74, Caldecott Honor Book, American Library Association (ALA), and Children's Book Showcase title, both 1974, Jugendbuchpreis (Germany), and Silver Slate Pencil Award (Holland), both 1975, all for *Cathedral: The Story of Its Construction;* children's Book Showcase title, 1975, for *City: A Story of Roman Planning and Construction;* Christopher Award, and *New York Times* Outstanding Children's Book of the

Year, both 1975, *Boston Globe-Horn Book* honor book, and Children's Book Showcase title, both 1976, all for *Pyramid; New York Times* Outstanding Children's Book of the Year, 1976, Children's Book Showcase title, and *School Library Journal* "Best of the Best 1966-1976" citation, 1978, all for *Underground; New York Times Book Review* Outstanding Book of the Year, 1977, New York Academy of Sciences Children's Science Book Award honorable mention, Caldecott Honor Book, and *Boston Globe-Horn Book* honor book, all 1978, all for *Castle;* Washington Children's Book Guild Award for a body of work, 1977; American Institute of Architects Medal, 1978, for his contribution as "an outstanding illustrator and recorder of architectural accomplishment"; ALA Best Books for Young Adults and New York Public Library's Books for the Teen Age citations, 1980, both for *Motel of the Mysteries; New York Times* Ten Best Illustrated Books, and Parents' Choice Award for illustration in children's books, both 1980, New York Academy of Sciences Award honorable mention, 1981, and Ambassador of Books-across-the-Sea honor book, English-Speaking Union, 1982, all for *Unbuilding; New York Times Book Review* Notable Book of the Year, 1982, for *Help! Let Me Out!; School Library Journal*'s Best Books and New York Public Library's Children's Books citations, both 1983, for *Mill;* nominated for Hans Christian Andersen Illustrator Medal, 1984; honorary Doctor of Literature, Rhode Island College, 1987; honorary Doctor of Humanities, Savannah College of Art and Design, 1987; *Times Educational Supplement* senior information book award, science book prize for under sixteen, The Science Museum/Copus (London), *Boston Globe-Horn Book* Award for best nonfiction book, all 1989, and American Institute of Physics best science book of the year award, 1990, all for *The Way Things Work;* Caldecott Medal, 1991, for *Black and White;* Charles Frankel Prize, 1995; Chevalier of Order of Arts and Letters (France), 1995.

■ Writings

SELF-ILLUSTRATED

Cathedral: The Story of Its Construction, Houghton, 1973.
City: A Story of Roman Planning and Construction, Houghton, 1974.
Pyramid, Houghton, 1975.
Underground, Houghton, 1976.

Castle, Houghton, 1977.
Great Moments in Architecture, Houghton, 1978.
Motel of the Mysteries, Houghton, 1979.
Unbuilding, Houghton, 1980.
Mill, Houghton, 1983.
BAAA, Houghton, 1985.
Why the Chicken Crossed the Road, Houghton, 1987.
The Way Things Work, Houghton, 1988.
Black and White, Houghton, 1990.
Ship, Houghton, 1993.
Shortcut, Houghton, 1995.
Rome Antics, Houghton, 1997.

ILLUSTRATOR

David L. Porter, *Help! Let Me Out!,* Houghton, 1982.
Electricity, Tennessee Valley Authority, 1983.
Robert Ornstein and Richard F. Thompson, *The Amazing Brain,* Houghton, 1984.

Contributor of illustrated articles to magazines, including *Washington Post.* Cartoonist for *Architectural Record,* 1990—.

■ Adaptations

The following works were adapted and broadcast by PBS-TV: *Castle,* October, 1983; *Cathedral,* 1985; and *Pyramid,* 1987; *The Way Things Work* was adapted to CD-ROM by Dorling Kindersley, 1994.

■ Sidelights

"I honestly think all of us would be better off if everyone took the time to draw, if for no other reason than the better we see, the more inevitable curiosity becomes," former architect and best-selling children's book author and illustrator David Macaulay said in his 1991 Caldecott Medal acceptance speech, published in *Horn Book.* Macaulay won the prestigious award for his intriguing work, *Black and White,* which tells four stories simultaneously and compels readers to look closely at what is going on within the illustrations. Macaulay, however, is best known for his nonfiction works that teach children about the wonders of architecture from past and present ages, as well as for his best-selling book, *The Way Things Work,* an illustrated guide that explains the mechanics behind everything from nail clippers to computers.

While many authors and educators denounce what they see as the dangers of verbal illiteracy in our times, Macaulay warned in *Horn Book* about what he calls "visual illiteracy—and by that I mean not really seeing what is going on around us. On one level, avoidance of informed looking and thinking results merely in inappropriate architecture, endless rows of neon signs, advertising agencies, political marketing consultants, Teenage Mutant Ninja Turtles, Barbie dolls, and Hallmark cards—in general, mediocrity. But on another, much deeper level, it threatens to turn us into isolated, insensitive, incapable, and ultimately helpless victims of a world of increasing complexity and decreasing humanity."

A Creative Child

Macaulay has been fascinated with the way the world works since his childhood. Born in Burton-on-Trent, England, in 1946, Macaulay was one of three children of an engineer who specialized as a textile machine technician. The author spent his early years in Bolton in a working-class neighborhood where the rows of houses all looked the same. Macaulay's resourceful parents had a penchant for making things rather than buying them. All the children learned to sew, and Macaulay learned to draw and make models and contraptions out of cardboard, yarn, tape, and string. When Macaulay was seven, "he received a Mechano Set—the English Erector Set—that was too advanced for him but that he was determined to use anyway," reported fellow children's book author Chris Van Allsburg in a *Horn Book* article. "Each evening, returning from work, Mr. Macaulay would find his young son waiting for him, ready to demolish the previous night's effort and build something new." The young boy loved to spend time by himself in his own imaginary world and playing with items he could find around the house. "I would take my little soldiers into the sitting room . . . put them into flower pots, and with threads and spools construct cable cars from the top of the curtain rods down to the corner of the room," Macaulay once related.

His parents also instilled in him a fondness for nature by taking the family out on picnics, as well as for literature by reading to them at night from *Alice in Wonderland, The Water Babies, The Wind in the Willows,* and *Robinson Crusoe* ("Oh, sure, *Crusoe* looks like a story all right," the illustrator remarked in *Horn Book,* "But it's really all about making things out of leftovers.") Macaulay's mother would fascinate him with the drawings she would make based on the story *Cinderella.* It was from her that he gained his love of drawing, though he did not become serious about this craft until after he left England. Before drawing, Macaulay actually distinguished himself in penmanship, winning a national handwriting award in 1956.

Life changed for the young Macaulay when he was eleven and his family moved to Bloomfield, New Jersey, because his father had been offered a job there. Two years later, they moved to Verona in the same state. It was in America that Macaulay first began to draw in earnest. After five years in New Jersey, his family moved once again, this time to Cumberland, Rhode Island, where Macaulay found the atmosphere more similar to the slow-paced life he enjoyed in England. By this time, he was in high school and was drawing all the time, often to impress his classmates. "I'd come home from school, would race through my homework, and then do another Beatles portrait, knowing that the next day at school everyone would rave over my effort, making me feel terrific," Macaulay once wrote. "[It was] a totally self-serving endeavor, but why else would anybody draw?" He was named best artist in the Cumberland High School yearbook.

But although Macaulay enjoyed drawing, he had a pragmatic side that told him it was unlikely he could ever make a living at it. Therefore, for college he applied to the engineering program at the University of Rhode Island, and to the Rhode Island School of Design, where he eventually enrolled to study architecture. "I was accepted by the School of Design first," recalled Macaulay. "Otherwise I may have ended up studying engineering and building bridges. In retrospect it looks predetermined and logical."

Macaulay found that architecture school was just the place to encourage that interest in how things work that his parents first instilled in him. "Architecture teaches you how to devise a way of thinking that allows you to believe you can tackle any problem of any scale," he once commented. "It fueled and educated my desire to understand how things work. Since then, I have realized that what I was learning in architecture—how to break down an immense problem into its smallest parts and put it back together logically with knowledge, expertise, and imagination—could also be applied to making books."

A Desire for Something More

Never thinking he would actually have fun with architecture, Macaulay "discovered that rigor and discipline don't necessarily exclude fun," according to Van Allsburg. "The design process was exciting and rewarding to him and an unexpected outlet for humor that made his architectural presentations favorites of his instructors and fellow students." Still, he never had a burning desire to see his models turned into actual buildings. After finishing school—the fifth year of which was spent overseas when he was selected for the European Honors Program and had the opportunity to see many of the architectural wonders of Italy—Macaulay taught art at a junior high school to avoid being drafted and sent to Vietnam. However, he did not enjoy his time as a teacher, which he once described as "the toughest year I've ever spent. Teaching was a tremendous strain. I realized immediately how difficult it would be to replenish myself and come back caring every day. It was impossible."

In addition to teaching, Macaulay was working part-time for Morris Nathanson, an interior decorator who suggested the possibility of picture book illustration. Inspired by such children's book creators as Maurice Sendak and Etienne Delessert, Macaulay decided he would indeed like to follow in their footsteps. He quit teaching and became a freelance illustrator for a textbook publisher while he worked on his children's books. The first of these efforts was a collaboration with Nathanson. Though the book was rejected, they did get some positive feedback, which encouraged Macaulay to continue. Macaulay then did four solo books, which were all fantasies for children. None were published. With the fourth book, however, editor Walter Lorraine of the publisher Houghton Mifflin praised Macaulay for the drawing he had done of gargoyles on a cathedral. This simple suggestion led to Macaulay's first published work, as well as a long-term business relationship with Lorraine.

Cathedral: The Story of Its Construction won numerous awards, including a Caldecott Medal Honor, the Dutch Silver Slate Pencil Award, and the Ger-

man Jugendbuchpreis. In the book, Macaulay creates an imaginary town, Chutreaux, in France that in 1252 undertakes the enormous task of constructing a cathedral. The construction takes decades and isn't completed until 1338. Macaulay shows the reader every step in the process, explains all the tools that were used, and even provides a floor plan. "The information in *Cathedral*, as in all of Macaulay's books, is given with clarity and directness," said *Dictionary of Literary Biography* contributor Nellvena Duncan Eutsler. While the actual construction process is very interesting, Macaulay also adds special touches to the book. For example, a careful observer will notice the roofs on the houses around the cathedral change from thatch to slate as the years pass and homes in the city improve. As Eutsler also pointed out, "The first double spread of the book introduces a whimsical scene with two ducks swimming in a stream and a fox jumping a riverlet."

"It is difficult to believe that David Macaulay's *Cathedral . . .*, was his first book," declared Valerie Anderson in the *Times Educational Supplement*, "for it conveys all the professionalism and authority of an established writer." Anderson later added that the author "certainly has a gift for putting across the complexities of construction engineering which should be the envy of most of our writers of children's non-fiction." The critic also particularly noted Macaulay's use of perspective "to give impressions of size and space and in *Cathedral* he demonstrates this par excellence."

However, despite all the praise the book received, some critics found some flaws. For example, Marcus Crouch complained in *School Librarian* that the "drawing is too clinical to convey the passion and excitement" of the great architectural achievements of the Middle Ages. Others, like *Children's Literature in Education* reviewer Geoffrey Hoare, have said Macaulay's drawings of people are particularly poor: "[Macaulay's] style ranges from careful explanatory diagrams through steady architectural observation . . . own to poor, hairy figure-drawing." Later, Hoare wrote, "The figure drawings lack all individuality and character." Macaulay himself has admitted that figure drawing is not his strong suit, but, after all, the star of his books are the buildings, not the people. As an educational tool that is fun to read, *Cathedral* contains much that is praiseworthy. It "is a book to treasure," according to Leon Garfield in *Spectator*.

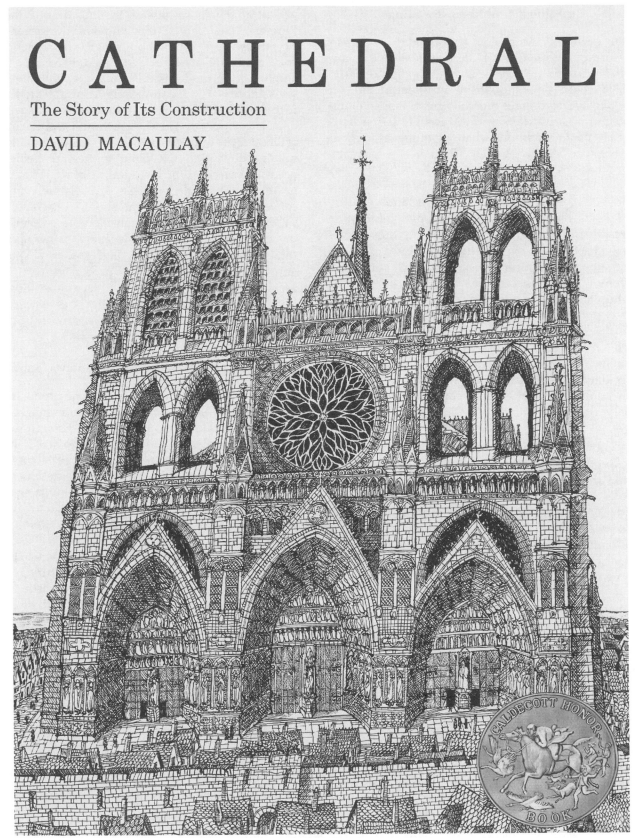

CATHEDRAL

The Story of Its Construction

DAVID MACAULAY

Set in the fictional town of Chutreaux, France, from 1252 to 1338, this 1973 Caldecott Honor Book shows the reader every step in the process of building a cathedral.

Buildings, Buildings, Buildings

After *Cathedral,* Macaulay continued his successful formula with *City: A Story of Roman Planning and Construction, Pyramid, Underground,* and *Castle.* All of these books describe in great detail the complicated processes behind great works of architecture. *City* differs from Macaulay's first book in that its focus is on urban planning as well as architecture. Asserting that "Roman . . . planning is the basis of any truly successful city," Macaulay shows how the organization of a Roman city is a model for efficient urban planning, and, in turn, that such planning fosters a happy citizenry. In *Pyramid* and *Castle,* Macaulay also creates imaginary structures to explain the procedures involved in their construction. *Underground* is somewhat different from his other early books in that the author takes his readers to a modern setting. For those people who have never taken the time to wonder about what goes on under the streets of their cities, Macaulay traces a labyrinth of pipes, tunnels, and piles to illustrate in a mere thirty-two pages the maze of construction that is hidden below the asphalt and concrete to help keep a city running.

As with Macaulay's first book, critics were impressed with all the instructive, easy-to-follow detail that the author and illustrator put into these books. Of *City,* a *New York Times Book Review* critic said, "Macaulay's book is as appealing and revealing as last year's 'Cathedral.'" And in a review of *Pyramid,* James Norsworthy wrote in *Catholic Library* that Macaulay transforms "a historical event into the true wonder which pyramids are." *Underground* was also lauded by reviewers. Alvin Eisenman, in a *Children's Book Showcase* review, said the author "has an exciting way of showing us all [the details of an underground system] in factual architectural drawings that somehow evoke the mood of science fiction." However, reviewers like *West Coast Review of Books* critic Barbara Karlin felt that *Underground* would not "attract as many readers as did [Macaulay's] three previous books." Karlin believed that the immense detail of the subterranean workings of a city would not be of much interest to a child who had not already set his or her heart on a future career as an engineer.

Despite the praise he has received, Macaulay is not without his detractors. In a *Times Literary Supplement* article, for example, W. H. Plommer picked at the flaws he saw in *City.* Among these, Plommer complained that the Latin inscriptions Macaulay puts on his buildings are sometimes grammatically incorrect; he also said that the "buildings around his forum are very crowded, with far too few surrounding courts"; Plommer further pointed out that the columns Macaulay depicts are Doric when they should be the more elaborate Corinthian; and there are several other minor points that the critic spotted as being in need of correction for historical accuracy. Plommer, however, admitted that these are relatively minor concerns—though ones that should be corrected. "The book is obviously a considerable enterprise," the critic stated. "David Macaulay draws everything clearly and honestly, and makes a special effort to elucidate technical processes. . . . His greatest strength, perhaps, is his almost Roman power of picturing complicated *ensembles* and making his pictures wholly convincing."

New Aspects Emerge in Macaulay's Books

Beginning with *Castle,* Macaulay uses more than just a straightforward approach to instructing readers on the wonders of architecture. Though *Castle* is at first similar to *Cathedral* and *Pyramid* in its approach, it ends not with the fortress's completion, but rather with its eventual destruction. Pointing out that the purpose of building the castle Macaulay depicts (military) is quite different from that of other structures, Jon Stott commented in *Children's Literature Association Quarterly* that it "is one of many bastions designed to subjugate the Welsh in the fifteenth century." But, even though the author writes that the castle "displays both superior strategical skill and the far-sightedness required for truly successful conquest," Stott noted that this statement in the early pages of the book is ironic. Its mission to help conquer the Welsh is ultimately a failure, and the castle is abandoned and falls into disrepair. "Interestingly," commented Stott, "eight of the book's last twelve pages deal with the Welsh attack" that almost overran the fortress. Stott also observed that the book's dedication reads: "to the past—farewell." "It is as if Macaulay found in the fifteenth century the end of the types of ideals that had led to the creation of the other works he has so admired."

Fittingly, Macaulay's *Unbuilding* is a lament and a complaint against "those of us who don't always appreciate things until they are gone," as the author writes in the book's dedication. In *Unbuilding* Macaulay imagines that a wealthy prince from the Near East has bought the Empire State Building with the plan to dismantle it brick by brick and then put it back together back in his homeland. Although this scenario is obviously fictitious, Eutsler speculated that it was inspired by the purchase 'of London Bridge, which was consequently shipped to America. So the idea proposed in this book is not unimaginable. Throughout the book, the author makes subtle criticisms against the values of today's society (grounded in a tunnel-vision interest in profit) versus those of the past as reflected in his earlier books. For example, the construction workers in *Unbuilding* are usually portrayed as being idle in comparison to the workers of ancient times; they are also blissfully unaware of what is going on around them, such as when Macaulay draws a picture of King Kong's hand in one illustration, but no one notices it. "The reference to King Kong is more than a visual joke," Stott pointed out. "It is an implicit comment on the modern world's failure to recognize the legends associated with its architectural monuments."

The ultimate irony in *Unbuilding*, however, is that the ship carrying the dismantled Empire State Building sinks before reaching its destination. The prince, however, is undaunted and makes plans to buy the Chrysler Building. Stott sees *Unbuilding* as a pessimistic work written by an author who finds much more to admire in the values of pre-Renaissance societies who built wonders that were for the glory of a people, rather than for pure economic reasons. In *Unbuilding* nothing is seen as permanent; nothing has any value beyond the dollar amount, a point made all the more poignant in the book's last scene in which the Statue of Liberty and the World Trade Center are surrounded by scaffolding. As Macaulay told *Contemporary Authors* interviewer Jean W. Ross, the lack of ingenuity in modern architecture is a symptom of the times. "These very big buildings are going up all over the place now, and it's just money, it's not even necessity—or if it is, it's necessity based on an erroneous set of values, in my view."

Macaulay's *Mill* is similarly a kind of paean to past values. The story begins with the construction of a wooden mill in Rhode Island in 1810. Macaulay shows how the iron and wood machinery of the mill are powered by a nearby river to

spin wool into thread for cloth. Two decades later, a stone mill powered by a water turbine is built across the river; another mill is completed in 1853, and it, in turn, becomes outdated when a mill powered by a steam engine is finished in 1872. But *Mill* does more than just describe the building of a succession of mills. Macaulay delves more deeply into the lives of the people who build these fictional mills, so the reader gets an intimate look at the day-to-day lives of people who lived in the nineteenth-century as they survive wars, economic depressions, and personal tragedies and triumphs. "In *Mill*," remarked Eutsler, "the reader has scanned through seventy years. . . . He has witnessed the hazards of small children working around the machinery and has seen some concern for the welfare of the worker. In addition, he has learned of many changes other than methods of building a mill." Eutsler later added, "Macaulay's ultimate purpose in the book is to provide the reader with a view of the life and times of a people in a small New England community."

Humor after the Cataclysm

Two books by Macaulay, *Motel of the Mysteries* and *BAAA*, again satirize contemporary society, though in a much different way than *Unbuilding* does. *Motel of the Mysteries* is set some two thousand years after North America has been destroyed overnight by a cataclysmic force that buried the continent. In the year 4022 A.D., an amateur archaeologist named Howard Carson falls into a shaft and discovers the many "wonders" of the past in the Toot'n'C'mon motel (a spoof of the tomb of King Tutankhamen.) Carson misidentifies various common objects like toilet seats and telephones, thinking they are religious and cult artifacts from a complex and mysterious society. The book, which was published in 1979, when an exhibit of the treasures of Tutankhamen was touring the United States, is a jab at the audacity the scientific community can demonstrate. Calling the book a "triumph," *Washington Post Book World* contributor Barbara Mertz wrote that *Motel of Mysteries* reminds "us of our human susceptibility to error."

Macaulay got the idea for *BAAA* one night while he was sleeping in a hotel room. He had been working on an idea for a book that would depict famous places with illustrations completely devoid of people. "Maybe it's a personal response to the neutron bomb," the author guessed in a *Saturday Review* article by Larry McCarthy; "I don't know." After having his sleep disturbed by a noise in the hallway, he couldn't get back to sleep. An idea began running through his head in which animals would come in and populate the cityscapes from which all the people had been erased. For some reason, the animals he picked were sheep, and the first draft of *BAAA* was written in a few days.

Macaulay imagines a depopulated city into which a flock of sheep wander. After some time, they learn to speak by watching VCR tapes, and then they begin to build a society similar to that of the humans who preceded them. Eventually, inevitably, the same problems that plagued humanity affect the sheep until they die out, too. The last scene shows a fish eyeing the empty city as possibly the next species to inherit it. Grimmer than *Motel of Mysteries*, *BAAA* is a very clear warning to humanity. Comparing it to such books as George Orwell's *Animal Farm* and Clifford Simak's *City*, *Washington Post Book World* critic Michael Dirda calls *BAAA* "an odd album, one that will appeal to thoughtful children even as it worries their parents." While some critics, such as one *Bulletin of the Center for Children's Books* reviewer, found the book "Pithy, hilarious, clever," others felt it was too pessimistic. *New York Times Book* review critic Judith Viorst wondered what sort of message Macaulay was trying to convey: "That the human race is composed of consumers and killers? That human beings, and any creatures adopting human characteristics, are doomed?" Viorst concluded, "Because David Macaulay's *Baaa* withholds all hope, I would not choose to buy it for children I love."

The Way Things Work

Although Macaulay had already built a successful career as an author and illustrator, he topped himself with his best-selling 1988 book, *The Way Things Work*. Written for people of all ages who are curious about the everyday conveniences they use, *The Way Things Work* explains not only the mechanics but also the physical principles behind mechanical devices of all kinds. *The Way Things Work* differs from the much drier technical books that have preceded it in two ways: Macaulay categorizes machines according to the physical principles by which they operate (the four sections in

Macaulay begins this unique 1993 work with a tale of archaeologists discovering the remains of a 500-year-old ship.

the book are entitled "The Mechanics of Movement," "Harnessing the Elements," "Working with Waves," and "Electrical and Automation"), and he adds a lot of whimsical humor to hold his readers' interest. Examples of the latter are the characters who make unexpected and amusing appearances to help illustrate various machines. Mary Poppins pops up in the demonstration of a radio telescope; angels fly about to enliven the text; and Macaulay created a wooly mammoth character who shows up in several places in the book and is tormented by a prehistoric inventor. "The mammoth came into the early sketches when I was trying to figure out how to present the simple mechanical machines . . .," Macaulay explained in a *Chicago Tribune* article. "He never quite left again. In retrospect he has become something of an empathetic victim of technology. I think we can relate to his trials and tribulations. The mammoth, the angels, the whimsy—I think it's all a natural response. My attention to detail and accuracy spills over to zaniness."

The combination of interesting information and fun spelled success for *The Way Things Work,* which reached an unexpected number three slot on the *New York Times* best-seller list. Reviewers gave it resounding praise. *New York Times Book Review* critic Mario Salvadori called the book "a superb achievement." And Faith McNulty, writing in *New Yorker,* said the book "approaches the subject with a great deal of humor, lots of amusing sketches, and sublime confidence in the reader's intelligence. A wonderful book for anyone, at any age, who really wants to know."

Macaulay spent a great deal of effort on the 384-page book. It took him and three other assistants four years—and much research—to produce. In a *Horn Book* article, Macaulay called the process of writing the book "rarely fun and often threatening. The deadlines were relentless, and no matter how much I completed there always seemed to be at least twice as much left to do. It was a challenging and exhausting task, and no one is more amazed than I am that the book ever got finished." The author consulted professional technical experts to help insure accuracy and to clarify things that he didn't understand well himself, such as the automatic transmission in a car. "It still stumps me!" Macaulay told Ross. "I have to look back at my own drawing and follow it very carefully to begin to understand [how it works]."

But in addition to the complex, *The Way Things Work* also explains simple things like nail clippers and lawn sprinklers. Understanding these devices is a valuable pursuit for anyone, Macaulay maintained. "We're surrounded by clever things that are really signs of human inventiveness. We are clever folks, and we need to be reminded of that; then maybe we'll use our cleverness more effectively in different ways. We seem to have developed blind spots, and certainly one of them is towards technology. It's our creation, and here we are becoming intimidated by this thing we've created, theoretically to make life more enjoyable or more satisfying. We create all these things, and then we think of ourselves as being too stupid to understand them. If *The Way Things Work* does

anything, I hope it says to readers, You can figure it out."

In 1994, publisher Dorling Kindersley released a multimedia CD-ROM version of *The Way Things Work* for children in grades four through eight. At first, Macaulay was skeptical of putting his book on CD. "I've always been very leery of what I consider spinoff products," he told Renee Olson in *School Library Journal.* "I don't like the idea of simply taking advantage of something's success and producing 10 slightly different variations on the theme." But curiosity got the better of him, and he agreed to the project. He was pleased with the results, especially the ability to hyperlink, which accentuated the relations between types of machines that he tried to create in the book, and the animations, which helped to illustrate mechanical principles. Still, when asked whether he would recommend the book or the CD (which actually contains only eighty percent of the book's informational content), Macaulay chose the former. "I think I would recommend the book because I feel strongly that the book does what I want it to do. The CD is a translation, it's an interpretation of the book. I don't have enough information to be able to back this up one way or the other, but if the entertaining aspects of the CD-ROM are overwhelming, then the information is going to be shortchanged, and that's a negative." As he told Joseph O. Holmes in *Publishers Weekly,* "In the end, it doesn't matter what the medium is. The content is of primary importance."

The Caldecott Medal

Macaulay followed the success of *The Way Things Work* with yet another success, *Black and White,* which earned him his first Caldecott Medal. *Black and White* is a book that demands its reader's attention. Each page is broken into four pictures, each in a different illustrative style and each telling its own story; yet the four stories are also—upon closer inspection—connected. The process of creating *Black and White,* the author said in his Caldecott Medal acceptance speech, "is perhaps best described as an example of visual Darwinism; it took almost as long to evolve as it did for monkeys to walk upright and run for office." The book broke many of the conventions of children's picture books, and Macaulay was rather surprised that such an unconventional work would be selected for the award. In his speech, he therefore

---

If you enjoy the works of David Macaulay, you may want to check out the following:

Ivan Banyai, *Zoom* (1995) and *Re-zoom* (1995).

The works of Maurice Sendak, who served as an inspiration for Macaulay.

The books of Chris Van Allsburg, including *Jumanji* (1981) and *The Mysteries of Harris Burdick* (1984).

---

thanked the Caldecott Committee for taking a chance and making a statement. "And when *committees* start taking chances, we all have reason to hope."

The next book Macaulay published, *Ship*, at first seems like a step backwards for the author (he returns to the formula of his early work by describing the process of construction—this time, it is a boat), but there is much more to this book than that. *Ship* begins with a team of archaeologists discovering the remains of a five-hundred-year-old ship called a caravel. Macaulay, using information compiled by historians and archaeologists, then reconstructs the caravel to show what it probably looked like, even though a real caravel has never been found. The second half of the book takes the reader to the year 1405, where the reader meets the fictional Spanish merchant who had the boat constructed and learns through his diaries all about the undertaking. "Though Macaulay barely portrays the actual voyage," commented one *Publishers Weekly* reviewer, "he has nonetheless crafted an exciting story." Jane O'Reilly, writing in the *New York Times Book Review*, concluded that "Macaulay has once again established a collusion between author and reader that carries his work into another dimension, far beyond the mere presentation of interesting material."

Humor once again reigns in Macaulay's 1995 book, *Shortcut*. Combining the silliness of the earlier *Why the Chicken Crossed the Road*, which suggested possible reasons behind this puzzle, and the nonlinear interconnectedness of *Black and White*, Macaulay makes a simple trip to the market a comical adventure. Albert takes his horse June on a trip to sell melons at the market. He decides to take a shortcut, and some of the innocent things they do along the way (such as untying a rope that is in their path—the same rope that is keeping Professor Tweet's hot-air balloon anchored) lead to chaos for other people. For example, when Tweet throws ballast out of his balloon after unexpectedly getting untied, the ballast sinks Bob's boat. Throughout the nine chapters, Macaulay shows how every event is interconnected and adds humor in the blissful unawareness Albert and June have toward all the havoc they cause. Calling *Shortcut* a book "reminiscent of old two-reelers where the comedian remains innocent of the hazards in his wake," *Bulletin of the Center for Children's Books* critic Deborah Stevenson praised Macaulay's line-and-watercolor illustrations and said kids would be sure to enjoy the story.

Although Macaulay's work varies between the flights of fancy shown in books like *Shortcut* to his highly informative nonfiction work, they are all imbued with a sense of humor. More importantly, however, all of Macaulay's work invites readers to see more deeply into the world around them. The author is concerned that modern technological society, with all its work-saving conveniences and easily accessed entertainments, is robbing people of their sense of awareness. In the 1990 *Horn Book* article, he called this "the age of the cover-up. We are encouraged less and less to see into things, to see the way things—political and mechanical—really work. This is where I come in. In studying architecture, I learned to see things from the inside out. . . . I've spent a great deal of time trying to create pictures that teach, that explain while entertaining. . . . *The Way Things Work* encourages us to believe we can reassert our control over an increasingly technological world, one we have too long taken for granted and upon which we have become frighteningly dependent." In all his books, Macaulay implores us above all else to *see* what is around us. "[As] soon as not seeing becomes a habit," he warned in his Caldecott speech, "we start accepting our visual environment without question. As technology becomes increasingly more complex, we are less and less able to actually see how things work. . . . Visual complacency rears its ugly head, and each time it does we humans lose a little ground."

■ Works Cited

Anderson, Valerie, "A Sense of Size and Space," *Times Educational Supplement*, September 10, 1976.

Review of *BAAA, Bulletin of the Center for Children's Books,* September, 1985, p. 13.

Dirda, Michael, review of *BAAA, Washington Post Book World,* September 8, 1985, p. 9.

Eisenman, Alvin, review of *Underground, Children's Book Showcase,* 1977.

Eutsler, Nellvena Duncan, "David Macaulay," *Dictionary of Literary Biography,* Volume 61, Gale, 1987, pp. 177-88.

Garfield, Leon, review of *Cathedral: The Story of Its Construction, Spectator,* September 14, 1974.

Hoare, Geoffrey, "The Work of David Macaulay," *Children's Literature in Education,* spring, 1977, pp. 12-20.

Holmes, Joseph O., "Making the Leap to CD-ROM," *Publishers Weekly,* October 31, 1994, p. 24.

Karlin, Barbara, review of *Underground, West Coast Review of Books,* January, 1977.

Macaulay, David, *City: A Story of Roman Planning and Construction,* Houghton, 1974.

Macaulay, David, *Castle,* Houghton, 1977.

Macaulay, David, in an article about *The Way Things Work, Chicago Tribune,* December 14, 1988.

Macaulay, David, "The Way Things Work," *Horn Book,* January, 1990, pp. 24-27.

Macaulay, David, interview with Jean W. Ross, *Contemporary Authors New Revision Series,* Volume 34, Gale, 1991, pp. 280-86.

Macaulay, David, "Caldecott Medal Acceptance," *Horn Book,* July, 1991, pp. 410-21.

McCarthy, Larry, "Bright Lights—Big Season: David Macaulay," *Saturday Review,* September-October, 1985, pp. 36-37.

McNulty, Faith, review of *The Way Things Work, New Yorker,* December 12, 1988.

Mertz, Barbara, review of *Motel of Mysteries, Washington Post Book World,* October 7, 1979, pp. 9, 14.

Norsworthy, James, review of *Pyramid, Catholic Library,* April, 1976.

Olson, Renee, "David Macaulay Talks about the Problems and the Promise of CD-ROM," *School Library Journal,* May, 1995, pp. 23-26.

O'Reilly, Jane, "The Way Things Work Underwater," *New York Times Book Review,* November 14, 1993, p. 23.

Peck, Richard, review of *City: A Story of Roman Planning and Construction, New York Times Book Review,* October 6, 1974.

Plommer, W. H., "Lovingly Reconstructed," *Times Literary Supplement,* December 5, 1975, p. 1458.

Salvadori, Mario, review of *The Way Things Work, New York Times Book Review,* December 18, 1988.

Review of *Ship, Publishers Weekly,* September 27, 1993, p. 63.

Stevenson, Deborah, review of *Shortcut, Bulletin of the Center for Children's Books,* September, 1995, p. 21.

Stott, Jon, "Architectural Structures and Social Values in the Nonfiction of David Macaulay," *Children's Literature Association Quarterly,* spring, 1983, pp. 15-17.

Van Allsburg, Chris, "David Macaulay: The Early Years," *Horn Book,* July, 1991, pp. 422-25.

Viorst, Judith, review of *BAAA, New York Times Book Review,* December 1, 1985, p. 38.

■ For More Information See

BOOKS

Children's Literature Review, Gale, Volume 3, 1978, Volume 14, 1988.

Holtze, Sally Holmes, editor, *Fifth Book of Junior Authors and Illustrators,* H. W. Wilson, 1983.

Kingman, Lee, editor, *Newbery and Caldecott Medal Books: 1976-1985,* Horn Book, 1986.

Moss, Elaine, *Children's Books of the Year 1974,* Hamish Hamilton, 1975.

Purves, Alan C., and Dianne L. Monson, *Experiencing Children's Literature,* Scott, Foresman, 1984.

Sutherland, Zena, and May Hill Arbuthnot, *Children and Books,* Scott, Foresman, 1986.

PERIODICALS

Booklist, September 1, 1985, p. 53; October 15, 1993, p. 437; February 1, 1995, p. 1020.

Bulletin of the Center for Children's Books, January, 1974, p. 81; December, 1974, pp. 65-66; January, 1980, pp. 99-100.

Growing Point, November, 1975.

Horn Book, October, 1973; October, 1974, p. 149; December, 1975; February, 1977; October, 1977, p. 544; December, 1980, p. 655; December, 1983, p. 726.

Junior Bookshelf, February, 1975; February, 1976, p. 50; August, 1984, p. 177.

Kirkus Reviews, August 1, 1974, p. 807; September 1, 1975, p. 1001; August 15, 1976.

Language Arts, May, 1976, p. 503; April, 1982, pp. 374-78.

Library Journal, January, 1995, pp. 147-48.

Literature Association Quarterly, winter, 1981, p. 27.

Los Angeles Times Book Review, January 7, 1996, p. 15.

New York Magazine, December 16, 1974, pp. 108, 111.

New York Times Book Review, December 16, 1973; October 5, 1975; November 13, 1977, p. 38; December 9, 1979, pp. 15-16; November 9, 1980, pp. 54, 67-68; September 25, 1983, p. 29; November 13, 1994, p. 56.

Publishers Weekly, September 10, 1973, p. 52; August 25, 1975, p. 294; July 26, 1976, p. 79; July 4, 1977, p. 77; July 17, 1995, p. 228.

Saturday Review, September 16, 1978, p. 49.

School Librarian, March, 1977; June, 1978, pp. 176, 179.

School Library Journal, December, 1973, p. 50; October, 1974; October, 1975; October, 1983, p. 160; January, 1995, p. 52; September, 1995, p. 182.

Time, December 8, 1975, p. 88.

Times Literary Supplement, July 23, 1982, p. 797.

Top of the News, April, 1974, p. 247.

Voice of Youth Advocates, February, 1995, pp. 367-68.

Washington Post Book Review, November 13, 1977, p. E2; November 9, 1980, p. 12; September 8, 1985, p. 9.

Wilson Library Bulletin, November, 1975, p. 195.

—Sketch by Janet L. Hile

Carson McCullers

genheim fellow, 1942, 1946; National Institute of Arts and Letters grant in literature, 1943; New York Drama Critics' Circle Award, Donaldson Annual Award for Best Drama, and Gold Medal from Theatre Club for best playwright of the year, 1950, all for *The Member of the Wedding*; Prize of the Younger Generation from German newspaper *Die Welt*, 1965, for *The Heart Is a Lonely Hunter*; University of Mississippi grant, 1966; Bellamann award, 1967.

■ Personal

Born Lula Carson Smith February 19, 1917, in Columbus, GA; died of complications resulting from a stroke, September 29, 1967, in Nyack, NY; daughter of Lamar (a jeweler) and Marguerite (maiden name, Waters) Smith; married Reeves McCullers, Jr. (aspiring novelist), September 20, 1937 (divorced, 1940); remarried McCullers, March 19, 1945 (committed suicide, 1953). *Education:* Attended Columbia University and New York University, 1935-36. *Hobbies:* Listening to records.

■ Career

Held various jobs during her twenties to support herself while taking college classes in creative writing. However, McCullers explained, "I was always fired. My record is perfect on that. I never quit a job in my life." *Member:* American Academy of Arts and Letters (fellow).

■ Award, Honors

Fiction fellowship, Houghton Mifflin, 1939; Bread Loaf Writers Conference fellowship, 1940; Gug-

■ Writings

NOVELS

The Heart Is a Lonely Hunter, Houghton, 1940, Random House, 1993.
Reflections in a Golden Eye, Houghton, 1941, New Directions, 1950, Bantam Books, 1991.
The Member of the Wedding, Houghton and Cresset Press, 1946.
Clock Without Hands, Houghton and Cresset Press, 1961.

SHORT STORIES

Wunderkind, originally published in *Story,* 1936.
Madame Zilensky and the King of Finland, first published in *New Yorker,* 1941.
A Tree, a Rock, a Cloud, first published in *Harper's Bazaar,* 1942, Creative Education, 1990.
The Ballad of the Sad Cafe (a novella first published serially in *Harper's Bazaar,* 1943), published as *The Ballad of the Sad Cafe: The Novels and Stories*

of Carson McCullers, Houghton, 1951, Cresset, 1952.

The Sojourner, first published in *Mademoiselle,* 1950.

A Domestic Dilemma, first published in *New York Post,* 1951.

Seven, Bantam, 1954.

Sucker, illustrated by James Hays, first published in *Saturday Evening Post,* 1963, Creative Education, 1986.

COLLECTED WORKS

The Ballad of the Sad Cafe: The Novels and Stories of Carson McCullers, Houghton, 1951, Cresset, 1952, published as *The Ballad of the Sad Cafe and Other Stories,* Bantam, 1991.

Collected Short Stories and the Novel, The Ballad of the Sad Cafe, Houghton, 1955.

The Mortgaged Heart: The Previously Uncollected Writings of Carson McCullers, edited by Margarita Smith, Houghton, 1971.

Collected Stories, Houghton, 1987.

OTHER

(Lyricist) *The Twisted Trinity* (opera), music by David Diamond, Elkan Vogel, 1946.

(Author of adaption) *The Member of the Wedding: A Play,* produced in Philadelphia, 1949, New York, 1950, London, 1957, New Directions, 1951.

The Square Root of Wonderful (play), produced in Princeton, New Jersey, and New York, 1957, London, 1970, Houghton and Cresset Press, 1958, Cherokee Publishing Company, 1990.

Carson McCullers Reads from "The Member of the Wedding" and Other Works (audiotape), Metro-Goldwyn-Mayer, 1958.

Sweet as a Pickle and Clean as a Pig (children's poetry), illustrated by Rolf Gerard, Houghton, 1964, J. Cape, 1965.

Contributor to *Vogue, Harper's Bazaar, Mademoiselle, Botteghe Oscure,* and other magazines. A manuscript collection of McCuller's is housed at the Humanities Research Center at the University of Texas, Houston.

■ Adaptations

Member of the Wedding, Columbia Pictures, 1952, and USA Network, 1997; *Reflections in a Golden Eye,* Seven Arts Production, 1967; *The Heart Is a Lonely Hunter,* Warners-Seven Arts, 1968; and *The Ballad of the Sad Cafe,* Merchant Ivory, 1991, have been adapted for motion pictures. *The Sojourner* was adapted for two different television plays: *The Invisible Wall,* "Omnibus," CBS-TV, 1953, and *The Sojourner,* NBC-TV, 1964. *The Ballad of the Sad Cafe* was adapted as a play by Edward Albee (McCullers was the author of narration) and produced in New York, 1963, Atheneum, 1963.

■ Sidelights

Along with such contemporaries as Tennessee Williams and Flannery O'Connor, Carson McCullers is considered a leading author of the American Southern literary tradition. While McCullers is best known as a novelist, she also mastered other genres including the short story, poetry, and drama. Her importance to American literature was established with the publication of her first novel *The Heart Is a Lonely Hunter* in 1940 when McCullers was twenty-three years old. Before reaching the age of thirty, she wrote two other major novels—*Reflections in a Golden Eye* in 1941 and *The Member of the Wedding* in 1946. Written within a period of six years, each of these three novels sold over half a million copies. McCullers's play adaptation of *The Member of the Wedding* won several drama awards and eventually all of her first three novels became successful films. Perhaps her most critically acclaimed work was a novella entitled *The Ballad of the Sad Cafe,* originally published in *Harper's Bazaar* in 1943 and adapted as a drama by Edward Albee in 1963. More recently, Keith Carridine and Vanessa Redgrave starred in the 1991 movie adaptation of *The Ballad of the Sad Cafe.*

Born and raised in Georgia, McCullers's stories are deeply rooted in her southern background and contain themes about spiritual isolation and the loneliness of the individual. McCullers's writings poignantly capture the painful solitude of the human heart, especially in situations involving troubled adolescence, racial and gender bigotry, and homosexuality. Her alienated and sometimes bizarre or grotesque characters symbolize man's essential isolation and the failure of communication. In "The Flowering Dream: Notes on Writing," McCullers explained that "spiritual isolation is the basis of most of my themes. My first book was concerned with this, almost entirely, and all of my books since, in one way or another. Love, and especially love of a person who is incapable of returning or receiving it, is at the heart of my selection of grotesque figures to write about—people whose physical incapacity is a symbol of their spiritual incapacity to love or receive love—their spiritual isolation."

McCullers viewed all of her major works as southern, believing that an author's voice reflects his or her birthplace. Choosing to set all of her novels in Georgia, McCullers felt "the voices reheard from childhood have a truer pitch. And the foliage—the trees of childhood—are remembered more exactly." When she did try to set a story someplace other than the south, she would "have to wonder what the time the flowers are in bloom—and what flowers?" In order to maintain the truest voice possible, she "hardly let characters speak unless they are Southern."

Musical Influences

McCullers infused her writing with the emotional energy of her own troubled life. Growing up in the small town of Columbus, Georgia, McCullers was deeply influenced by her mother, Marguerite Smith. Smith believed that her daughter was a genius and destined to become famous. Encouraged by her mother, McCullers began taking piano lessons at the age of five and regularly practiced eight hours a day throughout her childhood and adolescence. This isolation from her peers helped reinforce her feeling that she was different from others. Also, McCullers grew to become a tall young woman—5' 8 ½" by the time she was thirteen years old—which contributed to her sense of being freakish. In the *Concise Dictionary of American Literary Biography*, the literary scholar Robert Kiernan observed that "the considerable freedom and the constant approval that her mother gave her produced an effect of aloofness and eccentricity in her behavior that was greeted by Columbus adolescents with catcalls of 'Freak.'"

Convinced that she was to have a famous career in music, McCullers left Columbus for New York City in 1934 at the age of seventeen. She originally intended to study at the Julliard School of Music, but lost her tuition money on the New York subway. Abandoning her career as a concert pianist, McCullers enrolled in writing classes at Columbia University and New York University and supported herself with part-time jobs typing, clerking, and waiting on tables. It was during this period that one of her teachers helped her publish her first short story in *Story* magazine. This autobiographical work entitled "Wunderkind" tells of a teenager's realization that she is not a musical prodigy after years of playing the piano. The young female protagonist Frances is unable to interpret feeling in music despite long hours of practice. When she subsequently ends her music lessons, she also loses her circle of musical friends and her parent's special treatment. The story's sense of adolescent loss and insecurity reappear in later works by McCullers including her first novel, *The Heart Is a Lonely Hunter*, published three years after her marriage to the aspiring novelist Reeves McCullers.

While McCullers never acknowledged the influence of her mother on her work, McCullers did often attribute her sense of literary form to her early study of musical structure. In fact, she outlined *The Heart Is a Lonely Hunter* for her publisher using musical rather than literary terms, as if the story were a symphony. According to the Kiernan, McCullers described the organization of the story to her publisher in this manner: "Like a voice in a fugue, each one of the main characters is an entity in himself—but his personality takes on a new richness when contrasted and woven in with the other characters in the book."

Kiernan described *The Heart Is a Lonely Hunter* as "a fable about inescapable loneliness." Set in a small southern town similar to McCullers's hometown in Georgia, the novel tells the story of a deaf mute named John Singer. The ironically named Singer finds himself the confidante of four disparate townspeople—a radical white, a disillusioned black physician, a childless widower, and a gawky twelve-year old girl named Mick Kelly. One by one each of the characters share their dreams and frustrations with Singer, believing he understands and cares about them. But in reality, Singer seldom comprehends their intellectual rambles and is actually devoted to another male mute, Spiros Antonapoulos.

The character Mick Kelly represents McCullers's own adolescence. Much like McCullers, the tomboy Mick is obsessively preoccupied with music and dreams of escaping the small town to travel and become a composer. Pressed into caring for her younger siblings by her busy, distracted mother, Mick still manages to come in contact with music. She hides under windows at night listening to her neighbors' radios and even builds a violin from a cigar box. Eventually her family's poverty forces her to quit school and take a job at a dime store. Forced to abandon her ambitions, Mick's decision to help support her family symbolizes the death of her dreams and individuality.

In addition to the painful isolation related to gender discrimination and the effects of poverty, McCullers also explores the troubling issue of racial inequality in *The Heart Is a Lonely Hunter*. The character Dr. Copeland, a black physician, per-

ceives himself to be a failure because he has not fulfilled his dream of leading the struggle for racial reform. While Copeland knows he has helped his fellow blacks countless times as a doctor, he is disappointed that he has not changed their lives in a more meaningful way. Through Copeland's private and public musings on the true purpose of his life's mission, McCullers compels the reader to examine the pattern of racial prejudice in American culture.

Richard Wright, the black American novelist, praised McCullers's perspective and portrayal of American blacks in *The Heart Is a Lonely Hunter*. In his 1940 article, "Inner Landscape" for the *New Republic*, Wright commented that to him the most impressive aspect of the novel "is the astonishing humanity that enables a white writer, for the first time in Southern fiction, to handle Negro characters with as much ease and justice as those of her own race. This cannot be accounted for stylistically or politically; it seems to stem from an attitude toward life which enables Miss McCullers to rise above the pressures of her environment and embrace white and black humanity in one sweep of apprehension and tenderness."

McCullers also approaches the subject of homosexuality in *The Heart Is a Lonely Hunter* through the relationship between the two deaf-mutes John Singer and Spiros Antonapoulos. When Antonapoulos becomes hospitalized, the reader witnesses tender scenes involving Singer's loving preparation of gifts to take to his companion. After Antonapoulos dies, Singer, who is unable to bear the pain of his friend's death, commits suicide. To the other characters, who are forced to continue their lives without the essential emotional outlet Singer unknowingly provided, Singer's death is incomprehensible.

An acclaimed best-seller, *The Heart Is a Lonely Hunter* established McCullers's reputation as a leading American novelist. Many critics have characterized McCullers as belonging to the Southern Gothic school of literature. In 1957 reviewer Jane Hart described this school in the *Georgia Review* as "unconsciously established by William Faulkner, a school supposedly concerned with the grotesque and the abnormal, with an outlandish love for the morbid." However Hart emphasized that McCullers had a "tenderness" of seeing that gives her writing "the air of simple, star-like purity and beauty, the truth and humility of one who has

McCuller's debut novel, a harrowing tale of human isolation and loneliness, concerns five troubled individuals living in a small southern town.

Sondra Locke and Alan Arkin starred in the 1968 film adaptation of *The Heart Is a Lonely Hunter*.

learned to love . . . all mankind." Hart believed that the novel is "about the loneliness of all men, abnormal or normal, deformed or whole" and that if McCullers "used the grotesque it is because the loneliest of all human souls is found in the abnormal and deformed, the outward and manifest symbol of human separateness."

A Controversial Novel

McCullers's second novel, *Reflections in a Golden Eye*, did not meet the critical expectations raised by the success of her first novel. Written in 1939 during a troubled period in McCullers's life, many critics regard this novel as a reaction to her failing marriage to Reeves McCullers. While the couple's marriage was often unstable, it further

declined when they relocated from New York City to Fayetteville, North Carolina, where Reeves was stationed in the military. After Reeves had taken a male lover and McCullers also found a female lover, the couple divorced in 1940. McCullers published *Reflections in a Golden Eye* in 1941 with a dedication to Annemarie Clarac-Schwarzenbach, a lover she met after completing the novel.

The story is set on an army base, and as McCullers herself said in the book, the characters include two officers, a soldier, two women, a Filipino, and a horse. Captain Penderton, a sadomasochist, experiences latent homosexual yearnings for the inarticulate Private Williams while Penderton's wife, Leonora, is having an affair with Major Langdon. Langdon's wife Alison, a deranged recluse grieving the death of her deformed child, befriends the homosexual houseboy Ana-cleto. The unfulfilled spiritual and physical needs of these archetypical characters eventually leads to self-destructive and violent behavior.

Many contemporary critics gave the novel negative reviews due to the unsympathetic characterizations and unorthodox subject matter. Basil Davenport, in his 1941 review of *Reflections in a Golden Eye* for the *Saturday Review of Literature,* remarked that "the story is a vipers'-knot of neurasthenic relationships among characters whom the author seems hardly to comprehend, and of whose perversions she can create nothing." He went on to explain that "such a collection of sick and unnatural souls could become the stuff of tragedy only if handled with the greatest comprehension, and woven into a pattern which gave some logical conclusion to the bent of each character. Neither of these conditions is here fulfilled."

However several other prominent contemporary critics saw remarkable qualities in McCullers controversial second novel. In his introduction to the 1950 reprinting of *Reflections in a Golden Eye,* Tennessee Williams commented that this work "is one of the purest and most powerful of those works which are conceived in that Sense of The Awful which is the desperate black root of nearly all significant modern Art, from the *Guenica* of Picasso to the cartoons of Charles Addams." Williams gave McCullers a significant compliment when he wrote "I have found in her work, such intensity and nobility of spirit as we have not had in prose-writing since Herman Melville."

More recent critics have also praised the intensity and candor of *Reflections in a Golden Eye.* Pamela Bigelow commented in *Gay & Lesbian Literature* that McCullers's second novel "challenges American society's insistence on the inviolable sanctity of heterosexual marriage by revealing the dysfunctional underside of that institution." In fact, McCullers's insightful and painful view from within a damaging relationship foreshadowed Edward Albee's examination of marital despair and destruction in the 1962 classic *Who's Afraid of Virginia Woolf.* However, Bigelow also noted: "In retrospect, it is amazing that McCullers's popularity survived the publication of *Reflections in a Golden Eye,* which offered readers no sympathetic characters or relationships to ameliorate the shock value of its focus on Captain Penderton's sexual obsessions with Private Williams."

In the *Concise Dictionary of American Literary Biography,* literary scholar Kiernan speculated about why *Reflections in a Golden Eye* failed in comparison to McCullers's other work. He suggested that she attempted something "beyond her—to philosophize about persons in a military world." By writing about a situation she wasn't familiar with, McCullers may have created a falseness to her story. In his essay, Kiernan cited an example of McCullers's resistance to relying on literal facts in her creative writing. Apparently while working on *The Heart Is a Lonely Hunter,* she refused "to attend a convention of deaf-mutes with Reeves . . . because she did not want her imaginative concept of a mute destroyed." Throughout her writing career, McCullers preferred an imaginative concept of reality over facts.

Rebounds after Stroke

In 1941, the same year McCullers published *Reflections in a Golden Eye,* she suffered her first cerebral stroke during a vacation to her hometown Columbus, Georgia. Even though Reeves and McCullers had divorced in 1940, they remained in contact throughout their lives and it was Reeves who brought McCullers back to New York City. During this time she became close friends with the poet Muriel Rukeyser. Through Rukeyser, McCullers met and fell in love with David Diamond, the composer and musician. They eventually collaborated together on the opera *Twisted Trinity,* with McCullers writing the lyrics and Diamond composing the music.

Shortly after her first stroke, McCullers also befriended Elizabeth Ames, the executive director of the Yaddo artists' colony in Saratoga Springs, New York. Ames invited McCullers to be a guest at Yaddo during the summer of 1941. Over the years, McCullers returned many times to Yaddo, believing she did her best work there. During her first visit, she completed the novella *The Ballad of the Sad Cafe,* which many critics regard as her most outstanding achievement. Originally published serially in *Harper's Bazaar* in 1943, the novella was then published in book form in the 1951 omnibus volume *The Ballad of the Sad Cafe: The Novels and Stories of Carson McCullers.* While this book sold well and received many favorable reviews, critics singled out *The Ballad of the Sad Cafe* as being the most significant work in the volume. In fact, in his introduction to the volume, Tennessee

Williams viewed it as "assuredly among the masterpieces of our language."

Often considered to be the most accomplished work of McCullers's entire career, *The Ballad of the Sad Cafe* effectively blends realism and fantasy to create a type of southern folklore. The story revolves around Amelia Evans, a large woman who falls in love with a hunchbacked dwarf and con-man named Lymon. Inspired by this love, Amelia undergoes a transformation and opens a flourishing cafe in her small southern town. But when Amelia's handsome ex-husband Macy returns home following his release from prison, Lymon

HER FAMOUS NOVEL OF
A YOUNG GIRL SEARCHING FOR A WAY OUT OF
A DARK, CONFUSING WORLD

CARSON McCULLERS

THE MEMBER OF THE WEDDING

Twelve-year-old Frankie grows jealous of her brother's impending marriage in this 1946 work.

falls in love with him. Together the two men attack Amelia, destroy her cafe, and then leave town. After losing her lover, Amelia closes her cafe and withdraws from life.

Critics view McCullers's story about this strange and tragic love triangle to be her richest exploration of human isolation and love as an intensifier of loneliness. Once again McCullers relies upon physically deformed characters to suggest the human inability to give or receive love. While her characters are extreme, even grotesque, and their actions bizarre, there is a mythic beauty that encompasses the whole story. Albert Griffith observed in the *Georgia Review*, that the lyricism of McCullers's narrative style in *The Ballad of the Sad Cafe* "can render even sordid subject matter in poetic terms." Griffith believed that the mythic quality is conveyed by the presence of a narrator who transforms the story and that "in context, the grotesqueness remains but is turned towards a purpose, becomes part of a whole which is not grotesque, transcends the human and moves into the numinous."

Kiernan also observed that McCullers incorporates several important stylistic elements including "many traditional ballad motifs, such as natural and supernatural signs mirroring human events" and "characters who take their keynote from animals and birds." He noted that her success in controlling her unusual characters and plot is largely due to her use of an anonymous narrator who "with his quaint, storytelling language . . . casts the aura of folklore over the tale: the characters become archetypes in his hands rather than grotesques, and their story becomes something elemental, mysterious, and suggestive."

In writing *The Ballad of the Sad Cafe*, McCullers may have drawn from her own personal experiences with complicated love relationships. During her life, two different individuals threatened her continued intimacy with her former husband Reeves. Her female lover Annemarie Clarac-Schwarzenbach formed an alliance with Reeves, which greatly concerned and upset McCullers. Also, a few years later she discovered that Reeves had fallen deeply in love with her male lover David Diamond. Since Reeves and Diamond lived together in Rochester, New York while she was away at Yaddo for the summer, she feared she would be excluded much like Amelia suffered from the union of Lymon and Macy.

In 1946 at the age of twenty nine, McCullers finished and published *The Member of the Wedding*, which would become her last successful novel. McCullers had started work on this story as early as 1940, stopping numerous times to work on short stories. In fact, she wrote *The Ballad of the Sad Cafe* on one of her breaks from working on the manuscript for *The Member of the Wedding*. She completed her third novel with the support of a Guggenheim Fellowship, a National Institute of Arts and Letters grant, and summer fellowships at Yaddo between 1942 and 1945. Many critics who had been offended by the scandalous nature of her previous novel *Reflections in a Golden Eye*, praised McCullers for her exploration of the alienation and loneliness of the individual.

Much like in her first novel, *The Heart Is a Lonely Hunter*, McCullers uses characters in a symbolic manner to portray the issue of human isolation. Instead of focusing on broader social issues, McCullers dramatizes the effects of isolation on the individual in this story about a lonely adolescent girl named Frankie Addams. Feeling very much alone in the world, Frankie—a gawky tomboy much like Mick Kelly in *The Heart Is a Lonely Hunter*—confides in the family cook Berenice Sadie Brown and her six-year-old cousin John Henry West. She yearns to escape her mundane life and begins to fantasize about joining her older brother's upcoming wedding. Her conversations with Berenice and John Henry encompass many topics including sexuality, racial prejudice, and death. When Frankie's father stops her from joining her brother and his fiancee on their honeymoon, she undergoes a transformation from tomboy to precocious feminine teenager. Frankie changes her name to Frances, thus signifying the process of denying one's true self in order to accommodate society's expectations of a young woman.

Many critics view *The Member of the Wedding* to be McCullers's most accessible and realistic novel. Kiernan commented that in all of her work, McCullers strove to write what she herself described as "a lyric tragi-comedy in which the funniness and grief coexist in the same line." In his review of her writing, he felt that she most completely realized this goal in *The Member of the Wedding*. In her article "Carson McCullers's Tomboys" published in the *Southern Humanities Review*, Louise Westling applauded McCullers creation of "the wistful boy-girl" character. Westling remarked

that Mick Kelly and Frankie Addams "are *girls* who share artistic temperaments and serious ambitions." Their dreams "set them apart from other girls in their Southern towns, who spend their time reading movie magazines, primping, and having parties with boys." Through the characters of Mick and Frankie, McCullers "dramatizes the crisis of identity which faces ambitious girls as they leave childhood and stumble into an understanding of what the world expects them to become."

From Book to Stage to Screen

McCullers successfully adapted the novel *The Member of the Wedding* for the stage. Her life long friend Tennessee Williams first suggested she undertake the adaptation during their summer together at Nantucket, Massachusetts, in 1946. After critic Edmund Wilson commented that *The Member of the Wedding* contained "no element of drama at all," in his article "Two Books that Leave You Blank: Carson McCullers, Siegfried Sassoon" for the *New Yorker*, McCullers responded to her friend's suggestion by completing the first draft of the play by the end of the year. Unfortunately a series of strokes made it necessary for her to dictate revisions from her sickbed. By creating a stylistically innovative play, McCullers successfully retained the story's original theme and mood. Many critics noted it as being among the few successful dramatic adaptations of a novelist's own work. *The Member of the Wedding* ran for 501 performances and won the New York Drama Critics' Circle Award for best play of 1950. She sold the screenplay rights to Hollywood for $75,000, which made her financially secure for the first time in her life.

McCullers remarried Reeves in 1945, but their relationship became increasingly turbulent and violent. With her health progressively declining, McCullers attempted suicide in 1948. While her failed attempt renewed her commitment to live, her husband became increasingly suicidal and began to propose a double suicide to McCullers. During their travels in Europe in 1952 and 1953 McCullers grew terrified for her own safety and fled back to the United States. After Reeves committed suicide in a Paris hotel with an overdose of sleeping pills, McCullers refused to bring his body home for burial or even pay for the cost of having his ashes sent home.

If you enjoy the works of Carson Mc-
Cullers, you may want to check out the
following books:

Joanne Greenberg, *Of Such Small Differences,*
1988.
Elizabeth Kata, *A New Patch of Blue,* 1983.
Bette Greene, *The Drowning of Stephen Jones,*
1991.

Upon her return to the United States, McCullers
lived in Nyack, New York with her mother, Marguerite Smith. Tragedy continued to plague
McCullers, who was devastated by the death of
Smith in 1955. In her last play *The Square Root of
Wonderful,* McCullers attempts to reconcile her feelings of loss, guilt, and hostility surrounding the
death of Reeves and her mother. Critics considered *The Square Root of Wonderful,* which was produced in New York in 1957, as one of McCullers
least successful works. Her last novel *Clock without Hands* also received little critical praise when
it appeared in 1961. McCullers spent the last years
of her life in constant physical agony and under-
went numerous surgical procedures including surgery for breast cancer. Following a massive stroke,
McCullers died in Nyack in 1967 at the age of
fifty.

Although severe illness plagued McCullers throughout her life and greatly limited her
productivity after age thirty, she solidly secured
her place in American literature with the masterpieces she wrote while in her twenties. In her classic stories such as *The Heart Is a Lonely Hunter,
The Ballad of the Sad Cafe,* and *The Member of the
Wedding,* McCullers explored the condition of human isolation with remarkable compassion and insight. As she herself remarked in "The Flowering
Dream: Notes on Writing," "how, without love
and the intuition that comes from love, can a
human being place himself in the situation of
another human being? He must imagine, and
imagination takes humility, love, and great courage. How can you create a character without love
and the struggle that goes with love?"

■ **Works Cited**

Bigelow, Pamela, "Carson McCullers," *Gay & Lesbian Literature,* St. James Press, 1994, pp. 256-59.

Davenport, Basil, review of *Reflections in a Golden
Eye, Saturday Review of Literature,* February 22,
1941.
Griffith, Albert J., "Carson McCullers' Myth of the
Sad Cafe," *Georgia Review,* Spring, 1967, pp. 46-
56.
Hart, Jane,"Carson McCullers, Pilgrim of Loneli-
ness," *Georgia Review,* Spring, 1957, pp. 53-58.
Kiernan, Robert F., "Carson McCullers," *Concise
Dictionary of American Literary Biography: The New
Consciousness, 1941-1968,* Gale, 1987, pp. 347-
57.
McCullers, Carson, "The Flowering Dream: Notes
on Writing," *The Mortgaged Heart: The Previously
Uncollected Writings of Carson McCullers,* edited
by Margarita G. Smith, Houghton, 1971, pp. 274-
82.
Westling, Louise, "Carson McCullers's Tomboys,"
Southern Humanities Review, Fall, 1980, pp. 339-
50.
Williams, Tennessee, introduction to *Reflections in
a Golden Eye,* New Directions, 1950, pp. ix-xxi.
Wilson, Edmund, "Two Books that Leave You
Blank: Carson McCullers, Siegfried Sassoon,"
New Yorker, March 30, 1946.
Wright, Richard, "Inner Landscape," *New Repub-
lic,* August 5, 1950, p. 195.

■ **For More Information See**

BOOKS

Bloom, Harold (editor), *Carson McCullers,* Chelsea
House Publishers, 1986.
Carr, Virginia Spencer, *The Lonely Hunter: A Biog-
raphy of Carson McCullers,* Doubleday, 1975.
Carr, Virginia Spencer, *Understanding Carson
McCullers,* University of South Carolina Press,
1989.
Clark, Beverly Lyon and Melvin J. Friedman (edi-
tors), *Critical Essays on Carson McCullers,* G. K.
Hall, 1996.
Contemporary Literary Criticism, Gale, Volume 1,
1973, Volume 4, 1975, Volume 10, 1979, Volume
12, 1980, Volume 48, 1988.
Cook, Richard M., *Carson McCullers,* Ungar, 1975.
Dictionary of Literary Biography, Gale, Volume 2:
American Novelists Since World War II, 1978, Vol-
ume 7: *Twentieth-Century American Dramatists,*
1981, Volume 173: *American Novelists Since World
War II, Fifth Series,* 1996.
Edmonds, Dale, *Carson McCullers,* Steck-Vaughn,
1969.

Evans, Oliver, *The Ballad of Carson McCullers*, Coward-McCann, 1966.

Graver, Lawrence, *Carson McCullers*, University of Minnesota Press, 1969.

James, Judith Giblin, *Wunderkind: The Reputation of Carson McCullers, 1940-1990*, Camden House, 1995.

McDowell, Margaret B., *Carson McCullers*, Twayne Publishers, 1980.

Steinbauer, Janine, *Carson McCullers*, Creative Education, 1995.

Wikborg, Eleanor, *The Member of the Wedding: Aspects of Structure and Style*, Humanities Press, 1975.

PERIODICALS

Commonweal, May 24, 1946; June 15, 1951; October 13, 1961; December 3, 1971, p. 239.

English Journal, September, 1957; October, 1982, pp. 67-68.

Kenyon Review, Winter, 1947; August 15, 1971, p. 925; June, 1987, p. 832.

Mademoiselle, September, 1957.

New Yorker, February 15, 1941; March 30, 1946.

New York Times, June 16, 1940; March 2, 1941; January 6, 1950; January 3, 1972, p. 25; July 14, 1987, p. 23.

Saturday Review, November 13, 1971, p. 57.

Southern Literary Journal, Fall, 1972; Spring, 1977; January, 1988, p. 59; February, 1993, p. 34.

Time, February 17, 1941; April 1, 1946.

■ Obituaries

PERIODICALS

Antiquarian Bookman, October 23, 1967.
Books Abroad, Spring, 1968.
Current Biography, December, 1967.
National Observer, October 2, 1967.
Newsweek, October 9, 1967.
New York Times, September 30, 1967.
Publishers Weekly, October 9, 1967.
Time, October 6, 1967.*

—Sketch by Lorie McElroy

Terry McMillan

■ Personal

Born October 18, 1951, in Port Huron, MI; daughter of Edward McMillan and Madeline Washington Tillman; children: Solomon Welch. *Education*: University of California, Berkeley, B.S., 1979; Columbia University, M.F.A., 1979.

■ Career

University of Wyoming, Laramie, instructor, 1987-90; University of Arizona, Tucson, professor, 1991-92; writer. *Member*: PEN, Author's League.

■ Awards, Honors

National Endowment for the Arts Fellowship, 1988.

■ Writings

Mama (novel), Houghton, 1987.
Disappearing Acts (novel), Viking, 1989.

(Editor) *Breaking Ice: An Anthology of Contemporary African-American Fiction*, Viking, 1990.
Waiting to Exhale (novel), Viking, 1992.
How Stella Got Her Groove Back (novel), Viking, 1996.

Contributor to *Five for Five: The Films of Spike Lee*, Stewart, Tabori, 1991. Adapted screenplays for *Disappearing Acts* and *Waiting to Exhale* (with Ron Bass). Work has appeared in *Touching Fire: Erotic Writings by Women*, Carroll and Graf, 1989, and in periodicals, including *Callaloo*, *Esquire*, and *Other Voices*.

■ Sidelights

To her legions of fans, Terry McMillan, a writer who has been hailed by *Time*'s John Skow as the "first wildly successful black pop novelist," speaks the truth about the middle-class black experience. Her characters are sharply drawn and funny and her writing crackles with high energy. If sales of her books are any indication, it is obvious that McMillan has tapped into the concerns of a generation of young, black African American women.

In a review of the 1989 novel *Disappearing Acts*, Valerie Sayers of the *New York Times Book Review* predicted: "Terry McMillan has the power to be an important contemporary novelist." After the 1992 release of the phenomenally popular novel *Waiting to Exhale*, there was no longer any doubt that Sayer's prediction had come true. Although some critics remain wary about the literary merits of her writing—particularly her most recent novels—there's no denying the mass popularity of McMillan's books. As John Skow stated in his *Time* profile of McMillan, "The fact that an African-American author was writing about vivid characters with whom many black women could identify had the added effect of proving to booksellers that there is a sizeable, previously ignored market for semisoapy black fiction."

Terry McMillan is someone who knows first-hand about the trials and tribulations of growing up black in America. She grew up in Port Huron, Michigan, a blue-collar industrial town about sixty miles northeast of Detroit. The eldest of five children, she was born to working class parents. Her early years were lean and difficult since her father, Edward, was abusive and alcoholic. Terry's mother, Madeline, was a strong, independent-minded woman who worked at a variety of menial jobs in order to feed her children. "There were a couple of winter nights I remember my teeth chattering," McMillan is quoted by John Leland of *Newsweek*. "But I don't remember ever feeling poor. I hate that word. We never went hungry." McMillan recalled that although her mother worked hard, she always paid a great deal of attention to her children. "When we got good grades, it was a reflection on her. Even though she only got up to Eleventh Grade, that was her way of saying, 'I'm doing something right.' We didn't have time to fail. She didn't give us that space."

McMillan's parents divorced in 1964, when she was thirteen. Edward McMillan died three years later. Despite all of the hardships and abuse she endured, McMillan says her mother told her that she never regretted marrying him. "[Mom] was of that mind-set of, I have five beautiful kids, that's the one thing he did right. I don't share that attitude," Terry McMillan told Leland.

The only book the McMillan family owned was a Bible, and Madeline and Edward were not in the habit of reading to their children. Young Terry discovered the world of books only because she worked in a library. She shelved books as a teenager for $1.25 an hour. It was while doing this that she began to read, encountering the writing of the Brontë sisters and the biography of Louisa May Alcott. Books became McMillan's way to escape the drudgery of her life in Port Huron. Yet, she had not read any writings by black writers.

The first time McMillan saw a book by the African American novelist James Baldwin, she was embarrassed by the picture of a black face on the dustjacket. She was quoted in a *Washington Post* article as saying that she "did not read his book because I was too afraid. I couldn't imagine that he'd have anything better or different to say that [German essayist and novelist] Thomas Mann, [American philosopher] Henry Thoreau, or [American essayist and poet] Ralph Waldo Emerson. . . . Needless to say, I was not just naïve, but had not yet acquired an ounce of black pride."

Discovering Her Heritage

Once McMillan discovered there were black writers, she read everything she could find by and about them. As a student at Los Angeles Community College, she devoured the classics of black literature. After reading the *Autobiography of Malcolm X* by Pulitzer Prize-winning writer Alex Haley, she realized there was no need to feel ashamed about being a member of a race with such a rich cultural heritage. Oddly enough, it was her discovery of the writings of white humorist and short story writer Ring Lardner that gave her the courage to start writing in her own voice. "As soon as I read Ring Lardner, his voice jumped off the page," she told Leland. "What he was writing about was tragic, and I was cracking up. I realized that it was the same sort of thing I was trying to do in my stuff. Ring Lardner said, 'It's OK, Terry, to write the way that you talk.' Ring Lardner was the one who freed me up."

McMillan's first literary efforts were poems. Her first effort—a love poem—was published soon afterwards. Encouraged by this, she turned to fiction. She was a journalism major at University of California, Berkeley when, with the pivotal encouragement of writer Ishmael Reed and his Before Columbus Foundation, she published a short story called "The End." Its success convinced McMillan she had found a medium of expression that was right for her. "I really love the short story as a form," she told *Writer's Digest*.

McMillan's love affair with words and books may have been why she found herself on a different path than she had originally planned. She had expected to be married by age twenty-four, but instead found herself going to graduate school after earning her journalism degree in 1979.

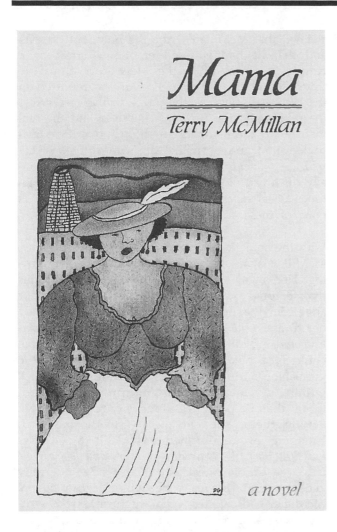

This 1987 novel, the author's first published work, is based on McMillan's life while growing up, as well as on the life of her mother, Madeline.

McMillan moved to New York to pursue a master's degree in screenwriting. She dropped out, however, because she found the environment at Columbia University racist, and instead took a job in a law office.

Unsure of herself and trapped in an unhealthy relationship, McMillan turned to alcohol and drugs. She struggled to overcome her self-destructive habits and finally succeeded. In 1981, shortly after her thirtieth birthday, McMillan quit using drugs and entered a ninety-day Alcoholics Anonymous program. She has been "clean and sober" ever since. McMillan told Laura B. Randolph of *Ebony* magazine what meant the most to her about freeing herself from her addictions was the renewed sense of ownership that she felt over her own life: "I mean feeling good about what I'm doing, how I've done it, the changes and struggles I've been through. That's what I mean when say there are certain things I own. Now, I own me."

The Dream of Getting Published

At age thirty-two, McMillan gave birth to a son she named Solomon. When her three-year relationship with the child's father ended soon afterwards, she supported herself and her son by working as a copy editor and typist. Through it all, she never abandoned her dreams of becoming a writer. One day McMillan showed her fellow members of the Harlem Writer's Guild a short story she had written called "Mama." They urged her to expand it into a novel. The idea seemed like a good one, so she spent time at a writers' retreat, where she was able to focus on her the project. During that time, the *Mama* manuscript grew to 400 pages. McMillan found a literary agent, but when a disagreement arose over the direction the book should take, she decided to look for a publisher herself. McMillan sent a collection of her short stories to Houghton Mifflin, with a cover letter that mentioned she was also working on a novel. An editor at the company was impressed with her work and asked to see her novel. Four days after McMillan sent the manuscript, she got a call from Houghton Mifflin saying the company wanted to publish the book. At age thirty-six, Terry McMillan's dream came true: she was a published author.

Mama is heavily autobiographical, being based on McMillan's experiences growing up and on a character who is clearly modeled on her mother, Madeline. The story chronicles the relationship between Mildred Peacock, who struggles to bring up her children after throwing out her alcoholic husband, and her eldest daughter Freda. Most first novels are lightly promoted by book publishers. McMillan did not want to see *Mama* ignored, so she began promoting it herself. She wrote more than 3,000 letters to African-American organizations, bookstores, universities, and colleges. Her efforts paid off handsomely. Not only did *Mama* get reviewed, but Michael Awkward, writing in *Callaloo*, praised the novel as a "moving, often hilarious and insightful exploration of a slice of black urban life that is rarely seen in contemporary black women's fiction." Other reviews were also positive, and the book became a huge hit.

By the end of 1987 McMillan had given thirty-nine readings, and six weeks after it was released, *Mama* was into its third printing.

McMillan's next book, *Disappearing Acts,* explored another topic that she knew well: the often difficult relations between men and women. McMillan summed up her feelings in an article that she wrote in *Essence.* "Maybe it's just me, but I'm finding it harder and harder to meet men," she said. "I grew up and became what my mama prayed out loud I'd become: educated, strong, smart, independent and reliable. . . . Now it seems as if carving a place for myself in the world is backfiring. Never in a million years would I have dreamed that I'd be 38-years-old and still single."

Disappearing Acts was different from *Mama* both in theme and structure. It tells the story of two lovers, Zora Banks and Franklin Swift. The narrative shifts back and forth between the two voices, giving readers both sides of the same story. Zora—named for one of America's first and best loved black novelists, Zora Neale Hurston—is an educated, black junior high school teacher. She meets Franklin, a high school drop-out who works in construction. Despite their different backgrounds, they fall in love, move in together, and try to build a relationship. The book, which most critics liked, touched a chord among many black women. Reviewer David Nicholson of the *Washington Post Book World* pointed out that professional black women had long been complaining about the difficulty of finding black male partners.

However, subject matter wasn't the only reason *Disappearing Acts* made such an impact. Many critics praised Terry McMillan's ability to capture Franklin's voice. Nicholson praised the novel as "one of the few . . . to contain rounded, sympathetic portrayal of black men and to depict the relationships between black men and black women as something more than the relationship between victimizer and victim, oppressor and oppressed."

When *Disappearing Acts* was optioned for a movie, McMillan was asked to write the screenplay for the Metro-Goldwyn-Mayer studio. (To date, the film has not yet been made.) The book also prompted a lawsuit from Leonard Welch, McMillan's former lover and the father of her son Solomon. Welch filed a $4.75 million defamation suit in August 1990, claiming McMillan had used him as the model for the Franklin character. Welch

claimed that McMillan wrote the book out of spite and that he had suffered emotional stress as a result. In April 1991, the New York Supreme Court found in McMillan's favor. As reported in the *Wall Street Journal,* the judge in the case wrote that although "the fictional character and the real man share the same occupation and educational background and even like the same breakfast cereal. . . . The man in the novel is lazy, emotionally disturbed alcoholic who uses drugs and sometimes beats his girlfriend. . . . Leonard Welch is none of these."

With the emotional torment of the trial behind her, McMillan again turned her attention to her writing. Her anger at reading a book of short stories that featured no African-American or writers nor any from the developing Third World prompted her to assemble *Breaking Ice: An Anthology of Contemporary African-American Fiction.* She regarded the book as a positive step toward addressing the publishing industry's lack of attention to black writers. As awareness of her proposal spread, more than 300 submissions poured in. From among them, she chose fifty-seven seasoned, emerging, or unpublished writers. In a *Washington Post Book World* review of *Breaking Ice,* novelist Joyce Carol Oates said it was a wonderfully generous and diverse collection of prose fiction. McMillan had selected such "high quality of writing," Oates said, "that one could hardly distinguish between the categories [of writers] in terms of originality, depth of vision and command of the language."

The Breakout Novel

McMillan's success continued with her next novel. *Waiting to Exhale* was the breakthrough book that vaulted her to dizzying heights of fame and fortune. In the words of James Wolcott of the *New Yorker,* the book was McMillan's "popular breakthrough after years of paying dues." Its plot was a return to her familiar themes of failed romances, the search for love, and strong female friendships. McMillan sensed that many of her friends were experiencing the same thing she had long felt: they, too, were educated, smart, attractive—and alone. "I asked myself, 'How did this happen?'" McMillan is quoted as saying on the world wide web site *Afronet.* "So the book became an exploration of this question. And because the story reflected more than my own singular experience, I created these four 'types' of women who deal with the same issue through their different situations."

McMillan's themes are men's fear of commitment and everyone's fear of growing old alone. *Waiting to Exhale* tells the story of four successful professional black women, each of whom is at a critical point in her life. Through a series of broken relationships with men, the women's friendships remain strong and true. In the *New York Review of Books*, Darryl Pinckney wrote: "The novel is . . . hilarious, to the verge of camp, but the thoughts and feelings it captures are too much like life not to make a striking impression. There's nothing self-aggrandizing or moralizing about it." When *Waiting to Exhale* was published by Viking in 1992, it immediately shot to the top of the bestseller lists. It hit the influential *New York Times* bestseller list the week it came out and remained there the next thirty-eight weeks. This time, there was no need for McMillan to initiate her own publicity. The publisher sent her on a twenty-six-city, six-week tour, including appearances on the *Oprah Winfrey Show*, *Today*, and the *Arsenio Hall Show*. Just three weeks after its release, *Waiting to Exhale* was already into its tenth printing. The paperback rights fetched a cool $2.64 million from Pocket Books, and sales since then have totaled almost four million copies.

The success of *Waiting to Exhale* made it abundantly clear that McMillan had found a huge untapped audience that crossed racial lines. Both black and white women loved the book, and so did many men, surprisingly. McMillan said that was the response she had hoped for, since her aim was not to insult men, but rather to help them understand why it's difficult for women to love them.

When film producers Deborah Schindler and Ezra Swerdlow read the book, they hoped it could touch a film audience the same way. "The minute we read it we knew it was a movie that had to be made, and that these characters had to be put on the screen," Schindler told *Afronet*. In fact, the producers were so impressed with McMillan's writing talents that they asked her to adapt the book into a screenplay. She did so, working with Academy-Award winning screenwriter Ron Bass, whose earlier credits included the critically acclaimed Tom Cruise film *Rainman*, and the two quickly found they had the same vision for the

If you enjoy the works of Terry McMillan, you may also want to check out the following books and films:

Connie Briscoe, *Sister and Lovers*, 1994.
Beebe Moore Campbell, *Your Blues ain't like Mine*, 1992.
E. Lynn Harris, *And This Too Shall Pass*, 1996.
What's Love Got to Do with It, Touchstone Pictures, 1993.

movie. When everything clicked into place, the film attracted big-name actors and a superb crew.

Looking back on the experience, McMillan said it was exciting and rewarding. "First of all, I was flattered," she is quoted in *Afronet*. "I didn't have any sense of ownership or possession in terms of the characters that, maybe, some writers do—where they feel, 'Gee, I created them; they're mine, and please don't do this and that to them.' I just thought, 'Here are some people I made up and, now, look, [actor] Whitney Houston's one of 'em. And [actor] Angela Bassett's become this person that I conjured up.' So it was kind of amazing."

Although some critics, like *Time*'s Richard Corliss, pronounced the movie lacking in artistic value—"tasty junk food," he termed it—audiences flocked to see *Waiting to Exhale*. The movie grossed $67 million, left audiences cheering, and reaffirmed that there is indeed a ready market for well-crafted stories about African Americans.

Handling Stardom

Nonetheless, the aftermath of the success of the book and the movie was not all positive for McMillan. She has complained about the demands made on her by fans and by some black groups. She has come under fire for her "one-dimensional" depictions of men, and her use of profanity in her novels has also alienated some critics. Also, her mother and her best friend died within a year of each other. Unable to continue working on a partially completed novel about her mother, McMillan sought escape. A trip to Jamaica turned things around for her, both personally and creatively.

There she met and fell in love with Jonathon Plummer, a resort hotel employee, who is about half her age. Their relationship—he moved to the United States to live with McMillan—provided the inspiration for her next book, *How Stella Got Her Groove Back.*

Stella is a beautiful, successful, single forty-two-year-old business analyst. Tired of waiting for love, she travels to Jamaica for a vacation. There she meets Winston, an assistant cook at a resort. They fall in love, and he returns home with her. Unlike the men in her other novels, Winston is responsible, polite, and caring. The melodramatic plot aside, the real story of *How Stella Got Her Groove Back* was the huge money McMillan was paid for the book: the first printing was estimated to have been as high as one million copies. McMillan received a $6-million advance from Viking, her publisher, and she got a lucrative seven-figure deal for the movie rights. Critics were uncertain about the literary merits of *How Stella Got Her Groove Back* but acknowledged the book's impact on the literary marketplace. "It's a dubious sort of good luck that her slightest and fluffiest novel has brought McMillan her greatest reward," wrote John Skow in *Time.* "The new book starring 'Winston' burbles along cheerfully but lacks the satirical bite of *Waiting to Exhale.*"

While Terry McMillan has been compared to acclaimed black writers like Alice Walker and Toni Morrison, her voice and stories are more mainstream with great appeal to what is known in the publishing industry as a "crossover audience." She is a storyteller whose stories touch only lightly on racial and feminist issues. McMillan's voice belongs to what has described as "the New Black Aesthetic"—one which does not deal with everything from the perspective of race. That this approach does not please everyone is evident, for some African-American literary critics have chided McMillan for her lack of attention to racial issues. At the same time, John Leland of *Newsweek* has pointed out that McMillan writes "intimately, sometimes mockingly, about a middle-class experience in which white America is largely irrelevant."

Whatever the critics may say, the reality is that Terry McMillan's example has spawned a new generation of black writers who are making their marks with an eager audience. "[We're] a new breed," she wrote in her introduction to *Breaking Ice,* "free to write as we please . . . because the way of life has changed."

■ **Works Cited**

Afronet Internet Website, "About the Author—Terry McMillan," http://www.afronet.com/Exhale/About_the_Author.html.

Awkward, Michael, "Chronicling Everyday Travails and Triumphs," *Callaloo,* Summer, 1988, pp. 649-50.

Corliss, Richard, review of *Waiting to Exhale, Time,* January 8, 1996.

Leland, John, "How Terry Got Her Groove," *Newsweek,* April 29, 1996, pp. 76-79.

McMillan, Terry, editor, *Breaking Ice: An Anthology of Contemporary African-American Fiction,* Viking, 1990.

McMillan, Terry, "Looking for Mr. Right," *Essence,* February, 1990.

McMillan, Terry, interview with Laura B. Randolph, *Ebony,* May, 1993.

Nicholson, David, *Washington Post Book World,* August 27, 1989, p. 6.

Oates, Joyce Carol, review of *Breaking Ice: An Anthology of Contemporary African-American Fiction, Washington Post Book World,* September 16, 1990, pp. 1, 7.

Pinckney, Darryl, review of *Waiting to Exhale, New York Review of Books,* November 4, 1993, pp. 33-37.

Sayers, Valerie, review of *Disappearing Acts, New York Times Book Review,* August 6, 1989, p. 8.

Skow, John, "Some Groove," *Time,* May 6, 1996, pp. 77-78.

Wall Street Journal, April 11, 1991.

Washington Post, November 17, 1990, section D, p. 1.

Wolcott, James, "Terry McMillan," *New Yorker,* April 29, 1996, p 102.

Writer's Digest, October, 1987.

■ **For More Information See**

BOOKS

Black Writers, 2nd edition, Gale, 1994, pp. 420-424.

Contemporary Literary Criticism, Gale, Volume 50, 1988, Volume 61, 1990.

Reference Guide to American Literature, 3rd edition, edited by Jim Kamp, St. James Press, pp. 580-582.

PERIODICALS

Cosmopolitan, August, 1989.

Ebony, July, 1996, p. 20.

Entertainment Weekly, May 3, 1996, p. 70.

Esquire, July, 1988, pp. 100, 102, 104.

Library Journal, May 15, 1996, p. 84.

Los Angeles Times, February 23, 1987, p. 11; October 29, 1990, section E, p. 1; May 31, 1992, p. 12.

McCall's, November, 1996, p. 44.

Newsweek, January 8, 1996, p. 68.

New York Times Book Review, February 22, 1987, p. 11; May 31, 1992; June 2, 1996, p. 21.

People, February 5, 1996, p. 35; April 1, 1996, p. 107.

Publishers Weekly, May 11, 1992, pp. 50-51; July 13, 1992; September 21, 1992.

Tribune Books (Chicago), September 23, 1990, p. 1; May 31, 1992, p. 6.

Washington Post Book World, May 24, 1992, p. 11.*

—*Sketch by Ken Cuthbertson*

Wilson Rawls

leges, and universities in seventeen states. Speaker at educational conventions. *Member:* Authors Guild, Authors League of America, Idaho Parent-Teacher Association (honorary life member).

■ Personal

Full name, Woodrow Wilson Rawls; born September 24, 1913, in Scraper, OK; died December 16, 1984; son of Minzy O. and Winnie (Hatfield) Rawls; married Sophie Ann Styczinski (budget analyst for the Atomic Energy Commission), August 23, 1958. *Education:* Attended schools in Oklahoma. *Religion:* Presbyterian.

■ Addresses

Home—c/o Sophie S. Rawls, 1904 Tamarack Lane, Janesville, WI 53445-0997.

■ Career

Writer of children's books. Became itinerant carpenter in teens and worked in Mexico, in South America, on the Alcan Highway in Alaska, on five of the major dam projects in the United States, in West Coast shipyards, for the Navy in Oregon, and for a lumber company in British Columbia. Full-time writer, 1959—. Lecturer at schools, col-

■ Awards, Honors

Evansville Book Award, Division III, Evansville-Vanderburgh School Corporation, 1974, Michigan Young Readers Award, Division II, Michigan Council of Teachers of English, 1980, Children's Book Award for the Older Child, North Dakota, 1981, Twelfth Annual Children's Book Award, Massachusetts, 1987, and Great Stone Face Award, New Hampshire, 1988, all for *Where the Red Fern Grows*; William Allen White Children's Book Award, Emporia State University, and Sequoyah Book Award, Oklahoma Library Association, both 1979, Golden Archer Award, University of Wisconsin-Oshkosh, and Maud Hart Lovelace Book Award, Friends of Minnesota Valley Regional Library, both 1980, California Young Reader Medal Award, California Reading Association, 1981, and OMAR's Book Award, Indiana, 1984, all for *Summer of the Monkeys*.

■ Writings

Where the Red Fern Grows, Doubleday, 1961.
Summer of the Monkeys, Doubleday, 1976.

The Wilson Rawls collection, which includes literary awards, taped interviews, manuscripts, and other materials, is maintained by the archives and Collections Department of the Cherokee National Museum, Tahlequah, Oklahoma.

■ Adaptations

Where the Red Fern Grows was adapted for film by Doty-Dayton Productions, 1974, and has been recorded on audiocassette by Recorded Books, 1994, and Listening Library, 1994. *Dreams Can Come True*, an audiocassette featuring a talk given by Rawls, was released in 1993 by Reading Tree Productions.

■ Sidelights

As soon as he could fashion letters, Wilson Rawls began writing on any smooth surface he could find—the sandy bank of a river, a dusty country road. Many years later, his work found its way into print. Two successful novels, *Where the Red Fern Grows* and *Summer of the Monkeys*, established an enormous following for Rawls. Perhaps it was the shape of Rawls's life, the struggle to achieve his literary ambition and his ultimate success, that make his work resonate with readers and critics alike. What he lacked in formal education Rawls more than made up for in sheer drive and love of writing; grit, tenacity, and patient determination finally overcame the obstacles in his way, to the pleasure of his fans.

The rural descriptions in Rawls's work are all from his own experience. Scraper, where he was born, is a small town in northeastern Oklahoma. Such a tiny and isolated community could not afford to support schools, but fortunately Rawls's mother taught him and his siblings to read and write. Once a school was built for the community's children, Rawls and his sisters could attend class, but only for a few months during the summer. The family eventually moved to Tahlequah, Oklahoma, where Rawls discovered his first library. As he told Harold Schindler of the *Salt Lake Tribune*, "I didn't just read those books, I memorized them."

Reading was a family activity for the Rawls. Using books provided by their grandmother, the children were encouraged to take turns reading

aloud, a few pages according to ability. Rawls had trouble identifying with fairy tales, especially those with female heroines, but his mother managed to find a copy of Jack London's *The Call of the Wild*. After the usual communal reading, she made a present of it to ten-year-old Wilson.

From then on, he knew that he wanted to be a writer. His family life was not especially conducive to this goal—even pencil and paper were extravagances—but Rawls did not allow the limitations of their poverty to get in his way. His father's adage that "nothing was impossible, as long as you never gave up," became a guiding principle. Rawls attended Central High School in Muskogee, Oklahoma, but the Depression got in the way of his earning a diploma. He moved to

In this 1961 autobiographical novel, both of Billy Colman's coon hound dogs, which Billy reared from pups and trained to hunt, are tragically killed by a mountain lion.

wherever work could be found, half of all his earnings earmarked for the family, the small remainder for him.

From his teens until late adulthood, Rawls's life was highly itinerant. He worked for a while with an oil company in Mexico, venturing down to South America when he heard work was to be had there. Returning to the north, Rawls contributed to construction of the Alcan Highway in Alaska and to five of the largest dams in the United States. He worked in West Coast shipyards, for the U.S. Navy and for a British Columbia lumber concern.

Never during all of this did Rawls stop writing. Real writing paper was still a treat, but Rawls inventively put any scrap to use, including brown packing paper. By his own estimate, he wrote "hundreds of thousands of words," as he told Schindler, many of these "in the smoky glow of a hobo campfire, in cheap hotel rooms and riding in Greyhound buses." He kept all this work to himself, convinced that "it was pure trash and no one would waste time printing junk like that. I also knew my grammar was poor and my vocabulary zero," he told Schindler.

But even though he did not try to get published, Rawls held on to his work, storing it in a trunk at his parents' house. While working in British Columbia, he heard about plentiful work in Idaho Falls, where construction was underway. Not only were they hiring, but the fishing was reputed to be excellent; Rawls did not need any convincing.

The 1956 move to Idaho proved fateful for Rawls: he met Sophie Styczinski, a budget analyst for the Atomic Energy Commission. Two years later, she became his wife. Courting her replaced writing for a while, and Rawls decided to throw over his desire to be a writer. Shortly before their marriage, he visited his parents, then in New Mexico, to sort through his things. Finding the manuscripts, he decided to rid himself of them forever. "I burned them . . .," he told Schindler, "five complete novels destroyed because I was ashamed to send them to a publisher."

Living the Dream

Rawls was fortunate in his choice of a mate; when he finally revealed his ambition to his wife, she

While in Oklahoma, fourteen-year-old Jay Berry Lee finds a tree full of monkeys, which he later finds out escaped from a local circus and have a reward on their heads.

supported him to the full. He reconstructed "The Secret of the Red Fern" from memory, all of it with no punctuation. His wife corrected the errors; her enthusiastic response and careful editing shaped the piece enough to submit to the *Saturday Evening Post,* where it appeared in three installments as "Hounds of Youth." Doubleday then published the entire story as *Where the Red Fern Grows.*

This largely autobiographical novel details protagonist Billy Colman's memories of his impoverished boyhood, in which two coon hound dogs played

If you enjoy the work of Wilson Rawls, you may also want to check out the following books and films:

Robbie Branscum, *Old Blue Tilley*, 1991.
Babara Corcoran, *The Sky Is Falling*, 1988.
Robert Newton Peck, *A Day No Pigs Would Die*, 1961.
The Journey of Natty Gann, Disney, 1985.

an important part. Rearing the dogs from pups, Billy transforms them into prize-winning hunters, their efforts allowing him to assist his family financially. Billy and the dogs become inseparable, enjoying several adventures, until one night when they tree a mountain lion. In an effort to protect Billy, both animals are mortally wounded. Returning to their gravesite several months after he has buried them, the grieving Billy is elated to see that a red fern, according to legend the plant of angels, has sprouted between the two graves.

Writing in *School Library Journal*, Kit Breckenridge praised *Where the Red Fern Grows* for its "superb pacing and handling of characters," deeming it a "powerful story." Breckenridge echoed Susan H. Williamson and Michael M. Williamson's earlier assessment in the same periodical that Rawls's book was "beautifully written" and that by "capturing the thrill of hunting, it is perhaps the best of its genre." *Booklist*'s Frances A. Miller found the story warm and filled with "challenge and adventure." In the *New York Times Book Review*, Paul Engle wrote that the novel has "careful, precise observation, all of it rightly phrased."

Despite the accolades, sales of *Where the Red Fern Grows* were slow. (Rawls joked that fewer than a dozen copies made their way to readers in the first seven years of the book's existence.) But all of this changed when Rawls accepted an invitation to speak at a University of Utah summer workshop for teachers. Impressed by his remarks on his book, the teachers not only read *Where the Red Fern Grows* but urged their students to follow suit. Not long after, the book began to sell very well. By 1974, the book was not only still in print, but a movie had been made.

Two years later, Rawls published his second book, *Summer of the Monkeys*. *Where the Red Fern Grows*

drew almost directly on the autobiographical details of Rawls's life but *Summer of the Monkeys* was all fiction. Set in the early twentieth century, this is the story of Jay Berry Lee, a fourteen-year-old Oklahoma Ozarks boy, who happens upon a group of monkeys, recent escapees from a visiting circus. Tantalized by the $100 reward, a huge sum at that time, he resolves to capture the runaways. But even with his trusty dog Rowdy and the help of his grandfather, this proves harder than Jay Berry thought. Ultimately, he discovers that the monkeys, unused to fending for themselves, defend themselves out of fear. He manages to lead them to safety in a storm, earning the reward and discovering that, though he had planned to spend it all on himself, the satisfaction of paying for an operation on his sister's crippled leg is far greater. Commenting on a 1992 re-issue of the work, Jody McCoy of *Voice of Youth Advocates* wrote that *Summer of the Monkeys* "continues to be a good read." She praised the characters for being "well and richly drawn . . . with a wealth of thought-provoking situations."

Drawing on his successful appearance at the teachers' workshop, Rawls visited more than 2,000 schools in twenty-two states, primarily in the West and South. He often brought the manuscript of *Where the Red Fern Grows* with him, emphasizing to his listeners that they could deal with grammar and punctuation problems later; getting their stories down on paper mattered most of all. He also spoke at many teacher and librarian conferences, continuing these public speaking engagements until illness prevented him from further travel in 1983.

When asked what advice he had for young people who wanted to write, Rawls once commented, "Do a lot of reading. Read and study creative writing. . . . Remember, the more you write and rewrite, the better you will get. And most important of all do not get discouraged. If you keep trying and don't give up, you will make it some day." Rawls was convincing testimony to this simple truth, a writer who refused to lose heart, whose doggedness won out in the end.

■ Works Cited

Breckenridge, Kit, "Modern Classics," *School Library Journal*, April, 1988, pp. 42-43.
Engle, Paul, review of *Where the Red Fern Grows*,

New York Times Book Review, September 8, 1974, p. 38.

McCoy, Jody, review of *Summer of the Monkeys, Voice of Youth Advocates,* October, 1992, p. 230.

Miller, Frances A., "Books To Read When You Hate To Read," *Booklist,* February 15, 1992, p. 1100-1.

Schindler, Harold, *Salt Lake Tribune,* April 7, 1974.

Williamson, Michael M., and Susan H. Williamson, "Stalking the Elusive Prey," *School Library Journal,* September, 1984, pp. 47-48.

■ For More Information See

BOOKS

Authors in the News, Volume 1, Gale, 1976, p. 387.

Holtze, Sally Holmes, editor, *Sixth Book of Junior Authors and Illustrators,* H. W. Wilson Company, 1989, pp. 240-41.

Silvey, Anita, editor, *Children's Books and Their Creators,* Houghton, 1995, p. 351.

Ward, Martha E., Dorothy A. Marquardt, Nancy Dolan, and Dawn Eaton, *Authors of Books for Young People,* Scarecrow Press, 1990, p. 583.

PERIODICALS

Best-Sellers, June 1, 1961.

Chicago Tribune, June 4, 1961.

Children's Literature in Education, June, 1995, pp. 135-50.

Deseret News, February 16, 1974.

Idaho Falls Post-Register, March 17, 1974.

Library Journal, February 1, 1961, pp. 612-13.

Milwaukee Journal, June 25, 1978.

Tulsa Daily World, April 15, 1976.*

—Sketch by C. M. Ratner

Conrad Richter

The Town; National Institute of Arts and Letters grant in literature, 1959; Maggie Award, 1959, for *The Lady;* National Book Award, 1961, for *The Waters of Kronos;* Litt.D., Susquehanna University, 1944, University of New Mexico, 1958, Lafayette College, 1966; LL.D., Temple University, 1966; L.H.D., Lebanon Valley College, 1966.

■ Personal

Born October 13, 1890, in Pine Grove, PA; died of a heart attack, October 30, 1968, in Pottsville, PA; son of John Absalom (a minister) and Charlotte Esther (Henry) Richter; married Harvena M. Achenbach, 1915; children: Harvena. *Education:* Attended public schools in Pennsylvania.

■ Career

Editor and journalist for newspapers in Patton, PA, Johnstown, PA, and Pittsburgh, PA, and private secretary in Cleveland, OH, 1910-24; writer, 1924-68. *Member:* National Institute of Arts and Letters, Authors League, PEN.

■ Awards, Honors

National Book Award nomination, 1937, for *The Sea of Grass;* Gold Medal for Literature from Society of Libraries of New York University, 1942, for *The Sea of Grass* and *The Trees;* Ohioana Library Medal, 1947; Pulitzer Prize for Fiction, 1951, for

■ Writings

Brothers of No Kin and Other Stories, Hinds, Hayden & Eldredge, 1924, reprinted, Books for Libraries Press, 1973.

Human Vibration, Handy Book, 1925.

Principles in Bio-Physics, Good Books, 1927.

Early Americana and Other Stories, Knopf, 1936, reprinted, Gregg, 1978.

The Sea of Grass, Knopf, 1937, reprinted, Ballantine, 1984, reprinted, Swallow Press, 1992.

The Trees (first volume in trilogy; also see below), Knopf, 1940, reprinted, Bantam, 1975, reprinted, Ohio University Press, 1991.

Tacey Cromwell, Knopf, 1942, reprinted, University of New Mexico Press, 1974.

The Free Man, Knopf, 1943, reprinted, 1966.

The Fields (second volume in trilogy; also see below), Knopf, 1946, reprinted, 1964.

Smoke over the Prairie and Other Stories, Boardman, 1947.

Always Young and Fair, Knopf, 1947.

The Town (third volume in trilogy; also see below), Knopf, 1950, reprinted, Harmony Raine, 1981, reprinted, Ohio University Press, 1991.

The Light in the Forest, Knopf, 1953, Bantam, 1984.

The Mountain on the Desert: A Philosophical Journey, Knopf, 1955.

The Lady, Knopf, 1957, reprinted, University of Nebraska Press, 1985.

Dona Ellen, Rauch, 1959.

The Waters of Kronos, Knopf, 1960.

A Simple, Honorable Man, Knopf, 1962.

Over the Blue Mountain (juvenile), Knopf, 1962.

Individualists under the Shade Trees in a Vanishing America, Holt, 1964.

The Grandfathers, Knopf, 1964.

A Country of Strangers, Knopf, 1966, Schocken, 1982.

The Awakening Land: I. The Trees, II. The Fields, III. The Town, Knopf, 1966.

The Wanderer, Knopf, 1966.

The Aristocrat, Knopf, 1968.

The Rawhide Knot and Other Stories, Knopf, 1978, reprinted, University of Nebraska Press, 1985.

Also author of monograph, *Life Energy.* Contributor to anthologies and magazines.

■ Sidelights

During a career that spanned more than forty years, Conrad Richter published fifteen novels and four collections of short stories about the American frontier. He is now considered to be one of the foremost regional writers of the twentieth century. As Dayton Kohler observed in *College English,* "There are no novels quite like Richter's in the whole range of historical fiction. Together they probably give us the truest picture of the everyday realities of frontier life." His books have been popular among adult and teenage readers alike, and six have been adapted for movies and television. Richter also earned critical acclaim, winning the Pulitzer Prize for fiction for *The Town* in 1951 and the National Book Award for *The Waters of Kronos* in 1961. *The Light in the Forest* has been a favorite young adult novel since its publication in 1953.

In the late 1980s and early 1990s Richter's work received renewed attention from reviewers and educators as well as general readers. His stories about hardy pioneers who conquered the frontier and Native Americans who lived close to nature portray conflicts that are still a part of American life—the clash of diverse cultures and the devastating impact of civilization on the environment. Yet his books also appeal to readers simply because he tells a good story. In the *New York Herald Tribune Book Review,* Louis Bromfield noted that Richter "has that gift—the first and most important in a novelist—of creating for the reader a world as real as the one in which he lives, a world which the reader enters on reading the first page and in which he remains until the last."

Richter's own life could have been the subject of a novel, and in fact he used many of his experiences to create plots and characters for his stories. He was born on October 13, 1890, in Pine Grove, Pennsylvania, the eldest of three sons of Absalom and Charlotte Richter. The family moved frequently as Richter's father, who was a minister, was assigned to a series of small coal mining towns throughout Pennsylvania. When Richter was growing up he loved to read adventure stories and books about science. Reportedly he also wanted to run away and live with the Indians. After graduating from Tremont High School in 1906 at the age of fifteen, Richter had a variety of jobs, including horse team driver, farm hand, timber cutter, door-to-door magazine salesman, bank teller, and clerk. In 1910 his prospects improved when he was hired as the editor of the *Courier,* a weekly newspaper in Parton, Pennsylvania. Finding that he enjoyed being a reporter, he soon moved to newspapers in Johnstown and then Pittsburgh. As a journalist he learned to write concise sentences that became his trademark in action-packed novels that were rarely longer than 200 pages. However, he was not to achieve real success for another twenty years.

Richter eventually drifted to Cleveland, Ohio, where he was a private secretary to a wealthy family. He also started writing fiction, publishing his first successful short story, "Brothers of No Kin," in *Forum* magazine in 1914. *Forum's* publisher singled it out as the best short story of the year, and the story was reprinted several times, but Richter was not paid immediately. When he finally did receive a check he was disappointed in the value placed on his creativity—only twenty-five dollars. According to Bernard Kalb in the *Saturday Review,* Richter later recalled, "I told myself that if this was what one got for the 'best' story of the year, I had better stick to business and write in my spare time." By 1915 he had settled into married life with Harvena Achenbach, who was from his hometown of Pine Grove. Rich-

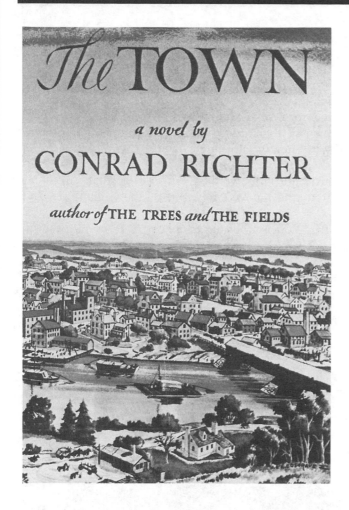

Richter won the Pulitzer Prize for Fiction in 1951 for this novel about a family of American pioneers during the nineteenth century.

ter continued to write stories for popular magazines, publishing his first collection, *Brothers of No Kin and Other Stories,* in 1924. Reviewer response was lukewarm, the main complaint being that the stories seemed to have been produced on an assembly line. As Edwin W. Gaston, Jr., reported in *Dictionary of Literary Biography,* Richter later admitted he had been "a young man intent on getting a bit of magazine money for his small family."

The New Mexico Years

The turning point in Richter's career came in 1928, when his wife's poor health forced them to move to Albuquerque, New Mexico. In New Mexico he found new subject matter for his fiction—the his-

tory and folklore of the rugged American Southwest. Nevertheless he increasingly drew upon his own experiences in the East. According to Gaston, "Occupations he assigned to characters in the early stories corresponded to many he himself had held, and places in which he set the works resembled those in which he had lived. The more he wrote, the more pronounced the practice became." Richter also started the practice of doing extensive research in order to provide authentic dialogue, characters, and settings, which became a distinctive feature of his fiction. He pored over old newspapers and scrapbooks, and he interviewed elderly local residents who had taken part in settling the Old West. The result was that Richter's second story collection, *Early Americana and Other Stories,* received an enthusiastic reception upon its publication in 1936. Stanley Young, writing in the *New York Times Book Review,* praised Richter's attention to realistic detail: "When he has made us feel how the Comanche moon looked on the roadless prairie, how the hoofs of loping horses beat on the bunch grass like a muffled drum, how the seasons come and go under the raw, hard sunlight, then he is ready, in as few words as possible, to unfold his dramatic story."

The following year, Richter gained national recognition with his first novel, *The Sea of Grass.* Set in New Mexico during the nineteenth century, it portrays the conflict between ranchers who ranged freely on the land and homesteaders who fenced in their farms. While some reviewers thought Richter's style was too romantic, most agreed that he had moved beyond the typical Western novel. Eda Lou Walton commented in the *New York Herald Tribune Books* that Richter "casts a kind of golden glow over a scene which other authors have given us in harsh, cruel, or tragic colors. Nor is he completely wrong in using the early American scene as a romanticist must. New Mexico is, indeed, a land of myth, a land of curious poetic superstitions. . . ." Richter wrote two other works about the Southwest. *Tacey Cromwell* is the story of a prostitute and a gambler in Arizona who want to become respectable, and *The Lady* was based on an actual unsolved mystery involving the murder of a judge and his young son in New Mexico.

While Richter was writing about the Old West, his imagination turned back toward the Pennsylvania-Ohio country where he grew up. From 1940 to 1950 he published the "Ohio trilogy," the novels for which he is best known. *The Trees, The Fields,* and *The Town* chronicle the lives of the family of Sayward Luckett Wheeler, one of the most memorable female characters in American pioneer fiction. Richter traces the development of the Northeastern frontier from untamed forests in *The Trees* to small farms in *The Fields* and finally to the prosperous community in *The Town*. Orville Prescott observed in his book *In My Opinion: An Inquiry into the Contemporary Novel* that all three segments of Sayward's story "are certain to rank among the fine novels of our time. . . . There is a rare quality in these glowing pages—the most finished yet unobtrusive artistry, and a profound understanding of the pioneer character as it was manifested in and affected by a way of life now vanished from the earth." When Richter won the Pulitzer Prize for *The Town* in 1951, it was assumed that he was being honored for his achievement in the entire Ohio trilogy. Fifteen years later the novels were published in one volume under the title *The Awakening Land*.

In 1948 Richter returned to Pennsylvania. During the last twenty years of his life he wrote several minor works. Among them are *The Free Man*, the story of a German indentured servant who becomes a soldier in the Revolutionary War, and *The Grandfathers*, a comic tale depicting hill people in Maryland. Richter's ninth novel, *The Light in the Forest*, is generally placed with those minor works. Since its publication in 1953, however, the book has been one of the most widely read frontier novels for young adults, and it was made into a popular Disney film in 1974. The story of John Butler, a white boy who is captured by the Delaware Indians at the age of four, *The Light in the Forest* presents the themes that have made Richter a renowned teller of adventure tales as well as a respected writer of serious fiction.

The Light in the Forest

Taking the name True Son, John Butler comes to love his Indian family and their idyllic life, which Richter describes as being in perfect harmony with nature: "They passed their days in a kind of primitive deliciousness. The past was buried. There was only the present and tomorrow. By day they lived as happy animals. Moonlight nights in the forest they saw what the deer saw. Swimming under water with open eyes, they knew what the otter knew."

When True Son is fourteen he is forced by an Indian treaty to go back to his natural parents. In a now-famous passage Richter describes the starkly different life that True Son will face in the white man's world: "Ahead of him ran the rutted road of the whites. It led, he knew, to where men of their own volition constrained themselves with heavy clothing, like harness, where men chose to be slaves to their own or another's property, and followed empty and desolate lives far from the beloved freedom of the Indian."

True Son is not able to adjust to the white world, so he returns to the wilderness. But circumstances

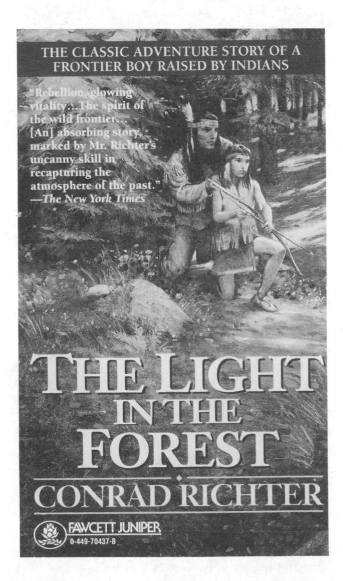

THE CLASSIC ADVENTURE STORY OF A FRONTIER BOY RAISED BY INDIANS

"Rebellion, glowing vitality... The spirit of the wild frontier... [An] absorbing story, marked by Mr. Richter's uncanny skill in recapturing the atmosphere of the past."
—*The New York Times*

THE LIGHT IN THE FOREST
CONRAD RICHTER

FAWCETT JUNIPER
0-449-70437-8

This 1953 work tells the story of John Butler, a white boy who is captured by the Delaware Indians at the age of four.

have changed profoundly, and he is faced with a painful dilemma. When he refuses to permit the Indians to use him as a decoy in an ambush of white settlers, he is banished from the tribe by his Indian father Cuyologa. True Son is then stranded between two worlds, and he must make the decision that will be his first step away from childhood toward maturity. Charles R. Duke stated in *Twentieth-Century Young Adult Writers* that the novel "dramatizes clearly the dilemma faced by people everywhere. Any individual who automatically accepts his or her culture as superior to others places restrictions on the ability to see good in others. . . . Through both the white men and the Indians in the story, Richter is able to show the prejudices that lead to misunderstanding and often violence and the effect that can have on young people such as True Son."

According to Duke, Richter was once asked about his purpose in writing *The Light in the Forest*. Richter replied, "I thought that perhaps if we understood how those First Americans felt toward us even then and toward our white way of life, we might better understand the adverse, if perverted, view of us by some African, European, and Asian peoples today." The "today" Richter referred to was the mid-1950s. Yet the need for understanding that concerned him then is equally meaningful at the end of the twentieth century, when the clash of cultures is still a pressing issue. *The Light in the Forest*—in fact, nearly all of Richter's best work—is timely in another respect. As Dorothy M. Broderick pointed out in *Voice of Youth Advocates*, the novel raises questions about the toll that human-centered civilization has taken on the environment. "What might our environment be like today," she asked, "if those arrogant white settlers had had just a smidgen of humility and been willing to learn from Native Americans? . . . Would we have national debates over preserving snails and owls at the expense of jobs and something called 'development' if we had begun our history by understanding that human beings were only one of God's creations?"

Coming to Terms With His Father

Near the end of his life Richter wrote the autobiographical novels *The Waters of Kronos* and *A Simple, Honorable Man*, which were the first two parts of a planned second trilogy. Richter was working on the third part, a novel about his own

If you enjoy the works of Conrad Richter, you may want to check out the following books and films:

James Fenimore Cooper, *The Last of the Mohicans*, 1826.
James Lincoln Collier, *The Bloody Country*, 1976.
Elizabeth George Speare, *The Sign of the Beaver*, 1983.
The Emerald Forest, Embassy, 1985.

life as a writer, at the time of his death in 1968. Both books are set in Pennsylvania and tell the story of an aging author named John Donner who re-examines his relationship with his father. In *The Waters of Kronos* Donner returns to visit the cemetery in his hometown of Unionville, only to find the town submerged under the dammed-up Kronos River. Then he hitches a ride with an old man driving a horse-drawn wagon and, as they descend the crest of a steep hill, Donner miraculously sees Unionville as it had been sixty years earlier. For the rest of the novel he meets the people and visits the places that were important in his childhood. Most significantly he come to terms with the death of his father. In *Conrad Richter's America* Marvin J. LaHood suggested that, through Donner, Richter "becomes aware of why his father prayed, prayers that as a boy he found painful and embarrassing. His father was fighting, with prayer, the forces of evil and death."

A Simple, Honorable Man directly parallels Richter's own experience, for in the novel Donner's father becomes a Lutheran minster who devotes his life to serving the poor. LaHood speculated that at the age of seventy Richter was finally "ready to write his father's fictional biography." Although he was able "to re-evaluate his relationship with his father in a more favorable light, there were still unresolved differences between them. In this beautiful tribute to his father, *A Simple, Honorable Man*, the crucial difference is one of faith."

Reflecting on Richter's career, Bruce Sutherland stated in the *New Mexico Quarterly* that the author's "understanding of people, a feeling for historical things which transcends mere knowledge, and the ability to think and write in terms of his characters and their environment places him among the chosen few who have made the past of America come alive." Similarly, Granville Hicks observed in *Saturday Review*, "I suspect that his fiction comes as close to historical truth as fiction can. . . . What his career hopefully suggests is that a man of talent and integrity may, with a little luck, thumb his nose at fashion and write the kind of books he wants to write."

■ Works Cited

Broderick, Dorothy M., "Two Grand Books Revisited," *Voice of Youth Advocates*, February, 1991, p. 346.

Bromfield, Louis, "Another Volume in Mr. Richter's Fine Frontier Saga," *New York Herald Tribune Book Review*, April 23, 1950, p. 5.

Duke, Charles R., "Conrad Richter," *Twentieth-Century Young Adult Writers*, 1st edition, St. James Press, 1994, p. 557.

Gaston, Edwin W., Jr., "Conrad Richter," *Dictionary of Literary Biography*, Volume 9: *American Novelists, 1910-1945, Part 2*, Gale, 1981.

Hicks, Granville, "Caught Between Two Ways of Life," *Saturday Review*, May 14, 1966, p. 28.

Kalb, Bernard, *Saturday Review*, May 16, 1953, p. 12.

Kohler, Dayton, "Conrad Richter: Early Americana," *College English*, February, 1947, pp. 225-26.

LaHood, Marvin J., *Conrad Richter's America*, Mouton, 1975, p. 326.

Prescott, Orville, *In My Opinion: An Inquiry into the Contemporary Novel*, Bobbs-Merrill, 1952.

Richter, Conrad, *The Light in the Forest*, Knopf, 1953.

Sutherland, Bruce, "Conrad Richter's Americana," *New Mexico Quarterly*, winter, 1945, p. 422.

Walton, Eda Lou, "Old Land of the Cattle Kings," *New York Herald Tribune Books*, February 7, 1937, p. 2.

Young, Stanley, "'Early Americana' and Other Recent Works of Fiction: 'Early Americana and Other Stories'," *New York Times Book Review*, August 2, 1936, p. 7.

■ For More Information See

BOOKS

Barnes, Robert J., *Conrad Richter*, Steck-Vaughn, 1968.

Contemporary Literary Criticism, Volume 30, Gale, 1984.

Edwards, Clifford Duane, *Conrad Richter's Ohio Trilogy: Its Ideas, Themes, and Relationships to Literary Tradition*, Mouton, 1971.

Gaston, Edwin W., Jr., *Conrad Richter*, Twayne, 1965, updated edition, 1989.

Lee, L. L., and Merrill Lewis, *Women, Women Writers, and the West*, Whitston, 1979.

Richter, Harvena, *Writing to Survive: The Private Notebooks of Conrad Richter*, University of New Mexico Press, 1988.

Stuckey, W. L., *The Pulitzer Prize Novels*, University of Oklahoma Press, 1966.

PERIODICALS

American Review, April, 1937.

Atlantic, November, 1943; June, 1946; April, 1947; August, 1950; June, 1964.

Books, February 7, 1937; March 3, 1940; November 1, 1942.

Book Week, August 22, 1943; March 31, 1946; June 7, 1964; May 22, 1966.

Boston Transcript, March 2, 1940.

Chicago Sunday Tribune, April 23, 1950; May 26, 1957.

Christian Science Monitor, March 10, 1937; June 1, 1940; May 4, 1946; November 5, 1968; October 23, 1978.

College English, February, 1947; November, 1950.

Commonweal, November 10, 1967.

Critic, June-July, 1964.

English Journal, September, 1946.

Midwest Folklore, spring, 1952.

New Mexico Quarterly, winter, 1945.

New Republic, March 18, 1940; December 9, 1978.

New York Herald Tribune Book Review, March 30, 1947; April 23, 1950; May 17, 1953; July 3, 1955; May 19, 1957; April 17, 1960.

New York Herald Tribune Books, August 2, 1936; February 7, 1937; April 22, 1962.

New York Herald Tribune Weekly Book Review, August 22, 1943; March 31, 1946.

New York Times, March 3, 1940; August 8, 1943; March 31, 1946; March 30, 1947; April 23, 1950; June 5, 1955; May 1, 1960; October 10, 1968.

New York Times Book Review, August 2, 1936; October 25, 1942; May 1, 1960; May 6, 1962; May 24, 1964; July 10, 1966; September 18, 1966; October 6, 1968; December 24, 1978.

Northwest Ohio Quarterly, autumn, 1957.

Old Northwest, December, 1975.

San Francisco Chronicle, May 1, 1950; May 15, 1953; June 22, 1955; April 18, 1960.

Saturday Evening Post, October 12, 1946.

Saturday Review, May 25, 1957; April 16, 1960; April 28, 1962; May 14, 1966; December 21, 1968.

Saturday Review of Literature, February 27, 1937; April 22, 1950.

Southwest Review, summer, 1958.

Spectator, May 17, 1940.

Springfield Republican, March 14, 1937; November 8, 1942; June 23, 1957.

Time, May 1, 1950; April 18, 1960; September 27, 1968.

University Review, summer, 1964.

Yale Review, June, 1946.

■ Obituaries

PERIODICALS

New York Times, October 31, 1968.*

—Sketch by Peggy Saari

Jon Scieszka

■ Personal

Last name rhymes with "Fresca"; born September 8, 1954, in Flint, MI; son of Louis (an elementary school principal) and Shirley (a nurse) Scieszka; married Jerilyn Hansen (an art director); children: Casey (a daughter), Jake. *Education:* Attended Culver Military Academy; Albion College, B.A., 1976; Columbia University, M.F.A., 1980. *Hobbies and other interests:* "Many."

■ Addresses

Agent—c/o Alida Welzer, Children's Marketing, Penguin USA, 375 Hudson St., New York, NY 10014.

■ Career

Writer. The Day School, Manhattan, NY, elementary school teacher, 1980—. Has also worked as a painter, a lifeguard, and a magazine writer, among other odd jobs.

■ Awards, Honors

New York Times Best Books of the Year citation, ALA Notable Children's Book citation, Maryland Black-Eyed Susan Picture Book Award, and *Parenting's* Reading Magic Award, all 1989, all for *The True Story of the Three Little Pigs!*; School Library Journal Best Books of the Year citation, *Booklist* Children's Editors' "Top of the List" citation, and ALA Notable Children's Book citation, all 1992, all for *The Stinky Cheese Man and Other Fairly Stupid Tales*; Best Children's Book citation, *Publishers Weekly*, Blue Ribbon citation, *Bulletin of the Center for Children's Books*, Top of the List and Editors' Choice citations, *Booklist*, all 1995, Best Book for Young Adults, ALA, 1996, all for *Math Curse*.

■ Writings

The True Story of the Three Little Pigs!, illustrated by Lane Smith, Viking, 1989.
The Frog Prince, Continued, illustrated by Steve Johnson, Viking, 1991.
The Stinky Cheese Man and Other Fairly Stupid Tales, illustrated by Lane Smith, Viking, 1992.
The Book That Jack Wrote, illustrated by Daniel Adel, Viking, 1994.
Math Curse, illustrated by Lane Smith, Viking, 1995.

"TIME WARP TRIO" SERIES; ILLUSTRATED BY LANE SMITH

Knights of the Kitchen Table, Viking, 1991.

The Not-So-Jolly Roger, Viking, 1991.
The Good, the Bad, and the Goofy, Viking, 1992.
Your Mother Was a Neanderthal, Viking, 1993.
2095, Viking, 1995.
Tut, Tut, Viking, 1996.

■ Adaptations

The True Story of the Three Little Pigs!, a sound recording read by the author, was released by Viking, 1992.

■ Sidelights

"Jon Scieszka," writes a critic in *Children's Books and Their Creators*, "enters classic fairy tales, turns them upside down, and exits with a smirk." In works such as *The True Story of the Three Little Pigs!*, *The Frog Prince, Continued*, *The Stinky Cheese Man and Other Fairly Stupid Tales*, and *Math Curse*, Scieszka and his collaborator/artist friend Lane Smith bring a postmodern sense of absurdity and a satiric edge to a classic category of writing. They take away the sense of easy familiarity and boredom that sometimes surrounds modern perceptions of the fairy tale genre. "What remains," the writer concludes in *Children's Books and Their Creators*, "is hilarious buffoonery within these energetic, yet sophisticated parodies."

The fact that Scieszka's parody plays to a more mature audience has astounded some critics. His works—sold as picture books intended for beginning readers—are equally funny to older children and young adults who have grown beyond the picture-book stage and are used to sophisticated humor. In doing this he follows the pioneering examples of other great writers in children's literature, such as L. Frank Baum, E. Nesbit, and Dr. Seuss. "What Scieszka has done," writes Patrick Jones and Christine Miller in *Twentieth-Century Children's Writers*, "is make a book equivalent of a happy meal—taking the things that most kids like in books like humor, adventure, fairy tales, and plain old silliness, and combining them into easy to read tomes which will indeed appeal to an audience of all ages." "Our audience is hardcore silly kids," Scieszka tells Smith. "And there are a lot of 'em out there."

Jon Scieszka attended Columbia University and studied writing there. He intended, says Amanda

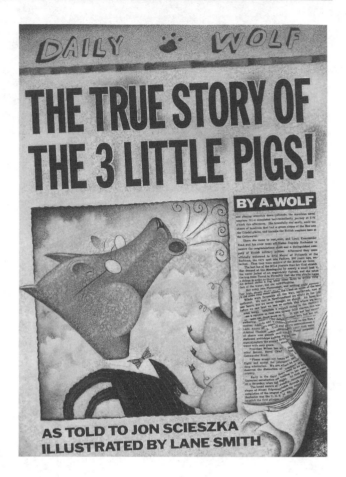

Scieszka retells the tale of the "Three Little Pigs," from the perspective of Alexander T. Wolf, a.k.a. the Big Bad Wolf.

Smith in a *Publishers Weekly* interview, to "write the Great American novel." The author reports, "Then I taught first and second grade and got sidetracked." Later he realized that a children's book is a condensed short story, and since he enjoyed writing short stories, he decided to try writing children's books. He remarked that it was surprising he hadn't thought of writing for children sooner, since he came from a large family, had always loved children, was the son of an elementary school teacher, and had enjoyed being a teacher himself.

After being introduced to author and illustrator Lane Smith, Scieszka left teaching for a year to develop book ideas with him. Regina Hayes at Viking Press saw the early drawings and text for *The True Story of the Three Little Pigs!* and decided to publish the story. "Lane and I got turned down in a lot of places," Scieszka tells Smith, "because people thought the manuscript of *The Three Little Pigs* was too sophisticated. That became a curse word—the 'S' word." "People don't give kids enough credit for knowing the fairy tales and being able to get what parody is," the author continues. "When I taught second-graders, that's the age when they first discover parody. They're just getting those reading skills and nothing cracks them up like a joke that turns stuff upside down." Teachers confirm this idea at book signings, saying how useful the book is in teaching point-of-view as an important facet of any story.

"Call Me Al"

The True Story of the Three Little Pigs! is the story of Alexander T. Wolf ("Call me Al"). A. Wolf has, he believes, been framed for the deaths of two of the three little pigs. This "revisionist 'autobiography,'" as Stephanie Zvirin calls it in her *Booklist* interview with Lane and Scieszka, presents the familiar story from a different aspect. "It turns out that Alexander . . . only wanted to borrow a cup of sugar for a birthday cake for his granny," writes Roger Sutton in the *Bulletin of the Center for Children's Books.* "After knocking politely on the first pig's door, Al's nose started to itch. 'I felt a sneeze coming on. Well I huffed. And I snuffed. And I sneezed a great sneeze. And do you know what? That whole darn straw house fell down.'" The scene is repeated at the wooden home of the second pig, and Al continues to the home of the third pig, where he is finally arrested, tried, and confined in the "Pig Penn."

Al maintains his innocence, state Kimberly Olson Fakih and Diane Roback in *Publishers Weekly*, by implying "that had the first two [pigs] happened to build more durable homes and the third kept a civil tongue in his head, the wolf's helpless sneezes wouldn't have toppled them." "He ably points out that wolves just naturally eat cute little animals like bunnies and sheep and pigs. It's just their normal dietary practice," explains Frank Gannon in his critique, "Everybody's Favorite Swine," in the *New York Times Book Review.* "'If cheeseburgers were cute,' says A. Wolf, 'folks would probably think you were Big and Bad, too.' It's hard to argue with him on that point."

One of the factors making *The True Story of the Three Little Pigs!* intriguing to readers is its dark humor. There is a sly contrast between Scieszka's

"innocent wolf" narrator and Lane Smith's sometimes morally-ambiguous pictures. Alexander's grandmother, notes Sutton, "looks a bit all-the-better-to-*eat*-you-with herself, and is that a pair of bunny ears poking out of the cake batter?" "At one strategic point the letter 'N' appears as a string of sausages," declares Marilyn Fain Apseloff in the *Children's Literature Association Quarterly.* "After the destruction of their homes, the first two pigs are shown bottom-up in the midst of the rubble; it is hard to tell if they are really dead or are just trying to hide. We have to take the wolf's word for their demise." One view of the second little pig frames his backside between a knife and fork. The reader's final view of Alexander shows

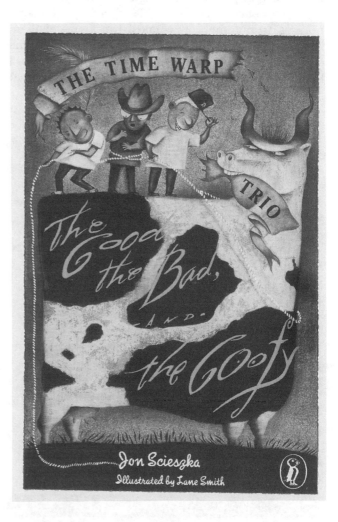

Intrepid Joe, Sam, and Fred of the Time Warp Trio team up for adventures in the wild, wild West, including being stampeded by crazy cattle and suffocating from cow fumes.

him, older, behind bars, and dressed in a convict's uniform, still trying to borrow that cup of sugar.

Enchanted Frogs and Time Travel

Scieszka's second fairy tale, *The Frog Prince, Continued*, was illustrated by Steve Johnson rather than Smith. As the title indicates, it takes up the story of *The Frog Prince* and traces it through its traditional happily-ever-after ending. It seems that the disenchanted Prince and his Princess are not well matched. "In fact," writes Linda Boyles in *School Library Journal*, "they're downright miserable. He misses the pond; she's tired of him sticking out his tongue and hopping on the furniture." The Prince decides to resolve his unhappy home life by finding a witch to change him back to a frog. He encounters several witches and magic makers from other fairy tales, but none of them have the power to resolve the situation. "At the end, tired and bedraggled and ready to re-count his old blessings," explains *New York Times Book*

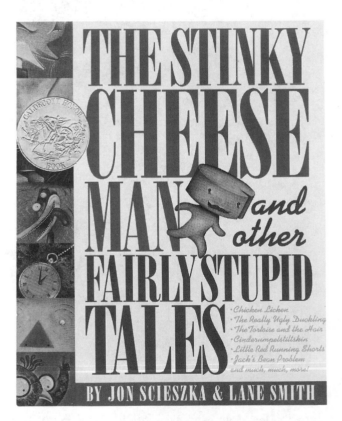

This 1992 award-winning book parodies popular fairy tales such as "Little Red Riding Hood," "Cinderella," and "The Ugly Duckling."

Review contributor Peggy Noonan, "he returns home to a by now anxious and rueful Princess, who is eager to kiss his moist amphibian mouth."

Several reviewers commented on Scieszka's continued use of a witty, mature outlook in *The Frog Prince, Continued*. "Like Sondheim's *Into the Woods*," declares Mary M. Burns in *Horn Book*, "Scieszka's tale is a sophisticated variant on traditional themes; it has a wry, adult perspective and yet is accessible to younger readers who enjoy—and understand—the art of parody and lampoon." Noonan also expresses the opinion that the book speaks best to older readers. "To fully appreciate *The Frog Prince, Continued*," she states, "you have to have a highly developed sense of irony and a sharp sense of the absurd, which most children don't develop before they can read, despite exposure to random television programming."

Scieszka and Lane Smith have also produced a series of books for younger readers called "The Time Warp Trio." The books are, according to Amanda Smith, "an introduction for children to other genres of literature." They tend to downplay the satire and parody of their picture books in favor of fast-moving plots and contemporary comedy. "I saw a need for something between a picture book and a chapter book," Scieszka tells Amanda Smith. "Kids get stuck in that lull there. When I taught third and fourth grades, I couldn't find cool-looking books to hand to boys, who, for the most part, were reluctant readers and didn't want to be seen as dummies." Scieszka and Smith wanted to make the books attractive to those readers, he continues, "so they'd pick 'em up and not feel bad about walkin' around with 'em. But still make 'em short enough, action-packed enough, disgusting enough." The titles take the three boys, Joe, Fred and Sam, to the court of King Arthur in *Knights of the Kitchen Table*, to face the pirate Blackbeard in *The Not-So-Jolly Roger*, and into the distant future to meet their own descendants in *2095*. The books, declares a reviewer for *Publishers Weekly*, "demonstrate Scieszka's perfect ear for schoolyard dialogue and humor—most notably of the bodily function variety."

"Almost Fairy Tales. But Not Quite."

Scieszka and Smith teamed up again for *The Stinky Cheese Man and Other Fairly Stupid Tales*, which takes on still more classic fairy tales. "With a relentless application of the sarcasm that tickled readers of *The True Story of the Three Little Pigs,*" declare Diane Roback and Richard Donahue in *Publishers Weekly,* "Scieszka and Smith skewer a host of juvenile favorites." "Blend 'Saturday Night Live' with 'Monty Python,' add a dash of *Mad* magazine with maybe a touch of 'Fractured Fairy Tales' from the old 'Rocky and Bullwinkle' show," states *Horn Book* contributor Mary M. Burns, "and you have an eclectic, frenetic mix of text and pictures with a kinetic display of typefaces." The stories range from "The Little Red Hen" and "Jack and the Beanstalk" to "Cinderumplestiltskin," "Little Red Running Shorts," and "The Tortoise and the Hair." Not only does Cinderella fail to win the prince, but Little Red Running Shorts out paces the wolf to Grandma's house, the Ugly Duckling grows into an Ugly Duck, and the Frog Prince turns out to be . . . a frog. Even the title character has a twist; unlike the more famous Gingerbread Man, the Stinky Cheese Man is avoided by everyone. "What marvelous liberties Scieszka and Smith take here," exclaims *Bulletin of the Center for Children's Books* contributor Roger Sutton, "playing around with the entire case of *Into the Woods,* but managing to be twice as funny as Stephen Sondheim."

One of the most noticeable aspects of *The Stinky Cheese Man and Other Fairly Stupid Tales,* is its unconventional arrangement of pages and its anarchic approach to storytelling. Jack and the Hen serve as commentators and narrators in the text. "The little reddish hen on the back makes fun of the ISBN, and one blurb from the flap brags that there are 73 percent more pages than 'those old

In this 1995 work a little girl almost drives herself berserk while under the spell of a math curse.

32-page "Brand X" books,'" explains Signe Wilkinson in the *New York Times Book Review.* "The title page reads 'Title Page' in blaring 2 ½-inch-tall generic black type." The Table of Contents appears in the middle of the book instead of the front. Jack complains when the first story begins on the endpapers of the book instead of the first leaf. Later he avoids being eaten by the giant by distracting him with a never ending story. The Hen—"a kvetch if ever there was one"—declares Burns—appears at odd points in the volume, complaining about the position of her story in the book. In a dark moment, after one of these appearances she is apparently eaten by the giant. "For those that are studying fairy tales at the college level," Wilkinson states, "'The Stinky Cheese Man' would be the perfect key to the genre, but no one would mistake it for the old-fashioned originals."

Although *The Book That Jack Wrote* was not a Scieszka-Smith collaboration—the illustrations are by Daniel Adel—it continues Scieszka's theme of taking traditional fairy tales and nursery rhymes, including the works of Lewis Carroll, and turning them upside down. Its pictures are more realistic but fully as surreal as any of the collaborations between Scieszka and Lane Smith. "The characters are borrowed largely from children's literature—a grinning Cheshiresque cat, a cow jumping over the moon, a pieman at the fair, Humpty Dumpty, and the Mad Hatter—but they bear only a passing resemblance to their traditional forms," states Nancy Menaldi-Scanlan in *School Library Journal.* "Readers who require logic will be stymied," declare Elizabeth Devereaux and Diane Roback in *Publishers Weekly;* "those who appreciate near-Victorian oddities and Escher-like conundrums will tumble right in." "This one,"

If you enjoy the works of Jon Scieszka, you may also want to check out the following:

The quirky tales of children's authors William Joyce, J. Otto Seibold, and Richard McGuire.
Stephen Sondheim's musical *Into the Woods*, 1986.
Back to the Future, starring Michael J. Fox, Universal, 1985.

---

says a *Kirkus Reviews* contributor, "will wow even the most sophisticated."

Like *The Stinky Cheese Man and Other Fairly Stupid Tales*, *The Book That Jack Wrote* operates on several different levels, according to the sophistication of the reader. The original rhyme, "The House That Jack Built," is very old—perhaps dating back to 1590, according to William S. and Ceil Baring-Gould in their *The Annotated Mother Goose*—and belongs to a class of poems known to scholars as "accumulative rhymes." It builds on a single statement and adds more and more detail with each line, like the Christmas carol "The Twelve Days of Christmas." In *The Book That Jack Wrote*, however, Scieszka and Adel turn this structure on its head by looping the last page to the first page—the title character appears on both pages crushed under a fallen portrait. So what appears to be a straight-line story is in fact a never-ending circle.

Math Curse, another Smith-Scieszka collaboration, "is one of the great books of the decade, if not of the century," states Dorothy M. Broderick in *Voice of Youth Advocates*. The narrator, a little girl, is caught up in a remark made by her math teacher, Mrs. Fibonacci: "You know, you can turn almost anything into a math problem." "The result," according to Deborah Stevenson in *Bulletin of the Center for Children's Books*, "is a story problem gone exponentially berserk." Soon the anonymous narrator can think of nothing except math problems. "It's a math curse: for the next 24 hours no activity remains uncontaminated by this compulsive perspective," explains Amy Edith Johnson in the *New York Times Book Review*. She finally "breaks out of her prison," Stevenson continues, "by using two halves of chalk to make a (w)hole."

As in Scieszka and Smith's earlier works, *Math Curse* slyly introduces mature elements of humor. Mrs. Fibonacci likes to count using the Fibonacci series of numbers. The author and illustrator credits are contained within a Venn diagram, and the price is written in Binary rather than Arabic numerals. Like a traditional math textbook, the answers to the questions are printed in the book: in this case, they appear upside-down on the back cover. "This isn't coating math with fun to make it palatable," says Stevenson, "it's genuine math as genuine fun." Scieszka and Smith, Johnson concludes, "capture a genuine intellectual phenomenon: possession . . . that can swallow up a student, generally in junior high school, as systems of thought spring into three dimensions and ideas become worlds—for a time."

"I think that turning something upside down or doing something wrong is the peak of what's funny to second graders," Scieszka tells *Booklist* interviewer Stephanie Zvirin. "Catching adults or the world at large doing something wrong empowers kids because they know the right thing—like brushing your hair with your toothbrush. If they get a gag like that, they know they're in the real world."

■ Works Cited

Apseloff, Marilyn Fain, "The Big, Bad Wolf: New Approaches to an Old Folk Tale," *Children's Literature Association Quarterly*, fall, 1990, pp. 135-37.

Baring-Gould, William S., and Ceil Baring-Gould, *The Annotated Mother Goose*, Bramball House (New York City), 1962, pp. 43-45.

Review of *The Book That Jack Wrote*, *Kirkus Reviews*, August 15, 1994, p. 1139.

Boyles, Linda, review of *The Frog Prince, Continued*, *School Library Journal*, May, 1991, pp. 83-84.

Broderick, Dorothy M., review of *Math Curse*, *Voice of Youth Advocates*, February, 1996, p. 376.

Burns, Mary M., review of *The Frog Prince, Continued*, *Horn Book*, July/August, 1991, pp. 451-52.

Burns, Mary M., review of *The Stinky Cheese Man and Other Fairly Stupid Tales*, *Horn Book*, November/December, 1992, p. 720.

Devereaux, Elizabeth, and Diane Roback, review of *The Book That Jack Wrote*, *Publishers Weekly*, July 4, 1994, p. 63.

Fakih, Kimberly Olson, and Diane Roback, review of *The True Story of the Three Little Pigs!*, *Publishers Weekly*, July 28, 1989, p. 218.

Gannon, Frank, "Everybody's Favorite Swine," *New York Times Book Review*, November 12, 1989, p. 27.

Johnson, Amy Edith, "Your Days Are Numbered," *New York Times Book Review*, November 12, 1995, p. 31.

Jones, Patrick, and Christine Miller, "Jon Scieszka," *Twentieth-Century Children's Writers*, 4th edition, St. James, 1995, pp. 851-52.

Review of *Knights of the Kitchen Table* and *The Not-So-Jolly Roger*, *Publishers Weekly*, May 17, 1991, p. 64.

Menaldi-Scanlan, Nancy, review of *The Book That Jack Wrote*, *School Library Journal*, September, 1994, pp. 193, 199.

Noonan, Peggy, "Those Moist Amphibian Lips," *New York Times Book Review*, May 19, 1991, p. 25.

Roback, Diane, and Richard Donahue, review of *The Stinky Cheese Man and Other Fairly Stupid Tales*, *Publishers Weekly*, September 28, 1992, pp. 79-80.

Scieszka, Jon, essay in *Children's Books and Their Creators*, edited by Anita Silvey, Houghton, 1995, pp. 581-82.

Smith, Amanda, "Jon Scieszka and Lane Smith," *Publishers Weekly*, July 26, 1991, pp. 220-21.

Stevenson, Deborah, review of *Math Curse*, *Bulletin of the Center for Children's Books*, October, 1995, pp. 68-69.

Sutton, Roger, review of *The True Story of the Three Little Pigs!*, *Bulletin of the Center for Children's Books*, September, 1989, p. 19.

Sutton, Roger, review of *The Stinky Cheese Man and Other Fairly Stupid Tales*, *Bulletin of the Center for Children's Books*, October, 1992, pp. 33-34.

Wilkinson, Signe, "No Princes, No White Horses, No Happy Endings," *New York Times Book Review*, November 8, 1992, p. 29, 59.

Zvirin, Stephanie, "Jon Scieszka and Lane Smith," *Booklist*, September 1, 1992, p. 57.

■ For More Information See

BOOKS

Children's Literature Review, Volume 27, Gale, 1992, pp. 152-57.

Contemporary Authors, Volume 135, Gale, 1992, pp. 388-89.

Holtze, Sally Holmes, editor, *Seventh Book of Junior Authors and Illustrators*, H. W. Wilson, 1996, pp. 289-90.

Something about the Author, Volume 68, Gale, 1992, pp. 211-12.

PERIODICALS

Booklist, January 9, 1989, p. 74; September 1, 1992, p. 57; October 1, 1993, p. 344.

Bulletin of the Center for Children's Books, July, 1991, p. 274.

Horn Book, November/December, 1996, pp. 713-17.

Kirkus Reviews, May 1, 1991, p. 614.

Los Angeles Times Book Review, January 7, 1996, p. 15.

New York Times Book Review, November 12, 1989, p. 27; October 6, 1991, p. 23; November 8, 1992, pp. 29, 59.

School Library Journal, October, 1989, p. 108; May, 1991, pp. 83-84; August, 1991, p. 169; December, 1993, p. 27.

Time, December 21, 1992, pp. 69-70.*

—Sketch by Ken Shepherd

Neal Shusterman

■ Personal

Born November 12, 1962, in New York, NY; son of Milton and Charlotte (Altman) Shusterman; married Elaine Jones (a teacher and photographer), January 31, 1987; children: Brendan, Jarrod. *Education:* University of California, Irvine, B.A. (psychology) and B.A. (drama), both 1985. *Politics:* "No." *Religion:* "Yes."

■ Addresses

Home—Los Angeles, CA.

■ Career

Screenwriter, playwright, and novelist. *Member:* PEN, Society of Children's Book Writers and Illustrators, Writers Guild of America (West).

■ Awards, Honors

Children's Choice Award, International Readers Association, 1988, and Volunteer State Book Award, Tennessee Library Association, 1990, both for *The Shadow Club*; American Library Association Best Book, 1992, Children's Choice Award, 1992, and Young Adult Choice Award, 1993, both International Reading Association, American Booksellers Association Pick of the List, 1993, Oklahoma Sequoyah Award, 1994, all for *What Daddy Did*; American Library Association Best Book for Reluctant Readers, 1993, for *The Eyes of Kid Midas*; California Young Reader Medal nomination, 1995-96, for *Speeding Bullet*; American Library Association Best Book for Reluctant Readers, 1997, for *MindQuakes: Stories to Shatter Your Brain.*

Shusterman's books, including *What Daddy Did*, have received numerous state reader awards. Two educational films he wrote and directed for the Learning Corporation of America—*Heart on a Chain* and *What About the Sisters?*—were awarded the C.I.N.E. Golden Eagle Award in 1992 and 1994.

■ Writings

It's Okay to Say No to Cigarettes and Alcohol, TOR Books, 1988.
The Shadow Club, Little, Brown, 1988.
Dissidents, Little, Brown, 1989.
(With Cherie Currie) *Neon Angel: The Cherie Currie Story*, Price, Stern, 1989.
Speeding Bullet, Little, Brown, 1990.
What Daddy Did, Little, Brown, 1990.

Kid Heroes: True Stories of Rescuers, Survivors, and Achievers, TOR Books, 1991.

The Eyes of Kid Midas, Little, Brown, 1992.

Darkness Creeping: Tales to Trouble Your Sleep, illustrated by Michael Coy, Lowell House, 1993.

Piggyback Ninja, illustrated by Joe Boddy, Lowell House, 1994.

Scorpion Shards, Forge, 1995.

Darkness Creeping II, Lowell House, 1995.

MindQuakes: Stories to Shatter Your Brain, TOR Books, 1996.

MindStorms: Stories to Blow Your Mind, TOR Books, 1996.

The Dark Side of Nowhere: A Novel, Little, Brown, 1997.

Also author of television adaptations, including *Night of the Living Dummy III* and *The Werewolf of Fever Swamp* for R. L. Stine's *Goosebumps* series; author of educational films for the Learning Corporation of America, including *Heart on a Chain* and *What About the Sisters?* Has written feature films for Apollo Pictures in addition to screenplays, including *The Time Machine Returns* for Turner Network Television, and *Evolver* for Trimark Pictures.

■ Sidelights

By the age of eight, Neal Shusterman was already on his way to a career as a writer. In a letter to E. B. White, he informed the author that *Charlotte's Web* required a sequel—and that he would be willing to collaborate in its writing. Although resolved to leave *Charlotte's Web* as it stood, White encouraged the young Shusterman to keep writing. This he did: in fact, by the time he reached his thirtieth birthday, Shusterman had published a handful of award-winning books for young adults. The author of imaginative mysteries and thrillers as well as biographies and realistic fiction, Shusterman considers young adult fiction to be an important genre. In an autobiographical essay on his Website, the "Neal Shusterman Home Page," he explained: "I've always felt that stories aimed at adolescents and teens are the most important stories that can be written, because it's adolescence that defines who we are going to be. That's the time when we choose paths for ourselves that are going to shape and define the rest of our lives."

Born and raised in Brooklyn, New York, Shusterman was an avid reader as a child. "There

were many books that had a powerful influence on the things I thought about, and how I made sense of the world," he explained. Among the books that influenced him as a child were *Jonathan Livingston Seagull* and *Charlie and the Chocolate Factory,* which he has praised for its imagination. After seeing the movie *Jaws* as a youngster, Shusterman wrote a story about man-eating sandworms that attack a seaside village. Determined to be the next Steven Spielberg, he handed the story to his teacher on his first day in the ninth grade. She proposed that he compose a story every month for extra credit. "I rose to the occa-

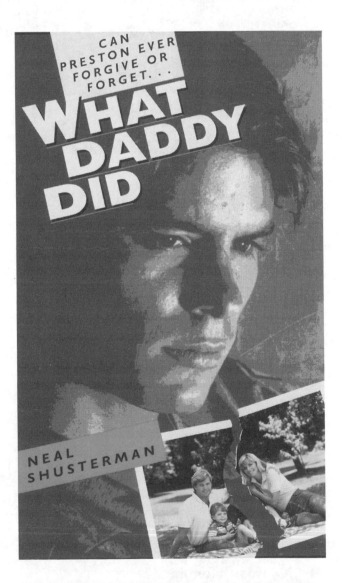

In this 1992 ALA Best Book for Young Adults, Preston Scott must face his father who was serving time in prison for killing the boy's mother.

sion," Shusterman recalled, and by the end that year, he stated, "I felt like a writer."

Shusterman moved with his family to Mexico City, where he graduated from high school and later attended the University of California, Irvine, earning degrees in psychology and drama. Not long after graduating in 1985, he launched his professional writing career, when the Syndicated Writer's Group—a national feature syndicate—picked up his humor column. Only twenty-two years old at the time, he became the youngest syndicated columnist in the nation.

A Novel Career

The Shadow Club, published in 1988, drew critical accolades and earned Shusterman recognition as a promising newcomer in the area of young adult fiction. Awarded the International Reading Association's Children's Choice Award, the novel explores themes of jealousy, rivalry, self-discovery, and self-worth. Seven ninth-grade students form a "shadow club" to commiserate about their common lot: each—from a class beauty to a track runner—is second-best to another student. Club members initially play innocent pranks on the students who overshadow their own achievements: a musician's trumpet is filled with green slime, for instance, and a leading actress discovers a snake in her thermos. Meanwhile, the "second-besters" become alarmingly loyal to each other in their mutual hatred for their rivals, and the pranks soon escalate into mean-spirited and even violent episodes. Although the Shadow Club members deny responsibility for the increasingly cruel tricks, the initiates—who started out as "really good kids"—begin to suspect that they have discovered "a power that feeds on a previously hidden cruel or evil side of their personalities," as David Gale observed in *School Library Journal.* Writing in *Bulletin of the Center for Children's Books,* Robert Sutton called *The Shadow Club* a "well-constructed" mystery "with a logical yet unexpected finale that provides moral weight as well as plot satisfaction."

Shusterman's next novel, *Dissidents,* covers familiar themes of rebellion and alienation, albeit in the unfamiliar setting of the Soviet Union. Kristiana Gregory, writing in the *Los Angeles Times Book Review,* called the story "an excellent glimpse of life on the other side of the globe," adding that

A boy struggles to control his hunger for revenge and desire of material things that he can obtain easily by wearing sunglasses that contain magical powers.

"Shusterman writes well. Contrasts between the United States and Soviet Union are wonderfully descriptive, from political twists to the perils of playing basketball on cobblestones." The action in *Dissidents* revolves around Derek, a fifteen-year-old boy who feels isolated and resentful when he is forced to live in Moscow with his mother—the U.S. ambassador to the Soviet Union—after his father dies in a car crash. Grieving over his father's death and nettled by his mother's lack of affection, Derek finds it difficult to adjust to the restrictions that accompany his new life. A misfit at school, he becomes fascinated with Anna, the daughter of a Soviet dissident. Determined to reunite Anna with her father, Derek confronts the KGB—as well as a number of personal demons. Kimberly Olson Fahib and Diane Roback noted in *Publishers Weekly* that "As adventure, this is a briskly paced, intriguing book," although they faulted Shusterman for a "patronizing attitude toward his material."

School Library Journal critic Lucinda Snyder Whitehurst called Shusterman's next work, *Speeding Bullet,* published in 1990, "a complex, multi-layered novel disguised as a boy's fantasy/adventure story." Nick Herrera, a high school under-achiever who is unpopular with girls, lives by the conviction that it is "better to fail by design than risk failing for real." After he rescues a little girl

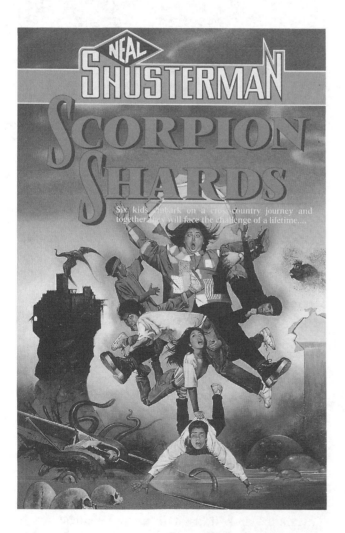

The battle of good and evil presides in this story of six teenagers who travel cross country to confront the evil forces that inhabit them.

from an oncoming subway train, however, he be-gins to suspect that he may have a calling: to rescue people in trouble. Nick performs another rescue—this time saving an old man from a burn-ing building—and soon becomes a local celebrity. He meets the mayor of New York as well as Linda Lanko, the beautiful daughter of a wealthy real estate developer, who introduces him to the upper echelons of New York society. While Nick continues to perform rescues, he eventually dis-covers that Linda has paid actors to pose as people in distress. When his friend, Marco, is trapped under a steel beam, Nick's rescue attempt results in his being shot, and he is ultimately forced to find a new source of strength. Diane Roback and Richard Donahue wrote in *Publishers Weekly* that Shusterman "here creates a fast-paced modern parable with compelling characters and true-to-life dialogue."

Shusterman turned to a fact-based story in his next book, *What Daddy Did.* Fourteen-year-old nar-rator Preston Scott was twelve when his father murdered his mother. When his grandparents for-give their son-in-law, Preston is forced to deal with the conflicting feelings he has for his father, who has been imprisoned for two years and is about to be released. "The account is an unbe-lievable testimony of love and forgiveness by fam-ily," Gerry Larson wrote in *School Library Journal.* Roger Sutton, writing in *Bulletin of the Center for Children's Books,* found that "the story is convinc-ing enough, realistically detailing Preston's anger and sadness, and his gradual forgiveness of his father." Larson noted, however, that "readers are made too aware that the author knows something they—and Preston—don't. It's a peek-a-boo kind of suspense that seems at odds with the interest-ingly complicated theme of forgiving and the un-forgivable." *What Daddy Did* garnered numerous awards, including the 1992 American Library As-sociation Best Book for Young Adults and the fol-lowing year's American Bookseller's Association Pick of the List award. Dorothy Broderick, writ-ing in *Voice of Youth Advocates,* claimed "many teenagers may actually stop and think about their own relationship with their parents," adding that "each reader will end up examining his or her own level of the ability to forgive and go on with life."

Shusterman readily admits that he wants his writ-ings to force readers to stop and think. "I sup-pose that's why I write—because I want to affect

If you enjoy the work of Neal Shusterman, you may also want to check out the following books and films:

Alden R. Carter, *Wart, Son of Toad,* 1985.
Robert Cormier, *The Chocolate War,* 1974.
Dean Koontz, *Cold Fire,* 1991.
Carol Matas, *Code Name Kris,* 1990.
Joyce Sweeney, *The Dream Collector,* 1989.
Heathers, starring Winona Ryder and Christian Slater, 1989.

people—somehow change them for the better," he wrote in *Junior Authors and Illustrators.* "I think most writers, deep down, have some hidden desire to change the world. They want to paint a picture of the possibilities—to show people the many things that are possible out in the world, or just within ourselves—both the good and the bad."

More True Stories and Tall Tales

With *Kid Heroes,* published in 1991, Shusterman continued to draw on true stories for inspiration. The book's more than fifty episodes relate the trials of young heroes, survivors and achievers, including a six-year-old who rescues her badly injured sister from the wreckage of a private plane; a thirteen-year-old homeless child who organizes a food and clothing drive; and a burn victim who loses both legs as a child, later to become a top wheelchair racer and the youngest member of the U.S. Olympic team. Following the publication of *Kid Heroes,* Shusterman was invited by Hasbro, along with actor Christopher Reeve and Admiral Richard Truly, the former head of NASA, to serve as a celebrity judge for the company's Real American Hero Search.

Shusterman received a 1993 American Library Association Best Book for Reluctant Readers citation for *The Eyes of Kid Midas,* a wish-fulfilling fantasy involving a seventh-grade student named Kevin Midas. "As the shortest kid in the grade, with the thickest glasses," the narrator informs readers, "control of his own destiny seemed about as far from Kevin as a slam dunk on a basketball court." When Kevin finds a magical pair of sunglasses on a class camping trip, however, he discovers that he can manipulate his—and others'—destiny: a bully jumps in the lake at his wish; an ice cream materializes in his hand; girls don't ignore him any more. Kevin soon realizes that his wishes, when granted, can be both dangerous and irreversible. Further, he discovers that the glasses have an addictive power over him, to the point where he feels ill when he removes them. "Shusterman has written a powerful fantasy based on every adolescent's desire to control his or her life," Frances Bradburn wrote in *Wilson Library Bulletin,* adding that "*The Eyes of Kid Midas* is middle reader horror at its finest, for it takes the most natural of early adolescent needs—the need to control one's own life—and exposes it for what it often is: an immature quest for greed and power." "Imaginative and witty, this fable for the '90s convincingly proves the dangers of the narcissistic ethos of having it all. With its original premise, unpredictable plot and whiz-bang finish, this book will handily captivate its audience," Diane Roback and Richard Donahue wrote in *Publishers Weekly.* Lyle Blake, writing in *School Library Journal,* found the story "hypnotically readable" although he noted that "The ending . . . may strike some readers as a simplistic cop-out, and the moral conclusion of his dilemma is the obvious one."

Adolescent insecurities spin grotesquely out of control in Shusterman's next novel, *Scorpion Shards,* the first installment of a projected trilogy. "As in *The Eyes of Kid Midas,* Shusterman takes an outlandish comic-book concept and, through the sheer audacity and breadth of his imagination, makes it stunningly believable," wrote Elizabeth Devereaux and Diane Roback in *Publishers Weekly.* Although the novel's six teenaged outcasts suffer from typical afflictions—from acne and obesity to confusing emotions such as lust and fear—their profoundly exaggerated problems are accompanied by supernatural powers. Tory, who suffers from acne, taints everything she touches; Travis, who enjoys destroying things, inadvertently demolishes five homes in a landslide; and Michael, who is obsessed with the opposite sex, incites jealous men to violence. Driven by internal demons, the six teens divide into two camps—one to eradicate the source of their powers, the other to exploit it. "This is a classic story about the battle between [good] and evil made especially gripping as the teenagers struggle with opposing forces literally within themselves. Readers will identify with their pain, their quest for identity, and the awesome responsibility each faces," Donna Scanlon observed in *Kliatt. School Library Journal* contributor Susan L. Rogers concluded: "The post-battle denouement finally allows stellar qualities to begin to shine, destruction to turn to repair, and readers to wish for a sequel to tell more about these interesting and unusual characters."

A Man of Many Talents

Shusterman's ability to captivate young audiences extends beyond the written word. He first tried his hand at screenwriting in 1987, when Apollo Pictures hired him to write two feature films. A member of the Writers Guild of America, he has written prolifically for film and television, producing scripts for *The Time Machine Returns*, a sequel to the H. G. Wells classic, and *Evolver*, a thriller for Trimark Pictures. His television credits include writing an adaptation for *Night of the Living Dummy Part III* and *The Werewolf of Fever Swamp*, two works from R. L. Stine's *Goosebumps series*. He also wrote a series of highly acclaimed educational films for the Learning Corporation of America, two of which—*Heart on a Chain*, about date violence, and *What About the Sisters*—garnered the C.I.N.E. Golden Eagle Award. He has also turned his talents to creating dramatic games, including two teen and two adult "How to Host a Mystery" games.

With *MindQuakes*, Shusterman produced a collection of supernatural stories that have been compared to the *Twilight Zone* genre. The volume's nine stories include that of an autistic child who paints pictures through which others can climb into an alternate world; a Loch Ness monster that lurks in a Jacuzzi; and a spiteful Christmas tree that causes trouble for Santa Claus. "Shusterman's mastery of suspense and satirical wit make the ludicrous fathomable and entices readers into suspending their disbelief," Elizabeth Devereaux and Diane Roback noted in *Publishers Weekly. Mind Storms*, a second collection, adds nine more off-the-wall stories to the collection, including the tale of a family that must avoid the morning's rising sun. "These stories range from humorous to poignant and capture the reader's imagination, exploring the themes with a certain degree of depth," Donna L. Scanlon wrote in *Kliatt*.

In *The Dark Side of Nowhere*, published in 1997, protagonist Jason Jonathan Miller gradually real-

izes that, below the surface, the picture-perfect community in which he lives is anything but "normal." After the funeral of his friend Ethan, who mysteriously died of a burst appendix, Jason encounters the school janitor, who gives him an unusual glove that can shoot steel pellets with lethal force. He keeps the gift a secret from his girlfriend, Paula, and soon discovers that the small town of Billington is entangled in a web of lies, including the true reason behind the monthly shots that are administered to the local teens. A *Kirkus Reviews* contributor stated that "Shusterman seamlessly combines gritty, heart-stopping plotting with a wealth of complex issues," and a critic in *Publishers Weekly* wrote that the author "delivers a science fiction page-turner in a classic mold."

Shusterman's works continue to grow in popularity. The reasons are clear: as a promotional piece from Little, Brown, and Company declared, his novels "deal with topics that appeal to adults as well as teens, weaving true-to-life characters into sensitive and riveting issues, and binding it all together with a unique and entertaining sense of humor."

■ Works Cited

Blake, Lyle, review of *The Eyes of Kid Midas, School Library Journal*, December, 1992, p. 133.

Bradburn, Frances, review of *The Eyes of Kid Midas, Wilson Library Bulletin*, March, 1993, p. 85.

Broderick, Dorothy M., review of *What Daddy Did, Voice of Youth Advocates*, June, 1991, p. 103.

Review of *The Dark Side of Nowhere, Kirkus Reviews*, March 15, 1997, p. 468.

Review of *The Dark Side of Nowhere, Publishers Weekly*, March 17, 1997, p. 84.

Devereaux, Elizabeth, and Diane Roback, review of *Scorpion Shards, Publishers Weekly*, December 4, 1995, p. 63.

Devereaux, Elizabeth, and Diane Roback, review of *MindQuakes, Publishers Weekly*, May 27, 1996, p. 79.

Fahib, Kimberly Olson, and Diane Roback, review of *Dissidents, Publishers Weekly*, May 12, 1989, p. 296.

Gale, David, review of *The Shadow Club, School Library Journal*, May, 1988, p. 113.

Gregory, Kristiana, review of *Dissidents, Los Angeles Times Book Review*, July 23, 1989, p. 11.

Larson, Gerry, review of *What Daddy Did, School Library Journal*, June, 1991, p. 128.

"Neal Shusterman Home Page," at http://www.storyman.com.

Roback, Diane, and Richard Donahue, review of *Speeding Bullet*, *Publishers Weekly*, December 14, 1990, p. 67.

Roback, Diane, and Richard Donahue, review of *The Eyes of Kid Midas*, *Publishers Weekly*, November 16, 1992, p. 65.

Rogers, Susan L., review of *Scorpion Shards*, *School Library Journal*, March, 1996, p. 221.

Scanlon, Donna L., review of *Scorpion Shards* and *Mind Storms*, *Kliatt*, January, 1997, pp. 10-11, 16.

Seventh Book of Junior Authors and Illustrators, edited by Sally Holmes Holtze, H. W. Wilson, 1996, pp. 295-96.

Shusterman, Neal, *The Eyes of King Midas*, Little, Brown, 1992.

Shusterman, Neal, promotional material from Little, Brown, c. 1996.

Sutton, Robert, review of *The Shadow Club*, *Bulletin of the Center for Children's Books*, May, 1988, p. 188.

Sutton, Roger, review of *What Daddy Did*, *Bulletin of the Center for Children's Books*, May, 1991, p. 227.

Whitehurst, Lucinda Snyder, review of *Speeding Bullet*, *School Library Journal*, February, 1991, pp. 93-94.

■ For More Information See

PERIODICALS

Booklist, February 1, 1996, p. 926.
Horn Book, May, 1991, p. 340.
New York Times Book Review, September 29, 1991, p. 27.
Publishers Weekly, May 12, 1989, p. 296.
School Library Journal, October, 1989, p. 137; December, 1992, p. 133.
Voice of Youth Advocates, June, 1988, p. 90; February, 1993, p. 358.
Wilson Library Journal, September, 1990, p. 103.*

—Sketch by Marie J. MacNee

Lane Smith

■ Personal

Born August 25, 1959, in Tulsa, OK; son of Lewis (an accountant) and Mildred (Enlow) Smith. *Education:* California Art Center College of Design, B.F.A., 1983.

■ Addresses

Home—New York, NY. *Agent*—Edite Kroll, 12 Grayhurst Park, Portland, ME 04102.

■ Career

Illustrator and author. Freelance illustrator, 1983—. Contributor of illustrations to periodicals, including *Rolling Stone, Time, Ms., Newsweek, New York Times, Atlantic,* and *Esquire.* Art director for film adaptation of *James and the Giant Peach,* Disney, 1996. *Exhibitions:* Works have been exhibited at Master Eagle Gallery, New York City; Brockton Children's Museum, Brockton, MA; Joseloff Gallery, Hartford, CT; and in the AIGA touring show.

■ Awards, Honors

New York Times Ten Best Illustrated Books of the Year citation, *School Library Journal* Best Book of the Year citation, *Horn Book* Honor List, American Library Association (ALA) *Booklist*/Editor's Choice List, and Silver Buckeye Award, all 1987, all for *Halloween ABC;* Silver Medal, Society of Illustrators, *New York Times Best Books of the Year* citation, ALA Notable Children's Book citation, Maryland Black-Eyed Susan Picture Book Award, and *Parenting's* Reading Magic Award, all 1989, all for *The True Story of the Three Little Pigs!;* Golden Apple Award, Bratislava International Biennial of Illustrations, 1990, Silver Medal, Society of Illustrators, 1991, and first place, New York Book Show, all for *The Big Pets; Parent's Choice* Award for Illustration, *New York Times* Best Books of the Year citation, ALA Notable Children's Book citation, all 1991, for *Glasses—Who Needs 'Em?;* Caldecott Honor Book, ALA, *New York Times* Best Illustrated Books of the Year citation, *School Library Journal* Best Books of the Year citation, *Booklist* Children's Editors' "Top of the List" citation, and ALA Notable Children's Book citation, all 1992, all for *The Stinky Cheese Man and Other Fairly Stupid Tales;* Best Children's Book citation, *Publishers Weekly,* Blue Ribbon citation, *Bulletin of the Center for Children's Books,* Top of the List and Editors' Choice citations, *Booklist,* all 1995, Best Book for Young Adults, ALA, 1996, all for *Math Curse.*

■ **Writings**

SELF-ILLUSTRATED

Flying Jake, Macmillan, 1989.
The Big Pets, Viking, 1990.
Glasses—Who Needs 'Em?, Viking, 1991.
The Happy Hocky Family!, Viking, 1993.

ILLUSTRATOR

Eve Merriam, *Halloween ABC*, Macmillan, 1987.
Jon Scieszka, *The True Story of the Three Little Pigs!*, Viking, 1989.
Jon Scieszka, *The Stinky Cheese Man and Other Fairly Stupid Tales*, Viking, 1992.
Jon Scieszka, *Math Curse*, Viking, 1995.
Karey Kirkpatrick, *Disney's James and the Giant Peach*, Disney Press, 1996.
Roald Dahl, *James and the Giant Peach: A Children's Story*, Knopf, 1996.

ILLUSTRATOR; "TIME WARP TRIO" SERIES; WRITTEN BY JON SCIESZKA

Knights of the Kitchen Table, Viking, 1991.
The Not-So-Jolly Roger, Viking, 1991.
The Good, the Bad, and the Goofy, Viking, 1992.
Your Mother Was a Neanderthal, Viking, 1993.
2095, Viking, 1995.
Tut, Tut, Viking, 1996.

■ **Work in Progress**

Illustrating *The Time Warp Trio Meet the XYZ Guys*, written by Jon Scieszka, for Viking.

■ **Sidelights**

Young readers are well acquainted with the work of Lane Smith. In fact, college students and adults, too, enjoy his satirical illustrations, which have often been described as "goofy" and even "disturbing." Winner of numerous awards, Smith is best known for his collaboration with the writer Jon Scieszka (pronounced "shes-ka") on such popular children's books as *The True Story of the Three Little Pigs!*, *The Stinky Cheese Man and Other Fairly Stupid Tales*, and the "Time Warp Trio" series. Smith's illustrations have also appeared in magazines such as *Rolling Stone*, *Time*, and *Ms.*, and he designed the characters for the Disney film *James and the Giant Peach.*

Smith is noted for his figures with large heads and small bodies, which he paints in dark oil colors that give them a distinctively strange, exaggerated quality, as if they stepped out of a dream—some might even say a nightmare. The artist traces his style directly back to his childhood interests and fantasies. In an essay for *Children's Books and Their Creators* he wrote that he is frequently asked by adults, "'Why *is* your art so dark? I am not quite sure why myself,'" he continued. "All I can say is when I was a child, I *liked* dark things. I liked the night. I liked being inside with my family and listening to the sound the wind made outside. I liked the scratching of the clawlike branches against the roof. I liked thunderstorms. I liked building tents and castles out of blankets and chairs, then crawling under them. I liked telling ghost stories. I liked Halloween." Not surprisingly, he also loved watching monster movies and reading horror fiction.

While Smith's work can be unsettling, it also shows a zany sense of humor, which may be at least partly inherited. Born in Oklahoma, he grew up in Corona, California, with his parents and his brother Shane. Smith once commented on the rhyming names to *Something About the Author* (SATA): "Shane and Lane. My mom thought that was funny. Yeah, a real hoot." He added that "*her* brothers were named Dub, Cubby, Leo, and Billy-Joe! My dad's brothers were Tom and Jerry (this is the truth)!" Smith developed an early fascination for the offbeat and the absurd. During summer trips back to Oklahoma on the old Route 66 highway, he enjoyed watching for unusual sights along the way. He told *SATA*, "I think that's where my bizarre sense of design comes from. Once you've seen a 100-foot cement buffalo on top of a doughnut stand in the middle of nowhere, you're never the same."

The Young Artist

Smith's artistic talent became evident during his years in grade school and junior high school. He made the wry comment in *Talking with Artists* that his future was determined by his lack of mathematical ability: "I guess I really knew I wanted to be an artist when my fourth-grade math test came back with a big 'D' on it." While Smith spent his time drawing and writing stories, he also read extensively. As he recalled in *Talking with Artists*, "I think one of my fondest memories is of lying stretched out on the library floor at Parkridge Elementary, reading Eleanor Cannon's *Wonderful Flight to the Mushroom Planet*. I loved the story and the art. To this day, whenever I smell hard-boiled eggs I think of how Chuck and David saved the planet with the sulfur-smelling eggs. From then on I drew only space stuff." As he grew older he became interested in cartoons, and he seriously thought about being a cartoonist.

After high school Smith enrolled at the California Art Center College of Design in Pasadena, where

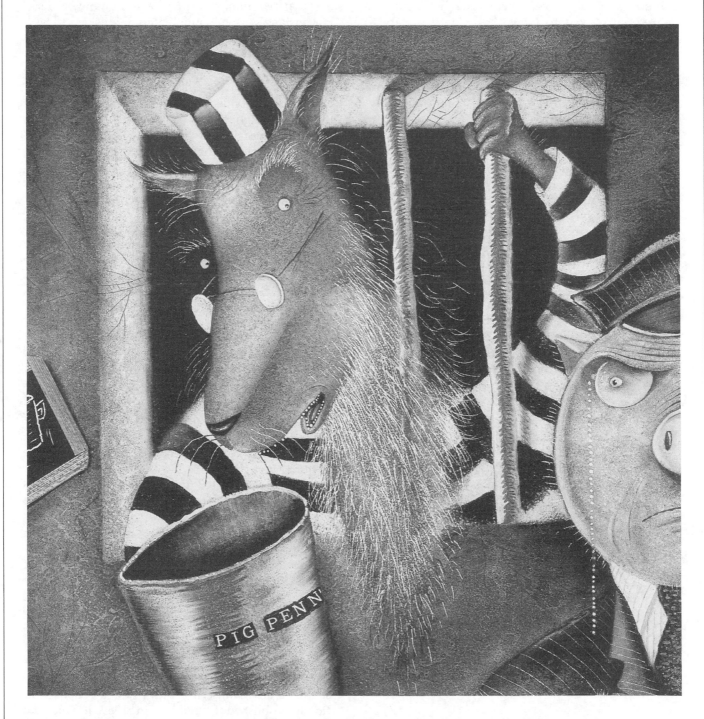

This retelling of the "Three Little Pigs" from the perspective of the Big Bad Wolf is the first of several works in which Smith teamed up with writer John Sciezka.

he studied advertising art. To earn money for tuition he worked as a janitor at Disneyland, cleaning out park attractions such as the Haunted Mansion and the Revolving Teacup at night. While in art school he developed an interest in Pop Art and European illustration, yet one of his teachers warned him he would never find a job in the United States. In 1984, a year after he earned his degree, he moved to New York City. Contrary to the teacher's prediction, Smith was soon a successful illustrator for some of the country's most popular magazines. He admitted in an essay in *Horn Book* that he had initially been worried about his employment prospects, but "the punk/new-wave movement came, and my work seemed to fit acceptably into that category."

Working on assignments from *Ms., Time, Rolling Stone,* and other magazines by day, Smith learned how to use oil paints at night. In college he had concentrated on drawing, so oil painting was a new medium for him. Smith's first real project was a series of thirty paintings, based on a Hal-

Smith's 1990 self-illustrated book details the dream-like journey of a little girl and her oversized cat.

loween theme, that illustrated the letters of the alphabet. He submitted the paintings to the children's book department at the Macmillan publishing house. Impressed by his work, the company hired children's author Eve Merriam to compose poems for each of the illustrations. Smith enjoyed his first experience in collaboration, finding that Merriam's poetry gave him new ideas. For instance, as he commented in his *Horn Book* essay, "I had *V* for 'Vampire,' and she came up with 'Viper,' which I liked a lot because I could use the *V* for the viper's open mouth." When their book, *Halloween ABC,* was published in 1987, reviewers responded positively to Smith's illustrations. Although the book was banned in some places because it was considered "satanic," it received several awards.

The Dynamic Duo Get Their Start

In the mid-1980s Smith met Scieszka, a teacher and aspiring children's author. They found they shared a wacky sense of humor, and they both enjoyed "Monty Python" movies and *Mad* magazine. Scieszka liked Smith's work, so they collaborated on a book titled *The True Story of the Three Little Pigs!* In their version of the traditional tale, which they tell from the wolf's point of view, Alexander T. Wolf is locked up in the Pig Pen for killing the three pigs. He says he has been misunderstood and victimized by the media, for he had called on the pigs only to borrow a cup of sugar to make a birthday cake for his grandmother. At the time he had a bad cold, and when he sneezed he blew their houses down. Alexander is quick to add that if the houses had not been so poorly constructed they would not have collapsed. Defending his decision to eat the pigs, he says, "It seemed like a shame to leave a perfectly good ham dinner lying there in the straw." In *Horn Book* Smith explained his approach to illustrating Scieszka's story: "I think Jon thought of the wolf as a con artist trying to talk his way out of a situation. But I really believed the wolf, so I portrayed him with glasses and a little bow tie and tried to make him a victim of circumstance."

At first Smith and Scieszka had little success in selling their manuscript, but when the book was finally published by Viking in 1989 it sold out within a few weeks. Children, teachers, and librarians all liked the contemporary twist to an old

In *The Good, the Bad, and the Goofy,* the Time Warp Trio—Joe, Sam, and Fred—travel back in time to the nineteenth-century American wild west.

story. While Kimberly Olson Fakih and Diane Roback in *Publishers Weekly* thought some readers might find Smith's pictures "mystifyingly adult," most critics were delighted by his quirky style. In a review for *Wilson Library Bulletin,* Donnarae MacCann and Olga Richard observed, "Using minimal but subtly changing browns and ochers, he combines great variety of creative modes: fanciful, realist, surreal, cartoonish." In an interview with Amanda Smith in *Publishers Weekly,* Smith expressed his surprise at the enthusiastic reception of the book, saying he was "stupefied when *The Three Little Pigs* took off."

In 1989 Smith also wrote and illustrated his own book, *The Flying Jake.* He dedicated it to his high school art teacher, Mr. Baughman, who had taught him how to experiment with different media to express various moods. The following year Smith published *The Big Pets,* which he described in *Children's Books and Their Creators* as "a surreal nighttime journey of a little girl and her giant cat." They travel to the Milk Pool, where children swim and other cats happily lap up the milk. The story also features children and oversized pets in the Bone Garden and the Hampster Hole. In *Children's Books and Their Creators* Smith said, "When I wrote *Big Pets . . . ,* I was expanding on

my own childhood fantasies of slipping out into the night for fantastic adventures while knowing there was a home base of security to come back to." Reviewers were charmed by the illustrations, finding them to be less threatening than the pictures in *The Three Little Pigs.* A typical response came from Diane Roback and Richard Donahue in *Publishers Weekly,* who noted that the "enticing illustrations . . . provide the perfect landscape for this nocturnal romp."

Smith's third self-illustrated book, *Glasses—Who Needs 'Em?,* was published in 1991. This story, which describes a boy's visit to an eye doctor to be fitted for glasses, is based on the author's own experience. Smith told interviewer Amanda Smith in *Publishers Weekly* that he had to get glasses in the fifth grade, but he rarely wore them because they made him look "too geeky." He said he wanted the character in the book to be "a little reluctant about [getting glasses] but still be kind of cool, so kids who wear glasses empathize and get some laughs out of the book, too, without its being heavy-handed." Writing in *Children's Books and Their Creators,* Smith credited designer Molly Leach with giving *Glasses—Who Needs 'Em?* the right visual effect by creating the opening lines of the story in the form of an eye examination chart. The words in the first line are in large letters, then they shrink down to the type size used in the rest of the book. "Not only did this device draw the reader into the story and establish the proper framework," Smith observed, "it also looked smashing! Leach has designed several of Smith's other books."

While Smith was writing and illustrating his own works, he continued his collaboration with Scieszka. The success of *The Three Little Pigs* had made them popular guests in schools. During their visits to classrooms, they read the students other stories Scieszka had written. A particular favorite was "The Stinky Cheese Man," which, Smith said in his *Horn Book* essay, got "a huge reaction" from the children. They "would just roll in the aisles. And then for the rest of the day you wouldn't hear anything else. . . . they would raise their hand and say, 'How about "The Stinky Car"?' Or they would come up after class and say, 'How about "The Stinky Cat"?' Because you know you are not supposed to talk about things being stinky." These responses encouraged Smith and Scieszka to publish *The Stinky Cheese Man and Other Fairly Stupid Tales* in 1992.

The Stinky Cheese Man contains "updated" versions of such classic stories as "Chicken Little," "The Ugly Duckling," "The Princess and the Frog," and "The Princess and the Pea." Here, however, Chicken Little is renamed Chicken Licken, and the animals are indeed crushed—by the book's table of contents, not the sky. The ugly duckling grows up to be an ugly duck, not a lovely swan, and the frog prince is revealed to be just a frog. "The Princess and the Pea" is retitled "The Princess and the Bowling Ball." *The Stinky Cheese Man* was an immediate hit, receiving praise from readers and reviewers alike. Smith received a 1993 Caldecott Honor Book award as well as several other citations for his illustrations. A contributor in *Time* magazine recommended *The Stinky Cheese Man* as "ideal kid stuff," and Mary M. Burns, writing in *Horn Book,* lauded it as "another masterpiece from the team that created *The True Story of the Three Little Pigs!*" *New York Times Book Review* contributor Signe Wilkinson claimed the book would appeal not only to children but to readers of all ages: "Kids, who rejoice in anything stinky, will no doubt enjoy the blithe, mean-spirited anarchy of these wildly spinning stories. . . . For those who are studying fairy tales at the college level, 'The Stinky Cheese Man' would be a perfect key to the genre. . . . Collectors of illustrated children's books won't want to miss it."

"Time Warp Trio" A Success

Smith and Scieszka launched their next project, the "Time Warp Trio" series, with the publication of *Knights of the Kitchen Table* and *The Not-So-Jolly Roger* in 1991. *The Good, the Bad, and the Goofy* followed in 1992 and *Your Mother Was a Neanderthal* was released the next year. The "Time Warp Trio" stories feature three boys—Joe, Sam, and Fred—who travel back in time and, with the aid of a magical book, encounter fantastic adventures. When they are transported to medieval England in *Knights of the Kitchen Table*, they save King Arthur's Camelot. Using their magic power to read, they defeat an evil knight, a giant, and a dragon. On their second journey, in *The Not-So-Jolly Roger*, the boys meet Blackbeard and his band of pirates, who threaten to kill the trio and make them walk the plank. In *The Good, the Bad, and the Goofy* they travel to the nineteenth-century American wild west, where they again use their powers to survive an Indian attack, a cavalry charge, cattle stampedes, and a flash flood. The

trio's fortunes change, however, in *Your Mother Was a Neanderthal*. After being transported back to the Stone Age, they find that not only are they naked, they also do not have their magic book. After Sam invents clothes, the boys embark on a series of escapades as they try to flee cavegirls, ultimately escaping to a happy ending.

The "Time Warp Trio" series received positive responses from reviewers who, like Smith-Scieszka fans, looked forward to each new installment. Elizabeth-Ann Sachs observed in the *New York Times Book Review* that *Knights of the Kitchen Table* is a "rollicking good story." Although she found *The Not-So-Jolly Roger* was "not nearly as much fun," she said Time Warp Trio enthusiasts would want to read it. Diane Roback and Richard Donahue expressed a similar reaction to *The Good, The Bad, and The Goofy* in *Publishers Weekly*. While they thought the story lacked the high-pitched "excitement of the trio's previous adventures," they expected readers to "gobble up this latest time-travel installment as they eagerly await the next one." Janice Del Negro, a contributor to *Booklist*, praised *Your Mother Was a Neanderthal*, especially Smith's illustrations: "Smith's pen-and-ink drawings add a rollicking, somewhat riotous air to the proceedings," she wrote. "This is the kind of book that kids tell one another to read—a surefire hit to the funny bone, whether read alone or aloud." Gale W. Sherman, in a review for *School Library Journal*, called it "Another great book from the dynamic duo!"

In 1993 Smith published his fourth independent work, *The Happy Hocky Family!*, a playful spoof on beginners' schoolbooks of the 1950s, which he described as his "favorite book to date." Smith created the seventeen-episode story of the Hocky family to help young readers understand the disappointments, mistakes, and accidents—as well as the positive experiences— that can happen in life. He used stick figures, basic outline shapes, and primary colors to depict the Hockys. In the *New York Times Book Review* Edward Koren noted that "Mr. Smith's draftsmanship, wonderfully expressive, still manages to create a family that is general and unspecific, one that could be of any racial or ethnic group. So who wouldn't be happy to drop in on the Hocky family and visit awhile in their book home?"

In 1995 Smith and Scieszka published *Math Curse*, a picture book, and *2095*, the fifth installment in

This 1992 Caldecott Honor Book, *The Stinky Cheese Man and Other Fairly Stupid Tales,* **features "Little Red Running Shorts" and other warped parodies of fairy tales for people of all ages.**

the "Time Warp Trio" series. *Math Curse* is the story of a girl who wakes up one morning to find every event during the day—getting dressed, eating breakfast, going to school—becomes a math problem that must be solved. She decides her teacher, Mrs. Fibonacci, has put a math curse on her, but that night she dreams of a way to get rid of the curse. Reviews of the book were glowing. Carolyn Phelan wrote in *Booklist*, "Bold in design and often bizarre in expression, Smith's paintings clearly express the child's feelings of bemusement, frustration, and panic as well as her eventual joy when she overcomes the math curse. Scieszka and Smith triumph, too, at the top of their class as artists and entertainers. . . ." Lucinda Snyder Whitehurst, a contributor to *School Library Journal*, liked the way the author and illustrator worked actual math problems into the story: "The questions, however, are not always typical workbook queries. For example, . . . How many yards in a neighborhood? How many inches in a pint? How many feet in my shoes?" She also observed that the book "can certainly be used as light-hearted relief in math class, but the story will be heartily enjoyed simply for its zany humor and nonstop sense of fun."

In *2095* Joe, Fred, and Sam are launched into the year 2095 by their magic book. Starting out in the 1920s room of the Natural History Museum, they eventually find themselves in the 1990s exhibition room at the museum. There they meet their great-grandchildren, who try to return them to the past. Julie Yates Walton, in a review for *Booklist*, noted that "the plot is a bit thin and meandering." However, she predicted that "readers will find sufficient distraction in the robots and levitation footwear of the future," and she praised Smith's black-pencil illustrations, which are "brimming with zany, adolescent hyperbole."

The Bright Lights of Hollywood

Smith undertook a completely new venture in 1996, when he designed the characters for the Disney animated version of Roald Dahl's novel *James and the Giant Peach*. At first he was reluctant to become involved in the project, which used live action, animation, and computer effects. In a *New York* magazine article Barbara Ensor quoted Smith as saying he knew it "could turn out to be a really bad thing where I'll commit for a year and I'll just keep getting stuff watered down."

If you enjoy the works of Lane Smith, you may also want to check out the following:

Florence Parry Heide's *The Shrinking of Treehorn*, illustrated by Edward Gorey, 1971.

The offbeat books of Maira Kalman, including *Sayonara, Mrs. Kackleman* (1989).

The works of James Marshall and Maurice Sendak, two authors who influenced Smith.

The art of Paul Klee and Kurt Schwitters.

However, he thoroughly enjoyed the experience, and all of his work was used in the film. Commuting from New York City to San Francisco one week a month for nearly a year, Smith designed the animated bugs and insects that are the characters in the story. He made highly complex drawings, paying attention to even the smallest details such as pleated skirts and antennae.

Smith did have some difficulty designing the James character. A composite of live action and animation, James had to look like ten-year-old actor Paul Terry. Smith told Ensor, "In real life [Terry is] kind of cute." Because Smith has trouble creating "cute" figures, the director, Henry Selick, finally designed James. Dahl's widow, Liccy Dahl, was thrilled with the film. She told Ensor she would never forget "that first moment when the bugs all came to life on the screen. . . . [Roald] would so have loved that. Ladybug! You just want to hug her. And Grasshopper is pretty dear to my heart." And Liccy Dahl had only praise for Smith: "Lane has got something that's extraordinary, the way he is able to put into their faces every ounce of their character." As a tie-in to the movie, Smith illustrated a picture-book version of *James and the Giant Peach*, which was written by Karey Kirkpatrick and published as *Disney's James and the Giant Peach* in 1996. That year Smith also did pen-and-ink artwork for a reissue of the original novel by Knopf. Reviewers were less than enthusiastic. Ilene Cooper, for instance, wrote in *Booklist* that "The art in both books is pure Smith, lots of Stinky Cheese Man-style faces. Kids new to the story or fresh from the movie won't mind a bit, but the contemporary artwork may cause a sigh among older readers who are fans of Nancy Burkert's [original] delicate and detailed illustrations."

As a result of his success with the animated *James and the Giant Peach*, Smith has been considering other Hollywood projects. He and Scieszka have reportedly discussed the possibility of making the Stinky Cheese Man a movie star. Smith told Ensor that in a screen version of *The Stinky Cheese Man*, "Stinky's role would be expanded. By virtue of his smell, he would create more and more havoc as the movie progressed, like a snowball that rolls down a hill and gets bigger and bigger. He starts out as a little stinky character that no one likes, but eventually he ends up sabotaging the whole fairy-tale land."

■ Works Cited

Burns, Mary M., review of *The Stinky Cheese Man and Other Fairly Stupid Tales*, Horn Book, November/December, 1992, p. 720.

Cooper, Ilene, review of *Disney's James and the Giant Peach* and *James and the Giant Peach*, Booklist, May 1, 1996, p. 1511.

Cummings, Pat, compiler and editor, "Lane Smith," *Talking with Artists*, Bradbury Press, 1992, pp. 72-75.

Del Negro, Janice, review of *Your Mother Was a Neanderthal*, Booklist, October 1, 1993, p. 346.

Ensor, Barbara, "Mr. Smith Goes to Hollywood," *New York*, April 8, 1996, pp. 50, 51-53.

Fakih, Kimberly Olson, and Diane Roback, review of *The True Story of the Three Little Pigs!*, Publishers Weekly, July 28, 1989, p. 218.

"Kid-Lit Capers," *Time*, December 21, 1992, pp. 69-70.

Koren, Edward, review of *The Happy Hocky Family!*, New York Times Book Review, November 14, 1993, p. 44.

MacCann, Donnarae, and Olga Richard, review of *The True Story of the Three Little Pigs!*, Wilson Library Bulletin, June, 1992, p. 118.

Phelan, Carolyn, review of *Math Curse*, Booklist, November 1, 1995, p. 472.

Roback, Diane, and Richard Donahue, review of *The Big Pets*, Publishers Weekly, December 21, 1990, p. 55.

Roback, Diane, and Richard Donahue, review of *The Good, The Bad, and The Goofy*, Publishers Weekly, May 11, 1992, p. 72.

Sachs, Elizabeth-Ann, review of *Knights of the Kitchen Table* and *The Not-So-Jolly Roger*, New York Times Book Review, October 6, 1991, p. 23.

Sherman, Gale W., review of *Your Mother Was a Neanderthal*, School Library Journal, October, 1993, p. 130.

Smith, Amanda, "Jon Scieszka and Lane Smith," *Publishers Weekly*, July 26, 1991, pp. 220-21.

Smith, Lane, "The Artist at Work," *Horn Book*, January/February, 1993, pp. 64-70.

Smith, Lane, comments in *Something About the Author*, Volume 76, 1994, p. 210.

Smith, Lane, essay in *Children's Books and Their Creators*, edited by Anita Silvey, Houghton, 1995, pp. 611-12.

Walton, Julie Yates, review of *2095*, Booklist, July 1 & 15, 1995, p. 1773.

Whitehurst, Lucinda Snyder, review of *Math Curse*, School Library Journal, September, 1995, p. 215.

Wilkinson, Signe, "No Princes, No White Horses, No Happy Endings," *New York Times Book Review*, November 8, 1992, pp. 29, 59.

■ For More Information See

PERIODICALS

Booklist, September 1, 1992, p. 57.

Bulletin of the Center for Children's Books, October, 1993, p. 58.

Entertainment Weekly, April 26, 1991, p. 71.

Horn Book, November/December, 1987, pp. 753-54; January/February, 1990, p. 58.

Kirkus Reviews, March 1, 1988, p. 369; August 1, 1991, pp. 1015-16.

New Yorker, December 25, 1995, pp. 45-46.

New York Times Book Review, June 12, 1988; November 12, 1989, p. 27; November 10, 1991, p. 54.

Publishers Weekly, July 24, 1987, p. 186; February 12, 1988, p. 83; May 17, 1991, p. 64; August 9, 1991, p. 56; September 28, 1992, pp. 79-80.

School Library Journal, June/July, 1988, p. 94; October, 1989, p. 108; June, 1991, p. 91; August, 1991, p. 169; October, 1991, p. 105; July, 1992, p. 64; August, 1993.

Washington Post Book World, December 6, 1992, p. 21.

Wilson Library Bulletin, November, 1992, p. 108.*

—Sketch by Peggy Saari

Jacqueline Woodson

tion, American Library Association, 1993, for *Maizon at Blue Hill*; Coretta Scott King Honor Books, American Library Association, 1995, for *I Hadn't Meant to Tell You This*, and 1996, for *From the Notebooks of Melanin Sun*.

■ Personal

Born February 12, 1964, in Columbus, OH. *Education:* Received a B.A. in English.

■ Addresses

Home—Brooklyn, NY. *Agent*—c/o Bantam Doubleday Dell, 1540 Broadway, 20th Fl., New York, NY 10036.

■ Career

Writer. Former faculty member of the Goddard College M.F.A. Writing Program; former fellow at the MacDowell Colony and at the Fine Arts Work Center, Provincetown, MA. Has also worked as a drama therapist for runaway children in New York City.

■ Awards, Honors

Kenyon Review Award for Literary Excellence in Fiction, 1992; Best Book for Young Adults selec-

■ Writings

FICTION FOR YOUNG ADULTS

Last Summer with Maizon (first book in a trilogy), Delacorte, 1990.
The Dear One, Delacorte, 1991.
Maizon at Blue Hill (second book in a trilogy), Delacorte, 1992.
Between Madison and Palmetto (third book in a trilogy), Delacorte, 1993.
Book Chase ("Ghostwriter" series), illustrated by Steve Cieslawski, Bantam, 1994.
I Hadn't Meant to Tell You This, Delacorte, 1994.
From the Notebooks of Melanin Sun, Scholastic, 1995.
The House You Pass on the Way, Delacorte Press, 1997.

OTHER

Martin Luther King, Jr., and His Birthday (nonfiction for children), illustrated by Floyd Cooper, Silver Burdett, 1990.
(With Catherine Saalfield) *Among Good Christian Peoples* (video), A Cold Hard Dis', 1991.
Autobiography of a Family Photo (novel for adults), New American Library/Dutton, 1994.

(Editor) *A Way Out of No Way: Writing about Growing Up Black in America* (short stories), Holt, 1996.

We Had a Picnic This Sunday Past (for children), illustrated by Diane Greenseid, Hyperion Books for Children, 1997.

Contributor to short story collection *Am I Blue?*, edited by Marion Dane Bauer, HarperTrophy, 1994; contributor to *Just a Writer's Thing: A Collection of Prose & Poetry from the National Book Foundation's 1995 Summer Writing Camp,* edited by Norma F. Mazer, National Book Foundation, 1996.

■ Sidelights

Jacqueline Woodson writes about invisible people: young girls, minorities, homosexuals, the poor, all the individuals who are ignored or forgotten in mainstream America. They are the people, as the author writes in a *Horn Book* article, "who exist on the margins." An African American and lesbian herself, Woodson knows first-hand what it is like to be labelled, classified, stereotyped, and pushed aside. Nevertheless, her stories are not intended to champion the rights of minorities and the oppressed. Rather, they celebrate people's differences. Her characters are not so much striving to have their rights acknowledged as they are struggling to find their own individuality, their own value as people. "I feel compelled to write against stereotypes," says Woodson, "hoping people will see that some issues know no color, class, sexuality. No—I don't feel as though I have a commitment to one community—I don't want to be shackled this way. I write from the very depths of who I am, and in this place there are all of my identities."

This sense of not really belonging to one community might be grounded in Woodson's childhood. During her adolescent years, she moved back and forth between South Carolina and New York City, and "never quite felt a part of either place," according to a *Ms.* article by Diane R. Paylor. But Woodson began to feel "outside of the world," as she puts it in *Horn Book,* even before her teen years. The turning point for her came when Richard Nixon resigned the presidency in 1974 and Gerald Ford took his place instead of George McGovern. "McGovern was my first 'American Dream.' Everyone in my neighborhood had been pulling for him." When Ford stepped into the

In this first book in the "Maizon" trilogy, Maizon Singh and her best friend Margaret struggle to keep their friendship strong while their lives lead them in different directions.

Oval Office, Woodson felt that she and all of black America had been abandoned. "The word *democracy* no longer existed for me. I began to challenge teachers, and when they couldn't give me the answers I wanted, I became sullen, a loner. I would spend hours sitting underneath the porch, writing poetry and anti-American songs."

This marked the young Woodson's first steps toward becoming an author. Writing soon became her passion. In the fifth grade, she was the literary editor of her school's magazine. "I used to write on everything," she said in a Bantam Doubleday Dell Web site; "it was the thing I liked to do the most. I never thought I could have a career as a writer—I always thought it was something I would have to do on the side." Her seventh-grade English teacher encouraged the young Woodson to write and convinced her that she should pursue whatever career she felt would make her happiest. Deciding that writing was, indeed, what she wanted to do, Woodson wished "to write about communities that were familiar to me and people that were familiar to me. I wanted to write about communities of color. I wanted to write about girls. I wanted to write about friendship and all of these things that I felt like were missing in a lot of the books that I read as a child."

The Maizon and Margaret Trilogy

In addition to the black community, Woodson has always had a deep empathy for young girls, who often suffer from low self-esteem in their preteen and adolescent years. "I write about black girls because this world would like to keep us invisible," she writes in *Horn Book*. "I write about *all* girls because I know what happens to self-esteem when we turn twelve, and I hope to show readers the number of ways in which we are strong." Woodson's first published book, *Last Summer with Maizon,* begins a trilogy about friends Margaret and Maizon that fulfills this goal. Set in the author's hometown of Brooklyn, the story tells of two eleven-year-olds who are the closest of friends. Their friendship is strained, however, when Margaret's father dies of a heart attack and Maizon goes to boarding school on a scholarship. While her friend is away, Margaret, who is the quieter of the two, discovers that she has a talent for writing. She also finds comfort in her family, who supports her in her attempt to deal with her father's death. Maizon, meanwhile, finds that she does not like the almost all-white Connecticut boarding school and returns home after only three months. Glad to be with her loved ones again, Maizon, along with Margaret, goes to a gifted school in their own neighborhood.

For a book just over one hundred pages, *Last Summer with Maizon* covers quite a lot of ground. Critics praise the work for its touching portrayal of two close friends and for its convincing sense of place. Julie Blaisdale, writing in *School Librarian*, also lauds the work for its "positive female characters . . . who provide the enduring sense of place and spiritual belonging" in the tale. *Bulletin of the Center for Children's Books* contributor Roger Sutton, while generally commending the

book, finds some flaws in it. He isn't convinced, for example, with the way Margaret eases her sadness by writing poetry. "Although underdeveloped," Sutton concludes, "this story will appeal to readers who want a 'book about friends.'" Similarly, *Horn Book* writer Rudine Sims Bishop points out the story's "blurred focus," but asserts that "the novel is appealing in its vivid portrayal of the characters and the small community they create."

Woodson continues Margaret and Maizon's stories with *Maizon at Blue Hill* and *Between Madison and Palmetto.* The former is not really a sequel but, rather, an "equal" to the first book in the trilogy.

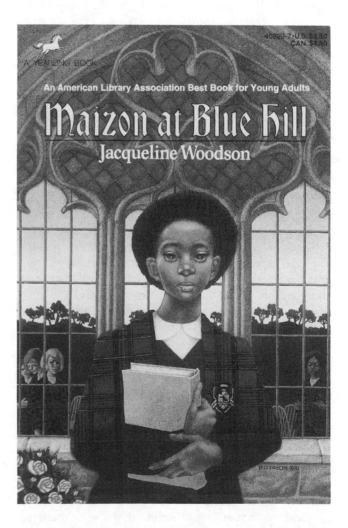

After starting classes at a private boarding school, Maizon misses her friends and family and has trouble adjusting to her new classmates in this second book of the "Maizon" trilogy.

Maizon at Blue Hill focuses on what happens to Maizon while she is at the Connecticut boarding school. Maizon, who is a very bright girl, likes the academic side of Blue Hill, but she is worried about fitting in socially. Most of the other girls are white and are either racist snobs or, at least, not eager to be her friend. Although she is welcomed by the small clique of other black students, Maizon sees this group as rather elitist, too. Her decision to return to Brooklyn is not made because she can't deal with any of these groups. She goes back because she wants to be in a place where she can just be herself.

An American Library Association Best Book for Young Adults, *Maizon at Blue Hill* has been acclaimed for Woodson's strong and appealing characters. "More sharply written than its predecessor, this novel contains some acute characterization," remarks Roger Sutton in *Bulletin of the Center for Children's Books*. Noting that the issues about self-esteem and identity that are addressed in the story spring appropriately from the characters rather than vice versa, *Voice of Youth Advocates* contributor Alice F. Stern asserts, "We are in the hands of a skilled writer here. . . . Woodson is a real find."

The last book in the trilogy, *Between Madison and Palmetto* picks up where the first book left off, with Maizon and Margaret entering eighth grade at the academy. Again, Woodson covers a lot of ground in just over one hundred pages, including Margaret's bout with bulimia, issues of integration as the two girls' neighborhood begins to change and white families move in, and the testing of Margaret and Maizon's friendship as Maizon spends more time with another girl named Carolyn.

As Elizabeth Devereaux and Diane Roback point out in their *Publishers Weekly* assessment of the novel, Woodson is primarily concerned again about themes of friendship and family. The critics applaud the author's gift with characterization, noting, however, that the effect is "somewhat diluted by the movie-of-the-week problems." In another *Voice of Youth Advocates* article, Stern similarly acknowledges that Woodson has "a lot of ground to cover" but notes that "she manages admirably." And a *Kirkus Reviews* contributor says that the episodes "don't quite add up to a plot," but the story is still a fine portrayal of a "close-knit community . . . [that] comes nicely to life."

The "Good" and the Controversial

In her *Horn Book* article, Woodson groups her books into two categories: her "good" books, which deal with relationships between family members and friends, and her more controversial books, which address issues of alcoholism, teenage pregnancy, homosexuality, and other issues that skirt the delicate problem of what is "appropriate" for children to read. She reflects here on how, after writing her second book, *The Dear One*, the invitations she had received to speak in front of people suddenly stopped. "Even after *Maizon at Blue Hill*, another relatively "nice book, school visits were few and far between. Yet I often wonder, If every book had been like *Last Summer with Maizon*, and I was a young woman with a wed-

Feni's life changes after Rebecca, a troubled, pregnant teenager, is invited by Feni's mother to stay with them in this 1991 work.

ding band on my hand, would I get to visit schools more often?"

The central character of *The Dear One* is twelve-year-old Feni, a name meaning "The Dear One" in Swahili. Feni lives in an upper-class African American home and basks in her family's attention. This all changes, however, when fifteen-year-old Rebecca is invited by Feni's mother to stay with them. Rebecca, the daughter of an old college friend, is a troubled, pregnant teenager from Harlem. Feni becomes jealous because she is no longer the center of attention. "But gradually and believably, with the patient support of Feni's mother and a lesbian couple who are longstanding family friends, the two girls begin to develop mutual trust and, finally, a redemptive friendship," relates *Twentieth-Century Children's Writers* contributor Michael Cart.

The Dear One is a unique book in that it deals with tensions not between blacks and whites but between poor and wealthy blacks. Woodson gives a sympathetic portrayal of Rebecca, who is uncomfortable living in what she considers to be a mansion, and who is also reluctant to change her lifestyle. She misses her boyfriend and her family back in Harlem; she envies Feni and resents the privileges Feni has been given. The novel also offers a fresh perspective on adult relationships. As Hazel S. Moore notes in *Voice of Youth Advocates*, "The lesbian couple seems to be intact, while the straight couples have divorced and suffered." Marion and Bernadette, the lesbian couple, provide Feni with wise advice to add to the support she receives from her mother.

Taking things a step further than *The Dear One*, *I Hadn't Meant to Tell You This* explores a relationship that spans both race and class when Marie, a girl from a well-to-do black family, befriends Lena, whom Marie's father considers to be "white trash." Both girls have problems: Marie's mother has abandoned her family, and Lena is the victim of her father's sexual molestations. Told from Marie's point of view, the book details the twelve-year-old's internal conflicts as she tries to think of how she can help Lena. In the end, Lena, who has been able to find no other viable solutions to her problem, runs away from home, and Marie must accept the fact that there is nothing she can do about her friend's tragedy. Woodson has been praised by critics for not resolving her story with a pat conclusion. Cart states, "Woodson's refusal

This 1995 Coretta Scott King Honor Book tells the story of Marie, whose mother has abandoned her family, and Lena, who is the victim of her father's sexual molestations.

to impose a facile resolution on this heartbreaking dilemma is one of her singular strengths as a writer." "Woodson's novel is wrenchingly honest and, despite its sad themes, full of hope and inspiration," conclude Devereaux and Roback in their *Publishers Weekly* review of the work.

The issue of homosexuality, which had been peripheral in Woodson's books up to this point, comes to the foreground in *From the Notebooks of Melanin Sun*. Thirteen-year-old Melanin Sun, the central character, has a close relationship with his mother, whom he admires as a single working mother who is also putting herself through law school. Their bond is strained, however, when Melanin's mother tells him that she is a lesbian

If you enjoy the works of Jacqueline Woodson, you may also want to check out the following books:

Alice Childress, *Rainbow Jordan,* 1981.
Simi Bedford, *Yoruba Girl Dancing,* 1992.
Bernie MacKinnon, *The Meantime,* 19884.
Brenda Seabrooke, *The Bridges of Summer,* 1992.
Rita Williams-Garcia, *Fast Talk on a Slow Track,* 1991.

and that she is in love with a white woman. This development makes Melanin question his relationship with his mother, as well as making him wonder about his own sexuality. Torn between his emotional need for his mother and his fear about what her lesbianism implies, Melanin goes through a tough time as his friends also begin to abandon him. Gossip in the neighborhood that Melanin's mother is "unfit" also spreads, making matters even worse. Again, Woodson offers no clean-cut resolution to the story, but by the novel's end Melanin has begun to grow and understand his mother. Critics have praised Woodson's portrayal of Melanin's inner conflicts as being right on the money. As Lois Metzger writes in the *New York Times Book Review,* "Ms. Woodson, in this moving, lovely book, shows you Melanin's strength and the sun shining through." "Woodson has addressed with care and skill the sensitive issue of homosexuality within the family . . . [without] becoming an advocate of any particular attitude," asserts *Voice of Youth Advocates* critic Hazel Moore.

Autobiography of a Family Photo

Most of Woodson's books up to this point have been aimed at preteen and teenage audiences, but more recently the author has also written a novel for adults, *Autobiography of a Family Photo,* and a children's picture book, *We Had a Picnic This Sunday Past.* The latter, as with all of the author's work, is about the importance of family, while the former addresses the issues of sexuality and sexual behavior for a more mature audience. However, its short length and central coming-of-age theme put *Autobiography of a Family Photo* within the reach of young adult audiences. Told in a series of vignettes spanning the '60s and '70s, the novel is a reminiscence told by an unnamed narrator. Her family has many problems, including her parents' troubled marriage, her brother Carlos's inclination to be sexually abusive her, her brother Troy's struggles with homosexuality that compel him to go to Vietnam, and other difficulties. Despite all of this, the narrator survives adolescence, undergoing a "compelling transformation," according to Margot Mifflin in an *Entertainment Weekly* review.

However, some critics have felt that, ultimately, the vignettes fail to form a unified whole. A *Kirkus Reviews* contributor, for example, comments: "Chapters build on each other, but the information provided is too scanty to really create any depth." Catherine Bush, writing in the *New York Times Book Review,* has the complaint that the novel focuses too much on the narrator's growing sexual awareness. "I found myself wishing that the narrator's self-awareness and longing could be defined less exclusively in sexual terms," Bush says. The critic nevertheless concludes, "But even in these restrictive terms, the novel is the best kind of survival guide: clear-eyed, gut true."

If there is anything that Woodson has never backed away from, it is portraying these truths about life in modern American society. She has written her "good" books about friendship and family that deal with safe, acceptable topics, but she clearly does not shy away from the controversial subjects like homosexuality and sexual abuse. This is not so much because Woodson is trying to force any kind of ideology on her readers as it is because of her interest in all kinds of people, especially the socially rejected, and to show that these people are significant, too.

"One of the most important ideas I want to get across to my readers," she says on the Bantam Double-day Dell Web site, "is the idea of feeling like you're okay with who you are." Once an outsider who felt uncomfortable with her position in the world, Woodson has now accepted and embraced her place in society. "I've been in the children's publishing world long enough to know I'm on the outside of it," she states in *Ms.* Even though Paylor calls her "one of the foremost African American women writers of young adult books," Woodson recognizes she will probably never have a best-seller. For her, it is enough to know that she has touched her audience.

■ Works Cited

Review of *Autobiography of a Family Photo, Kirkus Reviews,* October 1, 1994, pp. 1307-8.

Bantam Doubleday Dell Web Site, "Jacqueline Woodson," http://www.bdd.com./forum/bdd-forum.cgi/trc/index/wood (April 8, 1997).

Review of *Between Madison and Palmetto, Kirkus Reviews,* December 1, 1993, p. 1532.

Bishop, Rudine Sims, "Books from Parallel Cultures: New African-American Voices," *Horn Book,* September, 1992, pp. 616-20.

Blaisdale, Julie, review of *Last Summer with Maizon, School Librarian,* November, 1991, p. 154.

Bush, Catherine, "A World Without Childhood," *New York Times Book Review,* February 26, 1995, p. 14.

Cart, Michael, "Jacqueline Woodson," *Twentieth-Century Children's Writers,* 4th edition, edited by Laura Standley Berger, St. James Press, 1995.

Devereaux, Elizabeth, and Diane Roback, review of *Between Madison and Palmetto, Publishers Weekly,* November 8, 1993, p. 78.

Devereaux, Elizabeth, and Diane Roback, review of *I Hadn't Meant to Tell You This, Publishers Weekly,* April 18, 1994, p. 64.

Metzger, Lois, review of *From the Notebooks of Melanin Sun, New York Times Book Review,* July 16, 1995, p. 27.

Mifflin, Margot, review of *Autobiography of a Family Photo, Entertainment Weekly,* April 21, 1995, pp. 50-51.

Moore, Hazel S., review of *The Dear One, Voice of Youth Advocates,* October, 1991, p. 236.

Moore, Hazel S., review of *From the Notebooks of Melanin Sun, Voice of Youth Advocates,* October, 1995, p. 227.

Paylor, Diane R., "Bold Type: Jacqueline Woodson's 'Girl Stories,'" *Ms.,* November-December, 1994, p. 77.

Stern, Alice F., review of *Maizon at Blue Hill, Voice of Youth Advocates,* October, 1992, p. 235.

Stern, Alice F., review of *Between Madison and Palmetto, Voice of Youth Advocates,* June, 1994, p. 95.

Sutton, Roger, review of *Last Summer with Maizon, Bulletin of the Center for Children's Books,* October, 1990, pp. 49-50.

Sutton, Roger, review of *Maizon at Blue Hill, Bulletin of the Center for Children's Books,* December, 1992, p. 128.

Woodson, Jacqueline, "A Sign of Having Been Here," *Horn Book,* November-December, 1995, pp. 711-15.

■ For More Information See

PERIODICALS

Booklist, November 15, 1991, p. 619; July, 1992, p. 1931; March 15, 1993, p. 1344; September 15, 1993, p. 152; February 15, 1994, p. 1072; December 15, 1994, p. 736; January 15, 1995, p. 860; April 1, 1995, pp. 1404, 1412; March 15, 1996, p. 1284.

Bulletin of the Center for Children's Books, September, 1991, p. 26; December, 1993, p. 136; March, 1994, p. 239; July, 1995, p. 401.

Essence, February, 1995, p. 52; April, 1995, p. 56.

Horn Book, November, 1991, p. 746; January, 1994, p. 72; September, 1994, p. 601; July, 1995, p. 468.

Horn Book Guide, January, 1990, p. 325; spring, 1992, p. 81; spring, 1993, p. 78; spring, 1994, p. 84; fall, 1995, p. 314.

Kirkus Reviews, August 1, 1991, p. 1018; October 15, 1992, p. 1318; June 1, 1994, p. 782; May 15, 1995, p. 717.

Ms., July, 1995, p. 75.

New York Times Book Review, July 29, 1990, p. 33; May 10, 1992, p. 21; November 6, 1994, p. 32; April 28, 1996, p. 36.

Publishers Weekly, June 28, 1991, p. 103; January 20, 1992, p. 66; January 4, 1993, p. 74; November 7, 1994, p. 44; May 15, 1995, p. 74; December 11, 1995, p. 71.

School Library Journal, November, 1990, p. 121; June, 1991, p. 129; November, 1992, p. 99; November, 1993, p. 111; May, 1994, p. 136; August, 1995, p. 158.

Voice of Youth Advocates, February, 1991, p. 360; April, 1994, p. 32; June, 1997, p. 114.*

—Sketch by Janet L. Hile

Cheryl Zach

journalist, 1976-77. *Member:* Romance Writers of America, Society of Children's Book Writers and Illustrators (regional advisor), PEN, Southern California Council on Literature for Children and Young People, Phi Kappa Phi.

■ Personal

Full name, Cheryl Byrd Zach; pseudonyms Jennifer Cole and Jamie Suzanne; born June 9, 1947, in Clarksville, TN; daughter of Smith Henry (a military non-commissioned officer) and Nancy (a sales manager; maiden name, LeGate) Byrd; married Q. J. Wasden, June 2, 1967 (divorced, September, 1979); married Charles O. Zach, Jr. (president of a die casting company), June 20, 1982 (died, 1990); children: (first marriage) Quinton John, Michelle Nicole. *Education:* Austin Peay State University, B.A., 1968, M.A., 1977. *Politics:* Democrat. *Religion:* Episcopalian.

■ Addresses

Home—Bellflower, CA. *Office*—9157 Belmont St., Bellflower, CA 90706. *Agent*—Richard Curtis, 164 East 64th St., New York, NY 10021.

■ Career

Writer, 1982—. Harrison County High School, MS, English teacher, 1970-71; Dyersburg High School, Dyersburg, TN, English teacher, 1978-82. Freelance

■ Awards, Honors

Golden Medallion Award for best young adult novel, Romance Writers of America, 1985, for *The Frog Princess*, and 1986, for *Waiting for Amanda*; Rita Award finalist, Romance Writers of America, for *Looking Out for Lacey* and *Paradise*; Rita Award, Romance Writers of America, for *Runaway*; inducted into Romance Writers of America Hall of Fame, 1996.

■ Writings

YOUNG ADULT ROMANCE NOVELS

The Frog Princess ("First Love" series), Silhouette, 1984.
Waiting for Amanda, Silhouette, 1985.
Fortune's Child, Silhouette, 1985.
Looking Out for Lacey, Fawcett, 1989.
Paradise, HarperCollins, 1994.
Dear Diary: Runaway, Berkley, 1995.
Dear Diary: Family Secrets, Berkley, 1996.
Kissing Caroline ("Loves Stories" series), Bantam, 1996.
Carrie's Gold, Avon, 1997.

YOUNG ADULT ROMANCE NOVELS; UNDER PSEUDONYM JENNIFER COLE

Three's a Crowd, Fawcett, 1986.
Star Quality, Fawcett, 1987.
Too Many Cooks, Fawcett, 1987.
Mollie in Love, Fawcett, 1987.

"SWEET VALLEY TWINS" SERIES; UNDER PSEUDONYM JAMIE SUZANNE

Second Best, Bantam, 1988.
The Class Trip, Bantam, 1988.
Left Behind, Bantam, 1988.
Jessica, the Rock Star, Bantam, 1989.
The Christmas Ghost, Bantam, 1989.

"SMYTH VS. SMITH" SERIES

Oh, Brother, Lynx Books, 1988.
Stealing the Scene, Lynx Books, 1988.
Tug of War, Lynx Books, 1988.
More Than Friends, Lynx Books, 1989.
Surprise, Surprise, Lynx Books, 1989.
Growing Pains, Lynx Books, 1989.

"SOUTHERN ANGELS" SERIES

Hearts Divided, Bantam, 1995.
Winds of Betrayal, Bantam, 1995.
A Dream of Freedom, Bantam, 1995.
Love's Rebellion, Bantam, 1995.

"MIND OVER MATTER" SERIES

The Mummy's Footsteps, Avon, 1997.
Phantom of the Roxy, Avon, 1997.
Curse of the Idol's Eye, Avon, 1997.
The Gypsy's Warning, Avon, 1997.
The Haunted Beach, Avon, 1997.
The Disappearing Raven, Avon, 1997.

CHILDREN'S FICTION

Benny and the Crazy Contest, Bradbury, 1991.
Benny and the No-Good Teacher, illustrated by Janet Wilson, Bradbury, 1992.
Here Comes the Martian Mushroom, Willowisp, 1994.

OTHER

Twice a Fool (adult romance novel), Harlequin, 1984.
Los Angeles (juvenile nonfiction), Dillon, 1989.

Contributor of articles, poems, and stories to magazines and newspapers, including *Writer, Romance Writers Report,* and *Fiction Writers Monthly.* Zach's books have been published in French, German, Dutch, and Swiss.

■ Sidelights

Award-winning young adult author Cheryl Zach was walking on a street in Honolulu, Hawaii, in 1995 when she "had an epiphany—a moment when time seems to stop and you receive a sudden insight or revelation." As she explained in her essay in *Something About the Author Autobiography Series,* she realized, "I was living my dream. And I felt a surge of joy." Zach, who began her career writing young adult romance novels because of an agent's marketing decision and spent some time writing under a pseudonym for the "Sweet Valley High" series, may well be pleased about her success as a writer. Some of the series for which she has written have been very well received by young readers, and her work for the series "Southern Angels" has received positive critical attention. The first young adult author to be inducted into the Romance Writer's of America Hall of Fame, Zach has won praise for her ability to empathize with her characters, to write suspenseful works, and to integrate historical detail into the settings and plots of her novels.

Zach's parents were both from Tennessee, and she was born there after World War II. Due to her father's career in the U.S. Army, the family moved around a great deal. Zach spent her childhood in different parts of the United States, and in Europe. As Zach recalled in *SAAS,* she began to develop her skills as a writer when she was a young child by making up stories. Zach's love of history began in elementary school, when she read "an American history textbook . . . like a novel." In addition, Zach began to experience some of the situations which would emerge as themes in her novels for young adults. Notable among these was her temporary separation from her parents, when her father was stationed in Germany and her mother was in the hospital with tuberculosis. "I know that somewhere inside me lingers the feelings of a little kid whose parents have gone away." Finally, in part because her family moved around so frequently, she "felt different from the crowd" in high school, and "never, ever felt typical."

In this historical novel, Hannah, a slave, helps other slaves find their freedom via the Underground Railroad and attempts a daring escape herself.

Zach went to Austin Peay State University, where she majored in English and minored in history. She became active in drama, the college literary magazine, the drill team, band, and a sorority. It was at this point that she first began to submit articles and stories for publication to magazines and journals. She won the college English Award when she graduated in 1968. Despite winning this award and her limited success publishing articles, she was not able to begin her professional career as a writer immediately. Zach had eloped with a man in college, and in 1969, they had a son. "There are people who are able to write with small children, but I wasn't one of them," she remarked in *SAAS*. "With no help with childcare, I accomplished very little writing."

Still, Zach was able to begin work as a high school English teacher in Mississippi. There, in addition to the usual challenges of teaching young adults, Zach dealt with the problems of racial integration. She worked as hard as she could to become an effective teacher despite the tension in the school. She also, as she wrote in her sketch in *SAAS*, "discovered that I genuinely like my teenaged students, despite—or perhaps because of—the fact that my own adolescence was not a comfortable time. This empathy would later be an important factor when I once again began writing seriously."

Zach spent some time in graduate school before leaving with her husband and young son for Scotland. After a few years there, she returned to Tennessee and graduate school, and later, she worked once again as a high school teacher. She also had another child, a girl. "I taught sophomores and seniors, the last an age level I loved because in the twelfth grade we studied English literature and composition . . . my students were a joy." Despite her enthusiasm for teaching and her appreciation for her students, Zach was not completely satisfied with her career. "I still had a strong desire to write. I sometimes felt that something inside me would die if I gave up writing, and I would lose a piece of myself, perhaps never to be found again." She began to write obsessively, in between teaching, grading papers, and caring for her son and daughter. Zach also began serious attempts to publish her work. She attended writers' conferences and began to consult more experienced writers. One of the most important things she learned at these conferences was that "writing is a business."

A New Life

In 1979, Zach and her husband divorced. She remarried in 1982 and moved to Los Angeles. Although her children were teased about their accents and took some time to adjust (Zach later wrote *Here Comes the Martian Mushroom* based on her daughter's experience moving from a small town in Tennessee to Los Angeles), Zach soon found the move to be a beneficial one. She was finally able to devote herself full-time to writing. "After years of snatching thirty minutes here and an hour there, having the whole day to write made me so happy I almost floated off the chair. I wrote and wrote." Zach also took advantage of the many resources available to writers in the Los Angeles area: she attended conferences and met with literary agents. Finally, one agent suggested that she write an adult romance novel.

As Zach worked on the proposal for the adult romance novel, she kept thinking of another story that "had been suggested by something that happened while" she was "teaching high school. Taking a real event and then changing almost everything—which is how fiction writers work—I wrote a story about a high school girl who is the new

Part of the "Love Story" series, this 1996 novel features Jake Magee who plays matchmaker for his friend Caroline—until he realizes that he is in love with her.

girl at school (I know how that felt!) and who is elected class president as the result of a practical joke that backfires. She has to prove herself to the other kids, and even more to herself. I wrote this book mainly for myself." After Zach won a contract for the adult romance novel, her agent suggested they market the story about the new girl as a young adult romance.

Success with the YA Audience

As Zach completed the adult romance novel, yet another character captured her attention: "this girl—her name was Amanda—kept looking over my shoulder and I could barely write the book I was supposed to be writing. Finally, I had to stop and write the first chapter of her story, then finish the adult novel, then go back and write Amanda's book, which sold right away." Zach's first two romance novels for young adults—the ones she wrote as she worked on her first adult novel— met with immediate success and won Romance Writers of America awards.

Waiting for Amanda is the story of a young woman, Mandy, who is determined to make a life for herself and her younger sister after the death of their mother. The girls move to Kentucky to live with an elderly great-aunt, where Mandy gradually learns to cope with her anger and develops a romance with a local boy. According to Lorelei Neal of *Voice of Youth Advocates*, the story is "thought-provoking."

The Frog Princess begins with a prank. Despite—or because of—her unpopularity, Kelly is elected ninth-grade class president. Gradually, the uncomfortable, self-conscious girl rises to the challenges of her leadership position and even loses weight. As Judie Porter of *School Library Journal* noted, however, the story does not end as many young adult romance novels do. Instead of getting the popular guy, Kelly develops a relationship with one that's "not-so-popular." Betsy Hearne of *Booklist* appreciated the "nice glimpse" of Kelly's relationship with her single mother.

Zach's novel *Fortune's Child* takes up the story of a girl much different from Kelly. Melissa is rich, beautiful, and intelligent, and to top it off she is dating a football hero. Nevertheless, Melissa finds herself distressed when her father has an affair with his secretary. Her grades fall and her rela-

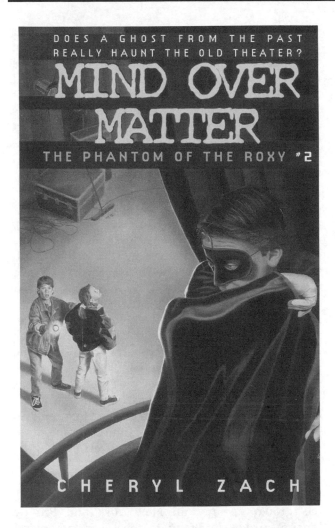

DOES A GHOST FROM THE PAST
REALLY HAUNT THE OLD THEATER?

MIND OVER MATTER

THE PHANTOM OF THE ROXY #2

CHERYL ZACH

In volume two of the "Mind Over Matter" series, twelve-year-old Quinn and his cousin Jamie pair up to find out who is behind the accidents at the old Roxy Theater.

tionship with the jock deteriorates. She begins some difficult soul-searching with an intelligent and attractive Vietnamese boy. In the process, explained Jo Ellen Broome of *Voice of Youth Advocates*, Melissa "learns the meaning of . . . true friendship." After writing *Fortune's Child*, Zach worked on a novel for a new series "about three teenaged sisters in California." The book, *Three's a Crowd*, was, according to Zach, "a best-seller on the teen list of one of the book-store chains." So she accepted an offer to work on the "Sweet Valley Twins" series, eventually completing five books.

With the intention of using her real name again, Zach wrote some of the books in the "Smyth vs. Smith" series. The stories in these books draw on Zach's "experiences as a step-parent. With so many step or blended families in America today, I thought this was a situation to which many teens could relate, and about whose hilarious and poignant moments they would enjoy reading." *Oh, Brother!*, the first book in the series, begins when the Smyth family (a woman and her teenaged daughter and son) moves to Florida to join the Smith family (a man and his teenaged son and daughter). Even before the wedding, the children of the Smyth-Smith union are at each other's throats. They gradually learn to get along, however. Meticulous Maxine and her new step-sister, Stephanie, grow closer, and Bill and Hal overcome their problems with one another. As Kimberly Olson Fakih of *Publishers Weekly* remarked, the novel "has a pleasant, readable style and premise many readers will relate to."

Zach is also the author of a nonfiction book for young people about Los Angeles, titled, aptly enough, *Los Angeles*. She explained that she "used some of" her "own photographs in this book." She and her husband would "drive 'till I found a likely spot, then I'd select a camera and snap a roll of film, while Chuck offered helpful advice. This would be my first hardcover book, and I dedicated it to my husband Chuck, just as I had also done in my very first novel."

It was around the time that *Los Angeles* was published that Zach's husband, who ran a tool and die company, was diagnosed with lymphoma (a type of cancer). As he needed a great deal of care, and as the couple wanted to spend more time together, Zach devoted less of her time to writing. Though Chuck Zach fought the cancer through chemotherapy, his health eventually deteriorated, and he died in 1990.

Returns to Her Roots

After her husband's death, Zach decided to return to live in her hometown in Tennessee. It was not until she was settled in Clarksville that Zach began to write again. She began work on a series "about four girls who live through the drama and danger of the Civil War. These books involved a lot of research, which I always find fascinating. I read old diaries and journals and stacks of history books. I traveled to Charleston where the war began . . . and visited battlefields and museums

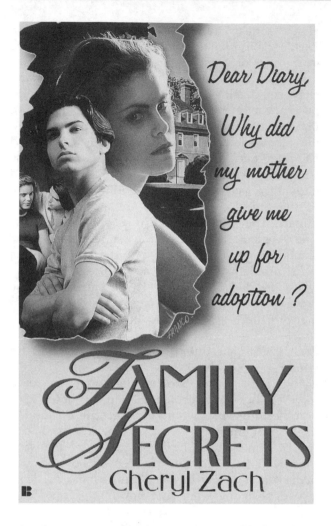

Dear Diary

Why did

my mother

give me

up for

adoption?

FAMILY SECRETS

Cheryl Zach

Sarah, a senior in high school who is battling leukemia, needs a bone marrow transplant, but due to strict adoption agency rules, she is unable to locate her natural parents.

and old homes . . . across the South." Zach's books in the "Southern Angels" series have won praise from various critics. In *Hearts Divided,* sixteen-year-old Elizabeth falls for a young Union soldier she meets at her boarding school. When war breaks out, Elizabeth's loyalties are torn: she's a Southern girl in love with a Northern soldier. Before too long, Elizabeth is forced to make a difficult choice. According to Sandra L. Doggett of *School Library Journal,* the novel's readers will "watch Elizabeth grow from a flirty teenager to an independent-thinking woman capable of making valuable contributions."

The heroine in *Winds of Betrayal* also finds her love life overturned by the Civil War. Victorine, a

young Creole woman, is very pleased with her arranged engagement to Andre, but she does not understand his lack of enthusiasm for the Confederate cause. As the war rages around her and she becomes a doctor's assistant, she realizes that her fiance's character is flawed. She also begins to fall in love with the doctor, despite the fact that he is not a Creole. "Historical detail is carefully woven into a tightly crafted plot that keeps the pages turning," observed Ann Bouricius of *Voice of Youth Advocates.*

A Dream of Freedom follows the story of a Hannah, a black slave. When the war comes, Hannah's employment as a seamstress in Charleston, South Carolina, ends, and she must return to her owner's plantation. Hannah, however, has learned a great deal from her life in the city, and she has met some interesting people, including a free man she begins to love. Hannah risks her life to free other slaves. As the war progresses and as she pursues her dream of freedom, Hannah becomes increasingly bold. *A Dream of Freedom* features more than just an adventurous heroine and a historical setting— according to Patsy H. Adams in *Voice of Youth Advocates,* readers "find drama, danger, intrigue, and love" in this novel.

Mystery and adventure in the Amazon distinguish the plot of *Paradise.* Ana, an American girl who has grown up in both New York and Rio de Janeiro, arrives in Brazil to meet her father and spend her vacation. When she learns that her father has gone to the Amazon, she follows him and finds a suspicious scene instead of her father. Ana gets lost in the jungle, but she is saved by a young college student who is working with his botanist mother in the Amazon. At first, Brad distrusts Ana; he grows to love her and believe in her as the two struggle to find Ana's father. "Ana is a brave heroine. . . . She becomes a champion of the rain forest. . . ." explained Sarah A. Hudson of *Voice of Youth Advocates.* As Barbara Jo McKee of *KLIATT* noted, Zach writes with detail about jungle wildlife, and "conservation facts abound. . . ." *Paradise* was a finalist for the Rita award from the Romance Writers of America.

Zach wrote another young adult romance, *Dear Diary: Runaway,* after reading "a riveting newspaper story." This novel explores the troubles of a girl through her diary entries. Readers enter Cassie's story when she is still just friends with

If you enjoy the works of Cheryl Zach, you may also want to check out the following books and films:

Betsy Byars, *Bingo Brown and the Lan-guage of Love*, 1989.
Jackie Koller, *The Primrose Way*, 1992.
Susan Beth Pfeffer, *The Sebastian Sisters Quintet*, 1987-1990.
Flirting, an Australian film with Nicole Kidman, 1989.

Seth, and follow along as Cassie and Seth develop a romantic relationship. Cassie becomes pregnant, and her strict father sends her to a girls' home. Feeling responsible for the pregnancy and his future child's welfare, Seth attempts to free Cassie. Although they have good intentions, the fleeing teenagers soon find themselves in a situation beyond their control. Anne O'Malley of *Booklist* described this "suspenseful teen romance" as "a page-turner." *Runaway* won a Rita award from the Romance Writers of America—as it was her third book to win an award (*Looking Out for Lacey* and *Paradise* had been Rita finalists), she was inducted into the Romance Writers of America Hall of Fame.

Although Zach continues to write fiction for young people in her comfortable study at home in Clarksville, Tennessee, she draws on and adds to a supportive community of writers and editors through electronic mail. She also speaks to other writers at conferences and workshops. In addition to receiving letters from her readers, Zach visits with children in schools. "It's great fun to meet some of my readers in a classroom setting," she commented in *SAAS*.

■ Works Cited

Adams, Patsy H., review of *A Dream of Freedom*, *Voice of Youth Advocates*, April, 1996, pp. 33-34.

Bouricius, Ann, review of *Winds of Betrayal*, *Voice of Youth Advocates*, April, 1996, p. 34.

Broome, Jo Ellen, review of *Fortune's Child*, *Voice of Youth Advocates*, February, 1986, p. 389.

Doggett, Sandra L., review of *Hearts Divided*, *School Library Journal*, October, 1995, p. 161.

Fakih, Kimberly Olson, review of *Oh, Brother!*, *Publishers Weekly*, September 9, 1988, p. 138.

Hearne, Betsy, review of *The Frog Princess*, *Booklist*, December 1, 1984, pp. 528-29.

Hudson, Sarah A., review of *Paradise*, *Voice of Youth Advocates*, April, 1995, p. 30.

McKee, Barbara Jo, review of *Paradise*, *KLIATT*, November, 1994, p. 17.

Neal, Lorelei, review of *Waiting for Amanda*, *Voice of Youth Advocates*, June, 1985, p. 124.

O'Malley, Anne, review of *Dear Diary: Runaway*, *Booklist*, January 1 & 15, 1996, p. 822.

Porter, Judie, review of *The Frog Princess*, *School Library Journal*, January, 1985, p. 89.

Zach, Cheryl, comments in *Something about the Author*, Volume 58, Gale, 1990, pp. 195-97.

Zach, Cheryl, essay in *Something about the Author Autobiography Series*, Volume 24, Gale, 1997.

■ For More Information See

PERIODICALS

School Library Journal, January, 1986, p. 81.
Voice of Youth Advocates, October, 1984, p. 202.
Writer, November, 1988.*

—Sketch by R. Garcia-Johnson

Acknowledgments

Acknowledgments

Grateful acknowledgment is made to the following publishers, authors, and artists for their kind permission to reproduce copyrighted material.

JANET BODE Cover of *Death Is Hard to Live With*, by Janet Bode. Laurel Leaf Books, 1993. Reproduced by permission of Laurel-Leaf Books, a division of Bantam Doubleday Dell Publishing Group, Inc./ Cover of *Heartbreak and Roses: Real Life Stories of Troubled Love*, by Janet Bode and Stan Mack. Laurel-Leaf Books, 1996. Reproduced by permission of Laurel-Leaf Books, a division of Bantam Doubleday Dell Publishing Group, Inc./ Bode, Janet, photograph by Stan Mack. Photo courtesy of Janet Bode. Reproduced by permission.

DAVID BRIN Cover of *Startide Rising*, by David Brin. Bantam Books, 1984. Reproduced by permission of Bantam Books, a division of Bantam Doubleday Dell Publishing Group, Inc./ Cover of *Sundiver*, by David Brin. Bantam Books, 1980. Cover art copyright © 1980 by Bantam Books. Reproduced by permission of Bantam Books, a division of Bantam Doubleday Dell Publishing Group, Inc./ Davidson, Dennis, illustrator. From a jacket of *Earth*, by David Brin. Bantam Books, 1990. Jacket illustration © Dennis Davidson. Reproduced by permission of Bantam Books, a division of Bantam Doubleday Dell Publishing Group, Inc./ Ruddell, Gary, illustrator. From a jacket of *Glory Season*, by David Brin. Bantam Books, 1993. Jacket illustration © Gary Ruddell. Reproduced by permission of Bantam Books, a division of Bantam Doubleday Dell Publishing Group, Inc./ Brin, David, photograph by Jerry Bauer. © by Jerry Bauer. Reproduced by permission.

STEPHEN CRANE Cover of *Maggie: A Girl of the Streets*, by Stephen Crane. Amherst, NY: Prometheus Books, 1995. Reproduced by permission of the publisher and Clifton Waller Barrett Library, Special Collections Department, University of Virginia./ Cover of *The Red Badge of Courage*, by Stephen Crane. Bantam Books, 1983. Reproduced by permission of Bantam Books, a division of Bantam Doubleday Dell Publishing Group, Inc., and Herb Peck, Jr./ Crane, Stephen, photograph. The Library of Congress./ Crane, Stephen, photograph. University of Virginia Library. Reproduced by permission./ Opening page of final manuscript of "The Red Badge of Courage," by Stephen Crane, photograph./ Scene from film "Red Badge of Courage" (older soldier marching with younger), photograph. Springer/Corbis-Bettmann. Reproduced by permission.

SHARON CREECH Desimini, Lisa, illustrator. From a cover of *Walk Two Moons*, by Sharon Creech. HarperCollins, 1996. Cover art © 1994 by Lisa Desimini. Cover © 1996 by HarperCollins Publishers, Inc. Reproduced by permission of HarperCollins Publishers, Inc./ Elliott, Mark, illustrator. From a cover of *Absolutely Normal Chaos*, by Sharon Creech. HarperTrophy, 1997. Cover art © 1997 by Mark Elliott. Cover © 1997 by HarperCollins Publishers, Inc. Reproduced by permission of HarperCollins Publishers, Inc./ Creech, Sharon, photograph by Matthew Self. Reproduced by permission of Sharon Creech.

LINDA CREW De Felice, Ron, illustrator. From a jacket of *Fire on the Wind*, by Linda Crew. Delacorte Press, 1995. Jacket illustration © 1995 by Ron De Felice. Reproduced by permission of Delacorte Press, a division of Bantam Doubleday Dell Publishing Group, Inc./ Kaufman, Stuart, illustrator. From a jacket of *Children of the River*, by Linda Crew. Delacorte Press, 1989. Jacket illustration copyright © 1989 by Stuart Kaufman. Reproduced by permission of Delacorte Press, a division of Bantam Doubleday Dell Publishing Group, Inc./ Robinson, Charles, illustrator. From a jacket of *Nekomah Creek*, by Linda Crew. Delacorte Press, 1991. Jacket illustration copyright © 1991 by Charles Robinson. Reproduced by permission of Delacorte Press, a division of Bantam Doubleday Dell Publishing Group, Inc./ Crew, Linda, photograph by Warren Welch. Reproduced by permission of Linda Crew.

JENNY DAVIS Cover of *Sex Education*, by Jenny Davis. Laurel-Leaf Books, 1989. Reproduced by permission of Bantam Books, a division of Bantam Doubleday Dell Publishing Group, Inc./ Marchesi, Stephen, illustrator. From a jacket of *Checking on the Moon*, by Jenny Davis. Jacket painting copyright © 1991 by Stephen Marchesi. Reproduced by permission./ Davis, Jenny, photograph by Bill Ringle. Reproduced by permission.

DICK FRANCIS Jacket of *Decider*, by Dick Francis. G. P. Putnam's Sons, 1993. Reproduced by permission of The Putnam Publishing Group./ Jacket of *Driving Force*, by Dick Francis. G. P. Putnam's Sons, 1992. Reproduced by permission of The Putnam Publishing Group./ Jacket of *Straight*, by Dick Francis. G. P. Putnam's Sons, 1989. Reproduced by permission of The Putnam Publishing Group./ Jacket of *Wild Horses*, by Dick Francis. G. P. Putnam's Sons, 1994. Reproduced by permission of The Putnam Publishing Group./ Francis, Dick, photograph by Jerry Bauer. © by Jerry Bauer. Reproduced by permission.

ROBERT FROST Cover of *Robert Frost: A Boy's Will and North of Boston*, by Robert Frost. Dover Publications, Inc., 1991. Reproduced by permission./ Feininger, Andreas, illustrator. From a jacket of *Robert Frost: The Road Not Taken and Other Poems*, by Robert Frost. Dover Publications, Inc., 1993. Cover illustration © 1993, Andreas Feininger. Reproduced by permission./ Frost, Robert, photograph. The Library of Congress.

BARBARA HALL Creighton, Kathleen, illustrator. From a cover of *The House Across the Cove*, by Barbara Hall. Laurel-Leaf Books, 1995. Reproduced by permission of Bantam Books, a division of Bantam Doubleday Dell Publishing Group, Inc./ Julia Duffy, Tom Poston, and Bob Newhart in the CBS television series *"Newhart,"* 1988, photograph. The Kobal Collection. Reproduced by permission./ Hall, Barbara, photograph. Reproduced by permission of Barbara Hall.

VIRGINIA HAMILTON Cooper, Floyd, illustrator. From a jacket of *Plain City*, by Virginia Hamilton. The Blue Sky Press, 1993. Jacket illustration © 1993 by Floyd Cooper. Reproduced by permission./ Cover of *Cousins*, by Virginia Hamilton. Scholastic Inc., 1991. Reproduced by permission./ Cover of *In the Beginning: Creation Stories from Around the World*, by Virginia Hamilton. Harcourt Brace & Company, 1988. Reproduced by permission of Harcourt Brace & Company./ Jacket of *The House of Dies Drear*, by Virginia Hamilton. Macmillan, 1968. Reproduced by permission of Macmillan Publishing Company, a division of Simon & Schuster, Inc./ Hamilton, Virginia, photograph by Jimmy Byrge. Reproduced by permission of Virginia Hamilton.

KEITH HARING Drawing on exhibition announcement by Keith Haring, photograph. Sidney Janis Gallery. Reproduced by permission./ Sculpture installation (with children) by Keith Haring, photograph by Tseng Kwong Chi. © 1997 Estate of Tseng Kwong Chi—MTDP/Artists' Rights Society (ARS), New York. Reproduced by permission of the Estate of Tseng Kwong Chi./ "Untitled," ink on the artist's hand, by Keith Haring, 1988, illustration. From a cover of *Keith Haring Journals*, by Keith Haring. Viking, 1996. Copyright © the Estate of Keith Haring, 1996. Reproduced by permission of the Literary Estate of Keith Haring./ Haring, Keith, Dusseldorf, 1988, photograph by Michael Dannenmann. Reproduced by permission of the Estate of Keith Haring.

FRANK HERBERT Alexander, illustrator. From a cover of *Destination: Void*, by Frank Herbert. Berkley Books, 1978. Reproduced by permission of The Berkley Publishing Group./ Sting and Kyle MacLachlan in the film *"Dune,"* 1983, photograph. The Kobal Collection. Reproduced by permission./ Tate, D. C., illustrator. From a cover of *Children of Dune*, by Frank Herbert. Berkley Books, 1976. Reproduced by permission of The Berkley Publishing Group./ Herbert, Frank, photograph by Jay Kay Klein. Reproduced by permission.

KRISTIN HUNTER Jacket of *The Lakestown Rebellion*, by Kristin Hunter. Charles Scribner's Sons, 1978. Reproduced by permission of Charles Scribner's Sons, a division of Simon & Schuster, Inc./ Koehn, Ilse, illustrator. From a jacket of *The Soul Brothers and Sister Lou*, by Kristin Hunter. Charles Scribner's Sons, 1968. Reproduced by permission of Charles Scribner's Sons, a division of Simon & Schuster, Inc./ McDaniel, Jerry, illustrator. From a jacket of *Lou in the Limelight*, by Kristin Hunter. Charles Scribner's Sons, 1981. Reproduced by permission of Charles Scribner's Sons, a division of Simon & Schuster, Inc./ Hunter, Kristin, photograph by John I. Lattany. Reproduced by permission of Kristin Hunter.

ROBIN KLEIN Gouldthorpe, Peter, illustrator. From a jacket of *Seeing Things*, by Robin Klein. Viking, 1993. Jacket illustration copyright © Peter Gouldthorpe, 1993. Reproduced by permission of Penguin Books Australia Limited./ Hannay, Lorraine, illustrator. From a cover of *Tearaways*, by Robin Klein. Viking, 1990. Reproduced by permission of Penguin Books Australia Limited./ Klein, Robin, photograph. Reproduced by permission of Robin Klein.

KATHERINE KURTZ Cover of *Camber of Culdi*, by Katherine Kurtz. Del Rey Books, 1976. Reproduced by permission of Random House, Inc./ Cover of *The Bishop's Heir*, by Katherine Kurtz. Del Rey Books, 1985. Reproduced by permission of Random House, Inc./ Herring, Michael, illustrator. From a cover of *The Harrowing of Gwynedd*, by Katherine Kurtz. Del Rey Books, 1989. Reproduced by permission of Random House, Inc./ Sweet, Darrell K., illustrator. From a cover of *Deryni Checkmate*, by Katherine Kurtz. Del Rey Books, 1972. Reproduced by permission of Random House, Inc./ Kurtz, Katherine, photograph by Beth Gwinn. Reproduced by permission of Katherine Kurtz.

DAVID MACAULAY Cover of *Cathedral: The Story of Its Construction*, by David Macaulay. Houghton Mifflin, 1973. Reproduced by permission of Houghton Mifflin Company./ Cover of *Ship*, by David Macaulay. Houghton Mifflin, 1993. Reproduced by permission of Houghton Mifflin Company./ Macaulay, David, photograph by Jan Bindas. Reproduced by permission of David Macaulay.

CARSON MCCULLERS Cover of *The Heart Is a Lonely Hunter*, by Carson McCullers. Bantam Books, 1967. Reproduced by permission of Bantam Books, a division of Bantam Doubleday Dell Publishing Group, Inc./ Cover of *The Member of the Wedding*, by Carson McCullers. Bantam Books, 1973. Reproduced by permission of Bantam Books, a division of Bantam Doubleday Dell Publishing Group, Inc./ Sondra Locke and Alan Arkin in the film *"The Heart Is a Lonely Hunter,"* 1968, photograph. The Kobal Collection. Reproduced by permission./ McCullers, Carson (at piano), photograph. AP/Wide World Photos. Reproduced by permission.

TERRY MCMILLAN Gottlieb, Dale, illustrator. From a jacket of *Mama*, by Terry McMillan. Houghton Mifflin Company, 1987. Jacket illustration © 1987 by Dale Gottlieb. Reproduced by permission of Houghton Mifflin Company./ McMillan, Terry, photograph by Jerry Bauer. © Jerry Bauer. Reproduced by permission.

WILSON RAWLS Ben-Ami, Doron, illustrator. From a cover of *Where the Red Fern Grows*, by Wilson Rawls. Yearling Books, 1996. Reproduced by permission of Yearling Books, a division of Bantam Doubleday Dell Publishing Group, Inc./ Cover of *Summer of the Monkeys*, by Wilson Rawls. Bantam Books, 1996. Reproduced by permission of Bantam Books, a division of Bantam Doubleday Dell Publishing Group, Inc./ Rawls, Wilson, photograph by Bacon. Reproduced by permission of the Estate of Wilson Rawls.

CONRAD RICHTER Cover of *The Light in the Forest,* by Conrad Richter. Fawcett Juniper, 1991. Reproduced by permission of Random House, Inc./ Jacket of *The Town,* by Conrad Richter. Knopf, 1950./ Richter, Conrad, photograph. Bettman Archive. Reproduced by permission.

JON SCIESZKA Cover of *The Stinky Cheese Man and Other Fairy Tale,* by Jon Scieszka. Viking, 1992. Used by permission of the Viking Penguin, a division of Penguin USA./ Jacket of *The True Story of the 3 Little Pigs,* by Jon Scieszka. Puffin Books, 1989. Used by permission of the publisher, Puffin Books, a division of Penguin USA./ Smith, Lane, illustrator. From a cover of *The Good, the Bad, and the Goofy,* by Jon Scieszka. Puffin Books, 1992. Cover illustration copyright © Lane Smith, 1991. Used by permission of the publisher, Puffin Books, a division of Penguin USA./ Smith, Lane, illustrator. From a jacket of *Math Curse,* by Jon Scieszka. Viking, 1995. Jacket illustration copyright © Lane Smith, 1995. Used by permission of the Viking Penguin, a division of Penguin USA./ Scieszka, Jon (outside), photograph by Brian Smale. Sharpshooter Creative Representation, Inc. Reproduced by permission.

NEAL SHUSTERMAN Archambault, Matthew, illustrator. From a cover of *The Eyes of Kid Midas,* by Neal Shusterman. Neal Shusterman, 1992. Reproduced by permission of TOR Books/Tom Doherty Associates, Incorporated./ Picart, Gabriel, illustrator. From a jacket of *Scorpion Shards,* by Neal Shusterman. Neal Shusterman, 1995. Reproduced by permission of TOR Books/Tom Doherty Associates Incorporated./ Zimet, Jaye and Robert Osonitsch, illustrators. From a cover of *What Daddy Did,* by Neal Shusterman. HarperKeypoint, 1993. Cover photograph © 1993 by Robert Osonitsch. Reproduced by permission of HarperCollins Publishers, Inc./ Shusterman, Neal, photograph. Reproduced by permission of Neal Shusterman.

LANE SMITH Smith, Lane, illustrator. From a cover of *The Big Pets,* by Lane Smith. Viking Penguin, 1991. Copyright © Lane Smith, 1991. Used by permission of Viking Penguin, a division of Penguin USA./ Smith, Lane, illustrator. From an illustration in *The Good, the Bad, and the Goofy,* by Jon Scieszka. Puffin Books, 1992. Illustrations copyright © Lane Smith, 1992. Used by permission of the publisher, Puffin Books, a division of Penguin USA./ Smith, Lane, illustrator. From an illustration in *The Stinky Cheese Man and Other Fairy Tales,* by Jon Scieszka. Viking, 1992. Illustrations © Lane Smith, 1992. Used by permission of the Viking Penguin, a division of Penguin USA./ Smith, Lane, illustrator. From an illustration in *The True Story of the 3 Little Pigs,* by Jon Scieszka. Puffin Books, 1989. Illustrations copyright © Lane Smith, 1989. Used by permission of the publisher, Puffin Books, a division of Penguin USA./ Smith, Lane (outside), photograph by Brian Smale. Sharpshooter Creative Representation, Inc. Reproduced by permission.

JACQUELINE WOODSON Cover of *I Hadn't Meant Tell You This,* by Jacqueline Woodson. Laurel-Leaf Books, 1995. Reproduced by permission of Bantam Books, a division of Bantam Doubleday Dell Publishing Group, Inc./ Cover of *The Dear One,* by Jacqueline Woodson. Laurel-Leaf Books, 1993. Reproduced by permission of Bantam Books, a division of Bantam Doubleday Dell Publishing Group, Inc./ Dillon, Leo and Diane Dillon, illustrators. From a cover of *Last Summer with Maizon,* by Jacqueline Woodson. Yearling Books, 1992. Reproduced by permission of Yearling Books, a division of Bantam Doubleday Dell Publishing Group, Inc./ Dillon, Leo and Diane Dillon, illustrators. From a cover of *Maizon at Blue Hill,* by Jacqueline Woodson. Yearling Books, 1994. Cover illustration © 1989 by Leo and Diane Dillon. Reproduced by permission of Yearling Books, a division of Bantam Doubleday Dell Publishing Group, Inc./ Woodson, Jacqueline, photograph by A. E. Grace. Reproduced by permission of Jacqueline Woodson.

CHERYL ZACH Cover of *Kissing Caroline,* by Cheryl Zach. Bantam Books, 1996. Cover art copyright © 1996 by Daniel Weiss Associates, Inc. Reproduced by permission of Bantam Books, a division of Bantam Doubleday Dell Publishing Group, Inc./ Cover of *Mind over Matter,* by Cheryl Zach. Avon Books, 1997. Reproduced by permission of Avon Books, New York./ Tadiello, Ed, illustrator. From a cover of *A Dream of Freedom,* by Cheryl Zach. Bantam Books, 1995. Cover art copyright © 1995 by Daniel Weiss Associates, Inc. Reproduced by permission of Bantam Books, a division of Bantam Doubleday Dell Publishing Group, Inc./ Cover of *Family Secrets,* by Cheryl Zach. Berkley Books, 1996. Reproduced by permission of The Berkley Publishing Group./ Zach, Cheryl, photograph by Kim Rager. Reproduced by permission of Cheryl Zach.

Cumulative Index

Author/Artist Index

The following index gives the number of the volume in which an author/artist's biographical sketch appears.